KU-212-757

Contents

Introduction

Connections is a unique and epic project. It unites some of the most important, exciting and significant contemporary playwrights with the talents, enthusiasm and experience of youth theatre companies throughout England, Ireland, Scotland and Wales. Most of the playwrights have not previously written for young actors; many of the young actors have not previously performed a challenging and innovative new play. But playwrights are the heart of theatre, and young actors are its future. The combination makes for imaginative and important new theatre; twelve specially commissioned one-hour plays are now being premiered in 150 productions, taking place everywhere between John O'Groats, Land's End and Malin Head, in schools, in local theatres and on rep theatre main-stages. Ten regional theatres will host festivals of local work; and the project culminates in a festival of twelve of the most interesting productions on the Cottesloe and Olivier stages at the Royal National Theatre in July 1997.

But first a brief history of the genesis of the Connections project. It grew out of young actors' hunger for plays which were contemporary, sophisticated, unpatronising and entertaining. Although many companies had brilliant histories of devising or improvising their own work, almost none had access to the finance to commission top playwrights. Nor was there a substantial existing repertoire of appropriate plays. Because new writing had slipped off the agenda of most theatres in the 1980s and early 1990s, many young actors were simply not able to see productions of important new work.

Yet, ironically, a new generation of exceptionally talented playwrights was having its work produced by a handful of new writing theatres. Their plays were uncompromising, richly imagined, heretical, beautiful, edgy, intelligent and faithful to the heart. Above all each writer created a distinctive and compelling dramatic poetry.

Connections was devised as a way of uniting these two powerful

creative forces in a nationwide project. The first Connections con-
cluded in July 1995 with a week-long celebratory festival at the
National's Cottesloe and Olivier theatres. Ten outstanding productions by companies based as far apart as Glasgow, Northern
Ireland and Stroud were showcased. The event was a wonderful
conclusion to an epic theatrical project which had embraced ten
regional festivals and involved thousands of young actors. The
imagination, integrity, variety, conviction and dramatic power of
the productions were wonderful vindications of the ideals of the
Connections project. The experience of performing premieres of
exciting new work – rather than *Oliver!* or *The Sound of Music*
yet again – was unforgettable for the actors. And important connections for the future were made all round: playwrights with
directors who might not have worked on a new text before, playwrights with actors and would-be playwrights, companies with
other companies, and actors with other actors from different parts
of the country. Playwrights saw perhaps twenty different productions of their new play, instead of the usual one; audiences
filled the theatres; surprise stars from film and TV awarded prizes;
and the Artistic Director at the NT, Richard Eyre, found himself at
the end of a Mexican wave of enthusiasm in the Olivier Theatre
on the last night.

The plays in this collection are new commissions for Connections
97. Continuing and developing the success of Connections 95,
they constitute a repertoire of exceptional new plays for young
actors. The list of writers embraces both distinguished, well-
established names (including the great Nigerian playwright and
Nobel Prize-winner Wole Soyinka), and some who have emerged
over the last few years as important writers:

Simon Armitage, whose four collections of poetry and TV
poems have earned him acclaim as the best young poet writing in
England; David Ashton, from Scotland, whose plays have been
produced in London, Ireland and Scotland; Simon Bent, from
Scarborough, who has had several plays produced at the National
Theatre Studio as well as at theatres in and around London; Jane
Coles, who has had several prize-winning plays on in London;
Siân Evans from Wales, whose work has been produced in Wales
and England, and on TV; David Harrower from Edinburgh,

whose first play *Knives in Hens* won him international acclaim; Bryony Lavery who has had many plays produced around the country and in London; Liz Lochhead, poet, playwright and performer from Glasgow; Gina Moxley from Dublin, whose *Danti-Dan* won rave reviews in Dublin and London; Philip Ridley, who has written many plays, feature films and prize-winning novels for children; and the American playwright Naomi Wallace, writing with Bruce McLeod; her most recent work in this country has been produced at the RSC and in the West End.

We were looking for a number of qualities in the playwrights we commissioned. We had to love the quality of their writing. Their work needed to suggest strong connections with a theatre by and for young actors. We wanted a broad sweep of writers whose stories and language, however local, would also possess a universality which would resonate with companies from different places around the country. We focused on writers of stature who had not previously written for young actors, but who were excited by the possibilities of the project. We looked at writers who had not written specifically for the stage before – Simon Armitage, for instance; the sheer drive of his language and his storytelling gift pointed out a powerful dramatic talent. Above all we wanted to create a portfolio which would be as richly diverse as possible, allowing the huge variety of companies to choose work which was appropriate to them in terms of cast size, content and style, but which would also be new writing of the highest calibre.

The commissioning and development of these plays deliberately reflected the process of a professional new-writing theatre. We drew up a wish-list of writers, and met them to talk through the project in more detail. We explained its particular and unusual circumstances: first, the plays were for young actors but should be written exactly as if for a professional company. Second, the plays could only be about an hour long. Third, this was a unique opportunity to write for casts as big as fifty, rather than the usual budget-restricted studio theatre chamber-casts of five or six. Fourth, they would have not one, but as many as thirty premieres of their work. And finally, and most importantly, the commissions were completely open. This is a writer-led project; we wanted the writers to work according to their own instincts. So we did not ask them to illustrate specific themes, issues or agendas. We wanted plays which would surprise and challenge, which were unpatronising, and which would match the writers' work for professional stages.

The writers immediately responded to the new possibilities of the project. It proved difficult to find Wole Soyinka, but he wrote back from America: 'It sounds an interesting project. I agree to participate.' We tried to set up a meeting without luck. Then, suddenly, one Monday morning he rang up; could we meet him in half-an-hour? Of course we could. Many months later *Travel Club and Boy Soldier* simply arrived in the post. The writers all suggested the bare bones of an idea, or a fragment of a story which they'd had in mind for some time; but once the actual business of writing took over, these initial notions were often radically transformed. We were thrilled with the results, and the way the writers had used this unique opportunity; Liz Lochhead's *Cuba* was a beautifully detailed and very funny large-scale theatrical extravaganza; Simon Armitage's *Eclipse* was an entirely original poetic drama; Simon Bent's *Shelter* was a beautifully nuanced study of friendship, failure and families. Jane Coles's *The Ultimate Fudge* went right into the heart of darkness of an English myth. David Harrower's version of *The Chrysalids* revealed it as a story about difference, purity and danger. David Ashton's *The Golden Door* was rowdy, jubilant, beautiful and dark.

I talked through the first drafts with the writers, and then each play was given a rehearsed reading by the National's youth company – these usually turned into impromptu workshops. The texts were made as ready as possible to go into rehearsal. The 150 theatre companies and groups involved in the scheme read them and decided which they wanted to produce in their own venues. Then, at the end of November 1996 we held a weekend of workshops. The purpose of this was to bring together the playwrights with all the directors, in workshops run by established directors who had worked with the writer on previous occasions. This was really the beginning of the rehearsal process, allowing each director to work on the text in depth, to ask questions, raise issues and problems, to get some of the scenes on their feet, and above all to get to know the writer – both in the workshop and in the bar.

The workshops were also an opportunity for some first principles to be stated. Character and story were emphasised over setting and spectacle. Most importantly, we insisted on fidelity to the writers' texts. These were not to be adapted or altered in any way without consultation with the playwright; problems encountered in rehearsal would need to be solved in rehearsal without recourse to any directorial changes. This may have sounded draconian – especially to companies used to the freedom of devising or improvising work – but the point was that each production should *realize the play* with integrity and imagination, rather than adapt it to a director's concept. All the experience and ability of the actors and directors needed to be brought to bear on the text, on language, and on character in a way which served the play by discovering the richness of its world.

But theatre is also a collaborative event; while we wanted the texts to be respected, we didn't want to limit the potential of each group to create their own production. In the end, the workshops were mutually beneficial and creative; the playwrights proved more than happy to discuss their work, and to be consulted about possible small changes and adaptations to particular insights or circumstances. What they wanted was to decide on their own solutions to various dilemmas – not to find their play had suddenly, unexpectedly and altogether incorrectly been relocated to Sarajevo, or turned into a musical. In Wole Soyinka's case he could not be present because he lives in exile in the USA; but group discussions in the workshop revealed answers and conclusions to the questions that arose. At the end of the weekend he was sent a short fax with a list of unresolved questions, which he answered by return with an equally short and open-hearted list of answers and permissions.

For all their individual and distinctive variety, these twelve plays share an outstanding excellence, richness, beauty and integrity in the writing. Themes and issues emerge inevitably and beautifully from situation and character, from the stories and journeys, and from the precision and poetry of each writer's dramatic language. Whether they are about a group of court women immured with the body of their dead Emperor in ancient China (*More Light*), or a group of antagonistic young people on the junk-strewn roof of a tower block enacting a story which will finally transform them all (*Sparkleshark*), these plays are imaginative explorations – of families and friendships, of social inclusion and exclusion, of history and language, and of the creative possibilities of theatre.

They are also dramatic adventures; vanishings and transform-
ations, grace and danger, violence and redemption, quests from
darkness into light; the power and demands of ritual and mythology, the anarchic energy and language of humour, the heroic
facing and vanquishing of monstrous fears; and perhaps above all
the creative force and necessity of stories and language.

The plays are also deliberately and defiantly challenging, both in
terms of their content and their theatrical ambition; for example,
More Light contrasts a highly wrought and oblique dramatic
poetry with sex, cannibalism and survival. *Asleep under the Dark
Earth* unites a history of social injustice with a story of magical
body-swapping. *Dog House* is a comedy with the darkest business
going on just offstage. *In the Sweat* is a drama of oppression, of
power and powerlessness, set in a disused synagogue. But this level
of challenge and ambition is crucial to the Connections project; all
the plays assume the ability, intelligence and insight of young
actors, as well as an equal ambition to collaborate in the creation
of theatre of imagination and integrity.

The plays from Connections 95 have since been taken up and
performed, independently of the project, throughout the UK and
in Europe. Through the publication of this collection, the twelve
plays in Connections 97 will also have a long stage-life after the
project itself is over. We're planning now for Connections 99 and a
further portfolio of twelve new plays by well-known and new playwrights. This time we hope to include a large-scale music theatre
piece and some new European writing. Connections will continue
to create an exciting repertoire of new plays for young actors,
putting new writing at the heart of young people's theatre on
stages throughout Wales, Scotland, Ireland and England.

Nick Drake
March 1997

ASLEEP UNDER THE DARK EARTH

Siân Evans

Characters

The play is set *circa* 1830 in rural mid-Wales

Bethan Tate, sixteen, daughter of landowner Henry Tate
Henry Tate, fifties, Bethan's father and recent convert to
nonconformism
Nia Richards, sixteen, daughter of farm labourers, friend
of Bethan
Deri Richards, eighteen, Nia's brother and friend of
Bethan
Caleb Jones, early thirties, travelling preacher
Pamela and **Clarissa,** fifties, Bethan's aunts
Mari, twenty, servant in the Tate household
Joshua, twenty-five, servant in the Tate household

Other Speaking Parts: farm labourers, church elders,
guests at the wedding, Bethan's ancestors and the chorus

Note
Deri's last speech is part of a poem by the eighteenth-
century spiritual writer Christopher Smart. Caleb's
wedding-night 'text' is taken from the writings of John
Fletcher.

Part One

SCENE ONE

Bethan is praying alone in the private chapel of her house.

Bethan Dear Lord, forgive me this morning the sins of
yesterday.

Arrogance. I was rude to one of the servants, Joshua.
I lost my temper. I thought I'd told him to repair my
shoes by Sunday and then I realized that I had not but I
scolded him anyway. Afterwards felt very bad. He did
not contradict me, though he must have known I was
mistaken. Father heard me and then he scolded him too.
Felt even worse. Thought of going to Joshua later and
apologizing but did not.

Ingratitude. Resentment. Saw Nia talking to Mari.
First time she's visited the house in two years. Ignored
her. It pained me. I was being obedient to father, which
is my first duty, but I felt that I had sinned in some other
way. Felt angry towards father. Saw Nia's face. Hurt.
Dreamed last night that we met, that we left the house
together, that we had . . . changed again . . . flown
away . . .

A man appears in the doorway and listens.

Regret. Yesterday longed for mother. Wanted to pluck her
from eternal bliss and bring her back to me. Didn't care
about her pain and suffering as long as she was here
with me.

And I have sinned against our guest Caleb. Though I
– cannot say how or why. I have felt no peace since he's
been here. He's kind and polite, but when he talks to me
I cannot answer. It's as though my tongue fills my

3

mouth. I am frightened that he will think this a slight.
Last night father noticed too and gave me one of his
black looks.

Forgive me. Fill me with thy love and understanding . . .

Her voice fades away in silent prayer as Caleb enters the
chapel and kneels next to Bethan. Bethan is acutely
aware of his physical presence.

Chorus O thou whom, unseen, I love, by what powerful
force dost thou attract my soul? The eye has not seen
nor has the ear heard, nor has it entered into the heart
of man to conceive what thou art, and yet I love thee
beyond all that my eye has seen or my ear heard –
beyond all that my heart comprehends.

Bethan turns to Caleb. He gets up and takes her face in
his hands.

Caleb It is a beautiful morning, sister, is it not?

SCENE TWO

Caleb preaching in the village square. He stands on a box
and holds a Bible in one hand. At first there are only a few
people listening. Some pass by, uninterested. Slowly the
crowd builds. Still people fidget. Children squabble and
fight. The longer he speaks, the more absorbed people
become. A young girl of sixteen, Nia, is among the crowd.
A boy with a blank expression stands very close to Caleb,
his face almost touching Caleb's face. Caleb tries to ignore
him.

Caleb You, old woman, my sister, and you, young man,
my brother, come closer and listen. Come, come. All of
you. What I have to say is so urgent, so critical, so vital
– that it will turn your life about.

Boy Ssh! Listen, everyone.

Caleb My mission is Jesus's mission.

Boy Did you hear that! Jesus's mission!

Caleb I've come to bring you the truth. The truth that lies here in my hand. The truth that no one dares tell you.

Man I've heard it all before. A hundred times over!

Caleb Not the way I'm going to tell it. Not *my* interpretation . . .

He lingers on this last word.

No. You may have heard Christmas Evans, you may even be old enough to have heard John Wesley, but you have not heard Caleb Jones!

Boy This is Caleb Jones. Caleb Jones.

Man So what is it then?

Caleb I tell you, there is not one quality of life for the master and another for the disciple.

Man (*laughing*) Oh yes!

Caleb He that saith he abideth in him ought to walk even as he walked.

Woman How's that then?

Caleb Brothers and sisters – do you know what we need?

Young Man Money!

Laughter all round. The Boy pushes the Young Man who said this.

Caleb I'll tell you what we need here. What we need is a new breed of Christians.
Reannouncers of truth!

The Boy claps.

Apostles of freedom for the people!
Heralds of a New Social Order!

The people are quiet suddenly.

We must harness our moral and spiritual energy like

horses to the plough!
We must use that energy and change those about us!
We must have Justice and Brotherhood!

Man Justice works one way here.

Caleb Then we must force a new path.

Woman How?

Caleb Nothing stands in the way of Jesus.

No-one can withstand the power of righteous anger.

The sheep are being devoured but the shepherds have not even seen the wolf.

The Boy howls like a wolf.

Our burdened brothers, our tired and battled sisters, our thousands of little children blighted by the struggle to survive, YOU are the Christ presence.

The broken-spirited must be healed, the bruised must be set at liberty.

A few cheers.

Woman Then why are you living in Henry Tate's house?

Everyone, including Nia, turns to look at the Woman.

Caleb Who asked that question?

The Woman holds up her hand.

I know what you're thinking, sister. You're thinking this man is a hypocrite! How can he preach to the shepherd and eat with the wolf? Is that your question?

Let me explain.

I can preach here every Sunday, rain or shine. But you good people, you come home from the fields exhausted. You need to sit and take shelter. You need a place to meet. To congregate, to join together and praise the Saviour, to talk.

You'll say, 'But we have a church!'

How many of you go? How many of you think, this

is a place where I can open my heart! This is a place where I feel at home!

We need a Meeting House. We need a chapel. And you'll say – but we need money to build a chapel. Is this man going to ask us for money?

No. Because I know that you have none. No. I went to the one person who I knew could afford to be generous. I put my hand on his conscience and squeezed it, sister.

A couple of people laugh and the Boy joins in, until his laughter becomes almost hysterical.

And let me tell you, brothers and sisters, Henry Tate has offered me the first hundred pounds to build our chapel.

Woman I'll believe it when I see it!

Caleb Where is your faith, sister? Without faith, faith that you will prevail – there is no life. No point in life. Will you have faith in me?

He holds out his arms to her. She doesn't move. He approaches her, picks up her hands. She grudgingly allows him to do this. He brings them to his lips.

Why has your faith gone?

The Woman softens and opens.

Woman I lost four of my five children. And now the fifth is grown, he wants to leave me for the city.

Caleb I will help you. Trust me.

The Woman smiles; she's close to tears. Caleb walks through the crowd, taking people by the hand; they offer up their stories.

Second Woman My boy said he'd send back his wages, but nothing's come. There's been no letter for three months.

Second Man This year the wheat and barley turned black with mould – dust in our hands. We have nothing.

7

Third Woman My son's fallen under the spell of a city woman and squanders all his money on her.

Third Man My daughter went and came back in shame. Now we have no money and another empty belly.

Nia thinks she sees Deri, her brother, in the crowd.

Nia Deri!

A young man turns and moves away.

Deri!

Caleb turns towards Nia, takes her hand and pauses. She's embarrassed. She looks round for Deri, but he's gone.

Caleb And you, sister, what is your grief?

Nia I'm no better or worse off than any other.

Caleb Have you lost your faith too?

Nia No.

Caleb Thank God. Everyone! This young woman has not lost her faith. If a young untutored girl has faith, then who shall fail?

He holds on to Nia's hands for a few seconds longer than necessary. She shivers. Caleb moves on. People fall over themselves to touch him. As he moves off, so they all follow him. He turns at one point and stares back at Nia.

Nia (*quietly, to herself*) How can I lose faith when I had none to start with?

SCENE THREE

A clearing in the forest. Nia stands alone and sings.

Nia
I left the unrelenting city
To find you, to find indulgence

A leaf licking the dirt from
My child's face.

To feel again that my hand is
And is not my hand;
To be swallowed by ferns;
Unborn, unpolluted.

To know spirits suck the cool dark air
Guiding our play, hide and seek
Hide and seek the invisible bud
Our invisible perfect self.

*She hears a noise behind her. Bethan is standing in the
clearing.*

Bethan?
Bethan I heard your voice.

*There's no response from Nia. Bethan makes as though
to continue her journey.*

Nia Wait. What are you doing here?
Bethan This is part of the estate!
Nia You used to be afraid to walk in the forest alone.
Bethan That was a long time ago.
Nia It was. Where are you going?
Bethan I'm on my way to the family at Maes Mawr . . . to
give them some fresh eggs. And you?
Nia I'm meant to be looking for Deri, but I know he's not
here.
Bethan So why did you come?
Nia To be alone.
Bethan Then I'll leave.
Nia Don't.
Bethan How can you like being in here?
Nia I thought you said you're not afraid any more.
Bethan I still only pass through. I wouldn't sit like you.
Not alone. How is Deri?

9

Nia Haven't you heard?

Bethan (*anxious*) Heard what? Is he sick? He's not been arrested?

Nia Arrested? Not everyone thought him as dangerous as your father. In any case, he stopped preaching revolution a long time ago. Now people are saying he's lost his wits. He hasn't. He just cries all day. He cannot work. He sinks on to his knees and prays anywhere, everywhere. Everyone laughs at him. My father wanted to throw him out. He would have if I hadn't pleaded with him. This morning we woke up and he was gone.

Bethan Gone where?

Nia We don't know.

Bethan I've heard nothing of this.

Nia Does it matter to you?

Bethan Of course.

Nia No one would guess that you and he . . .

Bethan Yes?

Nia That you once called him your soulmate.

Silence.

Bethan You've been away.

Nia I have. Merthyr.

Bethan You didn't stay long.

Nia Two months. Mother wrote and asked me to come home. Because of Deri. Two months is not long, not here, not for you. I worked next to an old woman – at least, I thought she was an old woman. She was twenty-five. She'd worked in the foundry for seven years. Most people have to leave after five – they're spent, useless. The noise had made her deaf and the dark and smoke had ruined her eyes. Her arms were covered with scars such as this –

Nia rolls up her sleeve to show a burn. Bethan touches it briefly.

Bethan And to think I envied you.

Nia You envied me? Why?

Bethan I thought you were brave to leave this place. I've hardly ever been off the estate. I'm sometimes . . . curious.

Nia Curiosity over such things is almost a pastime for the rich. Those that have the stomach for it.

Bethan You're happy to be back then.

Nia We may not have enough to eat but there I was too tired to eat. I missed the land, the sky. In Merthyr every day was the same. In winter we started before daybreak and finished after dusk. I lived in perpetual night. No birdsong, no flowers, no flickering sunlight, no autumn leaves to roll in, no glint of frost. I felt I was buried in some underground chamber and could not breathe.

Bethan I've lost count of how many have left. I'm glad you're not one of them.

Nia Why?

Bethan You don't understand.

Nia I understand very well. Your father tells you to ignore us and you obey. It's simple. You don't want to know how we live our lives now. All of us crammed into two suffocating rooms while you float through that house and enjoy your silence.

Bethan My life is not as you think it. I had freedom as a girl; now I have responsibilities.

Nia What responsibilities? Taking a few eggs to some poor family. How charming! They've probably stopped work this morning to prepare the cottage for your visit. They may have spent a day's wage buying tea to serve you. So that you can indulge your need to give. You understand nothing. (*She is staring at the basket of food.*)

Bethan Are you hungry?

Nia Of course I am hungry!

Bethan Here.

She gives her some of the food she was keeping for Maes Mawr. Nia eats.

Nia What will you say to the family at Maes Mawr?
Bethan That I have a chill.
Nia So their expenditure will have been in vain. And not even a few eggs and butter to show for it.
Bethan Nia! I did not forget you.
Nia And Deri?
Bethan Nor Deri.

Pause.

I am sorry, Nia. It was not my fault.
Nia What was not your fault?
Bethan Mother dying and Father breaking her promise.
Nia I suppose not.
Bethan I did try and change his mind. Do you believe me?

Pause.

Nia What did your mother imagine she was doing with us?
Bethan She thought she was performing a Christian act. She was.
Nia It was a whim, a fancy. Let's take a couple of peasants off the farm and educate them – then we'll send them back to the farm.
Bethan She had to fight Father to do it. He thought she was mad. 'It will never be enough. They will never be satisfied.'
Nia He was right.
Bethan She didn't abandon you. She died. At least now you can read and write.
Nia To what end? I can read Virgil as well as you.
Bethan Better.
Nia And how does it help me when I'm shelling peas or pulling swede and cabbage or tearing ticks out of sheep flesh?

Bethan Please! You can use our library whenever you like. I can speak to Father.

Nia Time, Bethan. I have no time.

Bethan You were sitting there dreaming a moment ago.

Nia I came to find Deri and no doubt I'll have to account for it when I return empty-handed. Please don't feel pity. I'm already too busy to think much of you.

Deri keeps asking these questions. They're driving him mad. But he carries his God in him like a bee's sting. I'm scared to pull it out in case it kills him.

Bethan We have a preacher staying with us.

Nia I know. Caleb Jones.

Bethan He might be able to help Deri.

Nia Will he be with you long?

Bethan He's a travelling preacher.

Nia And has he stopped travelling?

Bethan My father has offered him money to build a chapel.

Nia Then it's true. Your father!

Bethan He's been won over.

Nia And you?

Bethan is confused.

Ah! Oh, please tell me. If you have a secret, tell me. Let's share something secret again. How I'd love to have a secret to chew on when I'm knee-deep in mud, when my feet and hands are numb with cold.

Bethan There's nothing to tell. I think he's an interesting man. He's travelled all over the world and tells wonderful stories.

Nia Such as?

Bethan Stories from Africa and the East, where dead people visit the living, places full of superstition and magic. One woman told him she had spent three days beneath the water talking to the spirits and that when she emerged she had special powers. The fish and

13

mermaids told her their secrets. When he asked her to
show him the river she said it had gone, dried up when
the white man arrived. Can you believe that?

Nia Why not? You believe the miracles, don't you? That
Christ turned wine into water?

Bethan That's different. That's holy magic.

Nia What about us? What about our magic?

Bethan I don't know what you mean . . . It was a dream. I
don't believe it really happened.

Nia laughs.

Nia You're frightened!

Bethan Of course not!

Nia You weren't frightened then. Has this preacher put
the fear of God into you?

Bethan No! I don't see how anything like that can be
good, Nia.

Nia Then you admit it happened?

Bethan Yes.

Nia So you wouldn't do it again?

Bethan I don't know.

Nia It's not unholy, Bethan. How can anything which is so
wonderful be unholy. Becoming another of God's
creatures. Learning to soar above the trees, above the
farms and fields.

Bethan Nia!

Nia You have a coward's spirit. If you can be frightened
of something so innocent, no wonder you couldn't stand
up to your father!

Bethan If I was frightened of anything it was you!

Nia Me?

Bethan You always wanted what I had –

Nia Not true!

Bethan You said you wished you had no brothers and
sisters, no mother and father – that you could choose

your own mother and father, that you could live in a house like mine.

Nia I was a child – children say silly things.

Bethan I felt you would take the very breath from my body if you could and fashion it as your own.

Nia is silent.

Nia I didn't realize. I'm sorry.

Nia holds out her hand and Bethan hugs her.

Let's meet again.

Bethan How? Where?

Nia Here. Your father wouldn't know.

Bethan I'll see. Look. The stars are coming out. If I don't go now it'll be dark before I get home.

Bethan moves off. We suddenly notice Nia's brother, Deri. Nia is unaware of him. He is staring up at the stars. Nia too is captivated by them. The Chorus are the stars.

Chorus

Does fire exist in the vicinity of the moon?

Were angels created at the beginning of the world or before the beginning of the world?

What was there before creation?

What is creation?

Can God create other worlds?

Could the universe have existed since eternity?

Will the world end at some time?

Nia is by now aware of Deri. She tries to act normally, as though she had not spent all afternoon searching for him.

Nia There's some food left. Share it with me.

Deri You can take it home. The little ones need it more than me.

Nia Please.

Deri eats mechanically.

Red sky at night.

Deri Have you noticed how the dusk makes things glow with an inner light, as though they had absorbed the sun? Look at those trees, these flowers – I know they feel, Nia, they are sentient. Sometimes they seem to speak to me . . .

Nia Deri!

Deri I'm not mad, Nia.

Nia I know, but I'm frightened for you. When will you come home?

Deri I'm happier here.

Nia You can't live like this. It's too cold and damp.

Deri And you think our home is not?

Nia True.

Deri We lost a brother and a sister. They weren't sick, Nia.

Nia What do you mean? They died of pneumonia.

Deri And do you think they would have had pneumonia if they'd lived in a warm, dry house and had plenty of food?

Nia You sound like your old self suddenly.

Deri There are plenty to make speeches. Even the preacher Caleb talks about the New Social Order. I'll never see it.

Nia What do you think of him, of Caleb?

Deri Too few new people come into this place. That makes the least of them seem interesting.

Nia Is that all you have to say?

Deri His flesh and spirit seem in constant combat.

Nia Why?

Deri He has the brow of a saint and the mouth of a libertine.

Nia Nonsense.

Deri You've already formed an opinion then?

Nia I have no opinion. Bethan says she will talk to him about you. She thought he might answer some of your questions. He's travelled around the world.

Deri Has he? Why?

Nia Do you hate him?

Deri Not as much as you like him.

Nia Who said?

Deri No one. I can tell. He's not worthy of you, Nia.

Nia He's staying with Bethan.

Deri And you're jealous.

Nia (*angry*) I am not thinking of him in that way! Why must you always be so critical of me!

Deri Am I?

Nia I thought you might be jealous over Bethan.

Deri Bethan? I've forgotten her. Whatever feelings I might once have had, I buried them. And so long ago, I've forgotten where. I've forgotten everything. All anger and pain and hatred. These things kept me earth-bound. I shall probably leave soon.

Nia To go where?

Deri South again. To look for work.

Nia How long will you bear it this time?

Deri I have an inner strength I did not have then. I wasn't used to working in the earth. Now I look forward to it, that I might have some communication with the core, with the dark heart of her. You can hear her groan and sigh. They say it is the seam, the coal settling, the wooden stays creaking – that's how they explain it. You know how it is when you never see the sun? When we came out at night our eyes were so used to the dark that the stars seemed like a thousand suns and our ears were deafened by their music.

Nia What music?

Deri Haven't you heard it?

Nia What?

Deri The sounds of the spheres.

Nia No.

Deri What do they say? We are born with it in our ears but we cannot distinguish it from silence. (*He listens.*)

Nia Deri? Have you ever wished yourself in someone else's skin?

Deri My highest aspiration now is to lose my physical self and become spirit. Someone else's skin is no different to my skin.

Nia Deri, there is something I want to tell you. When Bethan and I were children and we played in the forest we had a game, a private game that no one else knew about. A magical game.

Deri What do you mean, magical?

Caleb enters.

Caleb Good evening, sister, brother.

Deri Preacher! Have you come to admire the stars too?

Caleb I'm looking for Bethan. She went out on an errand three hours ago.

Nia She's on her way home.

Caleb You saw her?

Nia Yes. We talked. She didn't finish the errand.

He looks at the basket.

Caleb So I see.

Nia I was hungry.

Caleb I'd better go and look for her. If she gets lost in this forest –

Nia Lost! She knows the forest better than anyone.

Caleb How so?

Nia We spent our childhood here.

Caleb You're old friends?

Deri We were. Bethan's mother paid for our 'education'. When she died Bethan's father threw us out and told Bethan never to speak to us again.

Caleb And she obeyed?

Nia Until today. We met by chance.

Caleb takes Nia's hand. She's moved.

Caleb This is a terrible wrong he has done you. I shall speak to him.
Deri No.
Nia Please, don't.
Caleb Such an injustice should not go unpunished.
Deri It's too late.
Nia What my brother means is, we're too proud.
Caleb But this evening Bethan broke the silence?
Nia Yes.
Caleb I'm glad. It shows generosity.
Nia Will you be staying here much longer?

Pause.

Caleb Bethan said nothing then?
Nia About what?
Caleb That we are to be married.

Pause.

Deri What?!
Nia No, she said nothing.
Caleb In a week's time.

Silence.

Deri Preacher! Before you go, I have some questions for you.
Caleb Questions? On matters scriptural?
Deri No. Matters spiritual.
Caleb I may be able to help, my interpretation –

He is interrupted by Deri. Deri's questions are firstly in earnest, then teasing and finally aggressive.

Deri Is the sky heavy or light?
Caleb (*smiles as though this were a sort of game*) Light.

Deri Is there something beyond the sky?

Caleb The stars, the planets, I suppose.

Deri Do the planets receive their light from the sun or from themselves?

Caleb From . . . the sun.

Deri Are the heavens fluid or solid?

Caleb Solid.

The Chorus joins in.

Deri Are the heavens moved directly by God?

Caleb Yes.

Deri Are the heavens moved by intelligences?

Caleb Yes.

Deri Do celestial bodies cause sound by their motions?

Caleb Sound? What sort of –

Deri Do celestial bodies act on the subliminal mind?

Caleb I –

Deri What was there before creation?

Caleb is silent. Hush. Deri speaks alone.

To what end was the world created?

Sharp intake of breath from the Chorus. Caleb is sweating. He laughs nervously.

Caleb A piece of advice, brother Deri. Do not dabble with the mystic writers – they are the most artful refiners that ever appeared in the Christian world. There is something like enchantment in them. When you get into them, you know not how to get out. (*to Nia*) So, goodnight. I shall expect to see you both at our wedding. And don't worry about Tate. He can refuse me nothing.

Deri I won't be here.

Deri leaves. Nia wants to follow him but stands before Caleb as though mesmerized.

Caleb And you?

Nia I –

Caleb Promise me you'll be there.

Nia I promise.

*Caleb continues to hold her hand, then leans forward
and kisses her on the cheek. As before, the gesture lasts
slightly longer than it should. Nia leaves.*
　　Caleb feels he is being sucked into a vortex.

Chorus
　O thou whom, unseen, I love,
　by what powerful force dost though attract my soul?
　The eye has not seen,
　nor has the ear heard,
　nor has it entered into the heart of man
　to conceive what thou art,
　and yet I love thee beyond all that my eye has seen
　or my ear heard –
　beyond all that my heart comprehends.

The Chorus release Caleb.

SCENE FOUR

Bethan and Nia in the forest two days later.

Nia Just think. You could spy on Caleb.

Bethan As if I would do such a thing.

Nia Aren't you curious to see what he does when you're
not there?

Bethan He works, he writes . . . Are you saying I
shouldn't trust him?

Nia That's not what I mean. Don't you want to see how
he is, how he behaves, how he speaks to others when
you're not present?

Bethan I wouldn't want to know. And the wedding is in three days' time. I have to meet the dressmaker at six o'clock. What if I couldn't get back in time? What if I became lost?

Nia You know that never happened before. We were always able to find our way back.

Bethan True. (*Pause.*) We would need two birds.

Nia I have them.

Bethan Already?

Nia One jackdaw, killed by the gamekeeper, and a song thrush. He must have killed that by mistake.

Bethan Where are they?

Nia Here.

Bethan You thought I would agree?

Nia I thought you might.

Bethan How can I?

Nia Just one last time. In a few days' time you'll be a married woman. You'll rarely step into this wood. Your husband will need you by him, at home. And if you have children there will be little time to indulge such fantasies. One last time, Bethan.

Bethan You're very subtle, Nia.

Nia Do you remember how it felt to fly? Over the fields, over the woods, along the mountain . . . you saw the eagle's nest. Do you remember?

Bethan I was above the eagle . . . looking down on the eagle . . . with the wind stinging my eyes, my mouth open, I could feel the mist, the cloud on my tongue. I never felt such freedom before, nor since.

Nia What else?

Bethan A blue sky such as I had never seen. Banks of blue that held me while the pale sun flowed round my shoulders. Silver and mercury, flying higher and higher through sphere after sphere, losing the earth, skimming the edge of this world. And then I felt that I was joined

22

to every other living thing, that I could never be alone. I was so happy.

Nia Come, you first.

Nia opens her bag and takes out the two dead birds. She places one on the floor before Bethan and one before herself. Bethan picks up the bird and holds it gently in her arms. Within seconds she falls apparently lifeless to the floor and the bird takes flight. Quickly Nia picks up the 'body' of Bethan and cradles it as Bethan did with the bird. Soon Nia collapses and 'Bethan' sits up. It should be obvious that Nia is now within the body of Bethan. She sits up and puts the other dead bird back into her bag. She then drags the body of Nia to a covered place and begins to dig.

Please forgive me, friend. I promise it will not be for long. You will have a lifetime together, all I want is a few days. (*She drags the body, her own body, to the pit and gently pulls it in.*) I cannot bear to look. Must I cover my own face with earth? (*She pulls up some flowers and plants them in the earth.*) Here. You only sleep, and while you sleep these anemones will flower above and send down their roots to caress your cheek. (*She washes her hands and face in the stream. A shaft of sunlight falls upon her hands. She notices how different they are from her own.*) The skin is so fine. The nails so smooth. (*Pause.*) I must go back to the house before she's missed. Before *I'm* missed.

Part Two

SCENE ONE

Nia as Bethan enters the house. The stairway is lined with portraits of Bethan's ancestors (the Chorus). She catches sight of herself in a large mirror and jumps with surprise. Then she stares at her reflection for a long time.

Her father enters and sees her.

Tate Are you become so vain?

Nia is startled. She turns and looks at him. He is taken aback by her frank stare.

Nia No, sir.

He looks away.

Tate You've missed supper. You know how I hate unpunctuality.

Nia Yes, sir.

Tate And your dressmaker will be here in a few minutes. Why were you staring at yourself?

Nia I was surprised.

Tate Surprised at what?

Nia (*hesitates*) How much I look like mother. (*She glances at one of the portraits.*)

Tate It's true. It startles me too sometimes.

He strokes her hair and kisses her cheek. She jumps.

You are in a strange humour this evening.

Nia Am I? (*She consciously copies one of Bethan's gestures.*)

Tate What is this on your dress? Mud?

Nia I was walking back through the forest and tripped on a dead branch.

24

Tate The forest? Again? Next time I'll send one of the servants with you. I've had enough of you playing peasant. The forest can be dangerous. The people in it too. (*Pause.*) You should go and eat.

Nia I'm not hungry.

Tate You're never hungry. You're not ill?

Nia No, sir.

Tate On the contrary, your voice sounds distinctly hoarse. You've caught cold. (*Pause.*) I hear that Nia is back.

Nia She came to the house on Sunday.

Tate Did she?

Nia I saw her speak to Mari. She was probably asking for work.

Tate Deri is back too. I didn't mention it because . . . because I saw no point.

Nia Of course not.

Tate Bethan, please, it would do you no good to see them, nor they to see you.

Nia How so?

Tate I've told you, they are an arrogant and bitter pair.

Nia Maybe they have good reason to be so.

Tate Maybe I have good reason too. Maybe your mother might still be . . .

Nia They had nothing to do with Mother dying.

Tate Not directly. I just think if she had thought of herself half as much as she thought of others . . .

Nia She died of typhoid.

Tate That she caught from one of the tenants.

Nia Are you saying that we should not practice Christian charity?

Tate (*pause*) I'm just saying in moderation, all things in moderation. Your mother always carried things too far.

Nia Why did you throw them out?

Tate Because they were a reminder, of her goodness. I used to think she did these things to spite me, to show

25

how I lacked conviction. Now, with Caleb's help, I no longer think so.

Nia Then you don't object to my seeing them?

Tate Six months ago I would have beaten you for such insolence. Now, now I am glad that you are so forthright. I think, I think it's too late. I think the damage is done. They are an arrogant pair. Nia is full of rancour. She always dominated you, Bethan, but you could not see it. And Deri – how could I allow him back in the house after the way he spoke to me, in front of the servants?

Nia You could use your influence, to find them work, something worthy of them.

Tate How can I? It's too late. Too many harsh words have been spoken.

Nia It's not too late.

Tate Bethan! This is the end of our discussion. I am still your father and you must still obey me. Once you are married, then you may answer to your husband, that is only natural, but until then you will do as you are told.

Nia You do not understand.

Tate raises his hand instinctively, then lowers it again.

Tate You have reason to be grateful for the change your future husband has wrought in me. Now go to your room.

Nia hesitates, not trusting her memory of the house layout. Mari passes carrying a lamp.

Mari! Take some coal to Miss Bethan's room and light a fire. I fear she has a chill.

He leaves. Mari gives Nia the lamp and exits. She returns quickly with a full bucket of coal.

Mari Miss Bethan? Are you waiting for me?

Nia Yes. Here, you take the lamp. I feel a little unsteady.

Mari walks on. Nia follows her.

(*to herself*) Ah! My body knows the way. I simply follow.
Now I belong here the house is not as I remember.
There's less pleasure than I imagined in this soft carpet.
When she called me 'Miss Bethan', so politely, I shivered
with delight. Why shouldn't I be addressed with respect?
I am as decent as any living being.

*Mari walks on ahead. As Nia follows her up the
staircase, the portraits she's passed react to her. They
hiss and make faces. The portraits (the Chorus) look
straight ahead and cannot see those on either side. One
of them is Bethan's Mother.*

Chorus (*in turn*)
Look, look at her dress. We know where she's been.
Her father forbids her. He absolutely forbids her to meet
    that girl, and her brother.
It was her mother's fault. Such a ridiculous idea!
Her mother was marginal. I mean, her sanity was always
    in question.
If this had been the Middle Ages she'd have been a nun.
That sort of person. A country mouse.
I don't mean to be uncharitable – God forbid!
This family has given so much to charity. Last year we
    were able to buy Bibles for every family on the estate.
Bethan's Mother A man cannot have public spirit, who is
    void of private benevolence.
Chorus (*in turn*)
Who said that?
You know who!
Well, I think it's a waste of time to lavish education on
    such people. How could she bring them up together?
Fortunately it doesn't seem to have damaged Bethan.
But it might have.
Of course. Miss Bethan is such a creature of refinement.

You should see the way she holds the knife and fork.
I find her a little dull. Like you know who!
And this man. This ridiculous preacher. If he's so
  wonderful, why's he interested in her?
(*together*) Ha! Ha!
Mother Come, come near, come near . . . near.

*This last sounds like someone calling her name. Nia
turns round. Mother puts her fingers to her lips.*

Take care. People are not always what they seem to be.
Nia What do you mean?

*Mari turns around. Nia is silent. They reach Bethan's
room. Mari opens the door and stands back so that Nia
can enter.*

Mari I'll make the fire before getting you ready for bed.
Nia I can manage myself.
Mari Maybe we should ask Dr Morris to call by. Do you
  have a fever?

She feels Nia's head.

No.

*Nia notices another mirror, this time full-length, and
stares at herself again. She undoes her hair and feels it.*

Looking forward to the wedding?
Nia Yes.
Mari Make sure you don't fall sick. I've seen that happen
  before. (*Pause.*) Is there anything else?
Nia No. I'd like to be left alone.

Mari leaves. Nia begins undressing.

What did she mean, take care? Did she know it was me?
  (*Pause.*) These shoes are too tight. (*She kicks them off.*)
  Vanity? Her feet are not so pretty, considering she does
  not stand in mud and water as I have to. (*She stands*

*before the mirror, twisting her body, trying to see herself
from every angle. Then she examines her hands and
arms.*) There's a livid scar here. How was that done?
And here, a bruise. (*She walks over to a cupboard and
opens it.*) Silk and muslin! In abundance! (*She throws
the dresses into the air and rolls about in them as she
might in a heap of fallen leaves.*)

SCENE TWO

The drawing room.

Clarissa We were concerned that everything was being
done according to form. Since your poor mother's
death, Henry has made a monumental effort, we realize,
but it cannot replace a mother's care. I only wish we
could have spent more time with you, but Bristol is quite
a distance and I've been kept quite busy with my girls –
all married now, of course. They did very well.
  Your trousseau, for example. What are you doing
about your trousseau?

Nia Er.

Clarissa Exactly! I might have guessed. Sailing towards
her wedding day with no trousseau!

Pamela Have you set the date?

Nia We marry on Thursday.

Clarissa and Pamela THURSDAY!

Silence.

Clarissa But, but . . . the Bishop is booked, I assume, and
all arrangements for the wedding breakfast have been
made?

Nia We want no fuss.

Pamela Is there another reason for such haste?

Nia No!

Clarissa No wedding breakfast! No cathedral!
Pamela What does Henry say about it all?
Nia He's happy.
Clarissa Of course, now he's seen the light!
Pamela (*mockingly*) Alleluia!
Clarissa Your mother had some strange ideas. She'd
approve of this, no doubt. This would be just her style.
She was more than a little . . . eccentric. Especially when
it came to the servants. How *are* your staff, my dear?

*Mari is standing behind them looking straight ahead.
Nia is embarrassed.*

Mmn?
Nia I believe Mari has a slight cold.

The aunts laugh.

Clarissa I mean, are they well behaved?
Nia I suppose they are.
Clarissa If you suppose they are, then they must be, but
take care. My friend Lady Buckley never concerned
herself with the servants. Only when her husband
questioned the amount of money she gave the
housekeeper and compared it to the quality of food they
received did they discover what was going on!
Pamela Which was?
Clarissa Well, if there was lobster to be served at dinner,
why, they had it downstairs as well, in equal portion!
Quince and lobster, chablis and champagne!
Nia We live very simply here.
Pamela So I see.
Clarissa You don't plan to entertain then?
Nia My future husband is a clergyman!
Pamela They're the worst!
Clarissa Pamela!
Pamela You're rather more like your mother than we'd
remembered.

Clarissa It's not always the case. My daughter Sophie is a
silly headstrong girl. You'd never guess we were related,
let alone mother and daughter. She never visits.

Pamela You never visit her.

Clarissa How could I with that booby of a husband!

Pamela A rich booby. And you chose him.

Nia clears her throat.

So, is your husband to be at home? I should love to meet
him.

Nia He was busy. I'm sure he'll be down soon.

The door opens.

Pamela Speak of the devil!

Clarissa Pamela!

Pamela Mr Jones, we are so pleased to meet you. (*She
eyes him up and down greedily*.)

Nia My aunts Clarissa and Pamela.

Pamela He's very tall for a man of God, don't you think?

Caleb Are men of God obliged to be short?

Pamela Every bishop of my acquaintance measures the
same in circumference as in height.

Caleb I am not a bishop! Some bishops are more
interested in their bellies than their souls.

Pamela We were saying, how exciting it is to have a man
of – conviction in the family.

Clarissa We attend church every week. In summer that is.
In winter it's very difficult. I'm very susceptible to cold. I
feel the cold terribly. It's a very cold church.

Caleb The Holy Spirit keeps me warm.

Pamela Indeed!

Clarissa It's draughty too. In the summer it's a joy to sit
there. It's so cool. In that terrible heat last summer, it
was the coolest place on the estate. Even cooler than the
cellar.

31

Caleb glares at them.

It's a beautiful building. Superb architecture. Fourteenth century.

Pamela Thirteenth century.

Clarissa End of thirteenth, beginning of fourteenth. It has a leper's window.

Pamela It does.

Clarissa Leprosy!

Pamela Eradicated!

Clarissa Wonders of modern medicine!

Caleb I'm afraid it is still common elsewhere.

Clarissa Well, 'The poor will always be amongst us.'

Caleb Is that so?

Clarissa You know, I have not sinned in thought, word or deed for a twelvemonth at least.

Caleb Really? And you?

Pamela Very little. Almost nothing. I lead a – busier life than my sister. Do you take confession?

Caleb Confession!

Pamela Of course, that's Roman! And celibacy. A very bad idea. You're not in favour of celibacy, are you, Mr Jones?

Clarissa Pamela, Mr Jones is getting married next week!

Pamela But he might be in favour of it as a principle. I understand it's becoming quite a fashion!

Caleb My theology is a little more rigorous than that.

Pamela I'm sure it's very rigorous.

Clarissa We were a little shocked that the wedding is so soon and that we only heard a few days ago. We understand that you want a simple ceremony with few guests. Of course, we should still like to give you something.

Caleb We're building a new chapel. If you would like to give us a wedding gift, then perhaps you might think instead of contributing towards that.

Clarissa I see.
Pamela I see.
Clarissa We were thinking of some of the family silver.
Pamela There are some beautiful pieces.
Caleb I should only melt it down and sell the silver.
Clarissa What!

Nia is enjoying their shock. It makes her feel closer to Caleb.

In that case I shall make out a note for the amount.

She opens her bag and takes out a book. She writes a figure and hands it to Caleb.

We wish you every happiness.

He takes it and pockets it, which shocks them even more.

Caleb Thank you.
Pamela We planned to visit an old family friend who lives in the vicinity. Do excuse us. Good day.

They leave. Nia and Caleb burst out laughing.

Nia Only two more days, and three more nights.
Caleb When I first asked you to marry me, you were the reticent one.
Nia Was I?
Caleb I thought you would refuse. You seemed almost nervous of me. Now you cannot wait even a couple of days.

She puts her arms around Caleb and he strokes her hair.

Patience! Patience! My little dove!

SCENE THREE

Nia is waiting for Caleb outside the chapel. She is wearing a very plain and simple wedding dress. People pass by and shake her hand. Some kiss her on the cheek. Mari stands behind her with some flowers.

Mari You haven't heard then?

Nia Heard what?

Mari That Nia Richards has gone missing.

Nia Don't her family know where she is? What about her brother, Deri?

Mari He's left.

Nia Left for where?

Mari How would I know? His father thinks he's gone to look for work. Work! Let's hope he's less workshy in the mine than he is on the farm.

Nia (*angry*) You know nothing about him!

Mari smiles.

Mari I always thought you had an uncommon interest in Deri.

Nia How long has Nia been missing?

Mari A few days.

Nia Is that all? I'm sure it's nothing to worry about.

Mari I'm not worried. I never liked her anyway. She always blamed me for taking her mother's job, but everyone knows you can't do this job and have a family. This family is my family, your family. I don't think anyone liked her apart from you. She's morose and sullen. She's always thinking. Even walking down the lane, sometimes she'll pass you and say nothing, and when you say, 'Hello' she'll say. 'Sorry – I was thinking.' People like that, they're always thinking about themselves. You can count upon it, she wasn't thinking of anyone else!

34

Nia (*hurt*) You don't understand —

Caleb enters. He seems flustered.

Caleb Your friend Nia is missing.
Nia Mari has just told me. It's only since Saturday!
Perhaps she's gone back to the town to look for work.
Perhaps she has a lover!
Caleb Bethan! Do you think so?
Nia I don't know.
Caleb Maybe we should send some of the men to search
for her.
Nia No! I think I know why Nia may have left.
Caleb And why is that?
Nia It may have something to do with our marriage.
Caleb How?
Nia She coveted my life here. Everything about my life,
including my future husband.

Caleb appears moved by this news.

I am not saying that she harboured any passion for you. It
is simply because you are mine. I believe she'll come
back once the wedding is over.
Caleb Despite what you say, I think we have a duty, you
as her friend have a duty, to make inquiries. She is a
vulnerable young girl, a pretty young girl. There are
people who would prey on her youth and innocence.
Nia Of course I shall. After the wedding. Caleb, have you
forgotten? We are about to get married.
Caleb Of course.

*Nia reaches out a hand to him. He is distracted. He
takes her hand and kisses it. She is reassured. The chapel
doors are opened. Caleb offers Nia his arm. They turn
together three times – this is the wedding ceremony. Nia
says the following as they turn.*

Nia Strange. Why should he worry so? Does he suspect?

How can he? He is a rational man of God. Just a few more days. Maybe then I should truly disappear. Go and find Deri. What will Deri do when he finds out I'm missing? I didn't mean to cause him pain. I'm glad he's gone. By the time he returns all will be back to normal. Bethan will not breathe a word. She'll be too frightened. The truth would have her dismissed as a witch. Who would believe her?

At the last turn the wedding guests throng around them, cheering and throwing confetti. A table is brought on for the wedding supper. It is obvious that the guests are disappointed with the simple food and drink.

Nia and Caleb sit at the centre of the table, Nia's father to the left. Local church men and other dignitaries, all in black, are seated either side.

Caleb stands to make a speech. He has an air of ironic detachment throughout his speech. He seems to be enjoying the discomfort of the guests. Nia also finds this amusing initially.

Caleb There are three things that are never satisfied – yea, four things say not, it is enough: the grave and the barren womb; the earth that is not filled with water and the fire that saith not, it is enough.

The guests begin to eat.

The eye that mocketh at his father, and despiseth to obey his mother, the ravens of the valley shall pick it out, and the young eagles shall eat it.

Some put down their knives and forks.

Such is the way of an adulterous woman; she eateth, and wipeth her mouth, and saith, I have done no wickedness.
Nia Caleb?

Nia pulls at his sleeve, he shakes her off roughly. She is shocked and angry. The guests look at each other – this is a very strange wedding. Henry tries to interrupt him.

Tate I think it's time to toast –

Caleb talks over him and Tate sits back down.

Caleb It is not for kings to drink wine, nor for princes strong drink, lest they drink and forget the law, and pervert the judgement of any of the afflicted. Give strong drink unto him that is ready to perish, and wine unto those that be of heavy hearts.

The revellers put down their cups.

For who can find a virtuous woman? Her price is far above rubies. The heart of her husband doth safely trust in her . . .

A loud commotion outside, a banging on the doors. Mari leaves to investigate. We can hear raised voices. Eventually two men burst in carrying the body of Nia. It is obvious that the body has been buried. There is earth everywhere.

Tate How dare you – on my daughter's wedding day.

Caleb pushes him out of the way and helps carry the body. Nia hangs back.

Caleb Lie her here. Is she dead?
Man No.
Caleb Then what? Asleep?
Man It seems. But she was buried. Our dogs uncovered her.
Tate Have you told her family?
Man We're on our way. We thought to rest here. We were – frightened. We don't understand. There are no marks,

37

no sign of an attack. We thought Bethan might know
something, them being such good friends.

Tate Were they now?

Nia We met by chance in recent months. Passing in the
forest. Friendship is too extravagant a phrase for our
acquaintance.

Man We often heard you laughing, like two jackdaws!

Nia stares at the man.

Caleb We should send for Dr Morris.

Tate Run and tell her family. Let them send someone to –
to collect her. Her brother?

Man (*hesitates and looks at other men*) He's missing too.

Nia swivels round.

Nia He's gone south, to the mines.

Man We've only his father's word, and that after his
daughter had gone missing.

Nia What are you implying?

Man We all know he wasn't himself recently.

Nia Nonsense! He adored his sister!

Caleb Bethan!

Nia She shall stay here.

Caleb I agree. Her family cannot afford to look after her.
It is the least act of Christian charity –

Tate Very well!

Caleb It is as if the soul has left her and flown away.

Nia Mari! Fetch me some water.

*They place the body on a couch, Nia draws closer
slowly. The other guests drift away.*

Tate I think you can leave this to Mari, my dear.

Caleb Let her do it. She is now the minister's wife. She
must be seen to express her humility.

Tate Even on her wedding day?

Caleb God makes no such exceptions. Do you doubt that

I have her best interests at heart?
Tate Of course not. (*He leaves.*)

*Mari comes in with a bowl of water and a sponge. Mari
and Nia begin to undress the body. Mari looks at Caleb
and he leaves. They begin to wash her.*

Nia You can go now, Mari. Please.

*Nia combs the hair. As Mari leaves Caleb is still
standing in the doorway. The two women look at him.*

Caleb I wondered if you were nearly finished?
Nia I will be there directly.

*Caleb goes. Mari goes. The Chorus (still as the wedding
guests) look through the windows.*

First Man Have you ever been to a wedding like it?
First Woman And when they brought in the girl!
Second Man Did you see the preacher's face?
Second Woman Such tenderness!
Second Man (*he giggles*) But not for the bride!
Third Woman Ssh! How can you! So much melancholy. It
hangs in this air like dust.

*They disappear. Nia finishes washing the body. She
kisses it on the forehead.*

Nia It is for this night that I have gambled my soul – and
yours.

SCENE FOUR

*The wedding night. Nia is undressing herself. Caleb,
already in his nightshirt, is sitting in a chair reading.*

Caleb I have prepared a text for this evening.
Nia I beg your pardon?

Caleb Something appropriate.

Nia A text? You wish to preach now?

Caleb My dear, I do not like your tone. I expect you are afraid. You have no need.

Nia There is no reason for me to fear my husband. I am not afraid, simply –

Caleb (*interrupting her*) Dying to pleasure, even the most innocent of pleasure, we shall live to God.

Nia Husband –

Caleb Of pleasures there are four sorts: pleasure of the mind – curious books, deep researches; pleasures of the heart – attachments, pure friendship; pleasures of the imagination – schemes and fantasies; and sensual pleasures – pleasures of the eye, ear, taste and smell, indulgence, etc. Pleasure, if indulged, spreads through and corrupts. It betrays with a kiss, poisons with honey, wounds in its smiles and kills while it promises happiness.

Pause. Nia puts her arms around Caleb's neck and he immediately disentangles himself.

You obviously don't understand.

Nia If you did not want me, why did you marry me? Is it because of my father? Because of his house? The land he owns? These servants? The money he will give you to build your church?!

Caleb Your father is a generous man and this new church will be my life – and yours.

Nia Then I am right!

Caleb You misunderstand.

Nia Then tell me the real reason.

Caleb To protect myself.

Nia From what?

Caleb From lust, from losing God.

Nia Then you did not love me at all?

Caleb Not in the way you mean. I did not mean to hurt

you. I may not have been entirely truthful and for that I am sorry. But it is for the good of both our souls – we will grow to love each other in God, without the pollution of base love.

Nia Pollution? Is that what you call it?

Caleb Bethan! Quiet! We will never speak of this again. You are now my wife and you will behave accordingly. As God is my master, so I am yours. The events of this evening have been disturbing and exhausting. I am going to sleep. I suggest you do likewise.

Nia And what of love?

Caleb Dear wife, I find it unseemly that while a young girl lies between life and death in this house, your chief concern is your own romantic fantasy.

Nia You love another.

Caleb is shocked at her guessing.

Nia (*screams*) You love Nia!

Caleb (*trying to cover his confusion*) What a ripe imagination you have!

Nia It's true, isn't it? Deny it then!

Caleb pulls the curtains around the bed and disappears behind them. Nia is alone. She catches sight of herself in the bedroom mirror. She begins to tear off her clothes and then tear at her hair.

She tries to collect herself. She takes the mirror off the wall.

(*shouts*) Mari! Mari!

Mari appears.

Mari What is it? What are you doing wandering around on your wedding night?

Nia I want you to take down all the mirrors in the house.

Mari All of them?

Nia Yes. And break them into small pieces.

Mari What? I can't

Nia Why not?

Mari Why not? Breaking mirrors! Think of the ill luck that will follow!

Nia Do as I say. There is no room for superstition in this house. Not now we have a man of God living among us. If I told him the servants clung to unchristian beliefs he might throw you out.

Mari I'll get Joshua to help me.

Nia Quickly. I don't want there to be a single glass left when I wake tomorrow. If my father protests, tell him it's Caleb's order. We are to be careful from now on, tell him. Dying to pleasure, even the most innocent of pleasure, we shall live to God.

SCENE FIVE

Nia stands on a hill watching the clouds scudding overhead. Night and day pass twice over. She screams the name of her friend.

Nia Bethan! Bethan!

No reply. Silence.

Where has she gone? She cannot be lost. She must have gone back to the spot and found the body gone. But why hasn't she come to the house? Where is she? What if she's been killed? What if some cruel boy has stoned her to death? What to do now? All my careful planning has come to nothing. My brother thinks me dead and is heartbroken. My husband does not love me. I have destroyed a life. I could take back my body now but what then, Bethan's lifeless body and Nia walking free. I'd be accused of murder, no one would believe me.
    WHAT HAVE I DONE?

Early morning. Mari enters the room where the body is laid out. Nia is sitting beside it.

Mari Miss Bethan, please. You must eat. Your sitting here won't help.

Nia Leave me alone!

Mari Miss Bethan. You don't see . . . she won't stay much longer.

Nia What are you saying?

Mari That I think she will pass over soon.

Nia How do you know? Are you the doctor now?

Mari No, but –

Nia But what?

Mari Nothing. I've already been reprimanded for my 'superstitions'.

Nia What is it?

Mari I'm not sure.

Nia TELL ME!

Mari I was woken up this morning, by a noise, just after dawn. A tapping on the window. I thought it was probably the branch – there's a chestnut tree close to my . . . I opened my eyes and you might think I was dreaming, but I swear I wasn't. It was a bird, a bird tapping at the window. It means death. A bird flying into the house, or trying to.

Nia Thank God . . . Thank God. Open all the windows and douse all the fires.

Mari It's February.

Nia If you refuse then I shall do it myself.

She flings open the windows. Caleb enters.

Caleb What is this?

Mari She's been sitting up all night with Nia.

Caleb Your solicitous nature is to be commended. Now dress and have breakfast. I want to discuss something with you in my study after breakfast. What is this window doing open? It is expensive enough to run this house without such profligate waste. (*He closes the window.*)

Nia (*to Mari*) My instructions. Not now, later.

Mari nods.

Caleb What was that?

Nia Nothing. And what will you do?

Caleb I've asked Dr Morris to come by. I'll wait here for him.

Nia reluctantly goes out of the room but leaves the door ajar. She peers through the crack at Caleb. He sits next to the body and strokes its hair.

My darling. Do not worry. I shall do all I can to discover the root of this sickness. My angel. I shall call the finest doctors in the land. Let them pay. It is my intention to bankrupt the old man, and as for his daughter, she once told me that her father beat her! Life with me and him will be fitting purgatory. Do not feel pity. She knows nothing of the lives of you and I, of our struggles. She idles her life away giving orders. Not now. Not any more. I shall make her work. I shall make her bones ache and her feet burn. She will minister to the poor night and day. She will help me build God's mansion with her bare hands. I told her I had travelled the world and this explained the colour of my face. She believed every word. I could have told her I'd seen two-headed men and she would have believed me. She's never stepped off this estate. I am this colour through working in the fields like you. My father was a labourer too – he died when the landowner's horse was lame and he made him pull the plough instead. His heart exploded.

44

I have insinuated myself into the hearts and minds of these parasites – I made them invite me into their home, I made *her* fall in love with me and now I have them, now I have this family here. (*He holds up the flat of his hand.*) If only you could have seen our wedding night! When my eyes and ears and thoughts were all for you; she stood there in our room, blushing and panting (*he laughs*) . . . and when I told her we would never be as man and wife because it was a sin in God's eyes, you should have seen her face. Her disappointment was palpable, Nia. I could not deny it. I thought she would burst into flames, such was her rage and frustration. In such a way I shall grind her down.

And yet somehow she guessed that you were the object of my longing.

I must go now, my angel. The doctor is to come later. Nia, if you can hear me, take hope. I have heard of such cases where a person lay as in a sleep for years and then awoke.

Caleb kisses Nia on the lips. Nia makes a noise and Caleb turns and sees her. He grabs her as she tries to escape and drags her into the room.

Would you spy on me too?
Nia I have something to tell you.
Caleb What?
Nia The reason why Nia's body lies there.
Caleb You know? Is it all your fault then?
Nia Her spirit . . . Nia . . . is in this body. I am Nia.
Caleb What?
Nia It's a trick, a game we played as children.
Caleb You're saying that you are possessed by Nia?
Nia I am Nia, Caleb.
Caleb And Bethan?
Nia Bethan's spirit is trapped, but it is trying to return. I must wait here till she returns. I hid the body, my body. I

45

was jealous. I wanted you. Just for a few days. But they brought the body here and she was nowhere, lost. Now Mari says there's a bird trying to beat its way back through the windows. We must keep all the windows open.

Caleb So you are Nia in Bethan's body and Bethan's spirit is flying around the rooftops . . . Is this what you are telling me?

Nia Yes, yes.

Caleb Who would have thought you would lose your reason – so soon! You Nia! You are nothing like her. You have neither her simplicity nor her wit. That *you* were jealous of *her*, I can believe.

Nia I'm telling the truth!

Caleb The truth? The truth is always plain, obvious. The truth has no magic, no dark corners. The truth is light, blinding in its simplicity.

For a moment the room darkens and there is a soft sound like the beating of wings. Caleb is frightened.

What is that?

Nia Do you see? Can you see?

Caleb A trick, a simple trick of light.

Nia No, it's Bethan. She's outside.

Caleb Is that what you want me to believe? That you are a young woman full of devils?

Nia No!

He grabs her hands.

Caleb But if you *are* telling the truth, then we must exorcize them!

Nia What!

Caleb I will send for the brothers. Joshua!

Joshua comes into the room.

Fetch brother Issac and brother Thomas and brother

46

Samuel. Bring them back here immediately. Tell them it's a matter of utmost urgency. Go!

Mari follows Joshua into the room.

Build a fire. Fire is purification. We will smoke out the devils.
Mari Miss Bethan?
Caleb I'm giving you an order. Do it!

Mari runs out to fetch firewood. Caleb sits holding Nia by the wrist. She struggles to free herself.

Now we wait!

SCENE SEVEN

A group of men in black file in. They form a circle around Nia. Two of the men hold Nia by the arms, Caleb has his hand on her head. He is reciting verses from the Bible. Another holds her feet, including the Boy who followed Caleb at the beginning. He's now dressed as the others and is one of the most enthusiastic helpers. Those less enthusiastic stand around, embarrassed, more than a little nervous.

Caleb (*this speech is simultaneous with the next exchange between First Man and Second Man*)
And they arrived at the country of the Gadarenes
And there met out of the city a certain man
who wore no clothes, nor lived in any house
but had suffered devils this long time.
He was kept bound with chains and fetters
and he brake the bands and cried with a loud voice
What have I to do with thee, Jesus, son of God?
I beseech thee, torment me not.
Boy Alleluia Jesus!
First Man Are we trying to sweat the devil out of her.
Can't we open a window?

47

Second Man And let more devils in?

First Man I think the devil not so prosaic as to come through a door or window. He can enter through the tiniest crack in the plaster, through the draught in the window frame. I need a clear head for this business and I can barely breathe.

Second Man opens the window while the others are preoccupied.

Caleb
O full of all subtility and all mischief
Thou child of the devil

The shadow passes the window briefly.

Boy Look, look. It's the devil. The devil himself has come!
Nia It's Bethan.

Caleb ignores it and carries on. Nia struggles to be free and get to Bethan.

Caleb
Thou enemy of all righteousness
will thou not cease to pervert
the right ways of the Lord?

The shadow passes again, larger this time. The men tremble and relax their grip on Nia. Caleb and the Boy hold on tight.

And now, he saith, behold
the hand of the lord is upon thee
and thou shalt be blind
not seeing the sun for a season
And immediately there fell on him
a mist and a darkness.

The shadow fills the window, blotting out the light.

First Man It's the end! Beelzebub is come!

Nia Bethan!

Caleb drops the book. Nia struggles free and runs to the window. The men huddle together terrified. Caleb pushes Nia out of the way and tries to close the window.

First Man What's he doing?

Second Man He's meant to be in charge. I have not done this sort of thing before. We might be making a terrible mistake!

Caleb Come and help me, you imbeciles!

Then Bethan's voice is heard.

Bethan Nia!

The Boy wails in fear. One of the men starts to recite the Lord's Prayer.

Caleb What kind of devilry is this? Come, help me!

The Boy reluctantly edges towards the window and clings to Nia. The shadow passes again. Caleb takes off his coat and climbs out of the window.

Caleb Nia! It is Nia!

Boy Caleb! Don't.

Caleb begins to scale the building in his attempt to reach the bird, which has now flown on to the roof.

Caleb Nia. Come back. I shall leave her. I shall have her committed to an insane asylum and then we can marry, then we can be together. Please come nearer. You can hear me. My angel, please come to me, come to me and I will give you back your body, come . . .

He crawls along the roof of the house. The shadow rises above him. He reaches out and falls. The Boy screams. The men watch, helpless. Having seen him fall, they all rush from the room except Nia.

The room fills with a flickering light of feathers. The bird has entered the house. The light changes and Nia rushes to the lifeless body and embraces it. Nia comes back to life, as Nia, Bethan as Bethan. They look at each other.

Bethan There was no other way to save us all.

Bethan moves to Nia and holds her.

Nia What have I done?

Nia cries. Bethan comforts her.

I'm sorry, I'm sorry, I'm sorry . . .

SCENE EIGHT

A sunny afternoon. Two months later. Bethan and Nia and Deri sit in the garden of the house. Deri is weaving a crown of spring flowers for each of them.

Bethan I have resisted asking you this, but tell me, how was it to be me?
Nia I was not you. I was too preoccupied with my own misery to imagine being another.

Pause.

Do you remember? You once told me that the magic made you feel as though you were joined to every living thing.
Bethan Did you not have that feeling?
Nia No. What was it like?
Bethan It was as though we were all creatures caught in a net, but we were also the net and held each other, gently. When I looked down at a bee drinking from a flower I was both the bee and the heart of the flower. And the earth that fed the flower and the rain that soaked the

earth and the cloud that hid the rain. And every flower
likewise. Do you understand?

Nia I think so.

Bethan takes Nia's hand.

Bethan By now, Father will be in Constantinople. I never
thought he would leave this estate. Look, he's sent me a
dried lily from the Black Sea. See how people change!

*Deri takes the lily from her and weaves it into her
crown.*

Deri
For flowers are good both for the living and the dead
For there is a language of flowers
For there is a sound reasoning upon all flowers.
For elegant phrases are nothing but flowers.

The Chorus slowly join in.

For flowers are peculiarly the poetry of Christ.
For flowers are medicinal.
For flowers are musical in ocular harmony.
For the right names of flowers are yet in heaven. God
   make gardeners better nomenclators.
For the poor man's nosegay is an introduction to a
   prince.

The Reality of Magic and Social Injustice

Siân Evans interviewed by Jim Mulligan

A precocious talent for writing at the age of nine, a supportive teacher at the age of eleven in the South Wales comprehensive school and then decline as the examinations system took over – this was Siân Evans's preparation for life as a full-time dramatist.

> In a sense that early talent faded away. I kept on writing poetry and short stories and, when I went to college, I worked on student newspapers but all the time I was watching from the sidelines. It wasn't until I left Wales and met other Welsh writers in London that I felt I might be able to write myself.

Since 1990 Siân Evans has had three plays produced and two television plays. The transformation in *Asleep under the Dark Earth* is based on an Indian myth in which two young men can take over the bodies of dead animals. When they exchange with two birds one of them tries to trick the other and to take over his body permanently.

> I think you find the transformation of people into animals in myths around the world. I am interested in magic and the way different worlds overlap. By magic I mean things that are outside everyday experience. And I think they are embedded in most cultures. In the West, of course, we seem to have lost these insights but even here some people have a link with these other realities. In a way it's like faith. If you believe it, it happens.

Siân Evans is convinced that metaphysical phenomena are as real as the physical world. She recalls how, as a child, she had experiences of people and places that were as real as the reality around but adults simply told her that such experiences were nonsense. She recalls two such experiences.

> When I was very small I would go to bed and close my eyes and I would 'travel', invisible, into other people's homes. I would watch and move from house to house and I would do things but as soon as someone suspected I was there I would leave and, almost like clicking my fingers, I would be back in bed. Later on as an adult in Malaysia where a relative was dying I was visited as I lay down by a presence who stroked my arm and murmured my name and words of comfort. You could say this is your subconscious talking to your conscious mind. Well, maybe it is, but it doesn't really matter. It is still useful information.

As a teenager in Wales, Siân Evans was deeply conscious of the divide between the social classes and the way she and other working-class people were patronized by educated, wealthy people who could not believe that working-class homes could have books and music and intellectual vitality. She brings this out in *Asleep under the Dark Earth*.

> Caleb is so contorted by hate that his notion of social justice is completely implausible. He would have to be mad to think that trapping Bethan in a barren marriage, stealing the family's wealth and gratifying his lust with Nia would improve the lives of the underprivileged. Of course, what happened to his family was terrible and tragic but you cannot restore social justice when you are driven by hate. In the end his death was inevitable because he was so poisoned by hatred he could not have survived.

Nia and her family have also suffered injustice. She feels genuinely aggrieved at the terrible injustice her family has endured but unlike Caleb she is able to learn from her experience.

She and Caleb connect so well because of her bitterness and desire for revenge. Her weakness is her envy and the play is about the way she learns that the lives of the people you envy are not what they seem. She has to go through the process of being somebody else in order to realize who she is and accept it. Her lesson is that, by rejecting herself in favour of someone else she almost lost everything – friendship, love, family. The climax of the play is her realizing this and trying to restore Bethan's spirit.

To Siân Evans the play is about the reality of magic and social injustice. She recognizes that the material situation of what were called the lower orders has improved over 200 years but the fundamental class divisions are as real as ever.

There is very little contact between the classes. Sub-cultures have an insight into the dominant cultures but it does not work the other way round. The ruling class preserves its boundaries by education whereas the working classes have far less choice.

The end of the play is ambiguous; we do not know what, if anything, has changed in the material position of Nia and Deri. Yet the characters have changed internally – Bethan's father has left the country on a spiritual pilgrimage, Bethan and Nia have gained a greater understanding of their flaws; Deri is ready to engage with the world and with the woman he loves. There is no revolution, but perhaps something more subtle.

I think there is a need for idealists or intermediaries like Bethan's mother. She may have been misguided in some ways but she did change people's lives. Real change will not always be achieved through violent revolution; those changes are often superficial and lead to terrible repression. I think a just social order can only be achieved by internal as well as external change, by attitudes in general changing. You can't take privilege away from people. They will just snatch it back. And you can only change people's attitudes through education and integration.

Siân Evans has never written anything specifically for children. In her plays she has children as protagonists and she believes these characterizations are her attempts to understand herself as a child. In *Asleep under the Dark Earth* she is exploring her own adolescence.

For me, adolescence was trying to come to terms with social injustic, passion and the huge questions about the cosmos. I don't believe I have changed much as a person since then. I remember asking those questions about the world and the cosmos. I don't know if any play can change people but I am certain that young people who take part in this play will have to confront the same questions that I asked when I was their age. I hope the play will provoke and stimulate. I hope they will have as much fun acting it as I had writing it. Most of all I hope they will be inspired to write themselves.

Siân Evans's work for theatre includes *Little Sister*, *Badenheim*, *Underdog* and *Four Doors*. A new play is due to open at the Theatre Clwyd in January 1998. TV work includes *Insect Life* and *Tiderace*. She is currently working on a screenplay for Gaucho Films. Awarded an Arts Council award for theatre translation and a Gulbenkian New Directions award for film, she also teaches the Playwright's Workshop at City University.

Production Notes

This is a tale of rivalry between two girls of different social standing who have magical powers. It is set in 1830 in rural Wales between autumn and spring. The settings vary from the Tates' private chapel to a village square, a clearing in a forest, the forest two days later, Bethan's bedroom in the Tates' house which is substantial, their drawing room, the outside of the private chapel, a hill, a room with a window and door where the body is laid and the garden of the house. These should be achieved as simply and fluidly as possible with minimal use of furniture and creative sound and lighting plans. Lighting needs to take into account the passage of time and location. For instance, the first forest scene takes place in the afternoon but Caleb enters into it at dusk. The arrival of the bird in the room in the confessional scene towards the end of Part Two involves the room being filled with 'a flickering light of feathers'. Costumes should reflect the period and the individual's social standing within the community.

CASTING

The characters' ages vary. Bethan Tate and her friend Nia are sixteen. They should be as physically different as possible with contrasting behavioural gestures and vocal range. This will make the transferral of Nia's body into Bethan's at the end of Part One clearer. The transformed Bethan can be played by either the actor playing Nia or the actor playing Bethan. For this to be successful, the physicality of the public and private personality and mannerisms must be well observed. The majority of the other speaking parts are adult but this shouldn't be of great concern to a young cast. Emphasis should be placed on playing the parts with commitment without applying ageing make-up and powdered hair to those playing the grown-up parts. The plot is strong and an audience is far more likely to suspend their disbelief if they understand the story and aren't distracted by these trappings. As well as the nine main characters, the speaking parts include farm labourers, church elders, guests at the wedding and a chorus. This can be as large or as small as you like and offers enormous scope to a cast with a wide age range. It has a variety of functions including being a ghostly congregation, a chorus of stars and Bethan's ancestors. Although the play is set in Wales, north of Merthyr, it would be a mistake to attempt the Welsh accent if it isn't the natural voice of the cast. It's more important to distinguish the various characters' social standing within the community.

QUESTIONS

1 What does the title of the play suggest?
2 What is Methodism? How do the characters' views on it differ?
3 The name Nia is that of a Celtic goddess who is represented by a dove. There are many other references to birds throughout the play, where are they and what is their significance?
4 Deri is isolated from the communal and religious experiences shared by the others. How does this affect him?
5 What moments in the play suggest that Bethan might be in love with Caleb?

6 How has Caleb's arrival changed the community? In what ways does his death allow others to flourish and occupy their natural spiritual plane?

EXERCISES

1 The chorus represents the unconscious thoughts of the community. Often it acts as an emotional barometer because it externalizes the characters' emotional states. It has the power to support or subvert the characters within the play and is highly judgemental. Look at the section where Deri leaves and Nia and Caleb are left alone in the forest a short time. What attitude does the chorus have to the two of them here and how does it serve the play at other times?

2 In pairs: a = Bethan; b = Nia. B (in character) takes several pieces of costume and puts them on slowly and carefully; A mirrors her movement and mannerisms. Gradually A now takes the lead and with more exaggerated actions admires herself in the reflection created by B. Apply this exercise to the section in Bethan's bedroom when her body has been taken over by Nia.

3 Split into groups of four or five and create a series of still images with one of the following titles:
– 'Take care, people are not always what they seem to be.'
– 'I felt you would take the very breath from my body if you could and fashion it as your own.'
– Deri in the forest.
– Nia and Bethan's magic before the play.
– Transferral of souls.
– Asleep under the dark earth.

4 In your group, write a paragraph which captures the atmosphere of any one of these titles. Find appropriate music to go with it.

Suzy Graham-Adriani
February 1997

THE CHRYSALIDS

adapted by David Harrower
from the novel by John Wyndham

Characters

David
Rosalind
Michael
Anne
Rachel
Mark
Petra
Joseph Strorm, David's father
Emily Strorm, David's mother
Katy, Sarah and **Petra,** his sisters
Axel, their uncle
Sophie Wender
Mary Wender, Sophie's mother
Alan Ervin
Mrs Ervin, Alan's mother
Inspector 1
Inspector 2
Fringe people

Note

During each monologue, the telepathy 'group' – David,
Rosalind, Michael, Anne, Rachel, Mark and later Petra –
can either be seen separately or together (although in
different locations across Waknuk). There are also
indicated moments in the text where it is important to see
the group together, to show that they are aware of what
David is thinking at that particular moment.

After Anne's speech in Scene Four she stops
communicating with the group, so is no longer seen with
them.

In Scene Five Sophie should have no socks on.

All the Waknuk characters wear a cross on their
clothing.

Rosalind
  I'm looking down on a city from above.
Michael
  Seen from the air, a city that looks on fire.
Anne
  So bright at first I have to close my eyes.
David
  This is the only dream I've ever dreamt.
Rachel
  A city that's burning in sunlight.
Mark
  Built on the shore of a shimmering lake.
David
  It's like no place I've ever seen.
Rosalind
  I can make out shapes now.
  Squareness of buildings, houses.
Michael
  My eyes are adjusting to the light.
Anne
  Colours emerge. Detail. Streets, trees . . .
Rachel
  And a sound is growing, rising through the air.
  Hypnotic.
David
  A humming . . .
  Like the sound of bees in a hive.
  Quiet, continuous humming.
Mark
  I've told no one of this dream.

This secret we've shared for years.

Anne

It comforted me once, it torments me now.

I try to dream of other things.

Rachel

But each night it returns.

The way secrets always return.

Michael

A city burning in sunlight.

I look down, helpless, suspended in midair.

Rosalind

Wanting only to fall to earth.

Mark

To feel the warmth of the ground on my feet.

Rachel

To walk through the streets.

In and out of shadows.

Michael

To find the source of that sound.

Rosalind

To find why it comes to me.

Why it haunts me.

Anne

To find an end to it.

SCENE TWO   A PURE PLACE

The Storms' house. At one side, Joseph talks to another man. Emily, Katy and Sarah watch them. David has come in with Petra, perhaps carrying wood.

David What is it? (*No reply.*) What's going on?

Katy I don't know.

David (*to Sarah*) What's happened?

Sarah How should I know?

Emily Be quiet, all of you. Sit down.

The man leaves. Joseph walks over.

There's been another raid, hasn't there?

Joseph Yes.

Katy Where?

Joseph The northern border. But they caught two of them.

Sarah Two of them!

Petra (*afraid*) Two Fringe people?

Sarah What are they like? Did he say?

David What about Uncle Axel? He lives on the northern border.

Joseph They attacked a farm. Nowhere near Axel. They beat the family unconscious. The parents and three children. Dumped them outside in a pile. Then took everything they could. Horses, cattle, grain. But these two were greedy. Caught in the kitchen, stuffing food into their mouths like animals. Stupid, greedy animals.

Emily Joseph, that's the tenth raid this year.

Joseph I know, Emily.

Emily How much longer do we have to live like this?

Joseph When the wall . . .

Emily The wall will take another year to finish!

Joseph And when it is we'll be rid of these people for ever. For ever. We'll have our land to ourselves. Until then we have to be strong. We have to be patient. We will get what we deserve. All of us know that, don't we?

Children Yes.

Joseph God is on our side. He will look after us. Now, let's eat. I want to sit with my family and eat.

Petra Why can't Uncle Axel come and live here? It might be him next.

Joseph Petra, I've told you. All of you. He can't be moved. The disease he has is contagious. It could spread and harm all of us. He has to be kept alone. You'll see him again when he's cured. Now . . .

He holds his hands out. They all join hands.

'God, we are eternally grateful for the food we eat, the earth in which it grows, the home in which we live. We thank you for making us what we are and blessing us with this special land. Amen.'

All Amen.

Joseph The food smells delicious. I'm so hungry, Petra, I could eat a tree.

Petra I could eat . . . two trees!

Joseph I could eat a . . . forest.

Petra I could eat a . . .

Katy There's blood on my hand!

Emily Is it cut?

Joseph What have you done?

Katy I don't know . . .

Joseph Go and wash it off, Katy.

Katy looks at David, sitting on her left.

Katy It's you, David! You're bleeding.

David examines his hand.

David It's a splinter. From chopping the wood.

Joseph Then leave the table. Now. Put a bandage on it.

Katy washes her hands. David starts putting on a bandage.

Sarah (*to Joseph*) Can we go and look at the Fringe people?

Joseph You want to?

Sarah Yes!

Joseph Petra, do you?

Petra No . . .

Emily They'll be behind bars, Petra. Tied up.

Sarah Beaten up!

Petra I don't want to see them.

Joseph I'll be with you. I want all of us to go. So you know what these animals look like.

Emily (*to David*) Will you hurry up?

David I can't hold it.

Petra I'm starving!

Joseph Help your brother tie it, Katy.

Katy You're hopeless.

David I've only got two hands.

There is instant silence. All look at Joseph.

Joseph Are you trying to mock me?

David No . . .

Joseph You think that's funny? At a time like this?

David I'm sorry.

Joseph Two hands – is that not enough for you?

David I just said I . . .

Joseph We heard what you said! Two hands are not enough. Do you want more? How many? Tell us how many more hands you want? Three? Four? Four hands to attack us and beat us and rob us. You want to be a Mutant, is that it?

David No . . .

Joseph No?

David No.

Joseph So you don't want to go and live in the Fringe with those animals? Because I can take you to the border now.

Petra David didn't mean it. He made a mistake.

Joseph Petra, why is your brother so stupid? (*to David*) Why are you? Is it deliberate? Petra, tell him what Purity is. Go on. You know it.

Petra 'Purity is the true image of God. One body, one head, two arms, two . . .'

Joseph Petra . . . 'Ten . . . fing . . .'

Petra '. . . ten fingers . . . two legs, ten toes.'

Joseph Good. Sarah, tell him what a Mutant is.

Emily Joseph . . .

Joseph He has to be told. He has to learn respect. How much we sacrificed for him. Sarah . . .

Sarah 'A Mutant is a thing hated by both God and man. A Mutant is, an inferior being. A Mutant is an obscenity.'

Joseph Do you think you'll remember that now? Leave the room. Get out of our sight.

David goes.

Now, we can eat.

Lights up on David.

David
I close my eyes and the pain fades
as I tell him what I've always been told
there is only us
there is only here
there is only now

they burnt the old maps on bonfires
in celebration
the maps of before
the evidence of how we once lived

and created a new map
the map that's in every room in every home
the map of now
our land and its border
a pure world sealed by a black line
the paper left blank beyond it

a sacred black line
sustaining us
defining us
carving out a shape that's been
cut into our hearts

cut into our minds
a line we must never cross

I tell him again
what I've always been told
there is only us
there is only here
there is only now.

Joseph steps forward. The intimation is that David has been punished.

Joseph This place you call home – we created it from nothing. We came here owning only what we wore. And we built this. For our children. If they forget that, it's worth nothing. They will inherit nothing. We will have created this land for nothing.

SCENE THREE   SIX TOES

Some days later. David walking alone in the forest. He sees a girl on the ground. Her foot is caught between rocks. She's in pain, angry at herself.

Sophie Stupid foot! You stupid, bloody foot! (*She suddenly freezes, aware of him.*)
David You want some help?

Sophie doesn't speak.

What've you done? Are you stuck? Do you want me to help you? I heard you. I heard you shouting. You're in pain. What's wrong with you?
Sophie No one comes here. What're you doing?
David Walking. Just walking. Is that all right?

Pause. She's staring at him.

What?

67

Sophie What?

David You're staring at me.

Sophie I'm not staring at you.

David So what've you done? Let me have a look.

He comes closer, crouches down. She warily lets him do this.

Sophie I fell. My foot's trapped between these rocks.

David How long have you been here?

Sophie Three or four hours.

David Your ankle's swollen. (*He begins searching his pockets.*)

Sophie What're you doing?

David I've got a knife. If I cut the shoe open I can pull your foot out.

Sophie No . . .

David It won't hurt.

Sophie No!

David It's the only way you'll get it out.

Sophie Leave me alone! I can do it. Go away.

David What's wrong with you? I'm trying to help you.

Sophie I don't need you!

David stands, moves back.

David You know what'll happen if no one else comes? You'll be there all night. You'll freeze to death. See you.

Sophie All right . . . But be careful.

He returns and begins to cut the shoe. He can feel her staring at him.

David My name's David – in case you were wondering. What's yours?

Sophie Hurry up . . .

David What are you doing here? It's so remote.

Sophie I was walking too, OK . . . Just cut it.

David That's it. (*He begins to move her foot out.*)

Sophie Don't look!
David What?
Sophie DON'T LOOK!

But by now he's seen.

David You've got six toes . . .

She pulls her foot away, covers it with her hands.

But the cross . . .
Sophie I know. The cross . . . Run, then! Run back home.
Tell the authorities. Stop looking at me like that! I make
you sick?, don't I?
David No. No, you don't . . .
Sophie Go. Leave me alone.
David I won't say anything.

She looks at him.

I promise. I promise you. I won't say a thing.
Sophie I have to go home.

*She tries to stand and does – just – but it's painful.
David goes to support her.*

No . . .
David You'll get nowhere on your own. I'll help you get
back.
Sophie You can't . . .
David Look at me. I want to help you. What else do I
have to say?
Sophie Do you not understand? No one knows I exist! I'm
illegal! If you want to help, go. Get away from here.
Forget you ever saw me.
David Here, take my shoe. Take it. In case you meet
anyone.

He leaves. She looks at his shoe, then shouts.

Sophie David!

David re-enters.

Help me. I can't do it alone.

He supports her again.

David Which way?
Sophie That way.
David But there's nothing that way. Just more forest.
Sophie That's where we live.

They start to walk, talking quietly to each other. They turn and are home. Mary, Sophie's mother, comes on. She stares at David with hostility.

Mary What's happened?
Sophie I'm all right.
Mary Who are you?
Sophie His name's David. My foot got trapped and he helped me. (*Pause.*) He's seen my foot. He knows. But he won't say anything. He promised. Didn't you, David?
David I gave Sophie my word.

Mary glances at Sophie. She is not meant to give out her name.

Mary He knows your name.
Sophie I told him my name. I trust him, Mum.
Mary You've never met him before.
Sophie Look, he gave me his shoe to cover my foot. He helped me back here.
Mary And now he knows where we live.
Sophie I know, but . . .
Mary We'll talk about it after.
David Sophie was in agony! Did you want me to leave her?
Sophie I went further than I'm supposed to. I'm sorry. It's my fault. But David . . .
Mary Go inside, Sophie.

Sophie Mum . . .

Mary Go.

Sophie Listen . . .

Mary Sophie, we can't risk it.

David Risk what?

Sophie Listen! Don't you think I know the danger? I know what could happen to us. But I made a decision. He wanted to help and I trusted him. I trust him. I could be wrong, but I don't think I am. I'm not a child any more. I have to make my own decisions.

Mary I know, Sophie. I know you do. (*to David*) I don't know who you are, David, but if Sophie trusts you . . . so will I. I hope you're someone who understands. I know there are still people in Waknuk who do.

David They'd send you to the Fringe, wouldn't they? The authorities.

Mary No, we'd be a warning to others. They'd beat us. Starve us. Put us on public display.

Sophie A Mutant and her mother.

Mary That's their word, Sophie, not ours. There are others, David, in other parts of Waknuk. People who'd rather live in hiding than have the Inspectors take their children from them. They'd rather die than have that.

Sophie I have to go inside. My foot's aching. Will you come too, David? Can he, Mum?

Mary Do you want to, David?

David Yes, I do.

Sophie I need your shoulder again.

They start to go.

There's so many things I want to ask you.

A crowd of people watching the Fringe prisoners, off.
Joseph, Emily, Sarah and Katy are at the front, David and
Petra further back. Joseph is trying to get them through
the crowd.

Joseph Let my children through! Come on! They've
queued. They want to see. David, let Petra through
first! Petra, here! Take my hand. They won't harm you,
Petra. Look at them. They can't do anything. They're
chained up.

Sarah I can't see their faces! I want to see their faces!

Various other shouts from the crowd.

Crowd 1 Kick them!
Joseph Guard! Turn them over.
Crowd 2 Drag them up here! We want to see them.

The crowd reacts as they see their faces. Some recoil,
others hiss or spit. Petra holds on to Joseph. David
pushes his way out and stands to one side on his own.
  Axel enters. He stands apart, watching David.
  Lights up on Anne.

Anne
He was the first of us to see them
and we waited for him to tell us
working in the fields
sitting in our houses
lying on our beds
in the east, west, north and south of Waknuk
All of us, waiting . . .
knowing what we wanted him to feel
desperate for him to tell us
how monstrous,

how repulsive,
how unnatural they were
how unlike anything we would ever see.
David
They're dressed in rags . . .
bloodstained, filthy rags
torn, ripped
hanging off them . . .
I can see ribs pushing against skin
the outlines of bones . . .
cuts . . .
bruises . . .
blood.
Axel David.

David breaks communication with group. Lights down on them. He's surprised it's Axel, his uncle, but shows genuine warmth towards him.

David Axel . . . But you're meant to be ill. Are you better?

Axel pauses.

Axel It's good to see you, David. I knew you'd be here. I knew he'd bring you here.
David I'll go and get them. They'll want to see you.
Axel No, David. No. I can't stay.
David Why?
Axel This. I can't watch this. Look at it. It's barbaric. Do you not think it's barbaric, David?

Pause. David has to decide to say what he's thinking.

David We're meant to hate them, Axel. They're meant to be animals. Obscenities. Nothing like us.
Axel The authorities have to tell us something, David. If they didn't we'd start to ask questions. And they don't want that. They don't want people who ask questions.

People who doubt. If they're not animals, what are they? And what are we?

David But why are they attacking us so much?

Axel Maybe because of the wall. Maybe because they're asking questions now too. Why do we judge ourselves superior? Why do we have the best land and food and cattle? Why are they cast out there in the forest, to live with nothing?

David is uncomfortable hearing this – so many people are nearby.

Questions are hard to listen to sometimes.

David But the wall has to be built. To protect us.

Axel That's what they tell us. As if living like this is natural! Nothing's natural. This land was fought for, tooth and nail. We have no right to it. The wall will solve nothing. It'll only make the Fringe people more determined. Things will only get worse.

David Axel, why are you talking like this?

Axel Because I may not get the chance again. It's important you know. And I want you to tell the others.

Pause. Rest of the group are seen, perhaps in half-light, to suggest that they're aware of what's going on.

David What others?

Axel The ones you talk to, David. Who have the same power as you.

David I . . . don't know what you mean.

Axel David, I know! I know about you. I know you have a power. I've seen it before. There were others, people like you, who lived here once.

David What happened to them?

Axel They left. All of them. I don't know where.

David You've known about us all this time?

Axel I don't know how many of you there are.

David But you never said anything.

Axel I didn't need to. You have each other. But I'm
worried about you now. Because of what's happening
now.

Pause.

David We don't communicate as much as we used to.
Every time we do we realize how different we are from
everybody else. We don't know how to feel. To be
ashamed of it or . . .

Axel There's nothing wrong with you. There's nothing
wrong with any of you.

David But what if they find out? What will they do? We
don't know. We don't even know what we are . . . We're
not Pure. We're not Mutants. What are we? Why were
we born like this?

Axel I don't have answers for that, David. I just wanted
you to know there's someone you can trust. I have to go
now.

David Axel, the others who left . . . Did they . . . go to a
city? A city beside a lake?

Axel David, I don't know . . .

Petra has come across.

Petra . . .

Petra Are you better now? I won't die if I touch you?

Axel No, Petra. No . . .

She goes to hug him, but Joseph has spotted them.

Joseph Petra! Come here! Axel, I warned you! I warned
you!

Axel I haven't seen the children in months.

Joseph Don't go near them! You hear me! Don't go near
any of them!

Axel I'm their uncle.

Joseph You stay away.

David You said he was ill . . .

Joseph He is ill.

David But . . .

Joseph Sick in the head. Poison in his head. What was he saying?

David Nothing.

Joseph Talking about those animals, was he? Or how the world was before? Everyone living together? Look where that got us, Axel. Back to dust.

Axel And I see it starting all over again.

Joseph Look at him. Sick old man living in the wrong time. An outcast.

Axel But still your brother, Joseph. Still that.

Joseph Never talk to my children again. You hear me? Never.

Some of the crowd have turned and are watching with hostility. Axel goes.

He's not ill. He's dead. You understand? Dead.

Lights up on Rachel.

Rachel
I am an only child
a perfect girl
loved beyond reason

with a certificate of Purity
signed by an Inspector
who examined me an hour after birth
and gave me life

if I had been less than perfect,
blemished in the tiniest way,
I'd have been taken away
across the border
by a man on a horse
and left in the traditional place
an old basket on the edge of a field

76

I imagine sometimes an imperfect child
raised by Fringe people as one of them
in dark forests beyond the black line
like the other child my mother had
the girl born after me
my sister

then I remember I am an only child
a perfect girl
loved beyond reason.

SCENE FIVE   HIDDEN

Some days later. David has come back to see Sophie. They sit by a river.

David I could lie here all day.

Sophie But you'll have to go soon.

David Not yet. I don't have to go yet.

Sophie This is as far as I'm allowed to go. I come here to watch the river. I try to imagine where it begins and where it ends.

David No one knows. What's it like, hiding your whole life?

Sophie I don't know. I don't know any other way. Apart from my mother, you're the only person I've ever spoken to.

David It's such a strange feeling.

Sophie That's why I keep asking you questions. You must be getting bored.

David No. No, I'm not.

Sophie I prayed you'd come back, David. My mother talked about leaving, how dangerous it was that someone knew, but I told her I wouldn't go. I had to know I was right about you. That my instinct was right.

David So, any more questions for me?

Sophie Not just now. I just like sitting here with you.
David I feel like swimming. Do you want to swim?

Pause. Both of them know what this means.

Sophie Yeah. Why not?

She begins to take her shoes off, David too. In her spirit of abandon, Sophie throws them to one side. David starts on his shirt. Sophie is watching the river.

How do things begin? This river begins somewhere. Who was the first person to say 'Purity is the true image of God'? And who were the first people to believe them?
David More questions . . .
Sophie What?
David Something my uncle said.
Sophie Your uncle?

Alan, an older boy, has entered.

Alan What's going on here?

Sophie freezes.

David Alan . . .
Alan Undressing . . .
David We're going to swim.
Alan Who's she? I've never seen her before.
David What're you doing here?
Alan Meeting my girlfriend. Along at the bridge. Only place we get to be on our own. Has she got a name? Hey, you got a name?
Sophie Sally.
Alan You his girlfriend? She your girlfriend?

Sophie begins edging over to her shoes, trying not to draw attention to herself.

David We saw a girl heading that way.
Alan What's wrong with you?

78

He glimpses her foot and tries to look more closely.
Sophie's got her shoes and moves away.

Who are you? Hey! Come here!

He starts to go after Sophie, but David stops him. They
struggle until Alan has him pinned down.

What's going on? She's one of them, isn't she? With a cross
on . . . What're you doing with her, you filthy
bastard . . .

Sophie hits him with a rock. He collapses. They stare at
him lying on the ground. David looks at Sophie.

Sophie I had to. He's not dead, is he?
David No.

Slight pause. Slowly lights come up on the group:
Rosalind, Mark, Rachel, Michael.

Sophie David . . . I have to go – now.

Alan groans, moving a little.

Rosalind David, what is it? I don't understand.
Sophie Now, David! I have to tell my mother. We'll have
to leave this time. He knows.
Mark You're not making sense.
Sophie Will you come with me?
David He needs help.
Rachel Your thoughts are too fast.
David I can't leave him . . .
Sophie David, please . . .

David makes a decision. He begins to leave with Sophie.

Michael What's happening?

Slow light down on group. Alan moves, slowly pulling
himself to his feet.
    As Scene Three, David turns and is outside Sophie's

house. Mary is beside him with packs and bags.

Mary (*shouting off*) Sophie, hurry!

David Where will you go?

Mary The Fringe. We've no choice. We can't stay in
Waknuk.

Sophie enters.

Sophie I'm ready now.

David There's other parts of Waknuk you can go to.
Remote parts.

Sophie We'd still have to hide.

Mary We don't want to do that any more. Don't look at
the house, Sophie. That's past now. We're going this
way.

David I'll come with you to the border.

Mary No. We have to go alone.

David This is all my fault.

Mary David, we always knew we'd have to leave one day.
Don't feel guilty. Or you, Sophie. We're not to blame.
(*She turns to David.*) Goodbye, David. Don't let them
harm you. If we get over the border, they won't come
after us.

Mary moves away. Sophie goes to David.

Sophie I'll never see you again, will I? (*She hugs him.*) As
soon as I get a friend I lose him. Goodbye.

David Take care, Sophie.

They begin to leave.

Mary Goodbye, David. Thank you.

*David is left alone. He looks at the empty house, looks
around him at the forest. He doesn't know where to go,
what to do. Lights slowly back up on the group.*

Rachel David . . .

Michael Where are you?
Rosalind What's happened?
Mark Are you all right?

A strange, abrasive sound begins. All hold their heads in pain. They shout for it to stop. Gradually it becomes a voice speaking with difficulty – Petra trying to communicate.

Petra (*voice-over*) David . . . David . . . David . . .
David Petra? Petra? Is it you? Petra! Can you hear me?
Petra David.
David PETRA!
Petra David?
David STOP! IT'S TOO LOUD, PETRA. STOP!

The sound fades.

Petra, I'm coming back. I'm coming home now.

SCENE SIX   ONE OF US

The Storms' house. Two Inspectors are there. They consult files. Emily sits with Katy and Sarah. Petra is on her own, to one side. Joseph also stands apart, preoccupied, hating the ignominy of the situation. Long silences broken by pages being turned.

Inspector 1 He was your . . . third child, is that right?

Maybe he directs the question to Joseph, but it's Emily who answers.

Emily Yes.

More silence. Then he looks around for Petra.

Inspector 1 And you're the youngest, aren't you? Petra?

Petra nods. Joseph strokes her lovingly and speaks gently.

Joseph Don't worry, Petra. It'll be over soon. I promise you.

Silence.

Inspector 2 Who inspected him? Can't read these initials.
Emily You did.
Inspector 2 Did I? (*He checks.*) So I did, so I did. Mm, I remember now. Busy year that one. Lot of boys for some reason, lot of boys born. Happens like that sometimes, doesn't it?
Inspector 1 What?

While Inspector 2 was talking, Petra has slipped away unnoticed.

Inspector 2 Well, sometimes it's all boys getting born, isn't it? Lots of boys. Then the next year it's all girls. Baby girls everywhere. Of course, sometimes it's the same. Same amount of boys, same amount of girls. Mm. It's interesting if you compare the figures. I've got them here somewhere . . .

We see the rest of the group.
Downstage David enters. Petra runs to him.

Petra David! The Inspectors are here! They say you hit a boy. His head was bleeding. They're in the house now.
David It's all right, Petra. Don't worry. Listen, that was you, wasn't it? Speaking to me.
Petra Yes. It's so difficult. The others have been talking to me. Rosalind and Mark and . . .
David They heard you too, Petra. All of us did.
Petra They're asking me things but I can't speak back! I can't make words like you.
David It's all right, Petra. We'll teach you. We'll teach you how to, I promise. But you can't tell anyone. No one. Do you understand?
Petra Yes.

David Your power's so strong. It's incredible. Stronger than any of us.

Petra Can you hear the others?

David Others?

Petra Behind you. I hear people whispering. Hundreds, it sounds like. But very quietly.

Sarah has come outside. She sees David.

Sarah He's here! He's here!

The family and the Inspectors come out and stare at him. Joseph walks slowly towards him.

Petra David, what will they do to you?

David (*urgently*) Petra, listen, can you hear words? Can you hear what these people are saying?

Petra No . . . They're too far away. They just sound like . . . bees. Just like bees buzzing.

Pause. David stares at her.

Joseph YOU, BOY! COME HERE NOW! GET ACROSS HERE NOW!

Later. David sits in front of the two Inspectors. They have been questioning him for some time. Joseph is to one side.

Inspector 1 So . . . This girl at the river . . . whatever her name is – you still don't know it?

David I've told you. I'd just met her.

Inspector 2 So you'd just met her? You'd gone out for a walk and just bumped into her?

David Yes.

Inspector 2 This was . . . five miles away from your home? Do you always go on such long walks?

David I like to be on my own sometimes.

Inspector 1 To remote areas? Without telling anyone?

Inspector 2 Knowing how dangerous the situation is just now?

David I got lost. Then I saw her. So I asked her for directions.

Inspector 2 While you were taking your clothes off?

David doesn't reply.

This boy, Alan, said you were getting undressed.

David I wanted to swim. So did she.

Inspector 1 You'd only just met her and she was undressing in front of you?

David We both wanted to swim.

Joseph He's lying. You're lying, boy!

Inspector 2 So why would you suddenly turn round and hit someone with a rock? I don't understand.

Joseph Tell him!

Inspector 1 Unless that person had seen something. Unless Alan saw something you wanted to keep hidden. It was a rock, wasn't it, David?

David He was threatening me. I pushed him over. He hit his head on the ground.

Inspector 2 He is lying, isn't he?

Inspector 1 Yes, I think he is.

Joseph Did she have six toes? Tell them! Was she a Mutant? Was she?

David She was the same as me! If she's a Mutant then I'm a Mutant. She's the same as me!

Inspector 2 I don't understand that. Are you saying she was a Mutant?

Joseph turns to the Inspectors.

Joseph Leave us alone. Wait outside.

The Inspectors leave. Lights up on group.

That was Axel I heard just now. Has he been talking to you again? Spreading his poison?

David No.

Joseph Then where does that stuff come from? Where do

you get it from? (*Pause.*) She was a Mutant. I know she was a Mutant.

When David answers it's an assertion, not an admission.

David She had six toes on her right foot. We were friends. We were friends because she's the same as me. She's no different from me.

Joseph Why is there only one way to make you learn?

Joseph moves towards him. Black-out.
    Later. David slumped in the chair. The Inspectors stand over him, reading what they've written. Joseph has gone.

Inspector 1 Mother's name Mary Wender. Girl's name Sophie. The girl has six toes. You knew them for about three weeks, visited them twice. They lived in the western forest. (*to Inspector 2*) Take some men out, burn the house. Check if there's any others hiding around there. They headed north . . . trying to get to the Fringe, presumably. Put more men on the border in case they haven't got there yet. (*to David*) An extra toe. You went through all this for an extra toe. See what trouble the Mutants bring?

Lights up on Michael.

Michael
    I knew them better than my brother and sister
    five others who shared this double life
    inhabitants of a secret world
    that was thrilling at first
    with a language that was ours alone
    where no one corrected or punished us
    for expressing what we felt

    then as the wall got higher, I turned away

85

the shouts for purity louder
– each of us turned away
slowly deserting the world we'd made
going back to ourselves and our families
becoming alone again.

until Petra . . .
came dazzling like sunlight
her thoughts chaotic, overpowering
drawing us all to her, together again
as she learned our language
as we taught her how to share her thoughts
as we returned to the world we'd lost.

SCENE SEVEN   BECOMING NORMAL

Mrs Ervin stands on her own. David approaches her.

David Mrs Ervin, my father's sent me to apologize for what happened to Alan. I disgraced myself and I've been punished for it.

Mrs Ervin I hope you have. You could have killed my son.

David I know. I'm sorry. Is Alan here? I have to apologize to him as well.

Mrs Ervin Alan's still in bed. He will be for at least a week. I'll ask him if he wants to see you, but I doubt it. Stay here.

She goes out. Anne enters. She doesn't see David.

Anne Mrs Ervin? It's me.
David Anne.

She looks at him, then looks away. He tries to communicate with her.

Anne . . .
Anne No. I only talk now.

86

David is confused. He whispers to her.

David But they might hear us.

Anne If you want to say something, talk to me. Talk to me like a normal person.

David Why're you being like this? We've been trying to contact you – all of us. Where've you been? We're communicating again. Like before. We . . .

Anne Stop it.

David Anne, what is it? Anne . . .

Anne I'm going to marry Alan.

David Marry him?

Anne It's been planned for months. I'm in love with him.

David is shocked. Mrs Ervin comes back in.

Mrs Ervin Hello, Anne.

Anne How is he, Mrs Ervin?

Mrs Ervin Much the same. He's asleep. (*to David*) You'll have to come back tomorrow.

Anne Can I do anything?

Mrs Ervin The fire needs building up in his room. No, Anne. Since he's doing nothing he can bring the wood in.

Mrs Ervin goes.

David Anne, you can't marry him!

Anne I'm going to marry him. I'm going to live with him. Like a normal person. I don't want to be like . . . this any more. One of you. I want to forget it all.

David You can't. It's part of you. Whether you like it or not. You can't forget about it.

Anne I'm going to tell him. I'm going to tell him about this. This . . . poison in my head.

David Anne, you can't!

Anne I have to. How can I live with him and not tell him? I love him. I want him to know.

David And what about the rest of us?

Anne What about 'us'? There's no 'us' any more! Maybe there was once, but not now. We hardly talk to each other now. We're all too ashamed of what we are.

David When Alan tells the authorities, they'll want to know if there's others like you. What will you tell them?

Anne Think about it, David. What if we all tell them? All of us.

David Are you serious? You know what it's been like living here the last few months.

Anne We're not Mutants! Look at us. They wouldn't treat us like them. Like those two prisoners they caught. We look the same as everyone else.

David That's why we're more dangerous! Don't you see? Because no one can tell.

Anne And you want to go on living like that? Living the rest of your lives like that? It'll drive you all mad.

Mrs Ervin (*off*) Anne, where's that boy gone with the wood?

Anne (*to David*) I've made my mind up.

David You know you'll never live your normal life.

Anne They'll believe us if they see we mean it. None of us wants to be like this, David. Not really.

Mrs Ervin (*off*) Anne!

Anne All of us secretly want to be pure.

Lights up on Rosalind and the rest of the group.

Rosalind
I walk into the room
and they're there where they always are
in the familiar evening
father, mother, sister and brother

I kneel down and put the last log on the fire
this is what I'll remember
no one looks up

88

nothing is said
each of them has their own place
their own involvement
in the quiet hour, before sleep
I watch my mother's hand holding a book
the room is filled with warmth and love
and trust
but not enough

I kneel down and put the last log on the fire
no one looks up
nothing is said
This has been every night of my life.

SCENE EIGHT   THE LAST MAP

Axel alone. David and Petra come on.

Petra Uncle Axel?
Axel Petra. My darling Petra.

They hug. Axel looks at David.

David, you shouldn't be here. You know what your father
   said.
Petra We came to say goodbye.
David Axel, we're leaving. All of us.
Axel Leaving? (*He looks at Petra.*)
David Petra's one of us.
Axel You, Petra?
Petra Yes.
David We only found out two days ago.
Axel But why are you leaving? What's happened?
Petra Anne's going to tell people about us.
David Anne Bishop.
Axel I don't know her.
David She's one of us too. But she says she's in love. She

89

wants to marry Alan Ervin.

Axel I know that family. They're vicious people.

David She's going to tell him. She wants to tell him. There's nothing we can do. She's closed her mind to us.

Axel Then you must go now, David. You shouldn't have come here. Where are the rest of you?

David We're meeting near the northern border. We're going into the Fringe.

Petra I can hear other voices, Uncle.

Axel You, Petra?

David She has a greater power than any of us..

Axel Little Petra . . .

Petra They're very far away, but maybe we can go there. Where they live.

David D'you think it's the people you talked about, Axel? The people who left.

Axel It could be, David. Yes, it could be. You have to contact them, speak to them, find out where they are.

Petra I can't do it yet.

David But we're teaching her.

Axel Good. You'll learn fast, Petra.

Petra I can already say 'cheese' and 'bacon and eggs' and . . .

David Petra, we have to go now.

Axel gives David a folded piece of paper.

Axel Here. I've had this near to hand for a while now. You'd better have it.

Petra What is it?

David It's a map . . . Of where?

Axel Look harder, David.

David It's here . . . It's here! It's one of the old maps! But they destroyed all these.

Axel So they told us. Remember, David?

Petra There's so much of it!

David And no border . . .

Axel Take it. It may be useless. I don't know what's out there now. I don't know what's left. You'll find out for yourselves. Petra . . .

He holds out his hands. She goes to him.

You know you'll be away for a long time? From the rest of the family? You know that?

Petra I don't want them to get angry. I wanted to wake them up and say goodbye, but David said they'd be upset. And we have to go. If we stay the Inspectors will hurt us.

Axel looks at David.

Axel Petra, they'll understand why you had to leave. Don't worry. You're going to a place where there's no fear. Where you can say and think whatever you want. That's the most important thing, Petra. That's why you have to leave here, Petra. You're special children.

Petra Are we?

Axel Now, go. Please. (*He hugs them.*) Go.

Petra Why can't you come with us?

Axel Me? And hold you back? No. You have to go alone.

Petra But we won't see you again.

Axel Maybe you'll come back one day. Come back to a different place. Now go. Quickly.

Lights up on Mark.

Mark
I crouch in silence and look at the border
our border
the first time I've seen it

the black line on the map in every home
the sacred black line
the world beyond it left blank
non-existent

thin wire running between sticks driven into
the ground some of the sticks have snapped
and the wire sags it creaks when the wind
blows soon there'll be nothing to look at
nothing but wall

for now, this is all there is
this is all I have to cross
to go from here to there

the simplicity of it here to there

out of one darkness into another.

SCENE NINE   TEARING OFF THE CROSS

*At the border. Darkness. Rosalind, Michael, Mark and
Rachel wait, hidden. David and Petra come on, out of
breath.*

David Rosalind. (*Pause.*) Rosalind . . .
Rosalind We're here. What happened?
David Two women on the path, talking. We almost ran
into them. We had to hide till they went. Everyone ready
then?

Silence.

What? What is it? We have to go.
Michael Rachel's not coming.
David What d'you mean?
Rachel I'm going back to talk to Anne.
David You can't!
Rosalind There's no time. I've told her.
David We have to leave now!
Rachel She wouldn't do this! Anne wouldn't do this!
David Rachel, I heard her. I saw her face. She meant it.
Rachel I just need to talk to her. She'll listen to me.

Mark It's worth a shot, isn't it? We don't even know where we're going. Or what's out there.

Petra Axel gave us a map! An old map!

Rosalind Let's see . . .

Michael Look at it all! There's villages and roads . . .

Rosalind Look, Rachel.

Rachel It's useless! All of that's gone! Listen, if Anne knew we were here . . . Hiding in the dark like animals. Going out there, into the Fringe. She wouldn't do this.

Rosalind She already has.

Rachel How do you know? I'm her friend. I'm her best friend!

Rosalind Did she tell you about Alan?

Pause.

Rachel No . . .

David Nothing you say will affect her. She doesn't want to be one of us any more. That's why she stopped communicating. She wants to tell Alan. She doesn't want it to be a secret. She doesn't want to live like this any more. Go back if you want to. You too, Mark. But we're leaving. Now.

As he's been speaking, he's torn his cross off. He throws it to the ground. Rosalind, Michael and Petra do the same.

Mark We can't split up now! David . . .

David What do you want me to do? I can't make your decision for you!

Petra I want them to come with us!

Rachel No! Wait! What if she . . .

Suddenly they hear Anne communicating. She's in great pain, her 'thoughts' weak and laboured.

Anne Rachel . . .

Rachel Anne? Anne!

Anne Go. All of you . . .
  They're coming for you!
  Get out of your houses!
  Run!
Rachel Anne, where are you?
Anne Coming for you now . . .
  Go!
  Get away from here, all of you.
  Please . . .
David We're going, Anne. We're going.
Rosalind Rachel, come on!
Rachel Anne . . .
Anne I'm sorry . . .
  you were right, David . . .
  . . . I'm sorry . . .
  they made me . . . made me tell . . .
  the pain . . . the pain's too much.
  I'm so sorry . . . so sorry . . .

The others have helped Rachel tear her cross off. They leave, Rachel distraught.

SCENE TEN THE SEARCHER

Joseph, an Inspector and other men enter. They are spread out, searching, perhaps with torches. One of them discovers the crosses lying on the ground and shouts.

Man Here! Look.
Joseph Six. It's them.
Man They've crossed over.
Inspector Looks like it.

Joseph walks forwards and looks over into the darkness of the Fringes. The urgency of the other men has now gone.

94

Joseph They can't be much further ahead.

Man Best place for them, out there.

Joseph Petra's my daughter. Not one of them.

Inspector We know that, Joseph.

Joseph (*to man*) You! Where are you going?

Man Home. Nowhere else to go.

Joseph They've got my daughter! (*to Inspector*) You know what Anne Bishop said. Five names. Not Petra's.

Inspector It's unfortunate, Joseph. I'm sorry. They must have tricked her.

Joseph You're sorry? You won't help me? None of you will help me?

Man Not out there.

Inspector Be realistic, Joseph. How can we go out there? We know nothing about it. It would be suicide.

Joseph If she was your daughter. Or yours . . .

Inspector Come back with us.

Joseph No.

Inspector Joseph . . .

Joseph NO! Go back home, all of you. Back to your families. Go!

They go. He searches for the smallest cross.

Petra . . . (*He slowly removes his own cross, folds the two of them together and puts them inside his shirt. He looks again at the border, then walks towards it.*)

SCENE ELEVEN   FACE TO FACE

Late the next day. Deep in a forest. Gloomy, stagnant light. The children come on, Michael leading. He stops and looks around. Hundreds of trees in every direction.

Michael When's this forest going to end?

Rosalind There's no light. It's like a giant tent.

Petra Can we stop for a while?

David Not yet. We have to walk some more.

Petra I'm so tired.

Mark Do you know where we are?

David (*pointing to map*) Somewhere about here. We should be out of this soon. On to some flat land.

Michael Then where?

Rachel is beside David. The others are spread apart; Michael the furthest to one side.

Rachel David, I'm sorry about yesterday. What happened with Anne. I put us all in danger.

David It's all right, Rachel.

Rachel It's like losing a sister. I never realized till then how much she meant to me. And how important it is we stay together, that we survive.

Rosalind notices that Petra is lying down now.

Rosalind Petra!

Petra What?

Rosalind You can't sleep.

Petra Why not?

Rachel Petra, you have to keep trying.

Petra They can't hear me!

David You have to concentrate.

Petra You keep going on and on about it. You don't know how hard it is. I've no strength left. I want some food.

Rosalind Forget about food. There isn't any. You're our only chance! Now come on!

Mark Rosalind . . .

Michael Ssh. I can see something . . .

Mark What?

Michael Down there!

David Be careful!

All go over except David, who's putting away the map.

Rachel It's light.
Michael Fire.
Rosalind Are they Fringe people?
David Don't go any closer!

*David starts to go over but is grabbed from behind by a
Fringe person, his hand covering David's mouth.
Another one takes the map from him. More Fringe
people appear, creeping towards the other children.
They are wild-looking, dressed in rags, dirt-encrusted.*

Mark I can't see anyone.
Petra I can smell food. David . . .

*Petra turns to see where David is. She stares in terror at
the Fringe people around them, unable to scream. The
others, in turn, realize. David is pushed into the centre
with them.*

Fringe 1 They're children . . .
Fringe 2 What're you doing here?
Fringe 1 Speak! Why are you here?
Fringe 3 It could be a trap . . .
David It's not a trap.
Petra You're Fringe people . . .
Fringe 2 Where are you from? This is one of the old maps.
Where did you get this?
David From my uncle. Axel.
Fringe 1 Where does he live?
Fringe 3 Look! On their clothes . . . The outline of
crosses! Look!
Fringe 4 They're from Waknuk!

*Hisses from some. Fringe 1 moves threateningly towards
them.*

Michael We've left Waknuk.
Fringe 2 They never leave. Them in Waknuk. Too afraid
of what's out here.

Fringe 3 Too afraid of us!

Fringe 1 Tell us why you're here! Tell us!

Rosalind We escaped.

Fringe 2 Escaped?

Fringe 3 (*to Fringe 1*) Like the other two.

Fringe 1 Escaped from what? You're children.

Fringe 4 You Mutants too, eh? Are you?

Some laughter, shouting.

Fringe 5 Show us! What's wrong with you? Or you?

David Wait . . . You said others. 'Like the other two.' Is it Sophie? Is Sophie here?

Petra (*to David*) Sophie Six-toes?

David Yes. And Mary, her mother? Did they make it? Tell me . . . Are they here?

Fringe 2 We have them. At the camp.

David Please, take me to them. Please.

The Fringe people confer.

Fringe 2 Come with us.

They go.

Sophie and Mary are lying by a fire. They look ill and very weak. David and others enter.

David Sophie? Sophie . . .

Sophie David . . .?

David suddenly turns on the Fringe people.

David What've you done! You bastards! What've you done to them!

Fringe 1 Shut it, you!

Hostile sounds from others.

Mary David! They found us. In the forest. We were starving to death. They brought us here. They've fed us.

98

David I'm sorry. I . . .

Fringe 2 Still got Waknuk in you, eh?

Sophie David, what's happened? Why are you here?

Fringe 1 Yes, tell us. Why are you here? You say you escaped. Why?

David looks at the group. A short silence.

Fringe 2 What is it?

Mary David . . . You can tell us. You're safe now.

Rosalind We've never told anyone before. We've never said it out loud.

Fringe 3 Said what?

Fringe 2 Nothing's hidden here. There's no judgement here.

Rachel We can speak to each other in our heads. All of us.

Mark We send thoughts. Without anyone knowing. No one can tell we're doing it.

Petra And I'm the best at it.

Michael We've kept it secret for years. But they know now.

David One of us confessed. Anne. She's . . . We had to leave her. They've hurt her.

Rosalind That's why we escaped. We had to.

A pause as they all take this in. The children don't really know what to do. Then Sophie steps forward to David and hugs him.

Sophie I knew there was something. I knew you understood.

Fringe 2 You lived there all that time among them? With your families?

Rosalind Yes.

Fringe 1 So much for purity.

Fringe 2 And are there more of you there?

Michael Not that we know of. There were others once, like us, but they left.

Rosalind That's where we're going. We think they live out there somewhere. We want to go and find them.

Sophie (*to David*) You're going on?

David We have to. We can't live anywhere knowing there's others like us out there somewhere. We have to go to them. We have to, Sophie. We have to find out why we're like this.

Fringe 2 You don't know where they are?

David No, but we have Petra.

Petra I can hear people in my head. Whispering.

David We think it's them.

Petra But they can't hear me yet.

Rosalind We have to go nearer.

Fringe 1 Here. Your map.

Sophie Can we come with you? (*to Mary*) Can we? Can we go?

Mary looks at the Fringe people.

Fringe 2 Do what you want. We've no prisoners here. You must go where you want to.

Mary You'll stay here?

Fringe 2 Yes.

Rosalind Why? Why not leave? Live somewhere else?

Fringe 2 No. We want what they have. What should be ours too. Land, homes, family, food. They cast us out once. So they could have a pure world. A world of their own. But it's dying. As we knew it would. Every day that world is dying. Because it's built on so many lies. We are part of them. We're part of each other. Look around you. Most of you will have a brother or sister here but not know it. They say we're not human but it's us who bring up their children. They need us. They couldn't exist without us. When their world finally dies, they'll need our strength. They'll need our truth. That's when we'll return.

Pause.

Petra Can we eat now?

Fringe 2 (*laughs*) Of course. Of course we can. We'll eat now. All of us.

They all sit as if to eat. The lights go down.
Later. The group are asleep. Beside them Sophie and
Mary. The Fringe people are asleep off.

Petra David? David?

David What?

Petra I'm still trying. I'm still sending thoughts.

David Go to sleep, Petra. Try again in the morning. Go to sleep now.

The light changes. Very early morning. A figure has
entered – Joseph. He makes his way across stage,
looking for Petra. He finds her, picks her up without
waking her and goes off.

SCENE TWELVE   CONTACT

The forest. Joseph has left the camp, carrying Petra, who's
still asleep. He's now out of breath. He has to put her on
the ground. She begins to wake.

Joseph You're getting heavy now, Petra. You're growing up. There was a time when I could lift you above my head.

Petra You're here . . .

Joseph I came after you. I thought I'd lost you.

Petra David said I couldn't say goodbye to you. I wanted to. But we had to go quickly. Where are the others.

Joseph They've gone, Petra.

Petra Gone? David's gone?

Joseph Come on. We have to hurry.

Petra I want to see David.

Joseph Petra, we're going home. I'm taking you home.
Petra But I can't go back! David said they'll kill us.
Joseph Not you, Petra. You're not one of them.
Petra I am, Dad. Dad, I am.
Joseph No . . .
Petra I am one of them! I speak to them in my head.
David and Rosalind and –
Joseph Your mother's worried to death about you, Petra.
She wants to know where you are.
Petra I can't go. I can't leave them. (*She tries to contact them.*)
Joseph Petra, listen to me . . .
Petra Why don't they speak? Where are they?

Joseph moves towards her.

Joseph You're not one of them! You're mine!
Petra I'm shouting at them!
Joseph Petra, stop!
Petra I'm screaming at them!

He grabs her, puts his hand over her mouth and holds her tightly to him.

Joseph Petra, you're my daughter. You hear? You're my daughter. I don't want to hurt you. We're going back. I'm taking you home. I'm taking you home to your family. Your mother and your sisters. Where you belong.

He begins to leave, still holding her. Offstage, David and the others shout her name.

All (*off*) Petra!

Joseph stops dead. He looks around, not sure which direction they're coming from. Their voices build until they all enter, running. Joseph stares at them. David goes towards him.

David We heard you, Petra. We heard you shouting and
  screaming. It's all right.

Joseph Not you, Petra, not you . . .

Joseph has released Petra and is moving away from her.

David She has a stronger power than all of us.

Joseph God, not you . . .

David What will you do now? Go back there, forget we
  ever existed.

Petra (*to Joseph*) What have I done wrong? What have I
  done wrong?

David Tell her.

Petra David says I can never come back. What have I
  done wrong?

David Tell her . . .

Petra Dad?

David I used to be your son. A minute ago Petra was your
  daughter. Now you can't even touch her. You can't even
  look at her.

*Joseph turns, looks at them both, then walks away.
Michael crosses to stare after him.*

Michael He's gone.

Long pause.

David We'll go back to the camp. Petra . . . Petra, what is
  it? (*to the others*) You go on. I'll bring her back (*The
  others start to go.*).

Petra (*very quiet*) David, there's a woman . . . There's a
  woman, David. I can hear her. But she's so quiet.

Mark It's one of the voices . . .

Petra She . . . heard me screaming . . . (*Pause. Then she
  nods.*) I've told her I'm all right.

Rachel I can't hear a thing.

Petra She's asking who I am.

David Tell her, Petra. Tell her about all of us.

Petra giggles.

Petra She's so quiet. It's like being tickled.
David Petra . . .
Petra I've told her. She wants to know where we are.
David Tell her the Fringe. The north.
Petra She lives in the east.
David How far away?
Petra Seven days.
Rachel Seven days! We don't have enough food for seven days.
Petra They'll come to meet us. They'll bring us food and water. She's speaking too fast . . .
Rosalind Tell her to slow down.
Petra East . . . Across the flat lands . . . it takes three days . . . then . . . mountains, we have to cross the mountains.
David There are no mountains on this map.
Petra We'll find our way, she says. She'll guide us. She'll guide us there.

They look at each other, aware of the task ahead.

Sealand. It's called Sealand.
David Petra, ask her . . . ask her if there's a city.
Petra Yes. Yes.
Rachel A city by a lake?
Petra She's showing me. She's showing me. . . I can see it!
Mark From the top of the last mountain, we looked down on it.
Rosalind On a city so bright at first we had to close our eyes.
Michael A city that looked on fire, burning in sunlight, lying next to a shimmering lake.
David Like no place we had ever seen.
Petra We walked through the streets.
   In and out of shadows.

Mark Felt the warm earth under our feet.

Rachel Towards the sound.

Michael Voices speaking a language we'd kept secret for years.

Rosalind The hypnotic sound of our dream.

David The sound of ourselves.

Children Denied Childishness

David Harrower interviewed by Jim Mulligan

To David Harrower it is a mystery how he became a playwright. While at college he wrote short stories but no plays and hardly went to the theatre. Afterwards, while earning a kind of living washing dishes, he wrote a short play for a competition as an experiment to see how much he could convey by dialogue alone. Four years later his play *Knives in Hens* was accepted and then produced by the Traverse Theatre in Edinburgh.

On first reading *The Chrysalids* David Harrower recognized the power of the story.

> The story and ideas coming from the novel were fascinating. What I tried to do was carve out the core of the story from Wyndham's writing to achieve a short, sharp narrative with, I hope, at times shocking moments that would reflect the savagery of the world that is Waknuk.

Waknuk is indeed a savage society. Wyndham invented an enclosed world that is surrounded by a fearfully vast wilderness. In this post-nuclear society only those who are without mutation are allowed to live in the community. Any person or animal with genetic mutations is banished to the Fringes where an alternative society has loosely formed. Wyndham never explains how a mutant baby finds its way into the Fringes but David Harrower explores how a symbiotic relationship between the two societies is essential and he has created a chilling moment when a man takes away a baby and leaves it in a field for collection.

David Harrower uses a rock-like language. He will

write a scene and then carve it, chipping away at extraneous material until he comes to the essence of what the characters are. As a result, on first reading his play young people may find the language sparse but David Harrower is confident the actors will come to realize the symbolism has a dramatic power.

This play has few stage directions and David Harrower expects that directors and actors will bring their own perceptions and interpretations to it but there are some themes that he believes are implicit in the play. Strangely, considering that the novel was written at the height of the Cold War, he does not see nuclear issues or the contemporary debate about genetics as being central. Instead his play deals with exclusion and inclusion, how society treats outsiders and the brutality a society can practise on its own citizens.

There are different forms of brutality in every society. Obviously there is the overt brutality of murder, torture and imprisonment that happens the world over. But there are also subtler forms of brutality to be found in this country: ways of treating people such as immigrants, asylum seekers, single mothers and, recently, beggars; and ways of portraying them to suggest they are upsetting the 'civility' of our society. It is possible to create a culture which suggests that these people are threatening a way of life we should be living, a mythical way of life. Waknuk contains both forms but the latter was more interesting to me as a playwright. I wanted to explore the idea that they actually need the mutants and when they cast them out they are using them to confirm the myth of Waknuk that's been built up over many years.

David Harrower heightened the dramatic tension by including the idea that the Waknuk people are building a wall to seal themselves in and the Fringe people are making more and more raids. There is a state of emergency in Waknuk and much black propaganda about maintaining the purity of the people. The children who are telepathic have felt different from birth and have used their powers imaginatively and creatively, saying things in their heads that would be proscribed in this restricted society. Over the years their power has been eroded so that at the start of the play they do not communicate very much. In a sense, it is only by being excluded from Waknuk that the children are able to use their powers and attain their freedom.

> Writing it, I felt a great emotion for the children and for the strength they have. The communication between them, the ability to think freely and imagine freely without fear of reprisal gives them this strength, something the other people of Waknuk do not have. It was difficult finding a way of creating this telepathic group but I eventually decided on monologues spoken by each of the children with a suggested stage direction that we see the other children lit or grouped around them at the same time. The monologues have a certain poeticism about them to show that the only way they can express themselves is in their heads, in secret. This is the only way they can use language without restriction.

The climax of the novel is when a space ship comes to rescue the children. David Harrower leaves out the space ship. Instead, when the children get to the Fringes, Petra makes contact with a woman. She does not communicate fully until the very end when the woman describes a place to her and how to get there. The play ends with the children setting off, a classic story of a journey going from darkness to light.

> I wanted to show a society that denied its children their childishness, took from them the ability to be

imaginative and surreal, blocked the process of discovering their own creativity and place in the world.

The Chrysalids, the play, is more than the story that John Wyndham created. It has poetry and insights and reflections on how a society can brutalize itself in the quest for purity and the pursuit of a high and essentially wrong moral code. David Harrower is not preaching about our society today. His first aim was to tell this story in the most entertaining way but it is more than likely that young people who take part in productions of this play will be forced to question some of the assumptions we make about social control.

David Harrower's first professional production was *Knives in Hens*. It opened at the Traverse Theatre and subsequently transferred to the Bush Theatre, London. David is currently under commission to the Royal Court, the National Theatre and the Traverse. His most recent play, *Quiet Night In* was commissioned by the Tramway and written in collaboration with KtC.

Production Notes

STAGING AND SETTING

The story focuses on a group of young people living in a post holocaust world who have the power to communicate telepathically. Their society is divided at birth by those who are physically 'perfect' and those who are not. The imperfect babies are taken across the border by a man on a horse and left in an old basket on the edge of a field to be looked after by the Fringe people. The power which sets them apart, if detected, would mean that they too would be banished. There are twelve scenes with a number of locations which can be achieved very simply. The action moves from the group itself which is always seen together, even when only one is speaking – this is a useful convention which will suggest very simply that the thoughts they're having are shared with the rest of the group – to the Strorm family household, a forest with rocks, a crowd scene where the inhabitants of Waknuk are gathered to see the spectacle of Fringe people being punished (the crowd should mask the cage so that the audience sees the Fringe people for the first time in Scene 11), by a river, at the border, deep in the forest and at the Fringe people's camp.

The design has to capture a sense of the borders, fear, divide and control. Within this landscape (created by image, colour, shadows, movement and sound) the space should allow fluid changes of locations, being flexible enough to move from interior domestic scenes to forest and into the Fringe land.

Lighting should take into account the shift from light to dark, the forest, river, and so on. It will need to pick out the telepathy group when it speaks. Petra's and later

Anne's voice is heard offstage and a decision will need to be made as to whether the audience can also hear the city people who communicate with the group or whether it is more effective to have it imagined. Special effects can be kept to a minimum because the excitement needs to lie in the telling of the story.

The inhabitants of Waknuk wear a cross on their clothing which is unspecified but not elaborate. They wear shoes. When the group members take off their crosses a mark must be left. The Fringe people are wild-looking, dress in rags and are dirt-encrusted.

CASTING

This is a play suitable for a wide age range (eleven to nineteen) offering parts for twenty or more. The telepathy group is made up of David Strorm (upper teens) and five others of roughly the same age as well as his sister Petra, who must appear to be considerably younger than the rest of the cast. Other younger characters are David's two sisters who are not telepathic, Sophie Wender and Alan Ervin. The Fringe people can be any age or sex. The adult characters are David's parents, his sympathetic uncle Axel (who at a push could be an aunt), Sophie's mother Mary and Mrs Ervin. We assume that the two inspectors are adult, but casting them young could be interesting; they can also double up as Fringe people.

QUESTIONS

1 Where in history and in the world today can we find examples of societies abandoning their babies because they don't live up to their ideas of perfection?

2 Why and when have walls been put up to define borders and with what consequences?

3 What is the immediate history of Waknuk?

4 What is its likely future?

5 What has caused the tension between Joseph and Axel?

6 What do Axel and Joseph believe? How do their views differ?

7 Why do you think that it is the youngest person who hears the 'city voices' most clearly?

EXERCISES

1 Find out from the script:
- What your character says about others.
- What your character says about himself/herself.

2 Write one sentence which describes the journey through the play any one character makes. Share your findings with the rest of the group.

3 Take the twelve scene headings and in groups of four or five create an image that best sums each up.

4 Sophie has so many things she wants to ask David. She asks, for instance, who was the first person to say, 'purity is the true image of God' and who were the first people to believe it? Imagine what other questions she might have asked and what his responses might have been.

5 In a large group, create the sound you imagine the telepathy group hear being communicated from the city that 'looks on fire' they describe so vividly at the start of the play. Let it progress from the faint and muffled sound they are first aware of to something more distinctive, and then to the lone female voice that Petra communicates with. Whether you decide to let the audience hear the sounds or not, Petra must know what she is describing.

6 *The Chrysalids* is written from the young people's point
of view and many of the older characters come out
unsympathetically – Joseph Storm, for instance. He is a
man of principle governed by the rules laid down by
society. Have his character tell the story from his
viewpoint.

Suzy Graham-Adriani
February 1997

CUBA

Liz Lochhead

Characters

B., the narrator, late forties, but appears ageless
Barbara Proctor, fourteen
Bernadette Griggs, fourteen
Dr Proctor, early forties
Mrs Proctor, early forties
Mr Griggs, early forties
Mrs Griggs, early forties
Mr Shaw, late twenties
Miss Arthur, mid-twenties
Mr Cairncross, forties
Old Prentiss, fifties/sixties
Eleanor/Girl Messenger, fourteen
Pamela, fourteen
Sandra, fourteen
Marianne, fourteen
Susan, fourteen
Linda, fourteen
Maureen, fourteen
Beth, fourteen
Jean-Ann, fourteen
Extra members of Chorus, if desired. Also two Chorus
members to play two Cleaners

Note: The pieces of dialogue in square brackets are
(Scottish) alternatives to the standard English text. These
are included to encourage any company performing the
play to similarly, here or elsewhere, localize the speech at
their own discretion. The events should sound as though
they happened in a Grammar School in *your* town in
1962.

*The narrator, B., is 'sorting through' in her parents' house
after the death of her (long-widowed) mother. 'Sadness
acting' of any sort is strictly to be avoided though. She is
flooded with memory and this is likely to be exhilarating
beyond all grief. B. drags a big dusty old cardboard box
across centre stage, stops, wipes her dusty hands on the
seat of her trousers, picks out a dusty old book, blows,
registers that it is a copy of* Palgrave's Golden Treasury,
*sees that tucked into it, though much bigger, is a real
large-size school photograph – we only see the back of it –
which she holds in front of her, perusing, as behind her,
central, lights come up on a still tableau . . .*

   *The Chorus in the form of that school photograph of a
grammar school form of fourteen/fifteen-year-old pupils
all girls,* circa 1962 *– that is, in the days of obligatory
school uniform and two or three years before hemlines
even thought of climbing towards the idea of the miniskirt.
Among them are Barbara and Bernadette as well as the
Chorus – made up of as many girls as the director wishes,
but the minimum number is nine more, the sum of those
individual characters (Eleanor, Pamela, Sandra, Marianne,
Susan, Linda, Maureen, Beth, Jean-Ann, the classmates we
will meet later, and then there are Mr Prentiss (or Mrs
Prentiss, whichever the director may choose) and Miss
Arthur and Mr Shaw on either side of Mr Cairncross in
the middle of the back row.*

   The girls of the Chorus begin to recite by rote.

Chorus
   I remember, I remember the house where I was born,

The little window where the sun came peeping in at
morn.
It never came a wink too soon, or brought too long a day
But now I often wish the night had borne my breath
away . . .

B. That's never us. It is though! There she is, and there's
me. Back row, to the left. There we are. Barbara and
Bernadette, Berni and Barb. *Un*believable.

*Barbara and Bernadette, summoned ghosts, split, one
each side, from their places in the photograph and
move slowly down midstage to the right and left as B.
sinks to her knees by the box, puts down the
photograph and peruses the dusty old book, smiling.
Speaks out clearly and evenly. She is well beyond tears
in all this.*

Palgrave's Golden Treasury . . . Every home should have
one. I didn't know we did . . . Not a lot of poetry round
our house, not that I can remember, not when I was
growing up. Maybe I should take it back to Sarah, little
souvenir of your Grandma, mmm? Must've been Mum's
. . . Oh look, a school prize!

She was so proud of you, Sairey, when you were born
that was the first thing I did she ever really approved of.
You two always got on like a house on fire. I know how
much you're going to miss her. I'll miss her. Oh, Mum, I
miss you so much. Where are you?

*B. hugs her arms around her stomach and rocks a beat
or two back and forward. Stops and pep-talks herself.*

Come on, come on, B. The sooner you get this done the
sooner you can go home. (*She picks up the photograph.*)
Take this? This'll make Will laugh. Wonder if my lot
would recognize me? Which one's Mum? Can you see
me? Which one am I? That's us, Bernadette and
Barbara, Barbara and Bernadette. Inseparable. Hah! So

they said. So we thought. Thing is we came from very different families.

In their two tight spots on either side of the stage, some more summoned ghosts, Barbara's family, the Proctors, Mum and Dad, and Bernadette's, the Griggses, Mum and Dad, appear very slowly, like almost identical tableaux coming to life. Different families? At first sight they could not be more similar. The Mums – both in party dresses of 1962 (ideally one a shiny sheath and the other a taffeta ballerina-length full-skirted effort) and both with faded flowery aprons on top – are ironing, in unison, and the Dads sit on armchairs behind newspapers.

Barbara and Bernadette, sobbing, heads down in shame as at the very end of the play, approach their home spaces.

In their separate homes, simultaneously, the Mums put down their irons and look fondly and sympathetically at their daughters. They too are in their very-end-of-the-play state.

Mrs Proctor and Mrs Griggs Darling, it isn't the end of the world!
Barbara and Bernadette Don't say that!

The mothers go to their daughters and put their arms around them.

B. It wasn't the end of the world! It felt like it at the time.
Mrs Proctor and Mrs Griggs You've got your whole future in front of you!

In unison, the Dads, also in their end-of-the-play state, lower their papers and, simultaneously, speak directly to their individual daughters –

Dr Proctor and Mr Griggs What's up with your miserable face? [What's the matter with your greeting face?]

Mrs Proctor / Mrs Griggs Jim! / Frank!

The Dads relent from their initial – if unexplained – anger, soften.

Dr Proctor and Mr Griggs We won't say anything about this again, you hear me? Hush! (Wheesht!) You've got your whole future in front of you.

Lights change.

B. Thing is, we didn't think that meant much. Because next week we'd be dead. The whole world would have blown itself to smithereens. The headlines outside the newsagents said so. WAR INEVITABLE. Everybody was really scared, the grown-ups didn't talk about it, not in front of us kids, but we knew they knew it too. It was the end of the world. Tomorrow. The day after. Next week. Next week at the latest. This was the time of Cuba.

This photo must've been *before* that . . . Must have been that summer, end of term, and the Cuban missile crisis was, what, October? Well, look at the picture, Barbara and Bernadette are still joined at the hip. Friendship is still very much an item. This is the class of '62.

There's Miss Arthur. And Mr Shaw. Heartthrob. It doesn't take much. It doesn't take much, not with a class of fourteen-year-old girls, does it? And Old Cairncross, the headmaster, right slap in the middle between them. And there we are. Barbara and Bernadette, Berni and Barb. 'Barbara Proctor the Doctor's Daughter'. And Bernadette Griggs, 'one of those Griggs that Breed like Pigs'. Seven of a family, six boys, one girl.

Lights begin to fade down on the family tableaux.

Did you ever have a better friend than she was? Say it's a Saturday night. A *normal* Saturday night before

President Kennedy put the shits up the whole world
with his game of nuclear poker with the Russians.

*By the last line of the Chorus's speech the Girls are
together, downstage. It's Saturday night. They're alone,
bored and browsing through a pile of magazines.
Reading aloud sometimes.*

Chorus Have you one basic dress that can be dressed up
for almost any occasion?
Are both your stocking seams straight, this minute?
Have you at least one pair of plain black court shoes?
Bernadette What to do on that rare, that spare, night in?
Barbara Pamper yourself, of course!
Chorus To whiten grubby elbows, rub with a cut lemon
daily.
Bachelor Boys –
Bernadette Hollywood style . . .

*Barbara drops her boring magazine, grabs Bernadette's
and peruses.*

Chorus Rock Hudson finds home cooking great fun and
has a gang of his friends over once in a while to try out
his speciality. Barbecue spare ribs. And boy oh boy, do
they taste good.
Barbara John Wayne favours fish dishes.

Bernadette snatches the magazine from her.

Bernadette Dirk Bogarde prefers a rag out of veal.

Barbara snatches it back, looks.

Barbara Eh? *Ragout*, you! It's French, Bernadette.
Bernadette I know.
Chorus Tab Hunter is happy with a hamburger.
Bernadette I'm starving, Barbara!
Barbara Look! Taffy-haired Janet Leigh is the lovely wife
of actor Tony Curtis . . .

Bernadette Are they not divorced?

Barbara Maybe, it's an ancient magazine. Mum's had them for donkeys. She kids on she only gets them for the waiting room. Hah! (*She looks some more in the film magazine.*)

Bernadette Hollywood, eh?

Barbara Oh, I know . . .

Bernadette This place is a dump. See, when I'm seventeen, I'm going to dye my hair platinum, buy the highest stilettos I can find and emigrate to the USA.

Barbara dreams and yearns through the next list, each place more exotic and wonderful than the last.

Barbara Canada . . . New Zealand . . . Australia . . . Bernadette, you can go to Australia for ten quid.

Bernadette No, America. I'm dead serious, Barbara!

Barbara I know . . .

Bernadette I mean it! I've got an auntie in the States. New Jersey. Call this bloody Saturday night!

Barbara Here *is* a dump, isn't it?

Bernadette Here? I would not pee on it if it was on fire. They should drop the bomb on it any time. Do the world a favour.

Barbara Bernadette!

B. Don't say that, don't say it! In three days' time that'll be exactly what looks like happening.

The family tableaux fade back up, the Mums still ironing. Barbara and Bernadette separate and home in.

Go back . . . earlier that day . . . oh, fourteen years old and every Saturday it's the end of the world about *something.*

The two girls begin to wail. In unison, the Dads lower their papers, exasperated, and, simultaneously, directly at their individual daughters –

Dr Proctor and Mr Griggs What's up with your miserable face? [What's the matter with your greeting face?]

Barbara and Bernadette Nothing!

B. . . . Well, maybe you've picked out the pattern. Misses Petite Capri pants or toreadors . . . You'd place the pattern, you'd make yourself take the time to pin it, *patience*, patience and *pins*. You'd cut them out really, really carefully . . .

Chorus Suitable fabrics: seersucker, glazed cotton, knits, needlecord and piqué. Allow extra fabric to match large-scale prints.

B. Or your first fumbling experiments with last-thru 6 to 8 shampoo semi-permanent hair colour.

Chorus Chestnut Charm, Northern Lights, Golden Sequins . . .

B. Hint of a Tint. You'd spend hours in the chemist's poring over the colour chart. Disaster. And the biggest disaster of all? No effect. Total waste of money!

The Mums put down their irons, fold their arms, sigh in unison at their daughters and shake their heads.

Mrs Proctor and Mrs Griggs What a waste of money. You must have a lot more money than sense, my girl!

Mrs Griggs Bernadette! Don't you be leaving dirty marks all over my good towels!

Bernadette No, Mum.

Mrs Proctor Just watch, Barbara, you don't do any damage to my good Singer.

Barbara Right, Mum.

Mrs Griggs Don't you be long there in that bathroom. Your Dad's to get in there and get himself shifted.

Mrs Proctor And mind my shears!

Dr Proctor and Mr Griggs Hush! [Wheesht!]

Mrs Proctor Well, Jim, my good dressmaking shears and she uses them to cut her fringe.

Mrs Griggs Dyeing your hair at your age, what will the teachers say on Monday?

Barbara and Bernadette Mu-um . . .

Mrs Proctor What are you supposed to be making anyway?

Mrs Griggs What colour is it supposed to be going to turn out?

Barbara Toreador pants.

Bernadette Golden Sequins.

Mrs Proctor Jim, did you hear that!

Mrs Griggs What your dad will say I don't know!

Barbara and **Bernadette** Mu-um!

Mrs Proctor / Mrs Griggs Huh, *Tor*-eador pants! / Huh, Golden *Se*-quins!

Mrs Proctor Toreador pants, what are they when they are at home? With a BTM like yours? Frighten the French!

Mrs Griggs Make yourself cheap! Ends up bleached-looking your dad will tan your hide, my girl. What the hair-oil is Golden Sequins as a shade for hair?

Dr Proctor / Mr Griggs Nora! I am trying to do my – / Betty! I am trying to do my –

Mr Griggs bites back a two-beat expletive during Dr Proctor's line.

Dr Proctor – crossword!

Mr Griggs – coupon!

B. Sometimes I think the whole different backgrounds thing was grossly exaggerated, although much was made of it at the time. OK, different class, different attitudes, different standard of living, granted. Different sides of the track maybe, but I'd say they were far more alike than – well, certainly *much* more alike than they thought they were.

As if to prove how true this is, the families come out with their similar and overlapping little list of favourite homilies.

Dr Proctor and Mr Griggs Cut according to your cloth –
Dr and Mrs Proctor / Mr and Mrs Griggs A stitch in time
saves nine.
Dr and Mrs Proctor Many a mickle makes a muckle.
Mr and Mrs Griggs Watch your handbag.
Mrs Proctor People who complain of playing second
fiddle should be glad they're in the orchestra at all.
Dr and Mrs Proctor / Mr and Mrs Griggs You've got your
whole future in front of you!
Chorus You have got your whole future in front of you so
see you watch your handbag and stick in at the school.
Mrs Proctor and Mrs Griggs Saturday night, eh?
Barbara and Bernadette Big deal.

*There is an equal note of ever so slight sarcasm in each
of the Mum's next speeches.*

Mrs Proctor I suppose Berna*dette*'s coming round?
Mrs Griggs I suppose you'll be going round to *Bar*bara's?
Mrs Proctor / Mrs Griggs Or are you going there for a
change? / Or is she coming here for a change?
Mrs Proctor / Mrs Griggs Sometimes I wonder if she's a
home to go to! / Her mother will be wondering if you've
a home to go to!
Barbara and Bernadette Mu-um!
Mrs Griggs Bernadette, doll, just because you passed your
exam and qualified for the grammar school [high
school] there's no reason to treat your brothers like dirt
and turn up your nose at everybody else around here.
Mrs Proctor Barbara, pet, I know you and Bernadette
have been the best of pals since you were so high [yon
high], but now that you are at the big school have you
not made any other nice friends?
Mrs Griggs Don't you want to be pals with them?
Barbara and Bernadette Uh-huh, but my best pal's
Bernadette! / Uh-huh, but my best pal's Barbara!

*The Mums shake their heads. Slowly lights fade on the
Mums and Dads.*

*We're back with the girls alone with their pile of
magazines on a Saturday night.*

Chorus To whiten grubby elbows, rub with a cut lemon
daily.

To lighten a sallow, winter-worn neck, make a bleaching
solution by mixing one tablespoon of twenty volume
peroxide to three drops ammonia.

Soak a wide strip of cotton wool, squeeze lightly and
wrap around the neck.

After twenty minutes, remove, splash skin with tepid
water and smear on a soothing cream.

Barbara I saw your big brother.

Bernadette Which big brother? My big big brother?

Barbara No, the nice-looking one, the next one.

Bernadette The apprentice? Nice-looking nothing!

Barbara Is he? With the bike. The butcher's boy.

Bernadette Butcher's boy? That's the third one and he is
ugly as a pig.

Barbara No he isn't.

Bernadette Is so.

Barbara Wish I had brothers . . .

Bernadette Pig ugly!

Barbara Wish I wasn't an only one . . .

Bernadette Wish I was an only one. My brothers are all
toerags. And this place is a dump.

Chorus Find your face shape here, then choose the style
famous London hairdresser Piers Von Spiers has created
specially for you . . .

Bernadette Barbara, would you say my face was round,
square, heart-shaped or oval.

Barbara Oval. Sort of a roundish oval. Or maybe it's
more of a squarish heart shape.

Bernadette I'm ugly.

Barbara Bernadette, you are not ugly. I'm ugly. I am pig ugly and Mr Shaw is getting married to Miss Arthur and I wish I was dead.

Lights change. The family tableaux begin to fade back up as B. speaks.

B. Don't say that, don't say it! Next week you'll wish you were back in this week, on a normal boring Saturday, making mountains out of molehills.

Back in their home spaces, Barbara, wailing, throws her botched sewing on the floor and, simultaneously, Bernadette, wailing just as loudly, flings down her towel in a temper.

Dr and Mrs Proctor / Mr and Mrs Griggs What's up with your face?

Barbara I cut the left leg-back out inside-out and squeegee.

Bernadette It's made no difference!

Barbara Supposed to be 'Simplicity'!

Mrs Proctor Nobody will notice.

Mrs Griggs Who's going to be looking at your hair anyway, you're only a little girl [wee lassie].

Dr Proctor and **Mr Griggs** I'll give you something to bloody cry for!

Mrs Proctor and **Mrs Griggs** Never mind, pet –

Mrs Proctor Bernadette's coming round, eh?

Mrs Griggs You're going round to Barbara's!

Barbara and **Bernadette** Where are you two going?

Mrs Proctor Just to the dinner dance at the golf club in aid of the Rotary.

Mrs Griggs Just round the pub [up the Miner's Welfare / the Club/the Legion, etc.] for a little [wee] drink.

Mrs Proctor and **Mrs Griggs** I didn't want to go . . . (*sigh*) It'll be no night out for me!

Mrs Proctor First it was where's his good black silk socks,

I says in your sock drawer beside your hankies, and I
suppose I'm to come and find your cummerbund and
your ready-tied bow-tie for you as per usual?

Mrs Griggs No night out for me, watching them pour
pints down their throats and arguing about outside lefts
and inside rights and bloody goalies. No –

Mrs Proctor and Mrs Griggs It'll be no night out for me
. . . (*sigh*) But it was your dad!

Mrs Proctor He'd bought the tickets.

Mrs Griggs Rose of Tralee came up first at the Dogs and
he promised Jack Thomson he'd buy him a pint.

Mrs Proctor and Mrs Griggs And it will be a night out, I
suppose.

Mrs Proctor A chance to give my silver shoes an outing –

Mrs Griggs Shift myself for a bit of a change [a wee change].

Mrs Proctor and Mrs Griggs And after all, it is Saturday
night!

*The Mums take off their aprons, smooth out their
dresses and twirl. The girls look on enviously.*
*As the Chorus speaks, the lights fade on the families and
the girls are alone on their Saturday night in.*

Chorus Single girls, how good a conversationalist are
you?

How bright will your visitors find the fireside chat this
winter?

Can you wash a woollen cardigan without shrinking it?

Do you know where the main stop cock is, for use when
there is a burst pipe?

Are you a stay-at-home with no wish to travel? (2 marks
for YES column A, or 2 marks for NO column C.)

Have you ever made (a) a dress, (b) a piece of basketry,
(c) a soufflé?

Barbara Did you not put that rinse through your hair?

Bernadette Uh-huh! Did you not finish your toreadors?

Barbara All right on Jackie Kennedy, but they'd never

have suited me anyway, an arse like mine.

Bernadette Can't you notice it a little bit [wee bit]?

Barbara It *is* nice and *shiny* . . .

Bernadette Look, I think it is just a rumour, about Mr Shaw and Miss Arthur. I hope it is only a rumour. For your sake.

Barbara Is it stuff just a rumour. He *is* getting married to her. Myra Simpson's big sister works beside Miss Arthur's cousin, who's a Saturday girl in Timothy White's the Chemist, and she's a bridesmaid. I only hope Arthur has the decency to wear a long white frock, piano legs like hers.

Bernadette She's got a nice face . . .

Barbara Up to a point. *Hellish* legs, you must admit it.

Bernadette I mean, I like her.

Barbara *I* like her. I *did* like her till she got her hooks in Mr Shaw.

Bernadette She's a good teacher.

Barbara He's a brilliant teacher.

Bernadette Barbara, you are only saying that because you fancy him.

Barbara I don't. You do.

Bernadette I don't. Not really. Barbara, I did do until I knew you did and then I decided you could because you've more chance with him than I do –

Barbara Bernadette, he's getting *married*.

Bernadette – and you're my friend. Barbara, we can't go around fancying the same people as each other any more, it just doesn't work out. So, he's getting married, that's nothing to us. Married, not married, that's not in our universe. But two best friends, Barbara, two best friends in love with the same man, disaster.

Barbara Can you do that, Bernadette? I don't think you can just decide about your feelings, that's not how it works.

Bernadette Oh yes it is, that's exactly how it works. Feelings is a decision.

Barbara I don't know . . . And anyway, I don't see how it matters if we both fancy the same person. I mean, we both fancied Richard Chamberlain last year, when everybody in the class went on to Ben Casey.

Bernadette That is totally different. Dr Kildare is a fictional character. But Mr Shaw is real.

Barbara Listen, Bernadette. I love him, and why I love him is he's such a brilliant teacher. With nice eyes.

Bernadette Whose pet are you.

Barbara I am not.

Bernadette You are. Teacher's pet. Mr Shaw's pet lamb [wee pet lamb] that's always the top of the class. *'I derived great pleasure from reading this essay. Eighteen out of twenty.' 'Barbara, would you read yours out loud?' 'I wish some of you would take a leaf out of Barbara Proctor's book.'* Barbara Proctor this, Barbara –

Barbara Look, drop it, will you, Berni? He's getting married.

Bernadette Are you sad?

Barbara remains silent, fuming with exasperation.

Tell you the truth, I'm sad he's getting married to Miss Arthur even though neither of the two of us has any chance anyway, even you that is his favourite, but . . . it's not the end of the world, you know.

Barbara Don't Tell Me What Is And Isn't The End Of The World. (*Pause.*) Read my fortune.

Bernadette I read your fortune on Wednesday. This is Saturday. You're supposed to give your future enough time to happen.

Barbara I didn't like that future. I want a different future.

Bernadette It's bad luck!

Barbara Get the book!

Chorus
>Your Fortune in the Cards.
>A Queen for a lady, A King for a gentleman,
>The suit according to his colouring – Hearts if very fair,
>>Diamonds if fairish,
>Clubs if rather dark, Spades if very dark,
>Will represent the person with whom you are, or are
>>destined to be,
>In love.

>*The cards are spread out before Barbara, who looks at them horrified, while Bernadette consults the 'luck book'.*

Bernadette Five of Clubs, a quarrel with a friend or at work. That's school, we don't go to work. A quarrel with a friend or at school. Seven of Spades, injustice, Nine . . . danger or risk. Nine of diamonds, news good or bad depending on the cards next to it. The Ace of Spades, reversed . . .

B. Two days after Bernadette wished the bomb would fall on this dump and Barbara wished she was dead and they brought bad luck on themselves tempting fate by asking for a different fortune too soon, it really began to look as if they were about to get their wishes.

>*Lights come up again on the ironing boards and home sets, the Mums still ironing and the Dads still with their papers.*

On Monday night after *The Archers* they announced on the radio that President Kennedy will address the American nation at midnight our time. On a matter of the Greatest National Urgency.

>*The Dads put down their newspapers, faces worried, listening. The Mums stop and upend the irons on their boards.*

Mrs Proctor and Mrs Griggs Uh-oh! (*They fold their arms and bite their lips.*)

B. He told how Russian missile bases were being built on the island of Cuba, just ninety miles off the Florida coast, easy striking distance from American soil.

Chorus . . . The purpose of these bases can be none other than to provide a nuclear strike capability against the West . . .

B. The United States were united in their hatred of Cuba, Communism, a revolution and a man called Castro. And very, very frightened by his alliance with Russia.

Chorus . . . capable of striking Washington DC, the Panama Canal, Cape Canaveral . . .

B. Kennedy demanded the 'withdrawal of Soviet offensive missiles from Cuba' and imposed a 'naval quarantine' – that was the word he used –

Chorus – a quarantine on all ships carrying weapons to Cuba.

B. Then it got to the bit when you knew it was really scary.

Chorus US strategic forces are on full alert. Any missile launched from Cuba will be regarded as a Soviet missile and will be met by a full retaliatory response.

Dr Proctor and Mr Griggs That sounds like that'll be the balloon about to go up!

Barbara and Bernadette What balloon?

Dr Proctor and Mr Griggs Never mind!

Mrs Proctor Hush, Jim [Wheesht, Jim], in front of Barbara.

Mrs Griggs Hush, Frank [Wheesht, Frank], you'll have all the kids [bairns/weans] terrified out of their wits!

B. You knew there was going to be a war, and they knew there was going to be a war, and all the bad dreams you'd ever had about the atom bomb and the four-minute warning and the noise of the sirens when they tested them – it was all coming true at last.

Dr Proctor That Khrushchev! We should've sorted out the Russians at the end of the last war.

Mr Griggs That bloody Kennedy, he's going to get us all killed trying to get himself re-elected president.

B. Next morning the newspaper headlines were all big black letters and the words CRISIS and CUBA. Yet everything, everything on the surface, was absolutely normal and you just went to school as usual. On the third day, the scariest day so far, of the Cuba Crisis, we went to Miss Arthur for Modern Studies.

The parents speak out from a different, earlier, time now, the time at the beginning of term when they first heard of the new subject. They are laughing.

Mrs Proctor Jim!

Mrs Griggs Frank!

Mrs Proctor and Mrs Griggs Do you hear that?

Dr Proctor 'Modern Studies', what's that when it's at home?

Barbara and Bernadette It's a mixture of Geography, History, Economics –

Mr Griggs At least it sounds like something useful and not that [yon] bloody Latin and Greek dead languages carry-on!

Mrs Proctor and Mrs Griggs Economics!

Mrs Griggs You'd know all about economics if you tried to keep you lot in school shoes on what they pay your father!

Barbara and Bernadette It's a mixture of Geography, History, Economics and Current Affairs.

Mrs Proctor speaks with mock humility but an amused scorn for such a ridiculous new-fangled non-subject.

Mrs Proctor Oh well, what did the poor child know!

*Lights change, the parents fade, all the girls in the
Chorus become a classroom seated in pairs, Barbara
and Bernadette in the middle. Miss Arthur is writing a
word on a central, invisible 'fourth wall' blackboard.
She turns to the class.*

Miss Arthur Block-ade. What does the word 'blockade'
mean? (*She looks about the class before picking at
random.*) Sandra?

Sandra Miss, it's where the navy stops ships landing their
cargo at an enemy port.

Miss Arthur Exactly. A blockade is a naval siege. Such as
President Kennedy is currently conducting on Cuba. But
he didn't actually use the word 'blockade' in his speech.
Any idea why? (*Pause.*) No? Nobody? Well, he used
another word instead? Anybody? He used the word
'quarantine'. What does the word 'quarantine' mean? I
mean normally. Marianne? No?

Marianne shakes her head. Linda volunteers.

Linda In a hospital, Miss.

Miss Arthur *What* 'in a hospital'? Yes?

Barbara Miss, it's where you isolate somebody that's full
of germs to stop them infecting anybody else.

Miss Arthur Very good. Yes. So it's an interesting use of
the word in this case, isn't it?

Maureen Miss, it means America wants to stop Cuba
from getting infected with Communism.

Eleanor Bernadette Griggs's dad's a Communist.

Bernadette He is not!

Beth Bernadette Griggs's dad says there is going to be a
war.

Miss Arthur Well, I fervently hope not, but Bernadette's
dad could be right . . .

Barbara Miss, there isn't going to be a world war, is
there?

Sandra and Maureen Will there be a war?

Bernadette Why do we still have to come to school? Why do we have to do hockey when there is going to be a war?

Linda, Jean-Ann, Susan and Marianne Miss, is there going to be World War Three?

Miss Arthur I *hope* not. Back to this language though.

Barbara Mr Shaw said there wasn't going to be a war.

Miss Arthur skates easily and neutrally over the personal nature of Mr Shaw's name being mentioned in her classroom.

Miss Arthur I very much hope he is right.

Bernadette pushes Barbara's taboo-breaking further, and more consciously than her friend.

Bernadette *Mr Shaw* said that the atom bomb has kept the peace since the end of the last war.

Miss Arthur Well, that's a point of view . . .

Linda Miss, are you in CND?

Jean-Ann Miss, is it true that you're a Ban the Bomber?

Maureen Miss, you look like a Ban the Bomber in your duffle-coat!

Susan Miss, are you engaged to Mr Shaw?

Miss Arthur, beleaguered, just answers nothing and shouts to regain control.

Miss Arthur NOW, THE AMERICAN BLOCKADE OF CUBA! Why didn't Kennedy use the word?

Bernadette Call a spade a spade.

Miss Arthur Exactly. Any ideas? Well, it was probably a matter of international law. Mr Gaitskell – Mr Gaitskell? Anybody?

Marianne The Leader of the Opposition.

Miss Arthur Right! Mr Gaitskell has raised the question of the legality of the American action in blockading

Cuba. A blockade is an act of war. Does one country have the right – in time of peace – to blockade another country by posting its navy in international waters? Also Gaitskell, and others – not the Prime Minister, not Macmillan, or at least not publicly, but many on the left – expressed their grave concern at the lack of consultation between the USA and its NATO partners. NATO, Jean-Ann Simpson?

Jean-Ann North Atlantic . . . North Atlantic . . .

Pamela North Atlantic Treaty Organization.

Miss Arthur Good, Pamela . . .

Bernadette My dad says Kennedy is crazy and he could kill us all trying to get re-elected.

Beth Everybody knows it's Khrushchev that's off his nut.

Eleanor He is! He's crazy. He's a Communist.

Pamela He wears funny suits.

Miss Arthur Is that important?

Eleanor Mrs Khrushchev wears big stupid bundles of lumpy fur coats and she looks worse than somebody out of the Women's Institute [Women's Guild].

Maureen Russian women have to drive tractors!

Pamela Mrs Kennedy looks like someone out of a woman's magazine. Jackie Kennedy looks like a million dollars.

Beth Khrushchev is a maniac.

Bernadette You just believe all the propaganda.

Beth It's the Communists that do propaganda.

Miss Arthur Ah, now we see – calm down, Beth, ssh! Bernadette – 'propaganda' is lies spread by the other side. 'Truth' is *our* side's view of the matter.

Bernadette 'Truth is beauty and beauty truth.' That's what Mr Shaw says.

Miss Arthur Good for him . . .

Barbara That's back-to-front, you. Anyway, it's John Keats!

Miss Arthur Good for him, but we were discussing the

136

current situation. Possible ways out. Of this dangerous situation. The United States could trade *their* bases in Turkey, which are after all just as close to the USSR as these ones the Russians want to build on Cuba are to American soil.

Sandra That's totally different!

Miss Arthur How is it totally different, Sandra?

Sandra It is! My dad says Churchill should've finished off the Russians at the end of the last war. He says the Russkies are worse than the Germans any day. Communism's worse than the Nazis.

Susan So does mine. He says the Yanks should bomb the Cuban bases and invade straight away, show Khrushchev who is the boss.

Miss Arthur Well, let's hope no one takes that course in the present incendiary situation . . .

Maureen My dad says what this country needs is another war to get this country on its feet.

Bernadette Then your dad's a maniac like President Kennedy.

Miss Arthur Now, now . . .

Bernadette Well, Bertrand Russell sent him a telegram telling him so!

Barbara So he did.

Barbara and Bernadette stand up and speak out in choric fashion as everyone else freezes, amazed.

Barbara and Bernadette 'Your action desperate. Stop. No conceivable justification. Stop. We will not have mass murder. Stop. End this madness. Stop.'

B. It got worse and worse, though. The Russian forces were on full alert. Khrushchev *was* crazy, we all knew that. He wore lumpy suits and Cossack hats and was bald and crazy like an angry baby. At the UN he took off his shoe and banged it on the table and shouted like a furious tyrannical baby determined to get his own way or bring the whole house down on everybody's head.

Lights change. The Chorus are singing the last verse of the hymn at school assembly.

Chorus
Hobgoblin nor foul fiend
   Can daunt his spirit;
He knows he at the end
   Shall life inherit
Then fancies fly away;
   He'll fear not what men say;
He'll labour night and day
   To be a pilgrim.

Mr Cairncross Let us pray. O Lord, Bless this school, and make all of us loyal, obedient and useful citizens in this our school community.
Lord, today in our school assembly, we pray for our country and the world. Bless our leaders in this time of international tension. God bless Mr Macmillan and President Kennedy. They know the course they have embarked on is right and just, and we pray that you will grant them courage to keep to this right course and to have the strength to prevail against those dishonourable peacemongers who would have them compromise with the forces of evil. We thank God for the strength of our leaders in the face of intolerable provocation.
We know that it is only when faced with our courage that our enemies will see the error of their ways.

Lights change. Barbara and Bernadette move out of that central position in the Chorus downstage to where they are talking alone together, probably in the same space as their 'Saturday night' scene.

Bernadette Jeez, that Cairncross is as mad as the rest of them, Barbara. Bloody headmasters . . .
Barbara I know. It's getting worse. There are all these

Russian ships stopped dead in the water just in front of the US Navy. If any of these lunatics fire, Bernadette . . .

Bernadette I know. Madmen. I think it's men that's mad.

Barbara You mean 'mankind'?

Bernadette No, men. Women wouldn't play at cowboys like this.

Barbara Women don't get the chance. Women don't get to be the president of the United States. Women don't get to be the prime minister.

Bernadette I'll tell you whose side I'm on.

Barbara Whose?

Bernadette Cuba's.

Barbara Cuba. But my dad says Cuba's just a prawn.

Bernadette A what?

Barbara I mean a pawn, Berni, you know what I mean. I mean just a toy. In Khrushchev's game.

Bernadette Exactly. That's why I'm on Cuba's side.

Lights change. Instead of Miss Arthur, Mr Shaw stands in front of the class. Bernadette and Barbara move back to their central places in the classroom.

Mr Shaw All right, 3A! Put away your *Merchant of Venice*s. We'll stop there, end of Act Two, till next week.

Barbara and Bernadette are talking in asides to each other.

Barbara If there is a next week.

Mr Shaw Take out your *Approach to Poetry*s. We've got twenty minutes or so left and we can continue on the Romantics. I'd like to get to Wordsworth by Christmas.

Bernadette Imagine this might be the final Double English we ever get and we've got to waste it on Poetry.

Mr Shaw Barbara Proctor and Bernadette Griggs, are you two chatting? If you've got something to say, share it with us all, please.

Bernadette Even on Death Row, eh, the guys get to pick

what they want for their last breakfast, don't they?

Mr Shaw Bernadette Griggs, stand up! Repeat what you just said!

Bernadette is embarrassed and apologetic.

Bernadette I . . . just said . . . 'On Death Row the condemned men get their favourite meal the day of their execution,' Sir.

Mr Shaw Fascinating! I won't ask from what lurid film on ITV you gleaned this riveting information. Nor will I ask you to explain its dubious relevance to the topic on hand. Which is the Romantic Poetry of the early nineteenth century. John Keats, Bernadette Griggs?

Bernadette A . . . a Romantic poet, Sir.

Mr Shaw OK, sit down, Bernadette. And no more chattering!

Bernadette No, Sir.

Mr Shaw A Romantic poet. Anything else? Anybody . . .

Eleanor He died, Sir.

Mr Shaw He died, Eleanor, like we all will someday. But yes, John Keats died very young, at the age of twenty-three, of consumption. But not before writing some of the finest, most beautiful, sensuous poems in the English language. (*Mr Shaw turns to an imaginary blackboard out front and 'writes' on it in invisible schoolmaster's copperplate.*) 'Beauty is truth, truth beauty.' John Keats, 'Ode on a Grecian Urn'. Write it down.

Bernadette Sir, we did last week.

Mr Shaw All right, Bernadette! Write it down again then. Beauty is truth, truth beauty. Think about that. (*Pause.*) Turn to page thirty-eight. Marianne, you start, a verse each. 'La Belle Dame sans Merci'. Translation, please.

No one volunteers until Bernadette, trying to get back in his good books, tentatively sticks her hand up.

All right, Bernadette . . .

Bernadette 'The Beautiful Ungrateful Woman'.

Mr Shaw How do you make that out? Oh, I see . . .
Literally! . . . Pamela!

Pamela 'The . . . Beautiful Woman without Thanks'?

Mr Shaw Yes, only here I think it means something much
closer to the English 'mercy'. First verse, Marianne!

*Mr Shaw picks at random by pointing to them, each
member of the Chorus, before each verse. Different
amounts of volume and commitment but somehow the
poem rings out clear.*

Marianne
O what can ail thee, knight-at-arms,
    Alone and palely loitering?
The sedge is wither'd from the lake,
    And no birds sing.

Eleanor
O what can ail thee, knight-at-arms,
    So haggard and so woe-begone?
The squirrel's granary is full,
    And the harvest's done.

Pamela
I see a lily on thy brow
    With anguish moist and fever dew,
And on they cheeks a fading rose
    Fast withereth too.

Maureen
I met a lady in the meads,
    Full beautiful – a faery's child,
Her hair was long, her foot was light,
    And her eyes were wild.

Susan
I made a garland for her head,
    And bracelets too, and fragrant zone,
She look'd at me as she did love,
    And made sweet moan.

Linda

I set her on my pacing steed,
  And nothing else saw all day long,
For sidelong would she bend, and sing
  A faery's song.

Beth

She found me roots of relish sweet,
  And honey wild, and manna dew,
And sure in language strange she said –
  'I love thee true!'

Jean-Ann

She took me to her elfin grot,
  And there she gazed and sigh'd full sore,
And there I shut her wild, wild eyes
  With kisses four.

Sandra

And there she lullèd me asleep
  And there I dream'd – ah! woe betide!
The latest dream I ever dream'd
  On the cold hill's side.

Bernadette

I saw pale kings and princes too,
  Pale warriors, death-pale were they all;
They cried – 'La Belle Dame sans Merci
  Hath thee in thrall!'

*Barbara, deeply affected both by the poem and the
nuclear threat, which seem to her suddenly somehow
powerfully connected, struggles to get her verse out.*

Barbara

I saw their . . . starved lips in the gloam,
  With . . . with horrid warning gapèd wide,
And I a– And I awoke . . .

*Barbara breaks down completely. Mr Shaw is
embarrassed, increasingly disconcerted as he fails to calm*

her, completely out of his depth. He feels responsible, though he would be hard pressed to explain why.

Mr Shaw Barbara, Barbara, pet, what's the matter? Do you want to go for a drink of water?

Barbara No. No, I don't . . .

Mr Shaw Bernadette, take Barbara for a drink of water, wash your face, huh? It's OK.

Barbara It's not!

Mr Shaw Take her to see Miss Houselander, tell her she's not feeling well.

Barbara I don't want to! I don't want to!

Mr Shaw What's wrong?

Barbara I'm frightened. (*She finds an almost defiantly clear voice to admit what, despite their questions in Miss Arthur's class, nobody's been actually admitting in so many words.*) I'm frightened there's going to be a war.

Mr Shaw Ah . . . (*All his natural kindness comes out and he drops all that grammar school teacher's pomposity.*) Listen, listen, don't cry. Don't worry. I don't think – really – we have anything to worry about. How many of you have been worrying themselves about the . . . international situation?

At first stragglingly slowly, following Barbara's defiant admission, gradually all the hands go up. He is very moved.

Mr Shaw Well, the situation is not good, I wouldn't pretend otherwise, but honestly –

Barbara Sir, I read a book about Hiroshima. The atom bombs they dropped at the end of the war . . . The people were turned to ashes. They were as thin as photographs, burned on to the buildings, like printed shadows on the brick and stone. And in Nagasaki a man saw a burning horse in the heart of the city and its foal ran by its side and there was no skin or flesh on it, just bare sinews and muscles, and its eyes peeled and its mouth screaming.

Mr Shaw Good God, what are your parents thinking about letting you read a book like that, sensitive girl like you?

Linda Is there really going to be a war, Sir?

Mr Shaw Now, I really think, honestly, that this is a game the world leaders are playing. They know exactly how far to go. They can take it right to the brink, then pull back. They don't want a war either. That's the last thing they want! A nuclear war is one nobody can win and they know that. Nuclear weapons have probably saved world peace ever since the end of World War Two. Because it's a balance. No one could win. They won't do it . . . Are you listening to me? I'm not frightened, and I assure you I am one of the world's great cowards . . . Dry your eyes. Come on, Barbara. Are you all right?

Barbara Yes, Sir.

Mr Shaw Good. Are you feeling better?

An eventual nod and a sniff.

Good. Well enough to read?

Another nod.

Excellent. Now will you read for us till the end of the poem?

Barbara breathes deep and reads clearly.

Barbara
I saw their starved lips in the gloam,
    With horrid warning gapèd wide,
And I awoke and found me here,
    On the cold hill's side.

And this is why I sojourn here,

> Alone and palely loitering,
> Though the sedge is wither'd from the lake,
> And no birds sing.

Lights snap change and back up on B. Alone.

B. In October 1962, at the height of the Cuba Crisis, we hid, after the Thursday After-school Chess Club, in the toilets, where the cleaners had already been, and waited till the school emptied.

Lights up on Bernadette and Barbara. They stand in front of a door which has on it, in gold letters, HEADMASTER. MR J. K. CAIRNCROSS, M.A. *They are shaking up aerosol cans with that satisfying rattle.*

Barbara Have you ever stolen anything before?

Bernadette No . . .

Barbara Me neither.

Bernadette Not even when you were little [wee], sweets out of the newsagent's?

Barbara No.

Bernadette My big big brother when he was little [wee]stole two Mars Bars and the policeman brought him home. By the ear. My father kicked his arse for him and it put us all off.

Barbara I enjoyed it.

Bernadette So did I.

Barbara Woolworths was the easiest, but these car paints out of Halfords are the best.

Bernadette Brilliant colour!

Barbara Were you scared?

Bernadette No.

Barbara Where did you say you were?

Bernadette I said I was going to yours to do my homework. What did you say?

Barbara I said I was going to yours.

Bernadette Barbara, do you promise?

Barbara Yes.

Bernadette Blood sisters?

Barbara Blood sisters till the end of the world, Amen.

Bernadette cuts her thumb with a penknife, wincing.
Barbara takes it, shuts her eyes, does the same. They
press their hands together and watch one loud drop
down to the floor. Barbara sucks her thumb, shakes the
aerosol up hard, and she is the one to fiercely aerosol,
large messy and scarlet across the headmaster's door,
the word CUBA. *They stand back and look, then*
Bernadette shakes again and this time sprays CUBA
LIBRE.

Bernadette Cu-ba Li-bre.

Barbara What's that?

Bernadette Free Cuba! I wish Kennedy and Khrushchev
would leave it alone and let them have their revolution
and their Fidel Castro and his Havana cigars.

Barbara Ssh!

They are both whispering.

Bernadette What?

Barbara There is somebody coming. There is!

Bernadette Hide!

Barbara Where?

They flatten themselves against the (imaginary) wall
either side of the door, breathing hard. They are afraid.
Looking in each other's eyes, a solemn and
preoccupied Mr Shaw and Miss Arthur, he with his arm
around her, come round the corner. Stop dead.

Mr Shaw What the hell is going on?

Lights change. Back up on B. alone.

B. Looking back now, I suppose Mr Shaw and Miss
Arthur had stayed late at school to make love. After all,

Mr Shaw lived with his widowed mother in a bungalow down Orchard Drive, everybody knew that. Miss Arthur – well, no doubt she had a similar impossible domestic parental situation.

Mr Shaw, as head of department, had a walk-in book cupboard with an armchair and cups and an electric kettle. I had seen all this when I was sent once to collect a set of *Far from the Madding Crowd*s. No doubt he had a tartan picnic rug too, and an old one-bar electric fire. I have made happy love myself in far more uncomfortable situations.

And it's true what they say about sex and death, isn't it? We were very close to death that week.

Anyway, I could tell they felt caught out themselves, catching us.

The girls sit side by side, with Mr Shaw standing over. Miss Arthur tugs at his arm, murmurs. But he doesn't waver.

Miss Arthur Stewart, just let them go . . . Think about it! Better off – from everybody's point of view – We weren't here, we saw nothing.

Mr Shaw What on earth is the meaning of this? Are you crazy? How were you going to get out of the school anyway? You were locked in!

Bernadette I don't know . . .

Mr Shaw You don't know! What the – has the whole world gone mad?

Miss Arthur I think that's rather the point, Stewart.

B. She dragged him away to one side. We just sat there. But we could hear every word they were saying nevertheless.

Miss Arthur They are really, really upset.

Mr Shaw They are upset! Hell, Joyce, we are all upset. I'd never have believed this. My best – (*here he catches himself before saying 'best pupil' and includes Bernadette*) *two* of my very best pupils –

Miss Arthur They won't do it again, Stew . . .

Mr Shaw By God they won't. Joyce, we have to report this to Cairncross first thing in the morning and God knows –

Miss Arthur Give me your keys, Stewart. (*She holds out her hand.*)

Mr Shaw What?

Miss Arthur Give me the car keys.

Mr Shaw Joyce?

Miss Arthur I'll drive them home. They're upset. Go to the Royal Oak. I'll meet you in the Royal Oak later.

He hands over the car keys. Lights change. Up on B. Alone.

B. She drove us home. She didn't say anything. She didn't come in and say anything to our parents, she even let each of us off at the end of our roads so we wouldn't be seen getting out of a car and have to answer any awkward questions. All she said to both of us was she would see us in the morning, we must come to school as usual, and that everything would be all right.

Lights change. Chorus together as a class again. Mr Prentiss's (or Miss Prentiss's) Latin class. Prentiss is the classic Classics teacher who can't keep order, old and deaf to all conversations, carries on regardless in a world of his or her own, therefore it is easy for Bernadette and Barbara to talk openly to each other with little sense of the 'aside'.

Prentiss '*Carpite nunc, tauri*' – '*tauri*'? Maureen Miller?

Maureen Bulls, Sir [Miss].

Bernadette She said it would be OK. Miss Arthur is magnificent.

Prentiss '*Carpite nunc, tauri, de septum montibus herbas dum licet*' – 'Seize while you may, O bulls, the grass of the seven hills.'

Barbara They'll tell. They're bound to.

Prentiss Seven hills, Susan Lockwood?

Barbara It doesn't matter. We'll be dead next week, like Bertrand Russell says.

Susan Seven hills of Rome, Sir [Miss]?

Bernadette The Russian ships have changed course. It said it on the news this morning.

Prentiss Seven hills of Rome, precisely. For, as we see, '*Hic magnae iam locus urbis erit.*'

Bernadette Glimmer of hope, that's what it said.

Prentiss Sandra? No? Jean-Ann?

Barbara I think there is no hope and there is no hope they won't report us.

Jean-Ann 'Here was the place of a great city' –

Prentiss '*Erit*', Jean-Ann, '*erit*'!

Barbara They're *teachers*.

Prentiss Future tense!

Bernadette I think we're safe.

Prentiss Future tense! 'Here *shall* be the site of a great city.' '*Roma, tuum nomen*' . . . 'Rome, your name' . . .

Bernadette Look at it this way, Barbara, what were they doing in the school together so late?

Prentiss '*Militat omnis amans et habet sua castra Cupido.*' 'Lovers are soldiers all, in Cupid's' – literally 'in Cupid's *camp*' . . . 'in Cupid's private army.'

Bernadette Imagine, Barbara, if the bomb fell and you'd still never even done it?

Prentiss 'Lovers are soldiers all in Cupid's private army.' Ovid.

A Girl enters and advances towards Prentiss's desk.

Ovid, the great Latin poet. Ah, a messenger approaches!

Messenger Girl Please, Mr Prentiss [Miss Prentiss], Mr Cairncross wants to see Bernadette Griggs and Barbara Proctor right away.

*Prentiss is jocular, not believing two model pupils can
be guilty of anything serious.*

Prentiss Right away! What have you two been up to, eh?
Barbara Proctor, Bernadette Griggs, to the headmaster's
office.

*They stand up and, clenching themselves, follow the
Messenger out of the room space as Prentiss continues.*

'. . . *ut eat sacer agnus ad aras.*' 'See the sacred lamb
advances to the shining altar.'

*Lights change, focus on B. and, as she speaks, the
classroom scene dissolves and the free-standing door, the
graffiti-ed door, is pushed on by two cleaners with mops
and pails. This time it is placed backstage and round the
other way so that downstage becomes inside Cairncross's
office. The cleaners open the door and get to work.*

B. Mr Shaw was inside with Cairncross. Behind closed
doors – well, they *would* have been closed, but two
cleaners were attacking our lovely graffiti with soap,
water and strippers, so they stood wide to the world.
And we could hear every word.

*Lights change. Barbara and Bernadette walk grimly
together towards the office door. Cairncross, in the
office with Shaw. Looks upstage and sees them. He
walks upstage and calls through the door to them.*

Mr Cairncross Sit down. You two sit down there until I
am ready to deal with you.

*The two chairs he indicates are side on, facing inwards,
in either near corner, just along the wall from the door
of what would be the outer hall of his office. Thus
Barbara and Bernadette are symmetrically placed facing
each other as they overhear Cairncross and Shaw.
Barbara looks at the floor. Bernadette often responds to*

what she hears by looking at the friend who won't meet her eye.

Mr Shaw Mr Cairncross, I really think this has been a case of one weak pupil being led astray by a stronger and far more wicked nature. Barbara Proctor is a very sensitive girl, a very gifted pupil. I don't think I've had a better in all the years I've been teaching.

Mr Cairncross The doctor's daughter? Jim Proctor's daughter? I know him well. Play golf with him. Her mother is a distinguished former pupil of this school, you know. Captain of the School, 1938-9. I know that because it was the year after I pipped Jim Proctor to the post for Dux of the Boys' Grammar [Boys' High]. Used to dance with her at the tennis club dances when I was home on leave during the war. Who's the other girl?

Mr Shaw Bernadette Griggs.

Mr Cairncross Griggs? I don't know any Griggses . . .

Miss Arthur approaches the girls and the headmaster's office.

B. Miss Arthur came along then. She went white when she saw us. She came and stood beside us. She took us each by the hand.

Miss Arthur takes Bernadette by the hand from her chair and leads her to the other side of the door and Barbara's place, where their threesome can clearly be seen. She takes Barbara's hand and she stands up too. Miss Arthur holds each girl by one hand, which she squeezes, steeling herself too.

Miss Arthur Courage . . .

Cairncross goes to the door.

Mr Cairncross Come in, you two. I told you to sit there! Miss Arthur! Don't you have a class . . .

*Miss Arthur still holds both girls by the hand. They
enter the study.*

Miss Arthur Not right now, Mr Cairncross. I've got a free
lesson.
Mr Cairncross Don't you have some marking . . .
Miss Arthur Don't punish these girls!
Mr Cairncross Miss Arthur!
Miss Arthur I warned you, Stewart, and I meant it. Here's
your ring.

*She takes it off and holds it out to him. He cringes,
mortified.*

Mr Shaw Joyce, for goodness' sake, this is neither the time
nor the place . . .
Miss Arthur Take it! Or I'll throw it on the floor. (*Pause.*)
Take it!

Mr Shaw takes the ring and pockets it.

Mr Cairncross Miss Arthur, leave us please. I have
something to discuss with you later. I have had
complaints, complaints from several parents about you
frightening the girls, frightening the girls and . . . and
. . . political indoctrination!
Miss Arthur I resign. Headmaster, I wish to give in my
notice.

*His jaw opens and shuts. He is amazed. Miss Arthur
walks out, head held high. Cairncross turns on the girls.
Their heads are down. They are quaking, silent.*

Mr Cairncross Now what do you two have to say for
yourselves?

Silence.

Nothing?

Silence.

Nothing! What is the meaning of this wanton
destructiveness?

*Bernadette's head goes up and she speaks out loud and
clear.*

Bernadette Cuba. Cuba Libre.
Mr Cairncross What is this nonsense?
Bernadette I wrote it on the wall. Kennedy is mad.
Kennedy is mad and Khrushchev is mad. I am a beldam,
I am a beldam sans merci. Cuba Libre!
Mr Cairncross Keep quiet! Barbara Proctor, what do you
have to say for yourself?

Silence.

I'm waiting.

Silence.

Come on!

Silence. It holds. Barbara stares at the floor.
*Bernadette looks at Barbara astonished, willing her to
speak. Gives up. Makes the decision to save Barbara's
skin if that's what she wants. Maybe there is scorn in
such a decision, maybe it is one last attempt to remind
her of her blood-sister promise, but anyway she speaks
out to save her friend.*

Bernadette It was my idea. Basically, it was my idea and
Barbara just went along with me.
Mr Cairncross Well? Well? What do *you* have to say?

*Barbara still stares at the floor. Silence. B. speaks out,
using loud and clear for the first time the word 'I' –
which she gives full emphasis and value to – owning up
to which role she played in this early personal drama,
revealing her identity.*

B. I said nothing. All I had to say was that it wasn't true.

Though it was, sort of . . . Indeed, it *was* Bernadette's idea to become CUBA, the two-girl gang, but I had been wild to be a part of it. I stole the red car paint, I made the first mark on Cairncross's door.

Lights slowly come up on the Mums ironing. The Dads in their chairs. The same domestic spaces as before.

And I was 'severely disciplined'. My parents were called in, I was stripped of my class vice-captain's badge, banned from any school outings, denied all privileges for the rest of the term.
While Bernadette was expelled.

Barbara and Bernadette, in a reprise of their first approach to their families, heads down in shame, go slowly to their Mums, who hold back for one beat, then embrace them. The girls weep silently in their mothers' arms.

Mrs Proctor Ssh, ssh, darling, it isn't the end of the world!

Dr Proctor puts his newspaper up in front of his face.

Mrs Griggs Never mind, darlin', it's not the end of the world.

Mr Griggs put his newspaper up in front of his face.
And both these symmetrical family tableaux, mothers with arms still round daughters, hold till the end of the play.

B. It wasn't. Cuba fizzled out. Touch and go, everybody said that. We'd been hours away from Armageddon. If Khrushchev hadn't withdrawn on Sunday . . . But they did, and the crisis was over, in exchange for a promise that America would never again invade Cuba and, unofficially, for some of those American bases in Turkey. The important thing was that nobody was to lose face. In America it was to be victory for Kennedy, and in

Russia victory for Khrushchev.

Bernadette and I were never friends again. When we were forced to pass each other in the street she would look through me and I would just look away. Usually she would be with some other friends of hers, from the rough school.

But, to this day, any time there is anything on TV about Kennedy . . . whether it is about him and Marilyn Monroe, or another theory about who it actually was that pulled the trigger that fired the fatal shot that killed the President on the motorcade in Dallas, every time, I think of Cuba.

And Bernadette. I think of her as 'La Belle Dame sans Merci' . . .

The Chorus as a photograph, as at the beginning of the play.

Chorus

I met a lady in the meads,
   Full beautiful – a faery's child,
Her hair was long, her foot was light,
   And her eyes were wild.

The Time When Next Week Might Be Cancelled

Liz Lochhead interviewed by Jim Mulligan

Liz Lochhead was educated in a school that was similar to the school in *Cuba* in that it was a senior secondary school with high academic standards – the equivalent of an English grammar school. But, like most Scottish schools in the public sector, it was for both girls and boys. She then went to art school to become a painter and came out a writer. In the twenty-five years since her first book of poems was published Liz Lochhead has written fifteen plays and her collected poems have been published.

> I wrote a version of *The Tempest* for the Unicorn Children's Theatre and a play about evacuees called *Shanghaied* to tour primary schools but I don't particularly write for children. I took the opportunity in *Cuba* to write a large-cast play that young people can perform but I wouldn't say it is a children's play. It's a play that young people will get a lot out of, I hope. Today's young people don't grow up thinking the world is going to end with an atomic explosion as my generation did. I wanted young people to be able to explore a time when people really did think that next week would be cancelled.

Liz Lochhead lived through the Cuban missile crisis in the sixties and recalls the sense of doom and outrage that was prevalent then. The philosopher Bertrand Russell did in fact send a telegram to President Kennedy that read 'Stop this madness'; politicians did indeed agonize over whether a naval blockade was different from a quarantine; and children brought the prejudices of their parents into classroom discussions. But, while she wanted to make young people aware of this historical event, Liz Lochhead also wanted to explore how this kind of tension could affect relationships and the decisions people make.

> External events make things happen in *Cuba*. If it wasn't for the Cuban missile crisis, the girls in the play wouldn't fall out, one of them wouldn't be expelled from school and Miss Arthur would not walk out of her engagement and her job. If you really believe the world could end next week stakes are very high and you are able to make that kind of decision.

The audience sees Bernadette and Barbara leading very similar lives. The ordinary and loving parents speak, dress and behave in a similar way. But, if they were asked, they would say they had nothing in common with each other. The headteacher recalls that the doctor's wife had been captain of the school and knows the doctor well but he does not know the other family. 'Griggs? I don't know any Griggses.'

> Mr Cairncross doesn't mean any harm when he says that, but the very fact that he says it without being aware of its implications says a lot about the subtle way class works in Scotland. The Scots are not as class-obsessed – or not in the same way – as the English. Because education is so prized, it is possible to become a teacher, for example, without leaving your working-class culture behind. In this play I'm interested in the minutiae of class differences, the way growing up in different families will determine the kind of life you will have.

In *Cuba* Liz Lochhead is exploring conformity, the effects of stepping out of line and what makes a rebel. Even in a school that places such store on academic success, the girls can cut loose in a lesson when a teacher lets her control slip a little but to defy authority in an overt way is unthinkable. The play, after all, is set in a time when young people accepted authority much more readily than they do now and ten years before Miss Arthur could have the support of the feminist movement.

Barbara stays on at school and loses her status but I don't think she suffers terribly. Bernadette gets betrayed and Miss Arthur makes her stand. The two of them have their moment of heroism. However, they don't beat the system, and remember Barbara, the one who keeps her head down, is the one who is telling her story and I think she partly regrets not being more heroic. She is remembering and telling herself the truth, perhaps for the first time, about that particular long-ago when a couple of people she admired made a stand. So the play has a poignant ending rather than a 'happy ending' or a 'heroic' one.

Liz Lochhead is adamant that she writes plays, not political tracts. Her plays do not have 'a message'.

Of course your own politics and the way you think go into what you write. You might write because you are convinced but you don't write to convince others. All you can hope is that for the duration of the play people will see the world as you see it and, by measuring it against their own experience, recognize what you have to say about the workings of the human heart as well as how the world works.

In her view, a successful play is one in which the forces that are pitted against each other are of equal weight.

All drama must have conflict. In *Cuba* the families and the headmaster are in a single state that remains unchanged throughout the play; the Narrator has an internal conflict and she is changed, albeit in a small way, by coming to terms with her long-ago act of betrayal; Mr Shaw and Miss Arthur are changed for ever by their conflict; and Barbara and Bernadette together are in conflict with the ways of the world until their own deepest natures force one to betray the other. You write a play to tell a particular story about real (though not necessarily realistic) characters and you hope people will recognize the forces that determine the choices people make.

Liz Lochhead's plays include *Quelques Fleurs, Blood and Ice, Dracula, The Big Picture, The Magic Island* (an adaptation of *The Tempest*, staged at the Unicorn Children's Theatre), *Shanghai'ed, Tartuffe* (a rhyming Scots translation of Molière's masterpiece), a translation/adaptation of the *York Mystery Plays* and the award-winning *Mary Queen of Scots Got Her Head Chopped Off*. She also writes for film, TV and radio. Her most recent poetry publication is in *Penguin Modern Poets Four*.

Production Notes

Cuba is set in 1962 in an all-girls grammar school at the height of the Cuban missile crisis. Cuba is the largest island in the West Indies and the first Communist state to be established in the western hemisphere. In October 1962 the USA accused the USSR of setting up missile bases in Cuba. There followed a tense confrontation between President John F. Kennedy and President Khrushchev resulting in the American blockade of Cuba. Finally, the USSR backed down and agreed to remove its missiles from the Caribbean island. The story is narrated by Barbara Proctor, now grown up, and recalls how she and her friend Bernadette Griggs felt they were living on the brink of a nuclear war and were moved to form their own protest. The incident ends badly and their loyalty is tested.

This is a play that will work extremely well on a conventional school stage which is often better suited for school assemblies and speeches. The chorus can remain throughout. Barbara's mum and dad and Bernadette's mum and dad form two almost identical tableaux in tight spotlights either side of the stage. Furniture should be minimal and needs to suggest the Proctors' and Griggs's rooms (ironing boards with different-coloured covers, and a chair for the father); a classroom and the headteacher's study (a free-standing door).

All the costumes, with the exception of that of the narrator's, are *circa* 1962. The school uniform should take into account that the hemline would be below the knee. The teachers would be conservatively dressed. The two mums are in contrasting party gowns protected by aprons at the start of the play.

CASTING

The total cast size is twenty or more, the majority of whom are fourteen-year-old schoolgirls. The two central characters are Barbara and Bernadette. Barbara comes from a more privileged background than her friend Bernadette. Both have a mum and dad. The chorus can be made up of as many girls as desired, but the minimum is nine, who are all named and have speaking parts. Two of the chorus also play cleaners. Prentiss, the Latin teacher, can be male or female and there are two more teachers, Miss Arthur and Mr Shaw, who are engaged to be married, and the headmaster, Mr Cairncross.

QUESTIONS

1 Why was Communism such a hot issue at this time? How do the two households' views differ on the subject?
2 In what ways have women's roles changed since 1962? What were Barbara and Bernadette's likely future prospects and how do they change?
3 What changes were happening in 1962? What were the major influences and when are they referred to in the play?

EXERCISES

1 Interview people who were at school at the time of the Cuban missile crisis, take a look at their school photographs.
2 Take several other verses of the hymn the chorus sing in assembly before the headteacher's address. Use it for

your company warm up and sing it with gusto, in canon, sweetly, and so on.

3 Experiment with changing the position of the chorus and see how this can help focus the action on stage.

4 As a group, discuss what you would do if you thought there was going to be no next week. Improvise the most outrageous idea.

5 In pairs, improvise the scene where Barbara and Bernadette plan their act of defiance. What other options do they consider? Who is the most enthusiastic about the plan? Decide how this will inform the way the actor playing Barbara will handle the scene in the headteacher's study.

6 In pairs improvise the scene (not seen) between Miss Arthur and Mr Shaw at the Royal Oak. What does it tell you about their relationship?

7 Place a chair in the middle of the rehearsal space and put Barbara on it. Have the rest of the class position themselves around her. Let distance and body language indicate the way the individuals feel about Barbara. Substitute Bernadette for Barbara, does the positioning of the other members of the class change?

Suzy Graham-Adriani
February 1997

DOG HOUSE

Gina Moxley

Characters

Ger, fourteen
Debs, fourteen, Ger's best friend
Mossie, sixteen, Ger's boyfriend
Jimmy, sixteen, a neighbour
Marian, fourteen, a neighbour
Connie, eighteen, father of Ger's sister Dee's baby
Barry, seventeen, a neighbour
Finn, twenty-two, Ger's brother
Aideen, twenty-one, Finn's wife
The Martin family a.k.a. **The Flying Saucers:**
Val, sixteen
Dessie, fifteen
Pats, fourteen
Bridget, twelve

The play is set in a cul-de-sac called Lime Lawn, the suburbs of Cork city.

SCENE ONE

Ger is standing at the gate to her house at the end of the cul-de-sac chatting to her best pal, Debs. Both are dressed in jeans and sloppy jumpers. Debs is sitting on her bike.

Debs Eight pounds twelve ounces. I don't believe you. Gawd, that's massive. It's gas, isn't it, so small going in and so big coming out.

Ger Don't let Connie hear you saying that.

Debs The idea of it.

Ger I know. You'd eat him without salt though, he's absolutely gorgeous.

Debs Yeah, but Ger, eight pound twelve ounces. That's not a baby at all, that's a teenager practically. She must be in flitters, is she?

Ger Shreds, girl. Something like sixteen stitches.

Debs Sixteen.

Ger And then they were worried that she might get toxaemia on top of everything else.

Debs What's that when it's out?

Ger Something to do with blood poisoning, or is it blood pressure? I'm not sure. They thought she might have to have a section, but in the end she was grand.

Debs That's good, no scar at least. She'll still be able to wear a bikini.

Ger Eventually, when she gets her figure back like. I'd say that's the least of her worries, Debs.

Debs Yeah. You'll have the barbed wire up for Mossie now. God, I wouldn't be able for it, would you?

They both shake their heads.

Ger (*laughing*) You'd want to have seen the state of
Connie, pacing up and down like a hen on stubble.
Then when the doctors came out and told him that he
was a father and it was a boy, he did a gawk in the
corridor. A big vom. I swear. All pints, of course.

Debs The place must've been reeking of stale stout. Poor
old Connie. I can just see him.

Ger The nuns weren't a bit happy with him being in there
in the first place like, but that really put the kibosh on it.
You know what they're like. The place is immaculate.

Debs Old wagons.

Ger Mercy is right. Whoever thought up that name for
them had some sense of humour, that's for sure.

Debs I know. Savages'd be nearer the mark. I'm sure he
didn't take a tack of notice. And were your ma and da
there?

Ger Sure, Da's up to his oxters with the engraving for
The City Sports. You can hardly see him in the shop
for cups, medals and plaques. He seems cool as a
breeze about it all though. The Ma was there all right.
Sort of.

Debs How so?

Ger She's on new tablets now, so she's a bit spacy. You'd
want to have heard her, 'My first was a surprise, the
second was an accident and the third was a mistake.
You're starting where I finished.' Just as well Dee was
half comatose, she'd have hit her otherwise. It was
awful really. She didn't say a word to Connie the whole
time. Like it's all his fault.

Debs It takes two to tango, sure. She'll get over it, Ger.

Ger I wouldn't mind like, but the child is the head cut off
him.

Debs Ah God, I'm dying to see him. He sounds divine.
Have they any names picked out yet?

Marian flounces up to them. She's around the same age

and is wearing a pastel-coloured dress. She's in a complete dither.

How's it going?

Ger Hiya, Mars. Great news.

Marian Did ye see Barry at all? Did ye notice him going by? I'm hanging round ages but I must've missed him.

Ger As I was saying, great news.

Debs Dee had her baby at last.

Marian is hardly listening, looking up and down for any sign of her crush, Barry. Ger and Debs realize this but keep talking anyway.

Ger A boy. Eight pounds twelve ounces. She was in absolute agony for eleven hours and got sixteen stitches.

Debs And he's the dead spit of Connie.

Marian Still no sign of a ring I suppose. It's your poor mother's the one I feel sorry for.

Debs Don't be such a bloody crab-jaw, Marian. (*to Ger*) Listen to her.

Ger Congratulations must be gone out of style, is it?

Marian turns around quickly and tries to make herself as inconspicuous as possible, pulling her hair around her face and looking at the ground.

Marian Talk to me talk to me talk to me.

Debs What? What's wrong with you? Oh.

Debs wolf-whistles as Barry jogs on. He's seventeen, athletic-looking and dressed in running shorts and vest.

Ger Hey Bar, Barry, come here.

Marian Ger, stop, will you, you dirty louser. I'm going to wet myself if he comes over.

Barry trots over to them.

Hi, Barry.

Debs Give her a goozer. Go on. A big smackeroo.

Marian looks at her in shock.

Barry Huh?
Debs Ger. She's an auntie.
Ger Dee had a little boy.
Debs Nothing little about him, he's a big bruiser.
Barry Fantastic. A boy. That's fantastic.

He lifts Ger and twirls her around, kisses her on the cheek and sets her back down. Marian glares at Ger.

Is he like me? Ha ha. Only razzing, only razzing.
Debs You missed your chance there, Barry boy.
Barry Sure, what could I do when Connie was in like Flynn? I couldn't wipe his eye on him.
Ger Wouldn't Debs here do you grand, for the time being? We'd hate to see you stuck.
Debs As my mother says, never go out with someone better-looking than yourself. Give me a small and wiry fella any day.
Marian Every day'd be more like it.
Barry Ye're gas, girls. Listen, I better make tracks, gang. I'm on in the bar at six. The place is jointed below. I keep telling them you don't need drink to enjoy yourself but sure, what can you do?
Debs Ah, don't go, Bar, you're great fun.
Barry Give Dee my best, Ger. Tell her I'll try and get in during the week.

He trots off. Marian is practically swooning.

Ger He's an old dote, isn't he?
Debs A dote. And not a bit affected.
Marian Where's he working?
Debs Starrie's, part-time.
Marian Really? He's a hunk, his hair even. Oh, God, I'm

getting palpitations, I'm sure. Am I red?

Debs Pucey magenta.

Ger You're like a beacon. They should give you a job at Roches Point.

Debs Attention all shipping.

Marian That green powder's supposed to cover it. I'm going getting my money back.

Ger You're not puce at all, you're grand.

Marian What did his lips feel like, Ger?

Ger Would you stop. I wasn't taking pleasure in it. Sure, I'm spoken for.

Marian Did you see the legs on him?

Debs Wasted on a fella if you ask me.

Marian I hope he didn't see me blushing. Was he looking, do you think? Oh, God. I have a spot on my chin as well.

Debs and Ger make eyes at each other.

Debs Right so, I'm gone. I'll give you a ring or you ring me.

Ger See you later anyway. Number thirteen is sold, by the way.

Debs So I hear.

Marian About time. The place'd give you the creeps empty.

Ger goes into her house and Debs pushes off on the bike.

Debs Hop on and I'll give you a backer.

Marian Ah, not in a dress.

Debs Sure, who'll be looking at you? Get on.

Marian reluctantly gets on the back of the bike, tucking her dress under her.

Marian Drop me at the end of Lime Lawn. I'll walk from there.

Debs From there to where? You're not going to follow him down to Starrie's, are you.

Marian No. I'm just going to the shop.

Debs doesn't believe her and pulls at her eye. Marian shrugs.

Debs Good. I'd hate to see you making a show of yourself.

They cycle off.

SCENE TWO

The Martins' kitchen is sparsely decorated. What furniture there is is old and rickety. The only light is whatever natural light comes through the window. Dessie and Bridget are unpacking boxes and putting stuff away. Val is sweeping the floor and Pats is sitting apart.

Val (*to Pats*) What's wrong with you? What have you a face like a boiled shite on you for?

Pats shrugs and smirks.

Dessie Shut up, you, will you? Don't mind her, Pats.

Pats Sweep around me.

Val sweeps viciously, hitting the brush against Pats's legs. Pats doesn't budge.

Bridget Is he going getting the lights turned on in this house at all, I wonder? Can't hardly see your fist in front of you.

Dessie 'When there's a sun in the sky what kind of a fuckin' eejit'd be paying for electricity? D'ya think I'm made of money.'

Bridget and Pats smile nervously at his imitation of their father. Val goes for him with the brush, just stopping short of hitting him.

Val Listen to him, Dessie the big man. Don't start shaping you, I'm warning you, 'cause if he hears you he'll break your face for you. Don't come crying to me. Place is bad enough with her causing ructions the whole time. Look at her, the puss on her.

Pats I can't even remember what I'm supposed to have done this time, what big mortaler I'm supposed to have committed.

Bridget He's gone out shooting. I saw him taking the gun with him.

Dessie That's all he's interested in since Mam died. Blasting birds out of the sky.

Bridget That and that dog.

Bridget nods. Pats stands directly in front of Val.

Pats (*shouting*) What did I do? Tell me. Blink, is it? Is that it? No, no, maybe I looked crooked at something. Did I? Or did I walk or talk or breathe at the wrong time? Whatever it was, you probably told on me anyway, you apple shiner, you. Well, I'm sorry, all right, sorry for having been born. OK? Are you happy now? Are you? Yeah?

Val sneers at her, calmly puts the brush away and throws a sleeping bag at her.

Val There you are, make yourself at home, number three.

Bridget Ah, Val.

Val Ah, Val what? When she starts acting like a human being, she'll deserve to be treated like one.

Pats He has more mass on that dog than he has on me.

Dessie Than he has on all of us.

Val Maybe that's because the dog has more manners. Rough, isn't it? Ruff, ruff, ruff.

Bridget Dogs don't have manners, do they?

The sound of a banjaxed car pulling up interrupts them.

171

Dessie That's him.
Val Move. Quick. Watch yourself, number three, or you'll be the one out in the shed next not Bran.

Bridget, Dessie and Val leave the room. Pats throws the sleeping bag on the floor.

SCENE THREE

Debs is sitting on the wall of the Martins' garden. Jimmy is loitering awkwardly and Marian is peering in at the house. Unseen by them, they are being watched by Val, Dessie, Pats and Bridget.

Marian Hey, look. The bathroom window is open.
Debs Mmm. Ger said she saw people going in and out all right.
Marian What are they like?

Debs shrugs. Jimmy looks in idly.

Judging by the state of the place they couldn't have moved in properly yet. No aerial up. Unless they don't have a telly. I mean the garden even, it's still covered in nettles and docks. No, they must've been just dropping off some of their stuff. It's an awful eyesore, dragging down the tone of the whole place.
Debs You'll have to go home when you want to go to the jacks in future so, Jimmy.
Jimmy Wha?
Debs Wha?
Marian Don't tell me he went to the lav in the garden, did he? That's disgusting, Jimmy.
Debs What are you talking about? We all did at some stage. Oh, sorry, I forgot, you don't go to the toilet.
Marian You think you're smart, don't you?

Ger and her boyfriend, Mossie, rush out of her house.

Ger God almighty, I don't know which of them is worse, Ma or Aideen.

Mossie They're like balubas inside there. (*He takes out a single cigarette and lights it.*)

Jimmy Sneaky flash, Mossie.

Mossie Can't help it, boy. They come out of my pocket lighting and all.

Jimmy Oh, congrats are in order, Ger, I hear you're an auntie.

Ger Thank you, you're a gentleman, Jimmy. It's more than some people would say anyway.

Marian gives her a filthy look. Ger smiles back at her.

Jimmy If she's an auntie, what does that make you, Mossie?

Mossie Careful, Jimmy boy. Very careful.

Marian rolls her eyes. The others laugh. Ger playfully hits him.

Ger Chance would be a fine thing, wouldn't it, Mossie?

Mossie jumps up and grabs her and pretends to maul her.

Debs Look at him dropping the hand like that. Watch it, Ger, or you'll get the quick baby off of him.

Marian There's a lot of it about.

Ger Ah now, Mossie, don't be giving Jimmy an education he wouldn't know what to do with.

Jimmy Wha? Go away out of that, girl.

Marian They think they're hysterical.

Ger and Mossie are still messing when Aideen and Finn come out of the house arguing. Aideen has a big teddy under her arm.

Ger That was fast.

Aideen If she asks me have I news one more time, I'm telling you I'll never darken that door again. I'm serious, Finn.

Finn Ah, she didn't mean have you any news, just . . .

Aideen Well, what did she mean so?

Finn Like any news . . . any ska.

Aideen Same thing.

Finn Ah, Aideen love, you're getting hyper.

Aideen She's sick. The woman is sick, Finn. She has babies on the brain.

Finn Ah now. She's just . . .

Aideen What does 'Any bun in the oven?' mean so? That she's hungry?

Ger bursts out laughing. A dog starts to bark next door. Marian is the only one who notices, but Aideen remains the focus of her attention.

Marian Ahh, they have a dog.

Ger She didn't say that, did she? Jesus. It's the new tablets she's on, I'm sure.

Aideen I'll be on them myself next.

Finn Come on if you're coming.

Aideen We won't be staying long. We're going out for a meal tonight and the table is booked for . . .

Finn . . . half seven.

Aideen Half seven.

They walk off. Mossie makes a face after them. Ger rolls her eyes.

Mossie Though there's dough there, there's love there too though.

Ger Come on, you.

Mossie gets up reluctantly. Ger grabs him by the hand.

Come on with us, Debs. There's room isn't there, Finn? Wait till you see the baby. Just wait till you see him.

Debs Call in and tell my old lady I'm gone down to the hospital, would you, Mars?

Marian nods reluctantly.

Ta. You're a dote.

They troop off to Finn's car, leaving Marian and Jimmy.

Marian You don't fancy a walk down as far as Starrie's, do you?
Jimmy Wha? The pub? Sure I don't drink.
Marian That's not what I asked you.
Jimmy Oh. Oh, OK so.

Marian, worried that Jimmy thinks she fancies him, goes off in a huff.

Marian Forget it. It doesn't matter.

Jimmy shrugs and as he ambles off Pats comes out into the yard. She's as surprised to see Jimmy as he is to see her. Their eyes meet.

Jimmy Eh . . . hiya. How's it going?

Pats half smiles at him and looks away. She goes back indoors. He walks on.

SCENE FOUR

Connie, Mossie, Debs and Jimmy are playing football. Jimmy is useless. Jumpers and jackets are used as goal posts. Marian is sitting on the wall watching out for Barry. Ger knocks on the Martins' door. There's no answer. She comes out shaking her head and joins the others in the game.

Ger They must all be gone out.

Marian I told you I saw the car going off. Car, if that's the right word for it. Crock is more like it. I wouldn't be seen dead in it. The noise of it alone would make you die of mortification.

Debs God love you.

The play is fast, with lots of pushing and shoving. Whatever scores there are are accommodated within the dialogue.

Marian What do you want calling them out for anyway?

Ger Just to be friendly, Mars. Maybe they wouldn't be too uppity to play a game of ball either. You know, neighbourly. To say welcome to Lime Lawn and that.

Marian Well, they won't be unless they tidy up the place. It's in a chronic state.

Mossie Do y'hear her, the residents committee on legs.

Marian What would you know about it? You're not even from this park.

Connie Woo hoo, stand back, there's fighting talk.

Marian Well, as for you, we all know what you're like.

Debs Heavy sausage! I don't think we approve of Connie being a daddy, would I be right?

Marian I never said anything about that.

Ger Exactly.

Barry walks on and the ball is kicked to him. They all salute him.

Barry How are ye, gang?

Jimmy Just what we need. Fall in with us, Barry.

Barry Hey, congratulations, Connie boy. I wouldn't doubt you.

Connie You know yourself, Barry, beginner's luck.

He's a good player and the game takes on a new seriousness. Marian doesn't take her eyes off him. She's on the verge of joining in when Barry kicks the ball to

Jimmy, who kicks it miles wide and over the wall into the Martins' garden. His team groan and the others cheer. A dog starts barking. Connie picks up a jumper from the goal.

What's that, Jimmy?

Jimmy My jumper. Why?

Connie Duh. It's not your jumper, it's the goal. You gom.

Mossie Good man, Jimmy, as smart with your foot as you are with your mouth.

Connie Like his old man. You'll have no bother getting into the cops, Jimmy boy.

Jimmy Wha?

Ger Ah, leave him alone.

They start chanting:

All
Queenie, queenie, who has the ball,
Is he big or is he small,
Is he fat or is he thin,
Or is he like a safety pin?

Jimmy goes into the garden to retrieve the ball. As he does so Pats comes out and picks it up. She and Jimmy nod at each other.

Jimmy Oh . . . eh, hiya.

Debs How come they know each other?

Mossie I knew it all along, Jimmy Wha?, the dark horse.

They all move towards the garden.

Ger Hiya. I'm Ger from number twelve, next door there. I called in earlier to say hello and see if any of ye wanted to come out for a game. There was no answer. We thought ye must be out.

Pats is very conscious of everyone looking at her and doesn't say anything.

Debs I'll do the honours so. I'm Debs, from number four, and that's Connie, he's Mossie, that's Barry from number nine and Marian from number one, and you seem to know Jimmy already.

They all say hello and still Pats stands there. The dog continues to bark.

Ger And what's your name?
Pats (*whispers*) Pats.
Debs Huh? Sorry?
Jimmy Pats.
Ger Pats what?
Pats Martin.
Jimmy Martin.
Mossie You're on the ball there, Jimmy.
Connie For a change.
Ger So, do you want a game?
Pats Eh . . . no. I was only going out checking on the dog.

She's just passing the ball to Jimmy when Val comes out into the yard and snatches the ball. Dessie and Bridget appear behind her.

Val That's it. Game over, ball burst. Get inside, you.

Pats walks away. Dessie and Bridget disappear with her. Everybody stares at Val. She smirks at them and is about to go, taking the ball with her. Jimmy edges his way back towards the others.

Connie Ah go on, don't be lousy, give us out the ball.
Val That's the thing about balls, if you want them you should hang on to them.
Mossie What did I tell you, Con?

They start sniggering. Val glares at them.

Barry Sorry about that. Could we have our ball back please?

Val continues to glare at them. They stare back.

Val See enough? Do you? Well, you'll know me the next time you see me.

Debs Never a truer word was spoken.

Val I'd advise ye to scatter off from here and ye're not to be sitting on our wall either.

She walks off with the ball under her arm. The gang huddle together.

Mossie Mother of Jesus!

Connie What a wagon.

Ger That softened your cough for you now.

Marian What did your other one say their name is?

Jimmy Martin. Pats Martin.

Mossie Martian'd be more like it.

Connie Now you're sucking diesel.

Mossie starts to whistle and hum at the same time, making a sound like a spaceship.

Marian Where are they from, I wonder?

Mossie Mars! I hate to break it to you, but that's where Martians come from, Marian.

Connie The Flying Saucers gang, what do you think?

They laugh, except for Jimmy.

Mossie Brilliant, boy. The Flying Saucers.

Connie And she's the mother ship.

He makes the spaceship sound and the others join in.

Barry Quite a nice-looking girl if she did something with herself.

Marian puts a brave face on it.

Debs I'd say she's up all night all right, wondering what you think of her, Barry.

Ger Well said, Debs.

Mossie Well, that's the game shanghaied anyway. The go of Barry though, lads, 'Can we have our ball back please?'

Connie What a laugh. You sounded like you were eleven, boy.

Barry It was worth a try anyway. I'd love to stay now for ye to be slagging me, but some of us have to make a living.

Marian is up like a bullet after him.

Marian I'll walk down a bit of the ways.

Connie Me too. Your ma's not below in the hospital now, is she, Ger?

Ger You're dead safe, she's having a bit of a lie-down. Depression is exhausting apparently! I think I'll get it myself sometime.

The noise of Pats's father's car can be heard approaching and it shudders to a stop. Barry, Connie and Marian go off. Jimmy follows a little behind. Connie makes the spaceship noise and walks robotically as he passes the Martins' house. They all laugh.

Mossie Gas man, Connie.

Ger Mmm. No wonder the Ma is up to ninety though. He's no more than a kid himself sometimes.

Debs Sure Dee's a rock of sense, they'll be grand. Oh look, look. There's the father going in.

Ger The face on him. God almighty. He's like a mastiff.

Mossie Your one, the mother ship, didn't lick it up off the ground obviously.

Debs The younger one is like a mouse though.

Mossie There'll be some crack around here yet.

Ger Come on in for a coffee if ye want to. I'm on dinner duty again for a change. Waste of time like, no one eats it.

The three of them go into her house.

*In the Martins' kitchen Val, Dessie and Bridget are sitting
at the table finishing their tea. Pats is also at the table but
it's obvious that she hasn't eaten. They all seem very tense
and are careful not to speak too loudly in case they're
overheard. Val waves her hand in front of Pats's face and
rubs her middle finger and thumb together.*

Val Know what that is?

Pats just stares at her.

The smallest violin in the world.
Dessie This is demented. He should be had up.
Val She has no one to blame, only herself, drawing a gang
of gurriers to the place.
Bridget They kicked the ball in. Sure, what did Pats do?
Dessie She was only checking on the dog, seeing what he
was barking about, did you tell him that?
Pats Feed the dog. Exercise the dog. Watch the dog. The
dog the dog the dog. Now I'm supposed to know what
the dog is thinking even.
Val Ruff, ruff, ruff. All I know is Daddy heard them
taking the piss out of him, whistling and laughing, when
he was coming in. He asked me who they were and were
we talking to them and I told him what happened. Full
stop.

*Bridget surreptitiously tries to pass Pats some food. Val
sees her and grabs it back. Val's usual tight grip on the
situation is beginning to crumble.*

Fuck it anyway. I thought things'd be different in a new
place.
Pats He couldn't stand the sight of me there, so why
should he be able to stand me now?

Dessie He used to eat with us then at least.

Bridget She's ravenous, Val. What he won't know won't bother him.

Val And then I'll get it. He said she's not eating till she cops herself on and stops causing trouble and that's that.

Pats It's all right, Bridget, I'm watching my figure.

Dessie How would he find out if you weren't such an arse-licker?

Val If you want to get thumped, Dessie, that's your own business, just leave me out of it.

A loud bang comes from the floor above. Everybody sits stock still, staring at the table. The noise stops after four thuds.

Bridget (*whispers*) How many was it?

Dessie holds up four fingers. Bridget points to herself and the others nod. She looks terrified.

(*loudly*) Coming, Daddy.

She shoots out of her chair. Val puts her head in her hands. Dessie looks furious. Pats remains relatively detached. They listen to Bridget run upstairs and almost immediately back down. She makes a face in an attempt to indicate the level of the father's anger.

Daddy says you're to go up to him now.

Pats gets up slowly, takes a deep breath and gives a brave smile. Bridget takes a leather strap from a drawer or the back of the door and hands it to Pats.

(*mouthing*) Sorry, Pats.

Dessie (*whispers*) Oh, Jesus Christ, we're off.

Pats shrugs and starts laughing.

Pats Here we go loopy loo. (*She leaves, taking the leather strap with her.*)

Val Loopy loo is right.

*In silence and with military efficiency they clear the
table. The routine should seem well established, each
one having their own job. The slap of the leather strap
can be heard from upstairs. Pats cries out once. Dessie
kicks at the ground, otherwise nobody reacts or looks at
one another. Val puts a bowl of sugar, an open jar of
honey and an open pot of jam on the table. She marks
the level of their contents with a piece of Elastoplast
which Bridget cuts from a strip. Dessie fills a glass of
water and places it, unmarked, between the jam and the
honey. Bridget places the sleeping bag on the floor.
They go out in order of age, leaving the kitchen in
moonlight.*

SCENE SIX

*Pats is standing in the kitchen, whimpering like a pup. She
holds her dress away from the backs of her thighs, which
are criss-crossed with red stripes. She searches for a cool
surface to relieve her stinging legs. She takes the glass of
water and holds it to her thighs. Standing over the jam and
honey, she holds her hair out of the way and inhales the
smells, careful not to let her nose touch the contents. She
takes a tiny sip of water, savouring it and making it last as
long as possible, and takes another sniff of the jars which
seem to intoxicate her. Bringing the glass with her she
unzips the sleeping bag and lies down on it. Her legs chafe
against the surface. She silently yelps. She finishes the
water in one go, covers herself carefully and lies down to
sleep.*

Ger, Debs, Jimmy and Marian are standing by the wall of the hall at a disco. The lights are flashing and the music's thumping but nobody is dancing yet.

Debs Don't know what we keep coming to this for, there's never any talent here.

Ger There is some here, OK, it's just that you've shifted all of them.

Barry comes in and Marian becomes very interested in the floor.

Barry How's the gang?

They all salute him, glad to be associated with an older, cooler person.

No sign of Mossie, no? It's not all off, I hope. Only slagging, Ger, only slagging.

Ger Naw, he's off with Connie somewhere. They're like two parrots on a perch since the baby was born. They'll get a right gonk when Dee comes home.

Jimmy Isn't he coming tonight?

Ger He said he'd see me inside.

Debs What's the point in jagging someone if they don't pay in for you? That's what I think, anyway.

Barry isn't really interested. He's scanning the room.

Marian Were you working earlier?

Barry doesn't hear.

Barry Very few here. A lot must be away on hols, I suppose. Well for some.

Jimmy Ah, it's early yet.

Barry Fair do's, Jimmy, ever hopeful. Might as well have a

look at the menu anyway. There's a few Spanish or is it
French students over there?

Debs Jimmy's holding out for one of the Flying Saucers,
aren't you, Jim?

Jimmy Wha?

Debs Wha? I saw you.

Barry They're only razzing you, boy. Catch you later,
gang. (*He moves off.*)

Marian Did you see the hairs on his chest, poking out of
his shirt?

Debs No chiffon scarf test for Barry, that's for sure.

Ger No test of any kind for Barry, I'm afraid.

Marian Oh, you're very pass-remarkable, aren't you?

Black-out.

    *Lights up and Ger, Debs, Barry, Marian and Jimmy are
dancing. Marian tries to edge closer to Barry, who dances
away every time. Jimmy is as good at dancing as he is at
football. Connie staggers in, followed by Mossie, who's
drunk as well, but not as bad. They're both holding
sparklers aloft. They dance over to the others, Connie
gives a sparkler to Jimmy. He obviously feels foolish with
it. Everybody shouts to be heard over the music.*

Ger Oh, Jesus. Cop on, will ye? If your man on the door
sees ye we'll all be out on our ear.

*Connie and Mossie are beyond caring and continue
dancing around the floor. Jimmy drops his sparkler and
leaves the dance floor.*

Barry The lads are in flying form, aren't they?

Debs So would you be if you had as much to drink as
they've had. Connie's palatic.

Ger So's Mossie. And he told me he had no money.
Bloody chancer.

Marian Who'd give him drink? He doesn't even look his
age, much less act it.

185

Ger Sure, they'd serve you in Flanagan's if you were
wearing a nappy.
Debs One more pint and he'll need one.

Black-out.
*Lights up and Jimmy and Marian are standing by the
wall. She's forlorn-looking. Connie is asleep on the
ground. Ger and Mossie are dancing slowly. He's
hanging out of her, running his hands up and down her
back under her top, her head is turned away to stop him
kissing her.*

Mossie What's wrong with you? You're not getting
cranky now, are you?
Ger The smell of booze off you would knock a horse.

*Marian catches Jimmy looking at her and pointedly
looks away in case he was thinking of asking her to
dance.*

Mossie They've decided to call the baby Rory.
Ger I know. Dee told me earlier. I'm her sister, remember?

*They continue to dance, Ger battling to stop him
mauling her. She rolls her eyes at Marian.*

Mossie What's up with you? Are you gone off me?

*Ger gives him a filthy look and looks away at Connie,
slumped on the ground.*

Mossie You're very quiet. What are you thinking?
Ger Nothing. Absolutely nothing, Mossie.

Jimmy goes over to Marian. She shakes her head.

Marian No thanks.
Jimmy Wha? I was only going to say I'm going to head
off.
Marian Why?
Jimmy The place is full of nothing, as usual.

Marian Right, see you so.

He leaves. She's very self-conscious, being left alone.

Mossie They're going to call the baby Rory.
Ger Go way. Really?

Black-out.
Ger is in the ladies' fixing her hair, etc., in the mirror, when Debs comes in. The music can be heard in the background. They talk to each other's reflections through the mirror.

Ger You're gone ages. Who were you dancing with?
Debs Dancing me eye. I was out the back having a tongue sandwich.
Ger Oh, God. I thought you said there was no talent here.
Debs Well, thought made a fool of me. He's a lasher, girl.
Ger Brilliant. Well, who is he? Where's he from? And do we know his father?
Debs Eh, I haven't a clue what his name is but he's from Bishopstown.
Ger It's worse you're getting.
Debs Ah no, give us a break. He told me all right, only I couldn't hear what he said and I didn't want to be doing a Jimmy on it, saying What? the whole time.
Ger How old about?
Debs He's wearing aftershave anyway, so I'd say about sixteen.
Ger Mmmm. Lovely. Unless it's just his old man's.
Debs Stop. I'm sure I have a beard rash. It'd be lovely to be going with someone before going back to school, for the winter like.
Ger Get off with him first anyway.
Debs Ah, he's walking me home and all. You'd never go out and find out his name, would you, Ger? He's standing over by Connie. Make something up. Tell him I'll be out in a minute or something.

Ger Well, what does he look like?

Debs He's a vision.

Ger Shouldn't be hard to find so. Over by Connie?

Debs nods, Ger goes to leave, looks out into the hall and comes back into the loo.

I don't believe it. Mossie's conked out on the floor next to Connie. I'll kill him. I can't stand him when he's like that.

Marian rushes in past her. She's in an awful state. She looks at herself in the mirror and bursts into tears. The girls put their arms around her shoulders.

What's up with you?

Debs What happened? Is it Barry? It is, isn't it?

She nods. One of them gives her a tissue.

Marian I asked him up for ladies' choice, it was a fast one, and he just said thanks at the end of it and went back dancing with the Spanish one. Now he's after getting off with her. I saw them going out, with his arm around her and kissing her hand.

Ger Her hand?

Marian He doesn't even do Spanish, what'll he be able to say to her?

Debs If he wanted a conversation he'd have stayed at home with his mammy.

Ger She'd talk for Ireland.

Marian What am I going to do? Who am I going to ask to my Debs now?

Ger How do you mean your Debs?

Debs That's not for another four years.

Marian I know but I . . . love him. I swear. I really do. I love him. What am I going to do?

Debs Don't mind him. Sure, she'll be gone back in a few weeks.

Ger Yeah, Mars. You're too good for him.
Marian I'm not. Oh, God, what am I going to do?
Ger Do you want to go home? Come on, I'll walk down
with you. You'll be OK, Mars. Really, you'll be grand.

She leads her out with her arm around her shoulder.

See you tomorrow, Debs, or give me a ring or I'll ring you.

Debs kisses her hand. She and Ger smirk at each other.

Good luck with yer man, what's-his-name.
Debs What about Mossie?
Ger What about him?

Black-out.

SCENE EIGHT

*It's dark and Ger is walking home from the dance alone.
She's a bit pissed off. As she nears her house she hears a
noise. She stops and looks around, thinking it might be
Mossie following her.*

Ger (*whispers*) Mossie?

*There's nobody there. She walks on. There's another
noise. She steps into the shadows. Pats comes out of
Ger's house with some food in her hands. She's stuffing
bread into her mouth. It takes Ger a couple of seconds
to figure out who it is.*

Pats.

Pats stands still like a rabbit caught in headlights.

Pats Sorry.

*She drops the food and disappears into her own house.
Ger looks back and forth from Pats's house to the food.*

Gingerly she makes her way across the Martins' garden and peers in the kitchen window. It's difficult for her to see in. She can barely make out Pats on the ground in the sleeping bag. On the table are the pots of jam and honey and the sugar bowl as before. She comes back out of the garden. It's as if she wouldn't have believed it had happened but for the food on the ground. She picks it up, places it in the Martins' garden, then goes into her own house.

SCENE NINE

The sound of the father's car can be heard taking off, backfiring as it goes. Pats comes into the garden. She's more relaxed than usual, though she looks thin and undernourished. She's in the same clothes as always. Ger is coming back from the shops with newspapers, fruit and milk. She spots Pats and stands aside and watches her. Pats checks to see whether the food she dropped the previous night is still there. She finds it where Ger has left it. She scoffs it.

Ger Hey, Pats, what's going on?

Pats looks up, startled, and is about to run away.

Hang on. Hang on. I'll only follow you in. I saw your crowd going off in the car. It's all right, I won't bite.

Pats Going off to see our cousins. There wasn't room for me.

Ger So?

Pats I have to stay to watch the dog.

Ger You know well what I mean.

Ger's caring tone has Pats on the verge of tears. She stares at the ground.

Pats Sorry. Don't say nothing, sure you won't. I'll pay ye
back.

Ger Look, it doesn't matter, it was only a bit of bread and
jam and some fruit. Just my mother isn't great at the
moment, it's . . . well it's her nerves, my sister had . . .
ah, anyway, you know what I mean, and she'd have a
hernia if she came down and found someone in the
kitchen.

Pats We just ran out of shopping and I woke up in the
night ravenous. I was half sleepwalking, I'm sure. Don't
ask me what made me go . . .

Ger I looked in the window and saw stuff on the table
though.

Pats Gooseberry.

Ger Gooseberry?

Pats Gooseberry jam. That's all we have and . . . I hate
that. I hate it. If there's anything I hate in the whole
world it's gooseberries.

*Pats is getting desperate. It's clear Ger doesn't believe a
word Pats is saying, so she tries a different tack.*

Ger So how are you getting used to Lime Lawn? Do you
like it?

Pats Lime Lawn? Ehm . . . grand, grand. Where we were
before was in the middle of nowhere. The country. I like
seeing people around. There's more noise. Cars and
noise. Yeah.

Ger And did you sleep on the floor in your last house as
well?

*Pats looks at her, shocked that she knows. Jimmy comes
along.*

Jimmy How's it going?

Ger Oh, hiya, Jimmy. Well, you didn't last long last
night. (*to Pats*) A gang of us were up at Highfield. It's a
dance.

Jimmy A bit boring. No point in staying holding up the
wall. None of the lads around, no?

Ger Probably down in the park airing their brains.

Jimmy I might take a wander down so, see what the crack
is like.

Ger Why don't you go with him, Pats, see some of the
local sights.

Pats and Jimmy What?

Ger Go on, why don't you?

Pats They don't . . . I've to be back before . . . I can't stay
out, like.

Ger It's only down the road. Jimmy's very responsible.
He'll make sure you're back on time. Won't you, Jim?

*She takes some bananas from a bag and hands them to
Pats.*

Here, look, why don't ye have a bit of a picnic while
you're at it? I'm all heart, aren't I?

*Ger goes off into her house. Pats and Jimmy smile at
each other and walk off in the other direction.*

SCENE TEN

*Pats and Jimmy are walking in the park. Initially he's very
awkward, not sure of what to be saying to her. Pats is
devouring the bananas. He watches her out of the corner
of his eye.*

Jimmy We used to have games of ball here before.

*She continues to eat and drops the skins whenever she
finishes one banana and starts another.*

We're not let any more though.

She looks at him quickly as if to ask 'Why?'

192

They're minding the grass.

They stop. Jimmy squats. Pats eats.

So. So . . . eh, this is the park.

Pats looks around as if noticing it for the first time. She starts smiling.

Wha?
Pats The trees here look so . . . on purpose. That's all.

She sits on the ground next to him. She's still eating but getting very drowsy. His shyness is steadily evaporating.

Jimmy The pond froze over one winter and my dad saved a fella who went through the ice on his bike.
Pats Why?
Jimmy Eh . . . 'cause he was drowning.
Pats Why did he have to save him though?
Jimmy Eh . . . 'cause that's the sort of thing cops are supposed to do, I suppose.

She turns to look at him sharply. There's an awkward couple of seconds' silence. She can hardly maintain focus; her eyes are beginning to close. As she lies back on the ground, she stuffs another piece of banana in her mouth.

You must like them, do you?
Pats Not really.

She falls asleep. Jimmy looks at her and leans closer as if he's about to kiss her. He stops short of it, gets up and picks up her discarded banana skins. He returns and stands over her for a moment before putting the skins in his pocket. As he bends to wake her, he notices the marks on the back of her legs. He taps her very gently on the arm. She sits up immediately.

Jimmy You said you couldn't be out long. You had to go home.

Pats It's only a house.

He offers his hand and helps her up.

Jimmy The things on your legs there, are you after hurting them?

She pulls down her dress, is about to answer, stops, looks him dead in the eye and considers her reply.

Pats No. I didn't hurt them. (*She walks off ahead of him.*)

SCENE ELEVEN

Debs cycles on with Mossie on the back of the bike. He's holding his head.

Mossie Take it handy, will you, girl? My head is opening.

Debs Sorry, Mossie, we hadn't time to carpet the road for you.

He hops off the bike. Debs gets off and gives Mossie the bike to hold.

I'll give her a shout. Pull yourself together a bit, will you?

Debs goes into Ger's. He leans the bike against the wall, sits down and shakily lights a cigarette. He takes one puff of the cigarette. He nearly gets sick and tops it, putting the butt in his pocket. He's in bits. Debs comes back.

She'll be out in a tick. God, you're green.

Mossie So she went home with Marian, is it?

Debs Yeah.

Mossie And I was out for the count?

Debs Yeah.

Mossie I know we had a good laugh but I can't remember a bit of it. Did I go home with Connie?

Debs Don't know.

Mossie Where were you?

Debs I left soon after Ger went.

Mossie With who?

Debs I don't know.

Mossie Some tulips, the whole lot of us.

Debs I just don't know his name, I remember everything.

Mossie Don't go on about it, OK? My head feels like it's full of sand, all moving around from side to side. Never again. Still, it's not every day Connie's a da.

Debs It is from now on.

Ger comes out of the house in bad form and sits with them. She's holding something in her hand. It is an egg.

Look what I found.

Ger What? The wreck of the *Hesperus*. Lucky you.

Mossie Sorry for last night, Ger. I was out of order. Totally, like. You got home all right, anyway.

Ger No thanks to you.

Mossie I'm in the dog house, am I?

Ger looks at him tiredly. Mossie takes the butt from his pocket and lights it.

Debs Well, I had a gala if you must know.

Ger Oh, yeah, sorry. Did you? That's brilliant.

Debs I'm seeing him again Tuesday. Still don't know his name, like.

Ger Good. I'm delighted for you.

They sit for a while, saying nothing. Ger rocks the egg in her hand.

Debs What have you an egg with you for, Ger?

Ger takes a piece of paper from her pocket and passes it to Debs. She matter of factly holds up the egg.

Ger This is the latest from my mother. It's a baby! Good,
huh?

Mossie What the . . . how do you mean, a baby?

Debs (*referring to the piece of paper*) This is like a
timetable or something. Two o'clock, feed and change.
Sleep for a while. Quarter past three, wakes crying.
Possibly teething . . . This is bananas.

She passes the paper to Mossie.

Ger She says she's determined to teach me the
responsibility involved in having a baby. She doesn't
want me to end up like Dee.

Mossie Ah, for God's sake, it's an egg. What's she on
about?

Ger She says she's not relying on the school any more to
tell us anything: Her claim is that they teach us Irish for
fourteen years and we come out not able to speak a word
of it, so what kind of balls – sorry, that's not the word she
used – hames are they going to make of sex education?

Debs I hate to admit it, but she does have a point there.

Mossie Yeah, but . . . that's bonkers, like. It's an egg.

Ger Not just any egg, Mossie, your egg.

She tries to give it to him.

Mossie Go away from me. Stop, will you?

Debs Ah, you should've had the old egg-cosy on, Mossie.
That's what happens. Even I know that much.

Mossie The woman is totally off her game. Quit messing,
Ger, take it away from me.

Ger Be careful, will you? It's the image of you and all.

Mossie This is giving me the creeps. Come on, you're
making it up.

Ger No, look. (*She shows him the piece of paper.*) Is that
my writing? Nope. It's my mother's. I'm not messing,
honestly, Moss. And I have news for you, you're looking
after it for the afternoon.

Mossie bursts out laughing. Ger pushes the egg at him and he pushes it away.

Laugh away, but I'm serious. Dee's coming home tomorrow and I have stuff to do.

Mossie Would you rev up, Ger. Come off it.

Ger That's the deal.

Debs According to this it . . . she, he, will be asleep for most of the afternoon, except for a bit of teething. Possibly.

Ger That's not that much responsibility now, is it? It's not like you'll be walking around with a pram.

Mossie But, Jesus Christ.

Debs Ah ah, not in front of the baby.

Mossie The Barrs are playing The Glen. I'm going to the game.

Ger So?

Mossie I am not going to the match with a fucking egg, do you hear me? Are you out of your mind?

Debs Tut tut, language, Mossie.

Ger Are you serious? You're not going to mind it?

Mossie Yes.

Ger Well, you better go so. Go off to your precious match.

Mossie Are you serious? You're not are you? You're only codding me. If it's over last night, I told you I was sorry.

Ger I'm serious, I said. Go on if you're going, otherwise give me a hand with this.

Mossie is backing away.

Mossie Fine, if you want to be like that about it.

Ger Yeah. Fine. See you. Good riddance to bad rubbish.

He goes off.

Debs Well, that shook him.

Ger Do him no harm to stew in his own juice for a bit.

Debs You were only messing, though? Testing him, like?

Ger Afraid not. You'd want to have heard the lecture I got. Dire, girl. There's nothing worse than your mother telling you about sex and things, sure there isn't.

Debs I know, it's chronic. If you pretend to be thick they tell you all sorts of gory mortifying stuff and if you act copped on then they think you're at it the whole time. (*She looks at the piece of paper.*) It's due for a feed and a change, Ger. Does she mean breast-feed?

Ger Are you out of your tree?

Debs What am I saying? It's an egg. God, I'm worse.

Ger Not that. But breast-feeding went out with the high bike.

Debs Oh . . . right. Well, I could baby-sit for you this afternoon if you like, I'm only washing my hair.

Ger Thanks anyway. I'll just put it in the fridge. It's only another one of the Ma's figaries, she'll forget about it.

Debs Here's Mars. I thought she'd still be mourning and weeping in the valley of tears.

Ger hides the egg and timetable.

Ger Say nothing to her about the other. I couldn't stomach her now.

Marian marches up to them, all business.

Marian I'm speechless. You won't believe what I'm just after seeing. Jimmy Wha? and your one from next door down in the park. Walking around, just the two of them, as if they were with each other, like. The cut of her. She looks like something dragged through a hedge backwards.

Ger Looks aren't everything, Mars, I thought you'd have figured that much out after last night.

Marian You mean Barry? Huh. I was telling my mother about it when I got in and she says he's heading the

same way as his father. I'm better off without him. Like
father like son, she said, a rag on every bush.

Debs Speak of the devil. Look at the walk of him. I ask
you.

Marian Jimmy had a lovely shirt on him actually. A kind
of a dark mauve. The colour really suits him.

*Barry comes on, delighted with himself. Marian isn't in
the least bit phased.*

Barry How are the girls?

Their greeting is subdued.

Fantastic night last night, girls, wasn't it? I'll tell you, I'm
knackered today, absolutely knackered.

Ger I better go in and give a hand. I'll see ye later on.

*Barry sits down next to Marian and Debs. Ger goes.
The sound of Pats's father's car arriving back. Debs
elbows Marian and they both get up.*

Debs We were just going ponemosing down the camino
actually, weren't we, Mars? See you around.

Barry Ponemos what? I'm not with you.

Debs Sorry, Barry, that's Spanish. I forgot you weren't
fluent.

Marian Adios, Barry. I'd get off that wall if I were you.
The Flying Saucers' da might get you.

Debs And mind the bushes.

Barry What are ye on about, girls? I can't keep up with
ye.

Marian We're only ragging you, Barry, only ragging.

They snigger and leave Barry looking a bit bewildered.

SCENE TWELVE

*Pats is standing in the middle of their garden in a state of
shock. Val, with her arms folded, is staring at her, fuming.
Dessie and Bridget are ranging around the perimeters
whistling and calling their dog, Bran. Their voices should
seem a bit tired and hopeless, as if they've been at it for
some time. All are worried-looking.*

Val I don't get it. You can't do anything right. There's no
hope for you, is there? And look at you, you don't give
a sugar, do you? I don't blame him getting annoyed with
you, you know that? I don't blame him.

Pats shrugs.

Did you check it? Did you check the shed door?
Pats It was closed last night, wasn't it? You'd swear I did
it on purpose.
Val I wouldn't put it past you.
Pats Yeah, of course, Val, I love getting a walloping. If he
wasn't hitting me, sure he'd take no notice of me at all.
Then I'd really get worried that he didn't like me or
something.
Val You're warped.
Pats He's the one who's warped. It's only a dog.
Dessie Leave her alone, Val, will you, for once. Pats, tell
him he just bolted when you opened the door and you
followed him down to the park but you couldn't catch
him.
Val Tell him what lies you like, but someone's going to get
a right kick up the arse over this and it's not going to be
me, I'll tell you that for nothing.
Dessie Tell us something we don't know.
Bridget What'll we do if he gets a belt of a car? He
hasn't a clue about traffic. I bet you he's in smush

200

somewhere. You'll be murdered.

Pats Stop. (*whistles*) Here, Bran. Here, Bran Bran Bran.

Her voice trails off hopelessly. There are four loud knocks on the window.

Val Bridget. Quick.

Bridget goes into the house. The others look at each other. Jimmy comes on, puffed.

Jimmy No sign, not a glimmer. Why don't I do out a poster thing and hammer them up around the place and up in the shops and that? Will I? I'm not bad at it, like.

Val We don't need no help from the likes of you. It's our daddy's dog is missing. Clear off, why don't you, and mind your own business? It's her own fault.

Pats It's OK, Jimmy.

Dessie Thanks anyway.

Jimmy begins to slope away reluctantly. Bridget comes back out.

Bridget Pats, he wants you to bring up his cigarettes to him.

Silence. Jimmy looks on, trying to figure out what's going on.

Dessie In the name of fuck, the man's an animal. I've had it.

Pats slowly walks towards the house. Dessie runs in ahead of her. Bridget stands by Val, who puts her arm on her shoulder.

SCENE THIRTEEN

There's a big fuss outside Ger's house. Dee has arrived home. Aideen and Finn carry bundles of presents from the

car into the house. Ger and Debs are admiring the baby in
Connie's arms. The dialogue is rapid fire and overlapping.

Debs Ah, God. He's gorgeous, isn't he?

Connie Of course he is. Isn't he the spit of me?

Ger It's his nose gets me. It's brilliant, isn't it?

Aideen Mind he doesn't get cold, Connie. Pull up that blanket around him.

Debs How's your ma? Is she still up to ninety over it?

Ger Herself and Dee are inside there laughing and crying and hugging every second minute, so I presume it's roses over the door again is it, Con?

Connie Ah, she's grand. She's calmed down again. I knew once he was home . . . And you'd want to see the cot his granddad made for him. Who's a lucky man?

Ger Yeah, imagine, that's what Dad was at the whole time. Pretending to us he was engraving. He's a big softie. Go on in and have a look at it.

Debs goes inside. Jimmy comes along, followed by
Marian.

Connie Well, what do ye think?

Marian Ah, look. Ah, look at him. Ah, God. The little nails on him. Perfect. Hello, baby. Hello, Rory.

Jimmy Eh . . . yeah. He's grand, isn't he?

Aideen Come on in, Connie. That child will get his death out there. He's used to the heat in the hospital.

Finn Do you hear the expert? You changed your tune fairly fast.

Aideen It'd be no harm for you to take a few lessons from Connie. You might need them someday.

Ger Come on in, let ye. There's lashings of sandwiches and everything. They'll be curling up if they're not eaten. Now, Mars, I should warn you, there's still no sign of a ring.

Marian Go away out of that, don't be stupid.

They go into the house. Jimmy hangs back.

Ger Jimmy?

Jimmy Eh . . . Mossie asked me to call up to see what the lie of the land was.

Ger Oh, did he now? And what are you going to tell him?

Jimmy You tell me.

Ger Tell him he should have the guts to do his own dirty work and not have you running his messages for him.

Jimmy I was out anyway, looking for the dog.

Ger Huh?

Jimmy Yeah, Bran Martin got out when myself and Pats went down to the park yesterday. Remember you said to her to go down with me? Now he's lost.

Ger Yeah and?

Jimmy Well, I think she got into fierce trouble over it because she was meant to be minding him. She seems to be picked on the whole time. I was out half the night looking for him. I'm not sure what's going on, like, but I'd say their da is ferocious if the sister is anything to go by.

Ger Did you call in?

Jimmy The sister told me to clear off and I don't want to make things any worse. They're all very cagey in front of her for some reason.

Ger Mmm. There's something fairly odd going on there all right. Did Pats say anything to you?

Jimmy She hardly opened her mouth. She just ate all the bananas you gave us.

Ger Like she was starving?

Jimmy I thought that was a joke, like. The picnic and that. Then she fell asleep sitting on the grass. Only for a few minutes. She seems real shy, very nice though.

Ger Oh, God, I don't know.

Jimmy The brother seems nice enough as well. I mean, I know it's their da's dog, but still.

Ger If you hang on a while I'll go in with you. I can't this minute 'cause of the baby and that. I don't want to be spoiling things. There's loads of grub inside.

Jimmy I should call over to Mossie, he'll be wondering.

Ger Sure, give him a buzz from my place.

Jimmy OK so. Your ma won't mind?

Ger Naw, she won't even notice.

They go inside.

SCENE FOURTEEN

Pats is sitting at the kitchen table. She's got three cigarette burns on her cheek. Dessie comes in. He has a black eye. They are both very jittery. A shotgun is leaning against the wall. He sits at the table and opens his hands. He's holding six shotgun cartridges. They both stare at them for a minute.

Pats But that's loads. Where did you get them?

Dessie I was putting them by . . . for a rainy day.

Pats Dessie, look, he said he was sorry . . . maybe he won't . . .

Dessie And you believe that bollox?

Pats I'm sorry you got it too, you shouldn't have stood up for me. I told you. What are we going to do if they have Bran with them when they come back?

Dessie Don't, Pats. Stop it. Don't back out on me now. You swore.

Pats He just lost his temper. I should've checked the shed. I know. I can't put a foot right. I can't help it. It's my own fault.

Dessie Stop it, Pats. He'll never burn you or me or anyone else again. Do you hear me? I want to see him die roaring.

Pats No. No, just only hurt him. Look that's what we said. Hurt him.

Dessie All right, all right. I know what we said.

Pats Maybe we should wait till he's better, till he's over his cold.

There's a knock on the window.

It's them. Jesus Christ, hide the bullets.

Dessie panics and fumbles, dropping the cartridges. They both scramble to pick them up, forgetting to hide the gun. Ger and Jimmy walk into the kitchen. Pats and Dessie pocket the cartridges.

Ger Hi. Sorry for barging in. We knocked. We heard voices so we knew someone was home.

She looks at Jimmy for help but he just nods. He's staring at Pats's face. She covers it with her hand.

Eh . . . anyway. We're, eh, having a bit of a do inside, my sister just had a baby, and, em, well, come in if ye'd like to. It's only the neighbours and ourselves, nothing grand. Ye're welcome.

There's an awkward silence.

Dessie Thanks. Thanks, OK.

Jimmy What happened to your face?

Pats Huh?

Jimmy Your face. What's that from?

Pats (*suddenly bright*) How do you mean? Oh, that. That's just . . . ah nothing. It's midge bites. Yeah.

Jimmy Midge bites?

Ger It doesn't look like it to me. It looks more like . . .

Pats There. On my face you mean? Oh, they're spots. I'm always at them, aren't I, Des? I know sure, I'm like a curranty scone, aren't I? I can't help it. I must be picking them in my sleep even.

Ger When you're asleep on the floor even?

Pats Go away. That was only once. For privacy.

Jimmy The same way that they're spots on the back of your legs, I suppose?

Pats What are you talking about? I said I didn't hurt them.

Jimmy Exactly. You didn't. But who did? I'm not that stupid.

Pats I don't know what you're saying. It's just from the chair or something.

Dessie Shut up, Pats, stop making excuses for him.

Jimmy We heard ye talking before we came in.

Ger Look, ye'll only get in worse trouble if ye start shooting people. We heard ye. It sounds mad even to be saying it. Shooting people, God. If your dad is . . .

Pats We were only messing, weren't we, Dessie? For God's sake.

Dessie takes the cartridges out of his pocket and puts them on the table. He holds out his hand and Pats puts her cartridges into it. He puts them on the table too.

Dessie We weren't. I wanted to blast that bastard sky high.

Pats We were only going to injure him a bit. Just a small bit. (*She starts to cry.*) More like a fright. It's my own fault 'cause I wouldn't cry.

Ger picks up the cartridges and gives them to Jimmy. Dessie puts his arms around Pats. They cling to each other, sobbing.

Ger Don't worry. It'll be all sorted out.

Dessie What's going to happen now? They're due back in a while.

Jimmy I'll give these to my dad and tell him the story.

Pats is half laughing, half crying.

Pats But I didn't go through the ice on a bike. Don't bring
the guards up. He'll kill me. Please, I beg of you. He
will, I swear.

Ger Listen, no one's going killing anyone.

Dessie They'll believe us, Pats. Sure, what would we be
making it up for. Look at the state of the two of us even.

Ger Did he do that to your eye too?

Dessie nods.

Pats Are you sure? Promise.

Jimmy Ah no. They'll believe you all right. My dad's
sound like that. Honestly.

Ger Do ye want to come into my place till . . . well, you
know?

Dessie We'll hang on here if that's all right.

Ger You're sure you've no more of those things for the gun?

Dessie shakes his head.

You better put it away anyway. In case he comes home
before . . .

Jimmy I'll go down and get my dad now, OK?

Ger Are you sure you don't want us to stay with ye?

Pats No. Thanks anyway. We'll be grand.

Dessie Yeah. We'll be grand.

Jimmy Yeah.

Ger and Jimmy leave.

SCENE FIFTEEN

Ger and Jimmy are standing on the road.

Ger God, it's unbelievable, isn't it? What's going on?
Imagine if they shot him. God almighty.

Jimmy I knew there was something weird going on but . . .

Ger I'll be inside if your da wants to talk or anything. Are we witnesses now? I hope we don't have to stand up in court or anything.

Jimmy I don't know, I doubt it. Just lucky we heard them in time, I suppose.

Ger Right. I'll go on in. I won't say anything – you know, with the party going on and all – but call in if you need me.

Jimmy I'll let you know what's happening. Thanks, Ger.

As he leaves, Mossie comes on, very sheepish-looking, with something behind his back.

Mossie Thanks for the phone call, Jimmy boy.

Jimmy Oh, yeah. You're welcome.

Ger Well, well, well. What a surprise.

Mossie Look, Ger. Sorry, all right? I know I was acting the gom. I should've copped that it was your ma's idea and . . . ah, I'm useless at saying stuff like this, but here, I bought you a present.

He takes the parcel from behind his back. It's roughly wrapped in plain paper.

Ger Look, Mossie, I'm not in the humour for you now. There's all sorts of shenanigans going on and I have enough on my plate.

He holds out the parcel. Ger takes it resignedly and shakes it.

What is it?

Mossie I wouldn't rattle it too hard. Open it, go on.

She tears off the paper. Inside is a half-dozen eggs. She bursts out laughing.

Ger Ah, Mossie. You eejit. I never knew you were such a romantic.

*She puts the eggs down and they kiss. While they're
kissing, Barry and Jimmy run on.*

Jimmy Quick, quickly ring an ambulance. There's been a
crash.
Ger Where?
Jimmy At the corner. Oh, God.
Barry It's The Flying Saucers' car.
Ger Jesus, Mary and Joseph, I don't believe you. Their
car. Crashed into what?
Barry It's wrapped around the telegraph pole below by
the traffic lights.
Jimmy Quick. Can I use your phone?
Ger Yeah, sure, come on.

They go into the house.

Barry The bloody madman. He swerved to avoid a dog
that ran out in front of him. Completely mad. He had
nowhere to go.
Mossie Is it bad?
Barry Oh, yeah. Serious, I'd say.

They follow into the house.

SCENE SIXTEEN

*In the Martins' kitchen Val, Dessie, Pats and Bridget are
sitting around the table eating. There is a new serenity
about them.*

Val Are you OK? Do you want more?
Pats I'm fine.
Dessie I will, if it's there.
Bridget Aren't you finishing that?
Pats No, have it.
Val Finish it.

Pats Really, I'm full.

There's a knock at the door. Bridget freezes as usual, then relaxes once she realizes it's the door.

That's probably Jimmy for me.
Bridget Where are you going?
Pats Just down as far as the park for some air.
Val Be back by half-five, will you? Auntie Kay is coming for us and we need to get cleaned up and that.
Pats I'll be back.

Black-out.

SCENE SEVENTEEN

A church bell rings. Lights up.
Graveyard. Dessie, Pats, Val and Bridget are standing around the grave. The rest of the cast are behind, mourners at The Flying Saucers' father's funeral. Everybody is solemn-looking, as if listening to a priest. Bridget steps forward and throws earth on the coffin. Val follows suit. Dessie steps forward and slowly lets the earth fall from his hand. Pats closes her eyes and steels herself to step forward. She does so and flings her handful of earth at the coffin. A dog barks in the distance. There is silence for a couple of seconds, then Pats starts to laugh, followed by Dessie and Bridget, then Val. Their laughter is infectious and is picked up by Ger and Jimmy and so on, until the entire congregation are hysterical.

Stomping the Bastard into the Ground

Gina Moxley interviewed by Jim Mulligan

Gina Moxley studied Fine Art, gave it up as soon as she qualified and began to act in the early 1980s. She wrote and performed comedy sketches for the street, stage, TV and radio. In 1992, as a result of a commission by Rough Magic Theatre Company, she wrote her first play, *Danti-Dan*. She finds acting and writing makes different demands – one is social and the other private and solitary – and she tends to alternate the two disciplines.

> I'm surprised at how much you instinctively know about writing drama once you've done a bit of acting. My writing is probably more character than plot driven as a result. Actors have all sorts of devices which help create a character so I have those systems in my head. I probably spend as much time walking around the room, building up the personalities as I do sitting down at the computer. I'm very conscious of being able to avoid the things I hate in the theatre like huge, elaborate set changes where these mysterious imps dressed in black come on and steal all the furniture. I also try to be democratic in terms of balancing the size of the parts. There's nothing as crap as being in a play with nothing to do.

Gina Moxley is aware of the strong tradition of memorable language, madness, savagery and, in particular, gallows humour in the Irish theatre. *Dog House* has all these elements. The play observes two families through the eyes of young people. The tensions of one family where the mother has taken to bed with her 'nerves' are counterbalanced by their seriously dysfunctional neighbours.

I was interested in writing something about parents not being the best people to be in charge of children and how kids cope. In the play Ger is quite open about the fact that her mother has temporarily excused herself from the world whereas the Martin family desperately try to cover up the terror of their situation. It's about the shifting parameters of normality too. I definitely didn't want to have adults seen; largely to avoid teenagers playing the parts with a head full of talcum powder but also because the character of the Martins' father in particular is more potent and threatening if absent. I trust the audience to join the dots themselves.

The young people on Lime Lawn are interested when the Martin family moves into an empty house. They observe that things are not quite right but they only gradually become aware of the real domestic horror that is taking place.

It is clear that, since his wife died, Mr Martin is obsessed with his dog and his gun and has ritualized his cruelty to his children. It is probably safe to assume that he has always subjected them to emotional abuse. For him the children no longer have names and his daughter Pats has become the immediate victim of his cruelty, but the others are made to participate. Val has become her father's henchwoman. She is the broker who negotiates and the conduit through which the cruelty is passed from the father to Pats.

Val is in a very peculiar position because she has been given the reins whether she wants them or not. She is aware that the choice of victim is totally arbitrary and that her father could turn on her at any time. She's watching her back by trying to maintain the status quo. Perpetrators of any kind of abuse seem to be very shrewd creatures, wizards at blurring moral boundaries and commanding allegiance. Here the father implicates

Bridget by making her the messenger. It's horrible but it sure as hell works.

While the young people on the street and in the dance hall are strutting, joking, getting drunk and forming liaisons, things in the Martin family are reaching crisis point. It is clear that someone in the family is going to die. Either the father will go too far or Dessie will snap and shoot his father. Just as the other young people become aware of what is happening and are starting to intervene by bringing in adult help, Mr Martin is killed swerving his car to avoid, he thinks, the dog he loves more than his children.

Something had to give. The father is hell-bent on his path. He is a furious force and Dessie is going to pulverize him in his sleep with a rock if things go much further. It's a kind of poetic justice when he's killed avoiding the dog that may not even be his own. After he's killed, the children have freedom for the first time. They are free to eat what they want and as much as they want. An aunt is coming and it's as if the sun has shone in that house for the first time. When there's a knock on the door it doesn't mean 'bring up the strap'.

The final scene has no dialogue. The stage directions describe a traditional funeral where the behaviour should be solemn. The audience must be expecting a decorous ending as Pats 'flings her handful of earth at the coffin'. 'Flinging at' might indicate an appropriate anger and then a dog barks. There is silence for a couple of seconds and then Pats starts to laugh and the laughter is picked up until the entire congregation is hysterical – a shocking end.

Not at all. There's no reason on this earth why these children should not be jubilant, stomping on the bastard, hammering him into the ground. Once Pats starts laughing it is an absolute relief. It's like the first time they've looked at each other, the first time they've laughed properly. Abuse and emotional neglect are pervasive and happen on a number of levels but *Dog House* is a play. It doesn't have any answers. I don't know if that's the responsibility of the theatre. If it's good drama then people are going to look at it and talk about it. That's as much as you can hope for. If it's bad it will just bore the arse off everybody.

Gina Moxley is both a writer and an actor. *Danti-Dan*, Gina's first play, was commissioned by Rough Magic and was produced in Dublin in 1995. Following a National tour it transferred to the Hampstead Theatre in London. In 1995 Gina received a literature bursary from the Irish Arts Council and was winner of the Stewart Parker Trust Award for New Writers in the Theatre in 1996. *Dog House* is Gina's second play.

Production Notes

STAGING AND SETTING

The play is set in a cul-de-sac of houses in the suburbs of
Cork City, Ireland. Companies can relocate to any
comparable place and adapt the language and idiom
accordingly. The settings include the cul-de-sac, the
Martins' kitchen, a makeshift football pitch, the disco, a
park and a graveyard. The set of the Martins' kitchen
requires a permanence and detail that is almost
naturalistic. We must have a sense of Mr Martin
occupying the room upstairs. All the other locations are
able to exist fluidly around the Martins' home. More
abstract props can be used to define the other scenes – a
row of front doors, the cul-de-sac, a mirror frame for the
ladies' toilet at the disco, and so on. At one point Debs
cycles on stage with Mossie on the back of her bike.

Sound effects include a dog barking, the various arrivals
and departures of the Martin family car which is prone to
backfire and the right level of sound required for a noisy
disco where the actors can still be audible. Lighting needs
to take into consideration indoor and outdoor locations,
the Martins' kitchen in moonlight, the time of day and the
disco. The costume is very straightforward and
contemporary but you might want to consider what effect
Mr Martin's neglect will have had on his children's
appearance. Pats wears the scars of her father's abuse and
appears with marks on the back of her legs and later
cigarette burns on her face, Dessie receives a black eye.

CASTING

There are thirteen speaking parts, six male and seven female. *Dog House* will suit a wide age range though most of the characters are aged fourteen and above.

QUESTIONS

1 Why is the play called *Dog House*?
2 Which of the characters are involved in a relationship and which of them would like to be but aren't?
3 What do you imagine the Martin household was like before the mother died; was it different?
4 Why do we never see Mr Martin?
5 Why is Pats picked on in particular?
6 Why does Val appear to support her father's tyranny?
7 What would Pats and Dessie have done if Ger and Jimmy hadn't intervened in Scene 15?

EXERCISES

1 In a circle and in character introduce the person to your right stating who they are and what their best features are.
2 Improvise a scene in the cul-de-sac before the Martin family arrives.
3 Have Ger, Debs, Mossie and the younger neighbours play a ball game using an imaginary ball. What does the game reveal about their characters and relationships; who is the most competitive, the most generous?
4 Contact a child helpline agency and find out how Mr Martin's abuse of his children could have affected them. In role as a group of experts, discuss the four Martin

children in turn. Decide how their experiences might have affected their behaviour and what help they are likely to need in the future.

5 Improvise a scene in the Martins' kitchen. What effects do Mr Martin's movements upstairs have on the four children. Find ways of making his unseen presence a real threat.

Suzy Graham-Adriani
February 1997

ECLIPSE

Simon Armitage

Characters

Six friends:
Klondike, the oldest
Tulip, a tomboy
Polly and **Jane,** twins
Midnight, male, blind
Glue Boy, a glue-sniffer

Lucy Lime, a stranger

SCENE ONE

A police waiting-room. Seven chairs in a row, Glue Boy, Polly and Jane, Midnight and Tulip sitting in five of them. Klondike enters the room and sits down on one of the empty chairs.

Klondike Tulip.

Tulip Klondike.

Klondike Midnight.

Midnight All right.

Klondike Missed the bus, then couldn't find it. Sorry I'm late.

Midnight Are we in trouble?

Klondike Anyone been in yet?

Tulip No, just told us to sit here and wait.

Klondike Oh, like that, is it? Glue Boy.

Glue Boy Klondike.

Klondike Extra Strong Mint?

Glue Boy Bad for your teeth.

Midnight Klondike, tell me the truth.

Klondike And how are the split peas?

Polly and Jane We're the bees' knees.

Polly Yourself?

Klondike Could be worse, could be better.

Midnight Klondike, we're in bother, aren't we?

Klondike Three times. Who am I? St Peter?

Off, a voice calls 'Martin Blackwood'.

Midnight Me first? I thought we'd have time to get it straight.

Polly Say as you speak . . .

Jane . . . speak as you find.

Klondike Say what you think, speak your mind. Clear?

Midnight Not sure.

Klondike Glue Boy, show him the door.

Tulip Klondike, why don't you tell him what's what? He's
pissing his pants.

Klondike
Let's all settle down. Midnight, stick to the facts.
The oldies were up on the flat with the van,
we were down in the crags.
They were waiting to gawp at the total eclipse of the sun,
we were kids, having fun.
It was August eleventh, nineteen ninety-nine,
they were pinning their hopes
on the path of the moon,
they were setting their scopes and their sights
on a point in the afternoon sky
where the sun put its monocle into its eye.
The first and last that we saw of her. Right?

Tulip Right.

Polly and Jane Amen.

Midnight Just tell me again.

Off, a voice calls 'Martin Blackwood'.

Tulip Stick to the facts. You were down on the sand . . .

Midnight
I was down on the sand.
The mothers and fathers were up on the land.
Was it dark?

Exit Midnight into interview room.

Tulip What a fart.

Klondike Oh, leave him. Blind as a bat. Sympathy vote.
He'll be all right. Anyway, who's said what? Tulip?

Tulip No fear, kept mum like those two did.

Klondike Polly, Jane?

Polly Thought we'd keep schtum till you came.

222

Klondike Good move.

Glue Boy What about you?

Klondike What about me? What about you?

Glue Boy No, nothing.

Klondike Well, that's all right then.

Jane What can you hear through the crack?

Polly He was egging himself, I know that.

Tulip Shh. No, not a word.

Klondike Can you see through the glass?

Tulip Give us a leg-up . . . No, it's frosted.

Polly Moon came up. Sun was behind.

Jane Nothing to say. Nothing to hide.

Klondike Correct. Let's all get a grip. No need for anyone
losing their head.

Tulip The copper who came to the house said we're in this
up to our necks . . .

Klondike
FOR CRYING OUT LOUD . . .
They were up on the tops,
we were down in the rocks.
Stick to the facts.
Pax?

Tulip Pax.

Polly and **Jane** Pax.

Glue Boy Pax.

Klondike Stick to what we know and we'll all be fine.
Now, a moment's silence for Lucy Lime.

All For Lucy Lime.

SCENE TWO

A police interview room.

Midnight
Martin Blackwood, they call me Midnight –
it's a sick joke but I don't mind. Coffee

please, two sugars, white – don't ask me
to say that I saw, I'm profoundly blind,
but I'll tell you as much as I can, all right?

Cornwall, August, as you know. There's a beach
down there, seaside and all that, cliffs with caves
at the back, but up on the hill there's a view
looking south, perfect for watching a total eclipse
of the sun. The mums and dads were up on the top,
we were down in the drop – we'd just gone along
for the trip, killing a few hours. You see
it's like watching birds or trains, but with planets
and stars, and about as much fun as cricket
in my condition, or 3D. There was Glue Boy,
Polly and Jane, Tulip and Klondike and me.
Thing is, we were messing around in the caverns
when Lucy appeared. Her mother and father
were up with the rest of the spotters; she wasn't
from round here. Thing is, I was different then,
did a lot of praying, wore a cross, went to church,
thought I was walking towards the light of the Lord –
when it's as dark as it is in here, you follow
any road with any torch. Lucy put me on the straight
and narrow. There's no such thing as the soul,
there's bone and there's marrow. It's just biology.
You make your own light, follow your own nose.
She came and she went. And that's as much as I know.

We were just coming up from one of the smuggler's
coves . . .

SCENE THREE

*A beach in Cornwall, 11 August. At the back of the beach,
a broken electric fence dangles down from the headland
above. There are cave entrances in the cliff face.*

Polly and Jane are sitting on a rock, combing each other's hair, etc. They are heavily made up and wearing a lot of jewellery.

Polly Your turn.

Jane OK. The three materials that make up Tutankhamun's mask.

Polly Easy. Solid gold, lapis lazuli and blue glass.

Jane Yes.

Polly Hairbrush. Thanks.

Jane Now you.

Polly Proof of man's existence at the time of extinct mammals.

Jane Er . . . artwork carved on the tusks of mammals.

Polly Correct.

Jane Nailfile. Thanks.

Polly These are a doddle. Ask me something harder.

Jane Who swam through sharks with a seagull's egg in a bandanna?

Polly A bandanna?

Jane All right, a headband.

Polly The birdmen of Easter Island. Easy-peasy.

Jane Lemon-squeezy.

Polly Cheddar-cheesy

Jane Japanesy

Polly Pass me the compact.

Jane Your go, clever clogs.

Polly On the same subject. The statues were studded with which mineral?

Jane Er . . . malachite. No, marble.

Polly No, white coral.

Jane Sugar. When's the test.

Polly Monday next I think he said.

Jane Oh, I should be all right by then. (*Pause.*) What time do you make it?

Polly Twenty past. Another couple of hours yet, at least.

Jane Mine must be fast.

Polly Let's synchronize, just in case.

Jane It might be yours. Yours might be slow.

Polly I don't think so. Anyway, it's solar-powered – it's been charging up all summer.

Jane Look out, here come the others.

Klondike, Tulip and Glue Boy come running out of one of the caves. Glue Boy is sniffing glue from a plastic bag, and continues to do so throughout. Klondike wears a leather bag on his back and is carrying the skeletal head of a bull. Tulip is wearing Dr Marten boots and a red headscarf worn like a pirate.

Klondike Bloody hell, it's a cow's skull.

Tulip How do you know it's not from a sheep?

Klondike You're joking. Look at the size of it. Look at the teeth. Some caveman's had this for his tea. Hey, girls, fancy a spare rib?

Polly Take it away, it stinks.

Jane And I bet it's crawling with fleas.

Klondike It's a skull, you pair of dumb belles, not a fleece.

Tulip He found it right at the back of the cave.

Klondike I reckon it fell through the gap in the fence – it's been lying there, waiting for me.

Polly It gives me the creeps.

Glue Boy It's a dinosaur. Ginormous Rex.

Klondike I'm going to frame it or something. Put it in a case.

Tulip takes off her red headscarf, unfurls it and uses it as a matador's cape.

Tulip Come on, Klondike. Olé. Olé.

Polly Where's Midnight.

Tulip Still coming out of the hole. Let's hide.

Jane Don't be rotten. That'd be really tight.

Polly Why don't we just stay here like statues. He can't see us.

Klondike He'd hear us, though. He's got ears like satellite dishes.

Glue Boy Like radar stations.

Tulip Everyone scarper and hide.

Glue Boy Everyone turns into pumpkins when Midnight chimes.

Exit Glue Boy, Polly and Jane.

Tulip Wait, my scarf.

Klondike Leave it.

Exit Klondike and Tulip, leaving the scarf behind. Enter Midnight from the cave, wearing dark glasses, and a crucifix around his neck, which he holds out in front of him in his hand.

Midnight Klondike? Tulip? That skull, what is it?

Enter Lucy Lime.

Klondike? Glue Boy. Come on, don't be pathetic. Tulip? Tulip?

Lucy Selling flowers, are we?

Midnight Polly? Jane?

Lucy Penny Lane? Singing now, is it?

Midnight I'm Midnight. Who are you?

Lucy I'm twenty-to-three. Look. (*She makes the position of a clock's hands with her arms.*)

Midnight I can't look. I can't see.

Lucy Oh, you should have said. I'm Lucy. Lucy Lime.

Midnight I thought you were one of the others. They said they'd wait for me somewhere around here.

Lucy No, I'm not one of the others. And you can put that thing down. I'm not Dracula's daughter either.

Midnight What, this? Sorry. I'm a believer. It's Jesus, watching over.

Lucy Well, don't point it at me. It's loaded.

227

An animal noise comes out of one of the caves.

What was that? A bat?

Midnight More like Klondike messing about.

Lucy Klondike?

Midnight Him and Tulip and Glue Boy and the twins. We all came here in a van to do this star-gazing thing, or at least everybody's parents did, but it's boring.

Lucy So you've been exploring?

Midnight Yes. Pot-holing.

Lucy How did you . . .

Midnight Go blind?

Lucy Lose your sight, I was going to say.

Midnight Looked at the sun through binoculars when I was ten.

Lucy By mistake?

Midnight For a bet. Burnt out. Never see again.

Lucy Sorry.

Midnight Not to worry. I've got Jesus, and the truth.

Lucy Truth? What's that.

Midnight When you can't see, it's better to follow one straight path.

Lucy Oh, right. (*Pause.*) Do you want them to come back?

Midnight I told you, they're written off.

Lucy No, the others, I mean.

Midnight Oh, they won't. They think it's a good crack, leaving me playing blind man's buff.

Lucy Ever caught moths?

Midnight What have moths got to do with it?

Lucy Oh, nothing. (*She sets fire to the silk scarf and tosses it up in the air. It flares brightly and vanishes.*)

Enter Klondike, Tulip, Polly and Jane.

Klondike Midnight, what's going on?

Tulip We thought we saw something burning . . .

Polly Or a meteorite falling . . .

Jane A maroon or whatever they're called, like a rocket . . .

Klondike Or sheet lightning.

Glue Boy Air-raid warning. Keep away from the trees. The strike of midnight.

Midnight Er . . .

Lucy It was a will-o'-the-wisp.

Tulip Who the hell's this?

Midnight Er . . .

Lucy Lucy Lime. Mother and father are up on the top with your lot. I've been keeping your friend company – thought you'd be looking for him.

Klondike Er . . . that's right. We got separated.

Lucy Lucky I was around then. Wouldn't have wanted the electric fence to have found him.

Polly (*aside*) Strange-looking creature.

Jane Not pretty. No features. Hairy armpits, I bet.

Polly Yeah, and two hairy legs.

Midnight sits on a stone away from everyone else and puts on his Walkman.

Lucy Mind if I join you?

Klondike Sorry?

Lucy Mind if I stay?

Tulip Feel free. Free country.

Jane I'm bored. Let's play a game.

Klondike Let's trap a rabbit and skin it.

Polly You're kidding. Let's play mirror, mirror on the wall . . .

Jane Spin the bottle. Postman's knock.

Glue Boy Pin the donkey on the tail.

Lucy What about hide and seek?

Tulip British bulldogs. No, numblety peg.

Lucy What's that?

Tulip That's where I throw this knife into the ground between your legs.

Klondike I know. We'll play bets. I bet I can skim this stone head-on into the waves.

Polly We know you can. I bet if we had a vote, I'd have the prettiest face.

Jane I bet you'd come joint first.

Tulip I bet I dare touch the electric fence.

Klondike Easy, you've got rubber soles. What do you bet, Evo-Stik?

Glue Boy Tomorrow never comes.

Klondike Sure, you keep taking the pills.

Lucy I can get Midnight to tell a lie. That's what I bet.

Tulip Your off your head. He's as straight as a die.

Glue Boy Straight as a plumb-line.

Klondike You've got no chance. He's a born-again Mr Tambourine man. A proper Christian.

Polly Says his prayers before he goes to bed . . .

Jane Goes to church when it's not even Christmas.

Lucy I don't care if he's Mary and Joseph and Jesus rolled into one. He'll lie, like anyone.

Tulip What do you bet?

Lucy I bet this. Two coins together – it's a lucky charm – a gold sovereign melted to a silver dime.

Klondike It's Lucy Locket now, is it, not Lucy Lime?

Lucy It's worth a bomb.

Tulip We can sell it and split it. OK, you're on. I bet this knife that you're wrong.

Lucy I've no need of a knife. I'll bet you your boots instead.

Polly I'll bet you this bracelet. It's nine-carat gold.

Jane I'll bet you this make-up case. It's mother-of-pearl.

Glue Boy I'll bet Antarctica.

Lucy You can do better than that, can't you?

Glue Boy OK, the world.

Tulip What do you bet, Klondike?

Klondike My skull.

Lucy Not enough.

Klondike And these Boji stones, from Kansas, under an ancient lake.

Lucy Not enough.

Klondike All right, if you win – which you won't – you can kiss this handsome face.

Lucy Everybody shake on it.

Klondike All for one, and once and for all.

Glue Boy And one for the road. And toad in the hole.

Lucy Glue Boy, is that your name?

Glue Boy One and the same.

Lucy Come with me, you're the witness.

Polly Why him? He doesn't know Tuesday from a piece of string.

Lucy Sounds perfect. Everyone else, keep quiet.

Lucy and Glue Boy approach Midnight. Lucy taps him on the shoulder.

Listen.

Midnight What?

Lucy Can you hear a boat?

Midnight Nope.

Lucy Listen, I can hear its engine. I'm certain.

Midnight I think you're mistaken.

Lucy There, just as I thought – coming round the point.

Midnight There can't be. Which direction?

Tulip (*to the others*) What's she saying, there's no boat.

Lucy Straight out in front. Plain as the nose on your face. See it, Glue Boy?

Glue Boy Er . . . ? Oh, sure.

Lucy It's a trawler. Is it greeny-blue, would you say?

Glue Boy Well, sort of sea green, sort of sky blue, sort of blue moon sort of colour.

Lucy I'm amazed you can't hear it, it's making a real racket.

Midnight Well, I . . .

Lucy Too much time with the ear-plugs, listening to static.

Midnight My hearing's perfect.

Lucy Fine. OK. Forget it.

Midnight I'm sorry. I didn't mean to be rude.

Lucy You weren't. I shouldn't have mentioned it. It's my fault – I should have thought. You can't hear the boat for the sound of the seagulls.

Midnight Seagulls?

Polly (*to the others*) There isn't a bird for miles.

Jane This is a waste of time. It's her who's telling the lies.

Lucy All that high-pitched skriking and screaming. Must play havoc with sensitive hearing like yours.

Midnight How close?

Lucy The birds? Three hundred yards, five hundred at most. Black-headed gulls, Glue Boy, don't you think?

Glue Boy Well, kind of rare breed, kind of less common, kind of lesser-spotted type things.

Lucy Don't say you're going deaf.

Midnight Who, me?

Lucy Glue Boy can hear them, and he's out of his head. Come on, Midnight, stop clowning around. I bet you can hear it all. I bet you can hear a cat licking its lips in the next town, can't you?

Midnight I don't know. . . I think sometimes I filter it out.

Lucy Yes, when you're half asleep. But listen, what can you hear now?

Midnight Er . . . something . . .

Lucy That aeroplane for a start, I bet.

Midnight Yes. The aeroplane.

Lucy I can't see it myself. Where would you say it was?

Midnight Er . . . off to the left, that's my guess.

Lucy What else? That dog on the cliff, half a mile back. Can you hear that?

Midnight Yes. The dog. Sniffing the air, is it? Scratching the ground?

Lucy Amazing. Wrap-around sound. What else? The boy with the kite?

Midnight
Yes, the kite.

The wind playing the twine like a harp.
It's a wonderful sound.

Lucy And Klondike and Tulip, coming back up the beach.
What are they talking about?

Midnight They're saying . . . this and that, about that
eclipse, and how dark and how strange it'll be.

Lucy And down by the rock pools, the twins?

Midnight Chatting away. Girls' things. Boyfriends, that
kind of stuff. It's not really fair to listen in on it.

Lucy You're not kidding. You're absolutely ultrasonic.
Glue Boy, how about that for a pair of ears?

Glue Boy Yeah, he's Jodrell Bank, he is.

Lucy And one last noise. A siren or something?

Midnight Car alarm.

Lucy No. Music.

Midnight Brass band. 'Floral Dance'.

Lucy No. It's there on the tip of my tongue but I just can't
place it. You know, sells lollies and things.

Midnight Ice-cream van. Ice-cream van. I can hear it.

Lucy You can?

Midnight Can't you?

Lucy No. Not any more. What was the tune?

Midnight Er . . . 'Greensleeves'.

Lucy 'Greensleeves', eh? Thanks, Midnight, that should
do it.

Midnight Sorry?

Tulip Nice one, stupid.

Midnight What? I thought you were . . .

Tulip Yeah, well, you know what thought did.

Polly Pathetic, Midnight.

Jane You should see a doctor, you're hearing voices.

Midnight But, all those noises . . .

Klondike She made them up, you soft bastard. I tell you
what, you should take more care of those ears.

Midnight Why's that?

Klondike 'Cos if they fall off, you won't be able to wear glasses.

Midnight I didn't invent them.

Polly You lying rat.

Jane You just lost us the bet, Dumbo. Do us a favour – stick to your Walkman.

Lucy Midnight, I'm sorry.

Midnight Get lost. Keep off me.

Polly Where are you going?

Midnight Anywhere away from here.

Klondike Well, get me a ninety-nine will you, when you're there.

Tulip And a screwball as well.

Midnight Go to hell.

Midnight takes off his crucifix and throws it in the direction of Lucy. Lucy picks it up and puts it in her bag.

Lucy Well, I think that clinches it, don't you? The bracelet, the case, the boots and the skull and the stone, if you please.

Everyone hands her the items. Lucy puts on the shoes and puts everything else in her bag.

Klondike Forgetting something?

Lucy I don't think so.

Klondike A kiss from me, because you did it.

Lucy No thanks, Romeo. I was only kidding.

Polly What a cheek. Not to worry, in the glove compartment I've got more jewellery, too good for that gold-digger.

Jane But you've got to hand it to her. I'll come to the car park to check out the courtesy light and the vanity mirror.

Exit Polly and Jane.

Glue Boy What did I bet?

Lucy The Earth.

Glue Boy I've left it at home in my other jacket. Double or quits?

Lucy No, I'll take it on credit.

Glue Boy A whole planet. In a top pocket.

Tulip Hey, where do you think you're going?

Lucy To see Midnight, make sure he's OK.

Tulip You've got a nerve.

Lucy Why? It was only a game.

Glue Boy Klondike, the sun . . .

Klondike Don't you think you've lost enough for one day?

Glue Boy No, the shadow. Here it comes.

Lucy It can't be. It's too early to start.

Tulip He's right, it's going dark. Klondike?

Klondike ECLIPSE, ECLIPSE. EVERYONE INTO POSITION. EVERYONE INTO POSITION.

Tulip We're short.

Klondike Who's missing?

Tulip Midnight. Gone walkabout. And the twins, where are the twins?

Klondike Get them back. Polly. Jane. POLLY. JANE.

SCENE FOUR

The police interview room. Polly and Jane make their statement, sometimes talking in unison, sometimes separately, one sister occasionally finishing the other sister's sentence.

Polly and Jane
    They were up on the tops, we were down on the deck,
    kicking around in pebbles and shells and bladderwrack.
    They were watching the sky, we were keeping an eye

on the tide, hanging around, writing names in the sand,
turning over stones, pulling legs from hermit crabs.

We're two of a kind, two yolks from the same egg,
same thoughts in identical heads, everything half
and half, but it's easy enough to tell us apart:
I'm the spitting image; she's the copy cat.

They were up on the top looking south, we were down
on the strand looking out for something to do. She came
and she went in the same afternoon, saw the eclipse,
like   us,
but mustn't have been impressed, so she left. Straight up.
And a truth half told is a lie. We should know, we're a
Gemini.

Oh, yes, and we liked her style and the way she dressed.
We were something else before the daylight vanished.
Whatever we touched was touched with varnish.
Whatever we smelt was laced with powder or scent.
Whatever we heard had an earring lending its weight.
Whatever we saw was shadowed and shaded out of
sight.
Whatever we tasted tasted of mint.
Whatever we spoke had lipstick kissing its lips.
We were something else back then, all right, muddled
up,
not thinking straight, as it were. But now we're clear.

Same here.

SCENE FIVE

*The beach. Klondike, Tulip, Glue Boy and Lucy are
standing looking at the sky.*

Tulip False alarm. Just a cloud.

Klondike Thought so. Too early.
Tulip What now?
Glue Boy I-spy.
Tulip Boring. Hide and seek. Come on, Klondike, hide and seek.
Klondike OK. Spuds up.
Lucy What, like this?
Klondike Yes, that's it.

They all hold out their fists, with thumbs pointing skyward.

One potati, two potati, three potati, four,
    five potati, six potati, seven potati, more . . .
Tulip
There's a party on the hill, will you come,
bring your own cup of tea and a bun . . .
Glue Boy
Ip dip dip, my blue ship,
sails on the water, like a cup and saucer . . .
Klondike
It's here, it's there, it's everywhere,
it's salmon and it's trout,
it shaves its tongue and eats its hair,
you're in, you're in, you're in . . . you're out.

The dipping-out lands on Lucy.

Tulip You're it.
Lucy OK, how many start?
Klondike Fifty elephants, and no cheating.
Glue Boy Fifteen cheetahs, and no peeping.
Lucy Off you go then.

Lucy turns her back and begins counting. Exit Tulip and Klondike.

One elephant, two elephant, three elephant . . .
Glue Boy Filthy underpants and no weeping.

237

Klondike returns and drags Glue Boy off. Enter Polly and Jane.

Polly Hey, there's what's-her-face.

Jane What's she playing at?

Polly Practising her times-table by the sounds of it. Let's tell her to get lost.

Jane No, I've got a better idea. Let's give her a shock.

Lucy . . . fifty elephants. Coming ready or not.

Polly and Jane BOO!

Lucy Don't do that. You'll give someone a heart attack.

Polly We're the two-headed . . .

Jane . . . four-armed . . .

Polly . . . four-legged . . .

Jane . . . twenty-fingered monster from the black lagoon.

Lucy And one brain between the pair of you.

Polly Now, now. No need to be nasty.

Jane Yeah, no one's called you pale and pasty, have they?

Lucy I just meant that it's hard to tell you apart.

Polly We like it that way.

Jane It's scary.

Lucy Anyway, this is the natural look.

Polly What, plain and hairy?

Lucy No, pure and simple. Basically beautiful.

Jane Says who?

Lucy Says people. Boys. Men.

Jane You got a boyfriend then?

Lucy Yes. Someone. What about you two?

Jane No one to speak of . . .

Polly We're not bothered. All those round our way are filthy or ugly and stupid.

Lucy Maybe you should do what I did then.

Polly What was that?

Lucy Well,

three men fishing on the towpath wouldn't let me past;

called me a tramp, threw me in and I nearly drowned.
I was down in the weeds with dead dogs and bicycle
frames.
Couldn't move for bracelets and beads and rings and
chains.
Don't know why, but I ditched the lot in a minute flat,
took off my clothes as well: cuffs and frills and scarves,
heels and buttons and lace and buckles and shoulder-
   pads,
climbed out strip jack naked on the other bank, white-
   faced
and my hair down flat. The three men whistled and
clapped
but I stood there, dressed in nothing but rain. They
stopped
and threw me a shirt and a big coat, which I
wouldn't   take.
One of them covered his eyes, said it was somebody's
fault;
a fight broke out and I watched. All three of them
cried,
said they were sorry, said they were shamed. I asked
them
to leave, and they shuffled away to their cars, I
suppose,
and their wives. I put on the coat and shirt, walked
home,
but never went back to dredge for the gold or the
clothes.
This is me now. Be yourself, I reckon, not somebody
else.

Jane What a story.

Polly Jackanory.

Lucy Well, that's what happened. You should try it. You
might be surprised.

Jane You're kidding. Us?

Polly Not on your life.

Lucy Why not?

Jane How do we know we'd look any good?

Polly We wouldn't.

Lucy You would. Well, you might.
Anyhow, better to look the way you were meant to be
than done up like a tailor's dummy and a Christmas
tree.

Polly
Better to look like us
than something the cat wouldn't touch.

Lucy No cat curls its nose up at good meat.

Polly
No, but I know what they'd go for first
if it's a choice between semi-skimmed or full-cream.

Lucy Suit yourselves.

Polly We will.

Lucy But don't blame me when you're twenty-three or
thirty-four or forty-five, and left on the shelf.

Polly We won't.

Klondike (*off*) You haven't found us yet.

Lucy Am I warm or cold?

Klondike (*off*) Cold as a penguin's chuff.

Tulip (*off*) Cold as an Eskimo's toe.

Glue Boy (*off*) Yeah, cold as a polar bear's fridge. In a
power cut.

Klondike and Tulip (*off*) Shut up.

Jane (*to Polly*) Why don't we give it a go?

Polly No.

Jane Why not?

Polly Because.

Jane It won't harm. Just for a laugh.

Polly I haven't put all this on just to take it all off.

Jane Come on, Sis, do it for me.

Polly What if we're . . . different?

Jane What do you mean?

Polly What if we don't look the same? Underneath?
Jane Don't know. Hadn't thought. Put it all on again?
Polly Straight away?
Jane Before you can say Jack Robinson. Before you can
  say . . .
Polly OK.
Jane Lucy. We're going to give it a whirl.
Polly Just for a laugh, though. That's all.
Lucy Excellent. Down to the sea, girls. Down to the shore.
(*sings*)

> Oh ladies of Greece
> with the thickest of trees,
> covered with blossom and bumble,
> snip off the bees
> and there underneath
> two apples to bake in a crumble.

> Oh ladies of France
> with warts on your hands,
> come down, come down to the waters.
> And where you were gnarled
> at the end of your arms
> two perfect symmetrical daughters.

> Oh ladies of Spain
> at night on the lane
> in nightshirts and mittens and bedsocks,
> strip off those duds
> and ride through the woods
> on horses carved into the bedrock.

*While singing, Lucy strips them of their jewellery and
some of their clothes, and washes their hair in the sea.
She puts the jewellery and a few choice items of clothing
into bag.*

How does it feel?
Jane Unreal. I feel like someone else.

Lucy Polly?

Polly Not sure. Up in the air.

Jane I feel lighter and thinner.

Lucy Polly?

Polly See-through. Like a tree in winter.

Lucy You look great. You look like different people.

Polly Sorry?

Lucy I mean . . . you still look the same, alike. Just different types.

Jane Here come the others. See if they notice.

Polly Oh no. Let's hide.

Jane Too late. What shall we say?

Lucy Say nothing. Just smile. They'll only be jealous.

Enter Klondike, Tulip and Glue Boy.

Klondike Couldn't you find us?

Lucy No. You win.

Tulip We were down in the caves with the dead pirates.

Klondike How hard did you look?

Lucy Oh, about this hard. Feels like I've been looking for hours.

Tulip We were camouflaged.

Glue Boy Yeah, we were cauliflowers.

Tulip Oh my God.

Klondike What's up?

Tulip It's those two. Look.

Klondike Wow. I don't believe it.

Jane What's the matter with you? Never seen a woman before?

Tulip Never seen this one or that one. What happened? Get flushed down the toilet?

Lucy They've changed their minds.

Tulip You mean you changed it for them. That's all we need, three Lucy Limes.

Glue Boy Three lucky strikes. Three blind mice.

Polly Shut it, Glue Boy.

Klondike I think they look . . . nice.

Tulip Nice? They look like bones after the dog's had them.

Lucy They had a change of heart.

Glue Boy Heart transplant.

Klondike I think they look . . . smart. Sort of.

Tulip Yeah, and sort of not. They don't even look like twins any more. Don't look like anyone.

Polly I told you we shouldn't have.

Jane Don't blame me. You don't look that bad.

Polly Me? You should see yourself. You look like something out of a plastic bag.

Jane So what? You look like an old hag. You look like a boiled pig.

Tulip Glue Boy, what do they look like? Mirror, mirror on the wall . . .

Glue Boy
Mirror, mirror on the wall,
who's the worstest of them all . . .

Jane Glue Boy . . .

Glue Boy This one looks like a wet haddock . . .

Jane I'll kill you.

Glue Boy But this one looks like a skinned rabbit.

Polly Right, you've had it.

*Polly and Jane pull Glue Boy's glue bag over his head
and start to kick him. He wanders off and they follow,
still kicking him.*

Klondike They'll slaughter him.

Tulip He wouldn't notice.

Lucy What a mess.

Tulip Yes, and you started it.

Lucy Me? It was all fine till you came back and started stirring it. Now it's a hornet's nest.

Klondike Leave it alone. It'll all come out in the wash.

Lucy (*holding up some of the clothes left on the floor*)

243

What about these? Needles from Christmas trees.

Klondike Tulip, go and put leaves back on the evergreens.

Tulip Why me? What about her – Tinkerbell?

Klondike I don't think that'd go down too well. Please?

Tulip OK, give them here.

Lucy Take this, a brush for back-combing their hair.

Tulip Beach-combing more like. How kind.

Lucy That's me, sweetness and light. Lime by name, but
   sugar by nature. Isn't that right?

Klondike Eh? How should I know? Got everything?

Tulip S'ppose so.

Klondike Won't take a minute.

Tulip (*to Klondike, privately*) You'll wait here, won't you?

Klondike 'Course.

Tulip Don't let her . . .

Klondike What?

Tulip Doesn't matter.

Klondike Go on, what?

Tulip Talk to you, you know.

Klondike No. I won't do.

Tulip Don't let her . . . Lucy Lime you.

Klondike Don't be daft. Go on, I'll time you.

   Exit Tulip.

Enjoying yourself?

Lucy I've had better.

Klondike Where are you from?

Lucy All over. (*Pause.*)
   I'm a walking universe, I am.
   Wherever the best view comes from,
   wherever Mars and the moon are in conjunction,
   wherever the stars and the sun are looking good from,
   wherever the angles and the right ascensions and
   declinations
   and transits and vectors and focal lengths and partial
   perigons

are done from, that's where I come from.
Traipsing round with mother and father. What about
you lot?

Klondike Yorkshire. Came in a van.

Lucy Bet that was fun.

Klondike I meant it, you know.

Lucy Meant what?

Klondike About that kiss. If you want to.

Lucy What about her? Don't you think she'd mind?

Klondike Tulip? No, she's all right. She's just . . .

Lucy One of the lads?

Klondike Something like that. Well, what about it?

Lucy Ever played rising sun?

Klondike Don't think so. How do you play it?

Lucy Well,
A light shines bright through a sheet or blanket,
somebody follows the sun as it rises,
it dawns at daybreak above the horizon,
the one looking east gets something surprising . . .

Klondike Really?

Lucy Something exciting. Something to break the ice with.

Klondike Let's try it.

Lucy Sorry, no can do. We need a torch for the sun.

Klondike (*producing a torch*) Like this one?

Lucy And we need a sheet.

Klondike (*taking off his shirt*) You can use this shirt.

Lucy And it needs to be dark. Sorry, can't be done.

Klondike I'll put this blindfold on. (*Without taking it off,
he lifts the bottom front of his T-shirt over his head.*)

Lucy OK, here it comes.

*Klondike kneels on the floor and holds his T-shirt up in
front of his face. Lucy, on the other side, presses the
torch against the shirt and raises it very slowly.
Klondike follows the light with his nose.*

Rain in the north from the tears of Jesus,

Rind in the west with its knickers in a twist;
Flies in the south sucking blood like leeches,
Sun coming up in the east like a kiss,
(*whispers*) from Judas.

Repeat.

SCENE SIX

The police interview room.

Tulip
When she left us for good I was nine or ten.
Ran off with the milkman, so Dad said. Ran off
with the man in the moon, as far as I care.
Grew up with uncles, cousins, played rugby-football,
swapped a pram for a ten-speed drop-handlebar,
played with matches instead, flags and cars, threw
the dolls on a skip and the skates on a dustcart,
flogged the frills and pink stuff at a car-boot sale,
burnt the Girl Guide outfit in the back garden,
got kitted out at Famous Army Stores and Top Man.
And Oxfam. I'll tell you something that sums it up:
found a doll's-house going mouldy in the attic –
boarded it up, kept a brown rat in it.
Put it all behind now, growing out of it, Dad says, says
I'm blossoming, and I suppose he must be right. Klondike?
No, not a boyfriend, more like a kid brother, really,
known him since as far back as I can remember.
Kissed him? Who wants to know? I mean no, Sir,
except on his head, just once, on his birthday.
Him and Lucy? Well, she took a shine to him,
he told her some things and I think she liked him.
She just showed up and wanted to tag along,
make some friends, I suppose, mess about, have fun;

she had a few tricks up her sleeve, wanted . . . all right,
if you put it like that . . . to be one of the group.
It's not much cop being on your own. Which was fine
by us. It's not that we gave it a second thought
to tell you the truth. She just turned up that afternoon
like a lost dog. She was one of the gang. Then she was
gone.

SCENE SEVEN

The beach. Lucy and Klondike playing rising sun.

Lucy
Rain in the north from the tears of Jesus,
Wind in the west with its knickers in a twist;
Flies in the south sucking blood like leeches,
Sun coming up in the east like . . . piss.

Lucy throws water in his face.

Klondike You bitch.
Lucy Someting to break the ice, you see. It was a riddle.

Enter Tulip, unnoticed.

Klondike It was a swindle.
Lucy Oh, come on. You can take it. Here, dry off on this.
(*She hands him his shirt and kisses him on the
forehead.*)
Klondike You shouldn't joke.
Lucy What about?
Klondike Rhymes and religion. Old things. Things in the
past.
Lucy I don't believe in all that claptrap.
Klondike It's just the way you've been brought up.
Lucy Yes, in the twentieth century, not in the dark.
Anyway, what about your lot? They're up there

believing in science and maths.
Klondike No, with them it's the zodiac.
Lucy Oh, I see. It's like that.
Klondike They've come to take part, not take
photographs.

Pause.

Lucy What's in the bag?
Klondike Bits and pieces.
Lucy Show me. Or is it a secret?
Klondike Just things I've collected.
Lucy Suit yourself. Only, I was interested.
Klondike Well, it's just that . . .
Lucy Oh, forget it then, if it's so precious. Makes no
difference.
Klondike All right then, since you've asked. (*Klondike
opens his bag, and reveals the contents, slowly.*)
This is the skin of a poisonous snake,
this is a horse stick, cut from a silver birch,
this is bear's tooth, this is a blue shell,
this is a wren's wing, this is a brass bell,
this is a glass bead, this is a fox tail,
this is a boat, carved from a whale bone,
this is a whistle, this is a goat's horn,
this is driftwood, this is a cat's claw,
this is a ribbon, a mirror, a clay pipe,
this is a toy drum, this is a meteorite,
this is fool's gold, this is buffalo leather –
Lucy All done?
Klondike
And this is the moon and the sun:
a hare's foot and an eagle feather.
Lucy How do you mean?
Klondike That's what they stand for.
Lucy Well, quite a bag full. When's the car-boot sale?
Klondike You couldn't afford them.

Lucy Wouldn't want them. Anyway, what are they for?

Klondike They're just things, that's all.

Lucy Things from a mumbo-jumbo stall?

Klondike Things for dreaming things up.

Lucy What?

Klondike I said, things for dreaming things up.

Lucy Tommy-rot. You're just an overgrown Boy Scout. Next thing you'll be showing me a reef knot.

Klondike Get lost, Lucy.

Lucy Dib dib dib, dob dob dob.

Tulip Klondike, show her.

Klondike No.

Tulip Why not?

Lucy Because he can't.

Tulip Show her.

Klondike Why should I?

Lucy Because he's a big kid, playing with toy cars.

Tulip You don't have to take that from her.

Lucy But most of all, because he's full of shite. Eagle feathers? Chicken more like.

Klondike All right.

Lucy
This is the eye of a bat, this is a leprechaun's hat,
This is the spine of a bird, this is a rocking horse turd –

Klondike I said all right.

Lucy
This is a snowman's heart, this is a plate of tripe –

Klondike ALL RIGHT. Pick something out.

Lucy Well, well, well. All this for little old me. I don't know where to start.

Eenie, meanie, meinie, mo,

put the baby on the po . . . no, not my colour.

Scab and matter custard, toenail pie,
all mixed up with a dead dog's eye,

249

green and yellow snot cakes
fried in spit,
all washed down with a cup of cold sick.
Here's what I pick.

Klondike The eagle feather.

Lucy None other.

Klondike Put it in the bag, then on the rock, then –

Lucy Let me guess. Light the blue touch and stand well
back?

*Klondike performs a ceremony around the bag. There is
a deafening roar and a brief shadow as a low-flying jet
passes overhead.*

Is that it?

Tulip What?

Lucy Is that it? A jet.

Tulip Oh, only a jet. What do you want, jam on it?
Klondike, you were brilliant. That was the best yet.

Lucy Hang on, let's get this straight. It's the feather that
counts, right? You made that plane come out of the
clouds by doing a voodoo dance around a bit of feather
duster in an old sack?

Klondike Not quite. Something like that.

Lucy Well then, how do you explain . . . this. (*She
produces a rubber duck from the bag.*) Quack quack.

Klondike What . . .

Tulip Where did you get it?

Lucy Down on the beach, washed up. Klondike, say hello
to Mr Duck.

Tulip You're a bitch.

Lucy
Sails on the water, like a cup and saucer. So much for
the jet,
lucky you didn't conjure up the *Titanic*, we might have
got wet.

Tulip I'm going to break her neck.

Klondike No, Tulip.

Lucy Rubber Duck to Ground Control, Rubber Duck to Ground Control, the signal's weak, you're breaking up, you're breaking up.

Tulip You think you're really fucking good, don't you?

Lucy I'm only having some fun. What else is there to do?

Tulip Oh, it's fun, is it? Well, I've had enough. I hope you're either good with a knife, or I hope you can run.

Klondike Tulip, leave her.

Lucy Sorry neither. You'll just have to do me in in cold blood. Mind you, I'm strong.

Tulip Where, apart from your tongue?

Lucy Here, from the shoulder down to the wrist. This right arm doesn't know its own strength.

Tulip Looks to me like a long streak of piss.

Lucy Ah, well, looks deceive. For instance, you don't have to look like a man to be as strong as one.

Tulip And what's that supposed to mean?

Lucy What will you do when your balls drop, Tulip? Grow a beard?

Tulip Right, you're dead.

Klondike Just stop. Knock it off, I said. If you want to show off, why don't you arm-wrestle or something, there on the rock?

Lucy No thanks, I don't play competitive sports.

Klondike Not half you don't.

Tulip Now who's chicken?

Lucy I've told you, I'm just not interested in winning.

Tulip Not interested in losing, more like. Come on, arm-wrestle, or maybe I just smash your face in anyway, for a bit of fun, for a laugh.

Lucy All right, but don't say you didn't ask for it.

Klondike Both of you down on one knee, elbows straight and a clean grip. Ready?

Tulip Yep.

Klondike Lucy?
Lucy As I'll ever be.
Klondike When I say three. One, two –

Enter Midnight, carrying a melting ice-cream in both hands.

Midnight Ice-cream. I got the ice-cream.
Klondike Not now, Midnight.
Midnight 'Greensleeves', up by the road. A screwball, right, and a ninety-nine. Or was it a cone?
Klondike Midnight, we're busy. Just wait there for a minute. And count to three.
Midnight Why?
Klondike Just do it.
Midnight OK then. One. Two. Three.

With her free hand, Lucy takes hold of the electric cable. Tulip is thrown over backwards with the shock.

What was that? Lightning?
Lucy No, something like it. Is she OK?
Klondike Just frightened, I think.
Lucy Ten volts, that's all. Hardly enough to light a torch, but it's the shock I suppose.
Klondike How come?
Lucy Meaning what?
Klondike How come her, and not you?
Lucy Easy. Insulation. Good shoes.
Klondike She was the earth?
Lucy Yes. Here, she can have them back – not my style, rubber boots. (*She takes off the boots and tosses them on the floor.*)
Klondike She was the earth.
Lucy Certainly was.
Klondike Just for a laugh.
Lucy No, self-defence.

Klondike I see. (*He picks up Tulip's knife.*) Well, that's enough.

Lucy What do you mean?

Klondike I mean, enough's enough.

Lucy Klondike, that's real. That's a knife.

Klondike That's right. That's right.

Midnight (*facing the opposite way*) Klondike. No heat.

Klondike No heat. Ice-cream. That's right.

Midnight No, no heat, on my face. No . . . no light.

Klondike No light?

Midnight No light. No sun.

Lucy Eclipse.

Klondike Eclipse? ECLIPSE. Everyone into position. Who's missing?

Tulip The twins.

Klondike Polly. Jane. POLLY. JANE. How long left?

Tulip A minute. No, fifty seconds. Less.

Klondike Who else? Midnight?

Midnight Here, right next to you.

Enter Polly and Jane.

Klondike Six of us. Six of us.

Tulip Glue Boy. Where's Glue Boy?

Klondike Where's Glue Boy?

Polly We saw him up by the tents.

Jane Out of his head.

Klondike Idiot. How long left?

Tulip Twenty. Less.

Klondike OK, OK. (*to Lucy*) You. It'll have to be you.

Lucy I'm going back to the . . .

Klondike Stay there and don't move.

Tulip Where shall we stand?

Klondike Don't you remember, the plan? (*He begins to move them into position.*) You there, you there, you there . . .

Midnight What about me?

Klondike You stand here.

Lucy Look, I'm not really sure . . .

Klondike Just stay put. You've had it your own way all afternoon, now let's see what you're made of.

Tulip Ten seconds.

Lucy Huh, me at the back then?

Klondike Pole position. Right where it happens.

Facing towards where the sun grows darker, they stand in a triangular formation, with Tulip, Klondike and Midnight at the front, Polly and Jane behind them, and Lucy at the back.

Polly Look out, here it comes.

Jane (*elated*) Oh yes.

Polly Time for the shades. Time for the shades?

Klondike Yes, the shades. Put them on.

Klondike, Tulip, Polly and Jane put on their protective glasses.

Midnight What?

Polly The specs.

Midnight Oh yes. (*He takes his off.*)

Tulip Five seconds, less. Three. Two. One.

Except for Lucy, they begin the chant.

All
Fallen fruit of burning sun
break the teeth and burn the tongue,

open mouth of the frozen moon
spit the cherry from the stone.

SCENE EIGHT

The police interview room.

Klondike
Dusk and dawn, like that, in the one afternoon.
For all the world, this is as much as I know.
We were standing there watching the most spectacular
    show
on earth, a beam of light from the bulb
of the sun, made night through the lens of the moon;
ninety-three million miles – point-blank range. Strange,
the moon four hundred times smaller in size,
the sun four hundred times further away;
in line, as they were for us for once for a change,
they're the same size. We were set. We were primed.
Like the riddle says, what can be seen as clear
as day, but never be looked in the face? This
was a chance to stand in a star's shade,
to catch the sun napping or looking the wrong way –
the light of all lights, turning a blind eye.
I'm getting ahead of myself – it's hard to describe.
When the shadow arrived from the east like a stingray,
two thousand miles an hour, skimming the sea spray,
two hundred miles across from fin to fin,
we felt like a miracle, under its wingspan.
We said nursery rhymes, like frightened children.
Midnight bats came out of the sea caves, calling,
birds in the crags buried down in their breasts
till morning, crabs came out of holes in the sand
with eyes on stalks to watch for the tide turning.
When it was done . . . we looked about, and she'd gone.
Never thought for a second she might be lost,
just reckoned she wasn't impressed with planets
and stars and shadows . . . figured she wasn't fussed.

Thought that she'd taken her lime-green self up top,
sidled away, shuffled off. Came as a big black shock
when they called and said she never showed up.
She wasn't us, although we liked her well enough.
She told us things, showed us stuff. It's almost
as if she did us a good turn by putting us all
on the right track. Sad. And that's the whole story.
I wish I could tell you more but I can't. I'm sorry.

SCENE NINE

*The police waiting-room. Tulip, Polly and Jane, Midnight
and Glue Boy, sitting, waiting. Enter Klondike from
interview room.*

Tulip Well?
Klondike Well what?
Tulip Any problems, or not?
Klondike No, none.
Polly What did you tell them?
Klondike Same as everyone else, I presume.
Jane What do they think?
Klondike How should I know? I'm not a mind-reader.
Tulip Well, I don't care. I don't see what else we're
supposed to say.
Polly Nor me.
Jane Me neither.
Midnight So we can go home?
Klondike No.
Midnight Why not? We're all done, aren't we?
Glue Boy Except for one.
Midnight Oh yes. Sorry. Forgot.

Off, a voice calls 'Paul Bond'.

Glue Boy That'll be me then.

Tulip Why are they asking him?

Klondike It's his turn. Everyone has to go in.

Polly Fat load of good that'll be. He can't remember his own name at the best of times.

Jane He was out of his brain that day, weren't you, Glue Boy?

Glue Boy High as a kite. Cloud nine.

Off, a voice calls 'Paul Bond'.

Oh, well. Cheerio.

Klondike Glue Boy?

Glue Boy What?

Klondike Whatever you know, get it straight.

Glue Boy Like you, right?

Klondike Right.

Exit Glue Boy into interview room.

Tulip See the news?

Polly No. In the paper again?

Tulip Yes, and on the telly as well this time.

Midnight *News at Ten*?

Tulip Don't know. I was in bed by then, but I saw it at six on the BBC.

Jane What did it say?

Tulip Said that they'd called off the search. Said they'd had aeroplanes over the sea, locals walking the beach, boats in the bay, dogs in the caves and all that for over a week, but they'd called it a day. Said that she might be thousands of miles away by now.

Polly Anything else. Anything . . . new?

Tulip No. Oh yes, they showed her mum and dad.

Klondike I saw that. Him in the suit, her in the hat, going on and on and on.

Jane How old?

Klondike Don't know, but you could see where she got it from.

Pause.

Tulip They're talking about a reconstruction.

Jane What's one of those when it's at home?

Tulip We all go back to the place and do it again, see if somebody remembers anything or seeing anyone.

Polly And they do it on film, don't they?

Jane Oh yes, and someone'll have to dress up as her, won't they?

Polly With her stuff, and her hair.

Tulip That won't be much fun.

Pause.

Klondike Not a problem. Can't be done.

Midnight You sure.

Klondike Certainly am. Not without the moon, and not without the sun.

Pause.

Tulip Anyway, when's the next one?

Polly Next what?

Tulip Eclipse. Klondike?

Klondike Don't know, I'll have to look at the list. Why, are you up for it?

Tulip Can a duck swim?

Klondike Polly? Jane?

Polly In.

Jane In.

Tulip What about him in there – Mr Pritt-Stick?

Klondike Mr dip-stick more like. Don't worry about him, he'll be all right.

Tulip What about you, Midnight?

Midnight Sorry, I wasn't listening.

Tulip Don't play the innocent with me, sunshine. The next eclipse – yes or no, sir?

Midnight Lunar or solar?

Klondike Solar. Total.
Midnight

Two days in a van with my mum's barley sugars and the
old man.

Two minutes at most of afternoon night when I'm
already blind.

Hanging around with you lot, calling me names, playing
tricks

of the light and stupid games, then egging myself for a
week,

can't eat, can't sleep, then twenty questions by the
police,

and all the rest, enough to put a normal person in the
funny farm

. . . go on then, you've twisted my arm.

SCENE TEN

The police interview room.

Glue Boy

I suppose you've heard it needle and thread times five.
Saying it over and over again – not much point, right?
Any road, I was all of a dither back then,
disconnected, fuse blown in the head, loose ends,
nobody home, fumes on the brain – know what I mean?
Hard to think of it all in one long line, it's all
squiggles and shapes. Fits and starts. Kills the cells,
you see, after so long, so that you can't tell. Well,
nothing to speak of coming to mind just yet. Except . . .
no, nothing, nothing. All gone funny. Not unless
you mean the bit between the last bit and the rest?
You should have said. Let's think. Let's think.
No point saying it over and over to death, no sense
wasting breath. Bits and bobs. Chapter and verse.

Unless . . .

no, nothing. What the others said. Just that. Oh yes,
then this . . .

SCENE ELEVEN

The beach. Klondike, Lucy, Tulip and Midnight, as before.

Lucy Klondike, that's real. That's a knife.

Klondike That's right. That's right.

Midnight (*facing the opposite way*) Klondike. No heat.

Klondike No heat. Ice-cream. That's right.

Midnight No, no heat, on my face. No . . . no light.

Klondike No light?

Midnight No light. No sun.

Lucy Eclipse.

Klondike Eclipse? ECLIPSE. Everyone into position.
Who's missing?

Tulip The twins.

Klondike Polly. Jane. POLLY. JANE. How long left?

Tulip A minute. No, fifty seconds. Less.

Klondike Who else? Midnight?

Midnight Here, right next to you.

Enter Polly and Jane.

Klondike Six of us. Six of us.

Tulip Glue Boy. Where's Glue Boy?

Klondike Where's Glue Boy?

Polly We saw him up by the tents.

Jane Out of his head.

Klondike Idiot. How long left?

Tulip Twenty. Less.

Klondike OK, OK. (*to Lucy*) You. It'll have to be you.

Lucy I'm going back to the . . .

Klondike Stay there and don't move.

Tulip Where shall we stand?
Klondike Don't you remember the plan? (*He begins to move them into position.*) You there, you there, you there . . .
Midnight What about me?
Klondike You stand here.
Lucy Look, I'm not really sure . . .
Klondike Just stay put. You've had it your own way all afternoon, now let's see what you're made of.
Tulip Ten seconds.
Lucy Huh, me at the back then?
Klondike Pole position. Right where it happens.

Facing towards where the sun grows darker, they stand in a triangular formation, with Tulip, Klondike and Midnight at the front, Polly and Jane behind them, and Lucy at the back.

Polly Look out, here it comes.
Jane (*elated*) Oh yes.
Polly Time for the shades. Time for the shades?
Klondike Yes, the shades. Put them on.

Klondike, Tulip, Polly and Jane put on their protective glasses.

Midnight What?
Polly The specs.
Midnight Oh yes. (*He takes his off.*)
Tulip Five seconds, less. Three. Two. One.

Except for Lucy, they begin the chant.

All
Fallen fruit of burning sun
break the teeth and burn the tongue,

open mouth of the frozen moon
spit the cherry from the stone.

Enter Glue Boy from opposite direction, still with glue
bag on his head. He collides with Lucy, who takes him
to one side and takes the bag from his head. She holds
his hands as he hallucinates.

Glue Boy Seeing things. Dreaming things.

Glue Boy blurts out his dream as Midnight leaves the
group, retrieves his crucifix from Lucy's bag and puts it on.

head through a noose dreams
    lasso roping a horse
needle threading itself
    bat flying into a cave
mole coming up through a grave
    cuckoo's head through the shell of an egg
dog on a leash dreams

Midnight rejoins the group, who are still facing the
eclipse, chanting. Tulip leaves the group and begins
putting on her boots. She also produces another red
headscarf from her pocket, and ties it around her
head.

sea-horse   trying on its shoes
    tom-cat   tortoiseshell   stood up
mermaid scaling the beach
    finding its feet   ditching its tail
square of the sky   shepherd's delight
    pulled down   worn as a crown
poppy blazing in a field of corn
    dead volcano   blowing its top
matchstick wearing heat to its head like a hat
    dream things   things like that

Tulip rejoins the group. The twins go to the bag to
retrieve clothes, jewellery and make-up.

double-vision dream   two trees
  Dutch Elms coming back into leaf
two snow-leopards   trying on furs
  leggings   coats of sheep that were shorn
two African rhino   stripped to the bone
  locking horns
nude Aunt Sally   birthday suit on a tailor's dummy
  rose-petal lips   ivory teeth
dreams   dolled up like Russians
  dressed to the nines   clothes of their mothers
those dreams   others

The twins rejoin the group. Klondike goes to the bag to retrieve the skull and the Boji stones.

nutcracker man coming out of his shell
  great auk treading thin air
phoenix roasting   driftwood fire
  unicorn meeting its match   point of a spear
head of a griffin   worn as a hat
  beak of a dodo worn on a boot
as a spur
  tusk of a mammoth   torn from its root
a tooth   a tree
  white hart hung by its hooves
Franklin's men   out of the deep-freeze
  dream things   those   these

Lucy and Glue Boy have become stuck together with the glue. They spin round violently trying to free themselves of each other.

Lucy Let go.
Glue Boy It's the glue. It's the glue.
Lucy LET ME GO.

The rest of the group are still chanting. The total darkness of the eclipse descends, then sunlight returns,

*and Glue Boy is found to be standing in the position
where Lucy stood.*

Klondike That's it.
Tulip Blown away.
Polly That was strange. Really strange.
Jane Funny, I've gone all cold.
Midnight I feel sick.
Klondike Happens to some people. I've read about that.
Tulip Come on, everyone up to the top.
Klondike Glue Boy?
Glue Boy Hello.
Klondike Where did she go?
Glue Boy Where did who go?
Tulip Princess Muck. Lady Di. Who do you think? Lucy
Lime.
Glue Boy Er, don't know. Lost her in the light.
Polly (*picking up Lucy's bag*) She's left her bag.
Jane Here, Glue Boy, better give it her back.

Glue Boy walks off with her bag.

Klondike Come on. We're wasting time.
Jane It seemed to go on for hours. How long did it last?
Tulip Two minutes thirty-five.
Polly Not according to mine. Yours must be fast.
Tulip So what did you make it then?
Polly Well . . . less.
Klondike Come on. Last one to the top gets a Chinese
burn.
Midnight I feel sick.
Klondike Somebody give him a hand. Polly and Jane.
Tulip Hang on.
Klondike Now what.
Tulip (*looking around*) Nothing. Just checking.

As everyone pauses, Tulip runs on in front of them.

Last one up's a chicken!

They all exit, Polly and Jane dragging Midnight with them.

SCENE TWELVE

The interview room. Glue Boy holding Lucy's bag, examining it.

Glue Boy
Sorry, I just wanted to be sure. Yes, this is the one,
the one that she had on the beach. It's been a bad week.
We're all cracking up with thinking what to think.
We've made up a rhyme to say at the service tonight,
something that fits, we reckon, kind of a wish or prayer
to cover whatever's gone on, wherever she's gone.
I could run through it now, if you like? You'll say
if you think we've got it all wrong? OK then, I will.

As he begins, he is joined in the chanting at various intervals by the others in the waiting-room.

under the milk token of the moon
under the gold medal of the sun
under the silver foil of the moon
under the Catherine wheel of the sun
born below the sky's ceiling
at home with the moon's meaning
nursed on the dew's damp
twilight for a reading lamp
tribe of the blue yonder
Cub Scouts of Ursa Minor
the east wind for a hair-dryer
Mercury for a shaving mirror
a-bed afoot Jacob's ladder
head down on Jacob's pillow

heaven's sitting tenants
meteorites for birthday presents
Masai of the stone deserts
stage-lit by daffodil heads
Orion's belt for a coat peg
Uranus for an Easter egg
tumbleweed of the world's park
hearers of the world's heart
ears flat to the earth's floor
thawed by the earth's core
needled by Jack Frost
high priests of the long lost
passed over by Mars
pinned down by the North Star
some type of our own kind
branded with real life
Lobby Ludds of the outback
seventh cousins gone walkabout
Navaho of the tarmac plains
snowdrifts for Christmas cakes
groupies of the new age
Venus for a lampshade
Jupiter for a budgie cage
Saturn for a cuckoo clock
guardians of the joke dogs
Jack Russells in tank tops
Sirius for a pitbull
Pluto for a doorbell
Neptune for night-nurse
civilians of the universe
Eskimos of the steel glaciers
St Christopher's poor relations
citizens of the reservations
under the bullet hole of the moon
under the entry wound of the sun
under the glass eye of the moon

under the bloody nose of the sun
under the cue ball of the moon
under the blood orange of the sun
under the sheriff's shield of the moon
under the blowtorch of the sun
under the stalactite of the moon
under the nuclear blast of the sun
under the hammered nail of the moon
under the cockerel's head of the sun
under the iceberg tip of the moon
under the open heart of the sun
under the cyanide pill of the moon
under the screaming mouth of the sun
under the chocolate coin of the moon
under the chocolate coin of the sun

The Biggest Geometric Event
You Could Ever Witness

Simon Armitage interviewed by Jim Mulligan

In his isolated cottage on the hills outside the last Yorkshire village before you cross into Lancashire, Simon Armitage writes poetry, radio documentaries and, latterly, *Eclipse*. He had a conventional education at a large comprehensive school followed by college and Manchester University. At school he read poetry but wrote little as a student. However, when he was working as a probation officer, he started to write.

> I was living a double life at the time. I was driving through the cutting over the Pennine Watershed into Lancashire to do my work and then I was coming back into Yorkshire, getting out of one set of clothes and into different clothes and writing, not with any particular ambition or objective. I was, and still am, obsessed with writing. I spend most of my time looking for things that will lend themselves to the purpose of poetry. And, although I write full time now, I have this mechanism in my brain where I try to think I'm not a writer and that way, if I'm not writing, I don't think I'm being lazy. If I tell myself endlessly that I am a writer and I suddenly stop I'll consider myself a failure.

Far from being a failure, Simon Armitage built up a collection of poems in magazines and had his first book published by Bloodaxe. Subsequently, Faber and Faber published three more collections.

> When I came to writing *Eclipse* initially I was going to write about something that happened in Hebden Bridge

where a girl was abducted. She was young and was hanging out with other young people and it happened on bonfire night which belongs to young people even though it is an ancient festival. There was a feeling that the kids knew something that they either wouldn't or couldn't tell. That was the territory I wanted to get into: knowledge without being able to see it, intuition, instinct. But I realized there were too many agonies associated with writing about a real event so I found a venue and a time for an exploration of disappearance – a beach on 11 August 1999 when we will witness the last total eclipse of the sun this millennium. That's the biggest geometric event you could ever witness.

The play is structured with only children appearing. Adults are present but not seen. Each child in turn goes into an interview room and makes a statement about the version of events which is either the one being remembered or one being created. Between the monologues there is a series of flashbacks to the day when the eclipse occurred and Lucy Lime appears and disappears. Each person has a different version of the event and up to the point of the eclipse four children give their versions, telling us about themselves and moving the narrative on. After the eclipse there are two more monologues.

I am aware that the children tip from being childish into being child-like and sometimes into having adult sensations and sayings. That is what is fascinating about children in that age between being young and becoming old. I think very young children have a particular special quality that relates to a primitive and ancient knowledge. As they grow up they lose this intuition just as the human race has lost some of its instincts. Lucy Lime is not meant to be a celestial creature who arrives on earth only to create havoc. Neither is she meant to be an ordinary child. She is somewhere in between. She brings modern ideas to the other children who are still caught up in old-fashioned ideas.

Lucy Lime is not entirely truthful. When she tells the story about her rebirth as she emerges naked from the canal with a new self-knowledge, she tells the story because she needs to convince the twins that they must give up their make-up and fripperies, she cheats at arm-wrestling and she wins the children's treasures by lying to Midnight.

Everyone lies up to a certain point. Lucy Lime says what she needs to say in order to be herself and to get others around her to accept her version of herself. I think we all have different versions of ourselves based on other people's ideas. Lucy certainly manipulates but then we all manipulate. She's just very good at it. They are frightened of her because, as a complete stranger, she is able to get them to do things they didn't think possible. They recognize she has power over them and they aren't sure where that process will end.

Simon Armitage uses different language registers in *Eclipse*: there are realistic scenes which veer off into the language of rhymes, dreams and fantasies; the monologues mix up the version of the eclipse with early life memories, earthy humour and carefully polished images; there is a song which is a mixture of balderdash and resonances of losing something and gaining something; there is Glue Boy's final rhyme.

The whole play is about occlusion, what is behind and what is in front, and I tried to write it so that some motifs came up constantly – disguise, masks, being in the dark, future present and future past. The last monologue is supposed to exist somewhere between a prayer and an alibi. Glue Boy explains that it is something they have concocted to say at a memorial service, so in a sense it is a token of their concern. But it

is also an alibi in the sense that something as difficult to
fathom as this could be concealing something else.
Many of the elements are of people living without a roof
under the stars. The very real is set against the very
abstract. Some parts are set in the here-and-now, others
are cosmological.

Simon Armitage believes that we have become
disconnected from the world we came from and this
process accelerates so that as we move further away from
our origins we move further away from explanations.
However, one way to make the reconnections is through
language used by poets. He sees poets as shamans who can
communicate with other realities of the self.

Most poets are after some version of the truth, not all of
them and not all the time and not always successfully.
I'm not anticipating anything from *Eclipse*. I'm just
interested in what will happen. After all, written down,
it's only half done. What will be interesting will be to see
how they perform it because every character has a
duality and can be played as completely innocent or
completely guilty. There are a number of ways this play
can be balanced. If they try to look for deep meanings it
might be too difficult. The best way is just to dive in and
have a go. That's what I did. I held my breath and dived
in. I don't think I've come up yet.

Simon Armitage is a Faber poet and a frequent
broadcaster on television and radio. His previous books
include *Zoom!*, *Kid*, *Book of Matches*, *Dead Sea Poems*
and *Moon Country* (with Glyn Maxwell). In 1993 he was
the *Sunday Times* Young Writer of the Year. Faber will
publish a new collection, *CloudCuckooLand*, in 1997.

Production Notes

The play is set in August 1999 in Cornwall. An unseen
group of adults is gathered on the headland, out of
scientific curiosity, to watch the total eclipse of the sun
while their teenage offspring are on the beach below, more
concerned with myth, magic and the inexplicable. A
strange girl appears to challenge each and every one of
them, then vanishes. The action of the play is intercut by
scenes in a police station where the friends try to make
sense of and come to terms with her disappearance.

There are cave entrances on the cliff face and a broken
electric fence dangles down from the headland above. The
design should concentrate on finding a few basic elements
(perhaps sand, a usable rock, circle, sky) to capture the
mysterious world of the beach and the contrast with the
controlled order of the police station. These two places
probably need to co-exist within the one setting, or at least
change easily.

Lighting and sound should take into account the sea
and the time of day (which is afternoon) and, of course,
the wonder of the great eclipse.

At one point Lucy sets fire to a scarf and tosses it up in
the air. This effect could be faked with paper which is
easily extinguished but you will need to consult your local
fire officer as to what will be allowed on stage. You may
have to create your own imaginative alternative. The
electric-shock effect can be achieved with a combination of
sound and acting.

CASTING

There is a cast of seven (three male, four female) aged
between fifteen and twenty-one who, apart from the
stranger Lucy Lime, know each other very well. Klondike
is the eldest. He carries a leather bag stuffed with objects
which he slowly reveals to Lucy Lime in Scene 7: among
other things, the skin of a poisonous snake, a stick from a
silver birch, a bear's tooth, a cat's claw and a meteorite.
When we first encounter him on the beach he carries the
skeletal head of a bull. He is a natural leader and is
sexually aware. Tulip is a tomboy and wears Dr Marten
boots and a red headscarf worn like a pirate; Glue Boy
uses a plastic bag. Midnight is male and blind. At the time
of the eclipse he is wearing shades and a crucifix: he is
going through a religious phase. The twins, Polly and Jane,
should be as similar as casting will allow. Some thought
needs to be given to their change in appearance from vamp
to soft and feminine, after their encounter with Lucy Lime,
and to which of the two images has stayed with them for
the scenes in the police station. Lucy is bright, assertive
and practical, she dresses simply and in green.

QUESTIONS

1 Why is the group so interested in the eclipse?
2 How is the eclipse celebrated in other cultures?
3 How do the group members know each other?
4 Is Lucy real or imagined, an angel or a demon?
5 In what ways are the group members in touch with their
  imaginations, their primitive instincts and the
  supernatural?
6 What causes Lucy's disappearance?
7 As individuals, how are they affected by their meeting
  with Lucy Lime?

EXERCISES

1 The group members have an easy rapport. They trade
   rhymes and play word games and together tell the story
   of what happened to them on the afternoon of 11
   August. Have the group collectively describe what
   happened after Lucy's disappearance which led to them
   sitting in the police waiting room.

2 Look at one of the monologues, for instance Klondike's
   in Scene 7. Have him direct it at: his parents; the police;
   the rest of the group; the audience. Decide how the
   delivery changes, which works best and why.

3 A lot of mystery and ambiguity surround the plot of
   Eclipse, this means that the characters have even greater
   need to tell the story clearly. 'Hot-seat' the actor playing
   Lucy by having her recount the events of the afternoon
   accurately from her point of view. Have the rest of the
   group question her closely in role.

4 All the objects in the play should fit the actions of the
   characters. They aren't magic or symbolic. Select a few
   of the actors and their most prized possessions. Have
   them describe how they came by them and why they are
   special to them. Have them experience the feeling of
   them being taken away and relate this to the loss of the
   bracelet, the case, the boots, the skull, the stone and the
   crucifix in the play.

5 Imagine yourself on a beach. Lie down in a circle with
   your eyes closed. Listen to the sounds close by and in
   the distance. Focus on a few very closely. Smell the sea
   and feel the sensation of the breeze and the sand on
   your body. As a group, without opening your eyes, find
   words to describe vividly the beach of your imagination.
   One by one, throw images into the circle. Some might
   overlap but don't allow pauses and let the images grow
   in strength and momentum.

6 Take the vivid poetic passage in Scene 12. Cut it up into about thirty chunks and number them chronologically. Have the group pick up a number of them at random and move into their own space in the room. Have each speak their small section imagining they are speaking to a group of ten, then twenty, then fifty, but with a very clear image of what they are describing in their heads. Now sort out the sections so that they can be spoken in the order that they were written. Have the group run through the section and listen to the different quality of the voices and the effect it has when spoken from different levels and parts of the room.

Suzy Graham-Adriani
February 1997

THE GOLDEN DOOR

David Ashton

Data

The Golden Door is a twelve-slot myth.

There are seven single actors but equally important is a team of performers who create all the music and various sound effects, also making and operating the strange mutant beings who inhabit the world-under. A possible idea is for them to be dressed in a team strip blending with the colours of the cave walls and dark red clay stalactite/ stalagmite formations which sprout out from odd angles. This would enable the team to appear and disappear as if by magic.

A short word on the single characters, but this is meant only as a small help for the beginning and is to be abandoned once the actors hit their stride.

The Tribe They call themselves the Jagged Ones, and each has a lightning streak marked down the face. None of these markings are the same size and colour, but depend on individual inclination. Their clothes are also to their own expression but it might be nothing too garish – a lot of the time they may not want to advertise their presence. So . . . the Tribe. In order of appearance (except for one):

Zip, storyteller, the keeper of the flame, myth-maker. He uses imagination like a weapon, and he has a great hunger for a world other than the one he lives in.

Reuben, headstrong, powerful. His first movement is to hit out at anything that threatens, but underneath is a childlike quality. He loves stories and yearns to believe them.

Skin, the youngest. Her fear often drives her to acts of misplaced bravado. She is not yet formed and desperately wants to be one of the gang. Imitates and adores Big Helen.

Moochie, the chef, the cook. Sly and conniving, he has a dirty mind which occasionally surprises him with its insights and bravery. Always looking for the quick way out, the easy option, he never finds it.

Big Helen, female warrior of the tribe. First instinct, kill; second, kill quicker. She has made herself hard as rock and despises weakness, but her emotions run deep and raw. Trusts no one except . . .

Cherokee, a Samurai Geronimo, the hunter. Silent, in speech and movement, he regards life as death-in-waiting.

And lastly, one who puts the cat amidst the pigeons . . .

The Princess Don't be fooled by the ankle socks and blonde hair, this girl does not blink easy. A deep and devious visionary.

SLOT 1   TRICKY ICARUS

Music/sound of a wild and scary vision.

A figure lies on the ground, that of a young girl. She wears a pretty patterned dress, with white ankle socks and black shoes. Her blonde hair is spread out on each side, obscuring the face.

We can see her because a door-shaped section of the roof has pulled back and a yellow rectangle of light is shining down on her. She is directly below and it appears that she may have fallen through from the opening above.

The section slides back, the light disappears and the music fades as darkness falls again.

SLOT 2   FINDING THE LADY

Echoey sounds, a dripping damp atmosphere as the blue-white light of the world-under filters in. The walls are of a red clay texture but the red is not vibrant. Spores and weird fungi sprout amongst inky black slabs – like the cross-section of a school-meal hamburger.

The girl still lies there, motionless. Dragging footsteps as a dark giant figure comes out of the rocks and moves towards her. Menace. Danger. Its shadow falls across the girl and the Giant makes the hungry rumbling noise of a meal in prospect.

Just as it is about to pounce, another, much smaller shadow is thrown across the sleeping girl. It is Zip. He produces a toy windmill and blows it so that the propellers whizz round. Then he looks up at the Giant with no fear whatsoever.

Zip So – a Giant, right?

The Giant growls assent. Zip carefully packs away his windmill.

A hungry Giant?

Another growl.

A *slimy* Giant.

Angry growl and a swipe which Zip nimbly avoids. He starts to storytell, keeping out of range the whiles.

There was once a Giant who kept everyone in fear, who *ate* everyone in fear. He would munch people's heads while they were still crying out. In fear. Chew off the top-knot and suck up the rest through the neck. He would suck and suck and suck till there was nothing left but skin. Which he would throw aside. Being fastidious. Like that.

The Giant laughs and nods his head. He likes this story.

Then one day, a little tiny man appeared. So small the Giant could hardly see him, let alone catch or chew or suck through top-knot!!

He moves towards the Giant and speaks softly.

The little tiny man had thousands of friends, all the same size, and they hopped up all over the Giant's body, making their way into every orifice. Every *known* orifice. (*Beat.*) Then, at a given signal – they each pulled out a horribly sharp tiny little needle, and at another given signal – they all plunged in!! Every *known* orifice. Agonistic. Total agonism. The pain was . . . the pain was . . .

The Giant lets out a terrified roar of pain, and anguish.

That bad. Right. Then the Giant saw his hands were covered in blood, and the blood was forming words . . .

He brought his hands together the better to see –

Zip brings his hands together, palms facing up towards him, and the hypnotized Giant does likewise.

And the words formed a message, and the message formed was . . .

He beckons the Giant to bend down, pauses for effect, then hisses the words into its ear.

'This – is only the beginning – '

The terrified Giant lets out a howl of agonized fear and stumbles away to hide from tiny men. Zip watches him go with some scorn.

What a craphead.

He moves to the girl and eases back her hair to reveal the face. She is fair of countenance, with blue eyes and cherry-red lips. She also has a silver band across her forehead with a diamond in the middle. He whistles softly in alarm.

A Princess. Oh dear. That's bad. That's just about as bad as it can get.

Snap out the lights. Bring in the dark.

SLOT 3   EVERYBODY FREEZE

Lights up. The damp dripping noises are occasional and in the distance. We are now at the cave headquarters of the Jagged Ones . . . Weird debris and the walls festooned with trophies of battles won. A large passage of graffiti slashed through clay announces JAGGED ONES RULE *and another the contemptuous* PUS BALLS EAT SLIME; *a third and more sober warns* THE WITCH – NO MERCY. *The*

*downward lightning flash of the Tribe is also cut into the
wall to indicate that this is their kingdom.*

    *The Princess, still apparently comatose, is now lying on
her back with her hands folded neatly on her stomach.
Three members of the Tribe, Reuben, Moochie and Skin,
are squabbling as they hover over her. Reuben is
threatened and aggressive, Skin is being contrary and
Moochie has his own sly agenda. Zip looks on from a
distance.*

Reuben We should kill her!
Skin Why?
Reuben Shut up, Skin –
Skin I can ask –
Moochie We should look up her skirt.
Skin and Reuben What?!
Moochie Just a thought.
Reuben We should kill her. Dead!
Skin We should wait. Till Big Helen gets back. She'll
  know.
Reuben Big Helen . . . (*derisive singsong*) Skin loves Big
  Helen, Skin loves Big Helen –
Skin Shut your gob gob, Reuben! Gob it shut!

    *She strikes a threatening pose which Reuben laughs at,
but Moochie is still on a different tack.*

Moochie We should just look up her skirt.
Skin Why?
Reuben What'll that tell us?
Moochie Where she comes from.

    Beat.

Skin You're a pervert, Moochie –
Moochie Makes sense to me.
Reuben We should just kill her –
Zip Go ahead, then.

At this interruption, the other two move away, leaving a suddenly defensive Reuben facing Zip.

Go ahead. (*Beat.*) Kill her.
Reuben What with?
Zip I don't know. You're the killer. A rock, a Cherokee ice-pick, a scabstone, a slab – with a slab, bash out her brains. Any squelchy bits land on you, Moochie'll lick them off.

Moochie makes a noise of disgust. Not his bag. Skin laughs provokingly at Reuben.

Reuben All right, I will.
Zip Go ahead. Bash, bash, bash.

A battle of wills between them, but Zip could also have another reason in that he may be trying to find out just how 'comatose' the Princess really is. Reuben picks up a large chunk of rock and stands irresolutely over her body. Zip speaks coldly:

Go ahead, Reuben.
Skin Big-time warrior –
Zip Shut up, Skin.

Reuben lifts the rock up into the air, but that's all. The stand-off is broken by the arrival of Big Helen and Cherokee. At first Big Helen doesn't notice the situation as she disgustedly dumps the contents of a bag out on to the ground. It is a pathetically small amount of dark-coloured mushrooms.

Helen Bad harvest, worse and worse. We are in deep doo-doo –

No response. Cherokee has immediately picked up on the scene and she follows his eyes to discover for herself. She points to the prone figure on the ground.

What's that?
Zip A Princess.
Helen Crap. Is she dead? (*Beat.*) If not, *why* not??

Silence. A sheepish Reuben cradles his rock in front of him as if it absolves him from blame as Helen turns to Zip.

You know the rules, Zip. She's not us, she's not Tribe, she's a Pus Ball, she gets splattered, splat, splat.

She signals to Reuben but Zip steps forwards.

Zip I'm curious. Like Moochie. I want to know where she comes from –
Moochie (*getting out of the heat*) I'm not *that* curious –
Helen She's a Pus Ball!
Skin She doesn't *look* like a Pus Ball . . .

Big Helen gives her a withering glance and Skin shrinks back out of the fray.

Helen Splat – her – Reuben!!

Reuben still hesitates. In the heat of battle OK, but this is different.

Zip (*suddenly*) I claim the Circle!

Big Helen growls in anger but he is unfazed and smiles sweetly at her.

That's the rules as well – Moochie?

He steps back and Moochie grins in a conciliatory way at a beady-eyed Big Helen, as he scrapes a circle on the floor. He does so, moves back, then Zip and Big Helen stand opposite each other just outside the ring. They bow to each other in solemn ritual, then Zip steps in and declaims his point. When finished he comes out smartly and she steps in to make her response.

It seems to me we ought to wait,
   Until the sleeper doth awake –
Helen
It seems to me we ought to splat,
She's not the Tribe and that is that –
Zip
It seems to me she's mystery –
Helen
It seems to me she's history!

Laughter. Zip nods grimly to acknowledge a good hit, and Helen holds her place for another jab before moving out. She speaks with relish:

I think I hear a dying groan –
Zip
Why should you fear what is unknown –

This riposte hits a sore spot in Helen. She jumps back into the circle and shoves her clenched fist under the nose of Zip.

Helen I fear nothing! Nothing here!

Then she realizes that she's broken ritual and has to step back out, losing much face. Zip piles it on. He clenches his own fist, then opens it to reveal an empty palm.

Zip
Then nothing do we have to fear –
That's how it seems, it seems to me.

With these ending words, he comes out. Helen has to complete. She steps in and makes a fist again, but it lacks the certain power of before.

Helen
That's how it seems, it seems to me.

She steps out. They bow to each other as previously.

Silence. Moochie has been overseeing the contest, and now makes a formal pronouncement.

Moochie Black for splat, Big Helen. Zip counsels red. Red for wait.

There are various small rocks of these two colours, scattered around. The Tribe will vote by placing one or the other within the circle.
Big Helen goes first: black. Zip follows with red. Reuben hesitates a second, then places black. Moochie, for his own strange reasons, shuffles up, slides in an apologetic red, then sidles off without meeting anybody's eye. Skin is caught in the full blast of Big Helen's glare. She agonizes, then picks up black and throws it hastily into the circle. That leaves it three to two, with Cherokee to come. In his capacity as umpire of the ritual, Moochie turns to him.

Cherokee?

The hunter and Zip exchange impassive looks. Silence. The tension is broken when Cherokee suddenly whips out a rock shard, chiselled into an ice-pick shape (his killing blade), and holds it high in the air.
Big Helen smiles triumphantly at Zip, but he watches on without reaction as Cherokee dances gracefully round the circle towards the sleeping girl. He is now poised above her with the blade held high. Indrawn breath. Just as he is about to make a move, the Princess stirs and comes awake. A savage grin from Cherokee. He ghosts away from her and, as he passes the circle, casually tosses in red. This is much to Big Helen's surprise, but Moochie, as referee, holds up three fingers of each hand.

A holding operation.

Which means Zip gets his way for now, but the matter

*is not yet finished. The Princess looks around slowly
while the Tribe gather over her. A certain grim
amusement from Zip, as he takes the lead addressing the
girl.*

Zip In the nick. How fortunate.

No response. No sign of fear either.

You are with the Jagged Ones. Ones who would wish to
    bite through your belly button –
Moochie Oh yes!
Zip
    If you do not wish these pretty ankle socks stuffed
    in mouth so that your shrieks of pain may
    not disturb the larvae suppurating in the scalding
    guts of a dead leech, answer me this –
Reuben And you better get it right, baby girl –
Zip Where – come you from?

*A moment's silence, then she points gravely up towards
the roof of the place. They turn their faces up, and both
wonder and terror are writ large. If true, she is from a
place they have never seen but fear, and dream of, as the
dark fears and dreams of the light . . . the world-over.
    Lights out. A jagged, dangerous chord of sound. It
cuts off abruptly.*

SLOT 4   BEDLAM BOOGIE

*Lights up. A moment later. They are frozen in exactly the
same attitudes as before. Skin moves uneasily, then
suddenly screams as a slimy tentacle slithers round her
neck. From deep-freeze to total mayhem, more tentacles
emerge from all over the place, trying to take hold and
drag them off into the darkness. The Tribe are at once*

*galvanized into fighting mode. Big Helen howls happily –
this is her addiction.*

Helen Grabbers – greasy, slimy Grabbers – come and eat
your death, my darling ones!!

*She starts wrestling furiously with the tentacles. A grisly
mixture of comedy and danger – Moochie scuttles off to
safety; Zip's weapon is to blow his toy windmill, which
for some reason terrifies the Grabbers into drawing
back; Cherokee cuts Skin clear with a slash of his razor-
sharp blade and the severed tentacle wriggles off into
the shadows. The Princess seems bewildered by all this
and a wodge of tentacles hover above her, but just
before they pounce, it is the surprising figure of Reuben
who hurls himself at her, knocking her to the ground
and to safety. Cherokee slashes into a thicket of
Grabbers and there is a high-pitched squeal of pain,
followed by a mass exodus of tentacles. Reuben and the
Princess are left lying on the ground together. She seems
so fragile in his arms that he doesn't know where to put
himself. Finally, she speaks her first words.*

Princess Thank you . . . Reuben.

*Zip picks up on her use of the name, while an
embarrassed smile spreads across Reuben's face. This
tender moment is broken by a howl of dismay from
Moochie.*

Moochie They got the harvest – we are minus the Mush!

*In Tribe patois, 'Moosh' is the name for the various
fungi which sustain their lives. They look desperately
around and, sure enough, the harvest plus bag have
disappeared. A loud groan as they realize the
consequences of this theft.*

Skin Oh, no . . . not bloody leeches again!

Princess Leeches?

She has addressed this puzzled remark to Reuben but Big Helen picks up on it.

Helen That's right. Leeches. What d'you eat up there – angel droppings?
Princess Rice. And vegetables. And warm bread.
Reuben Rice?
Skin And veggy veg –
Moochie And warm bread?

They all are glassy-stomached at the prospect. Helen turns savagely to Zip.

Helen Trouble. Nothing but. We should splat!
Zip And then what – put her in the pot?
Helen That's a possibility. (*She turns back to the innocence-personified of the Princess and spits the words at her.*) Well, down here, Milady . . . we eat leeches. A nice big fat slimy leech stew – if we're lucky.

No one looks too thrilled at this prospect as Helen starts leaving preparations.

Jagged Ones, let's move out!!

The rest of the Tribe trail after her. Reuben dallies a moment and the Princess smiles at him. He leaves in rapid confusion. She follows him with her eyes, and then finds herself under the dispassionate gaze of Zip. A moment between them before he turns and exits. For a second, she thinks she's alone and a very different look comes over her face, but when she glances up, she is being observed from on high by Cherokee. An ironic smile, then he gestures that she follows the rest, and he will follow her.

> *Lights out. Darkness follows, with a chord music/ sound, vibrating of things to come.*

Moist slurping noises. The Tribe are crawling through what seems like a long slimy intestinal tunnel. Big Helen and Zip are in the lead, Moochie beside the Princess, Reuben and Skin behind them, with a watchful Cherokee bringing up the rear. As they scrape along, Moochie explains some gourmet ground rules, with great enthusiasm.

Moochie You see it's either Mush. Or leech. Mush is the natural preference, but there's less and less, drying up, dying out, hard to find. (*Beat.*) We may have to diversify from leech.

Princess Into what?

Reuben (*glumly from behind*) Blindworm –

Moochie Or gently broiled maggots, sky's the limit –

Big Helen Freeze.

At this hissed command, they all do so. She listens. In the distance can be heard a louder slurping noise. She nods as it confirms that they are on the right track. She signals them to go on. Moochie talks very quietly since they're getting near the target.

Moochie Dangerous. Down here. Many monsters.

Skin (*from behind*) I don't like maggots –

Moochie Shut up, Skin –

Princess Who are the Pus Balls?

Moochie Two tribes. Them, Us. We fight. But they haven't been around lately. Maybe they've checked out.

He chuckles happily at that. Big Helen stops and signals Cherokee up to join her. He slides by them all as if they don't exist, his mind totally fixed on the hunt. As he joins the leaders, Moochie looks keenly at the Princess. Both Reuben and Skin have dropped back, so the two are alone for a moment.

Tell me something –
Princess What?
Moochie Why did you . . .

*He points a finger to above, then turns it to indicate her
arrival amongst them.*

Princess Why did you want to look up my skirt?
Moochie Curiosity.
Princess Same here.

*That's all he is going to get, he realizes, as Big Helen
calls back and they bunch up together.*

Helen No more jaw!

*Moochie puts his fingers to his lips in warning. They are
at the catchment area. They crawl to the end of the
squelching tunnel and look out. There, slithering around
in a pool of goo, are some leeches the size of footballs,
squeaking happily to each other. Moochie leans to
whisper into the Princess's ear, rather enjoying the
sensation.*

Moochie Once leeches are beyond a certain age, they are
. . . non-edible. You got to get them young. Like these –

*Reuben comes up and whispers in her other ear, having
envied Moochie's audience with royalty during the
journey.*

Reuben But the trouble is . . . Mamma Leech. She doesn't
like to lose her babies . . .

*A signal from Big Helen and they all fan out so that
they surround the leeches. Big Helen is very much the
leader, so they await her command. She delicately draws
her finger across her throat in signal. They all follow
suit, then they pounce.*
   Chaos. The leeches are black and oily, so a wild

*sliding comedy ensues, punctuated by grunts of effort
and high-pitched squeaks of leech alarm. Just as they
seem to be caught, out they pop, and the whole business
starts all over again.*

*One of them slithers on to the Princess. She freaks
and throws it up into the air, where it is neatly speared
by Cherokee's knife blade. A pitiful mewing noise from
the dying leech. This is answered by a much louder
high-pitched squeal. While they've been occupied, the
vengeful Mamma Leech appears and sucks Skin and
Moochie into her cavernous maw. Muffled shrieks as the
rest of the Tribe pull them free. Although Skin seems
shaken but unhurt, Moochie lies motionless as an
anxious Zip leans over to lift him up.*

Zip Moochie – you functioning??
Moochie (*sly smile*) Quite enjoyed that.

*Zip gives an annoyed growl and lets Moochie thud back
on to the floor. They round up the remaining leeches
and Reuben shepherds Skin and the Princess out as they
back down the slimy tunnel. Zip, Big Helen and
Cherokee keep Mamma Leech at bay. As Moochie slides
past them, Big Helen spots a piece of material like a
long snake scarf which is wound round him, sticking
with leech slime. She hauls it off.*

Helen Where d'you get this??
Moochie In her belly. Mamma. Must have been.

*His eyes widen as he recognizes the material and he
shoots off down the tunnel to get out of trouble. Big
Helen has also recognized it and her face contorts with
pain. She howls in fury and hurls herself towards
Mamma Leech.*

Helen You killed my friend – you killed her! You – bloody
scummy slag – you Witch!!

*Zip and Cherokee grab her to hold her back. She still
has the scarf in her hand and raises it up, tears
streaming down her face.*

Helen Look – see – she ate her bones – she sucked her dry
– my love, my loved one! (*screams*) You hag – you
bastard witch!!!
Zip (*gently*) She's not the Witch, Helen. The Witch is
something else.

*Big Helen stumbles off down the tunnel, howling like a
banshee. Zip and Cherokee are left looking at each
other. This is a bad moment.*

Something else.

*They leave abruptly. Silence. Then the mournful high-
pitched squeak of Mamma Leech, grieving for her lost
offspring. Lights out.*

SLOT 6   ONE EYE BUT IT'S EVIL

*Lights up. We are back at the cave. A more peaceful scene
but deep undercurrents. Moochie is hunched over a pot of
sorts which is steaming on some sulphuric moss. This is
the leech stew and he is sprinkling some dubious-looking
herbs into the mixture. Big Helen, the limp scarf draped
round her neck, is sitting moodily at the side with Skin in
timid attendance. Zip is sitting alone, preoccupied with his
thoughts, and Cherokee is high up, overlooking the whole,
and also watching out for sneak attacks from enemies.
Reuben is by the Princess, talking quietly to her. They are
watching Big Helen, who is smoothing at the scarf as if it
were a pet animal.*

Reuben Rattler – she was Big Helen's . . . (*He links his
two fingers.*) They were blood sisters. She went off to

tangle with the Witch. Rattler. A no-win situation. The Witch must have gutted her, then left her out for Mamma Leech.

Moochie has suddenly been struck by a thought. He beckons Zip over and speaks softly so that Big Helen will not hear.

Moochie It has just struck me. If Mamma Leech slobbered all up Rattler, and these (*points to pot*) are of Mamma born, we may be about to eat bits of a dead comrade.

Zip looks at him for a long moment, then turns and walks back to where he was before. Moochie shrugs and goes back to his bubbling concoction. Reuben and the Princess have observed but not overheard the exchange. She picks up the thread of their conversation.

Princess Who is this . . . Witch?

Reuben sighs in frustration, then signals towards one of the Tribe.

Reuben Zip – he tells the story. Names the demons. I'm . . . action-bound.

She laughs quietly at this and he is emboldened to try his hand at naming, even if it's only the Tribe, indicating each as he speaks.

Big Helen, she's . . . more action. Skin is – a pain that's growing. Moochie is . . . Moochie, and Cherokee – cuts down to the bone.

Though he could not possibly have heard, Cherokee flashes a savage grin towards the Princess. She accepts it, then suddenly stands and walks towards Zip.

Princess (*to Zip*) Tell me about the Witch . . .

Most have a very uneasy reaction to this name, except

for hatred from Big Helen. Zip is silent for a moment,
his eyes move to the graffiti, THE WITCH – NO MERCY,
then he suddenly jumps up and into action.

Zip Do I hear a voice? Is it a voice I wish to hear? We all
hear voices –

He and the whole tribe suddenly let out a primitive
scream, causing the Princess to jump back in surprise.
Zip mockingly indicates for her to sit and be regaled.
She does so, arranging her dress primly around her.
Though he does love to tell stories, there is another
motive in that, by reciting the litany of the Tribe, he is
also restoring some flagging spirits.

We are the Jagged Ones, a mean and deadly organism! We
take your heart and slice in deep, till drops of blood do
stain your pretty little dress . . .
Princess Go on, please.

Her polite and prim reply rocks him back for a second,
then he redoubles the stream of words.

Zip We rule this world. World-under! Our enemies, we
piss on them –
Skin With mighty jetting water –
Zip Shut up, Skin – the Pus Balls, pale coward creatures,
we crack them every time, run them ragged, stamp their
guts, their slimy guts, we stamp them, chase them to the
Hollow Lands and there we stop!

He does so. Silence all round.

Princess Why?
Zip Because in Hollow Land resides . . . the Witch.
(*Beat.*) A shadow on the wall, at the corner of the eye,
back of the neck, a dancing ghost. She blows fear. Into
you. On the wind. Fear. Dancing. The like of which –
was never felt before.

Silence. Dread. He has named a demon. As if it were
dancing amongst them.

Princess Is she with them – the Pus Balls?
Zip She's not with us.
Moochie Come and get it!

He has been completely absorbed in his cooking. Zip
represses a shudder, calling back.

Zip In a minute. No rush.
Princess What does she look like?
Zip A shadow on the wall.
Reuben Skin claims a sighting.
Skin I did! Black hair, white face, humpty back, one eye,
red and evil, but I piss on her –
Zip and Reuben Shut up, Skin!!

Zip drops his declaiming attitude and gives a sidelong
glance at the withdrawn, so far silent Big Helen as he
speaks soberly:

Rattler couldn't take it. The stopping. The fear. She
tooled up. Into the Hollow Land. To kill the Witch,
she went.

They all look as Big Helen clutches the scarf to her,
hands clenching in pain. Moochie gives his noxious stew
a final flourishing swirl.

Moochie Come and bloody get it, pronto!

As the rest troop off unenthusiastically, Big Helen looks
at the Princess, tears forming in her eyes.

Helen She was my friend. My baby . . .

She turns away abruptly and follows the rest.
*   The Princess looks up to where Cherokee is watching*
intently.

Princess Does she blow fear into you as well, Mr
  Cherokee?

*He leaps down lightly to land, so that they are face to
face, very close. He smiles, places the tip of his finger on
the diamond in the middle of her silver headband, then
traces his finger down the side of her face. He wheels off
smoothly to join the others, who are gathered dubiously
around Moochie's pot.*

  *The Princess is alone for a moment. Her face is grave
and thoughtful.*

  Lights out.

SLOT 7   DREAMING OF THE LIGHT

*Poisonous, menacing sound/music as we bring up first a
light on the face of the Princess. She raises the leech stew
in a rough container to her lips. Her expression, on
tasting, indicates this to be a truly dreadful experience.
Music fades and we expand the light to include everyone
else. We are still at the cave, a few moments later. The
Tribe are sitting in a circle of which she is a part. The pot
of stew is in the middle, and they all look queasy except
for Moochie, who finishes off his portion with gusto.*

Moochie Any more for any more? (*No response.*) Ah,
  well . . . (*He helps himself to some more and slurps it
  down. Licks his lips judiciously.*) Not bad, not half bad
  . . . better tomorrow – once it gets a chance to settle.
Reuben (*painfully to the Princess*) Rice . . . and
  vegetables . . . ?

*The Princess nods. The Tribe look up once more to the
direction from whence she fell.*

Tell us . . . what it's like? Up there . . . world-over?

Helen She's not allowed, not to name, not to bring forth, she's not Tribe!

Reuben (*hotly*) She is an' all! She's sitting in the circle, she ate the bloody stew – sorry, Mooch – she's been past the Grabbers, Mamma Leech –

Zip And the Giant. (*ironic*) Dead to the world at the time of course, but . . . past.

Moochie And with Rattler gone – sorry, Helen, but . . .

Big Helen smiles but it has a chilling edge.

Helen That's all right, Moochie. She can take Rattler's place. She can be Tribe. *If* she walks blind. (*at Zip*) *Another* rule. And I call it.

Zip, for once, has been outsmarted and his face shows so. Cherokee grins and Moochie whistles softly.

Moochie That's deadly, but . . . if she wants –

Rules are rules. Zip takes a deep breath and confronts the Princess.

Zip Well, my sweet lady. To be Tribe. If that's your wish. Will you, won't you, walk it blind?

She glances round the faces and knows better than to ask for meaning. A moment, then she nods acceptance.
    Big Helen lets out a roar of delight, but there are danger and death in the air as she wraps Rattler's scarf firmly round the eyes of the Princess, rendering her totally unable to see. Helen smiles triumphantly at Zip as she does this. The Tribe then form a circle with the Princess stuck firmly in the middle. Silence, then Zip speaks in formal tones.

East, west, north, south – is your heart in your mouth?

A moment, then she nods again, and, as if that were a signal, the Tribe explode into action, howling frighteningly as they propel her faster and faster round inside the circle. She is buffeted with many blows and there is a violence which seems almost out of control. Then, just as suddenly, they stop, leaving her dazed and dizzy, swaying and gasping for air as she struggles to keep her balance. Three of the Tribe, Cherokee, Big Helen and a reluctant Skin, stand round her with their razor-sharp shards, pointed at her body, while Reuben stands behind with his arms outstretched. If she makes the wrong choice, she will be impaled on one of the blades. Zip speaks again.

You're walking blind. North, south, east, west – which way is best?

An electric moment. She sways heavily towards Big Helen's knife, then back again. For another moment she almost falls on to Skin, but then, when all seems lost, she appears to lose her balance and fall back fortuitously into Reuben's arms!! This time the howl is of relief and acceptance. The scarf is ripped off and thrown to a grim-faced Helen. Celebration as the Princess gasps for breath, the sweat streaming down her face – this was not something she sailed through. Zip steps in front of her, speaking to Reuben.

Bring the marking sticks.

Reuben moves off swiftly to return with a handful of different-coloured sticks which Zip offers solemnly to the Princess.

Make your choice.

She unhesitatingly picks one of vivid blue. Zip sounds a warning.

You'll be sticking out a mile.
Princess It's my colour.

301

Zip So be it. (*He takes the stick and carefully marks a lightning streak down her face. A grave moment.*) Tribe. I name her . . . Princess.
Whole Tribe Princess. So be it. Named. Tribe.

Silence. The Princess is supposed to say something solemn, but she's too knackered.

Princess May I sit down, please?

A nod of permission. She plumps down somewhat indecorously, but they're not finished with her by a long chalk. Zip moves in again.

Zip So, Princess. Now you can tell, and may the smallest lie rot your tongue black. What is it like up there?
Reuben Bring it forth, baby girl – what's it like?

A desperation to know. Even from the still hostile Big Helen and copycat Skin. A forcefield of fear and awakened curiosity, so the Princess must choose her words with care. The ordeal she's just been through gives edge to the delivery, no lyricism.

Princess Green. Warm. Light.
Zip Light?
Princess Light shines. In the morning. All day. Light . . . streams down. From the sky. A blue sky.

The Tribe ponder this terrifying prospect. Finally Moochie breaks the silence.

Moochie Weird.
Skin I piss on it –
Princess Shut up, Skin –

But she smiles as she says this. Zip lets out a howl of frustration. His passion/terror to know causes him to speak with rare ferocity.

Zip All right – spit it out, Princess – wet your knickers for

us, come on – spit it out – everything!!
Princess I can't tell everything –
Zip Everything – yes!

*The Tribe suddenly let out a concerted roar as they
move to surround her.*

Whole Tribe YES!!!

*The shout hangs in the air. She tilts her face upwards
and lets the words and images tumble out of her mouth.*

Princess It's so . . . beautiful. The sun shines, white clouds
. . . chase each other across the sky. River. A cold clear
river runs down from green hills. Fish . . . chase each
other –
Reuben Like the clouds!
Princess Like the clouds – Water. A pool of water, so still,
see your face, look at your face, so cold and clear.
Everything grows, ripe. Full of juice. And always. The
light. Shining. Out of. Into. All things. Everywhere, you
see that light.

*A long silence. Big Helen chokes with pain at the
pictures in her mind.*

Helen Liar – black tongue –
Princess So beautiful. You swim in the river. Cold. Clear.
So clean. Then lie . . . with the green grass all round.
The warm sun falls on you. The light pours in.

*They are all wrapped in this vision, but Zip is also a
storyteller.*

Zip Why'd you leave it then, Princess?
Princess There was a Golden Door. They told me not to
open –
Zip They?
Princess The King and Queen. They told me not to. But I
did. And I fell. All the way down. The next thing –

Zip I know about the next thing!

Princess No, you don't. (*Beat.*) The next thing . . . is how I get back. Up there. World-over.

Silence. A challenge in the air. Moochie worries over an item of the vision.

Moochie Water?

The Princess nods.

Cold?

The Princess nods.

Clear?

The Princess nods.

Clean?!

A final nod from the Princess.

Not sure I like the sound of that . . .

Reuben Are there like . . . other people? Besides kings and queens and stuff?

Princess Farmers. They grow. Plenty food for everybody. Bags of space. For everybody.

Reuben Is there . . . animals?

Princess Deer. Rabbit. And all the birds of the air. You could go there, Reuben.

Reuben Huh?

Princess I need to get back. I need to find the Golden Door. Will you help me?

He is bewildered and doesn't know how to respond. No one can quite look at each other, but Big Helen shoves through to face right up to the Princess.

Helen Listen, you black-tongued bitch. No help. Nothing. Leave us be. Where we are – is good!

Princess Damp. Dark. Cold. Stinking. That's your world.

Wouldn't you like to breathe some clean air, Helen?
Moochie There's that word *clean* again –

*Something in the last description of the world-over used
by the Princess has touched a chord in Skin's starved
little heart. She suddenly jumps to the side of the
Princess and pronounces defiantly:*

Skin It seems to me – we ought to help!
Zip (*amused*) Does it, now?
Reuben Yes, it does.

*He joins the other two. Moochie coughs in embarrassed
fashion as he slinks over to add a fourth.*

Moochie We could just . . . look through the door. We
don't have to go in. If we don't like it.

*Zip shakes his head at the developing situation and
addresses the Princess.*

Zip Just about as bad as it can be . . .

*Cherokee looks deeply into the eyes of the Princess,
smiles sardonically, then reaches out his hand to pull her
up.*

Looks like you're on your own, Helen.

*As he says this, and for his own reasons, he steps over to
join the group. Big Helen is desperate. A sudden
outsider in her own tribe.*

Helen It's a lie! She's not real. It's a dream. Not *real*. She is
a bitch-liar!!
Reuben *She* would've come. Rattler. Your friend. She
would've come, Helen.
Skin She was getting hemmed in.
Moochie Desperate bad.
Zip She thought . . . if she killed the Witch. It would lift
some of the darkness. Inside her head.

Helen She never told me – I would've helped her . . . (*She is stricken by what has been said and clutches at the scarf.*)

Princess (*softly*) Come on, Helen . . . I'll teach you how to dream.

Helen Bitch!!!

But her tears betray her and she almost stumbles in, to be caught and held by the group. For a second, she rests in their arms, then she wrenches free and gets as far away from the Princess as she can. The Tribe all face out in a circle with the Princess in the centre.

Reuben Tell us again, Princess . . .

Princess The sun always shines. White clouds . . . chase each other across the sky. A cold clear – river . . . runs down from green hills . . .

She talks. They listen. Some believing, some in doubt, some in fear . . . the light fades to black.

SLOT 8   TAKE A DEEP BREATH

Lights up. The Giant sits on a rock and groans dismally. He slowly reaches down, takes a handful of muddy earth, then puts his hand aloft and sprinkles it over his great shaggy head. He repeats the action, lamenting the whiles.

We are back where we saw the Princess at the beginning. Zip and Moochie, acting as scouts, pop their heads round some stuff and watch the Giant., They both look pretty done in as they converse in whispers.

Moochie What's he doing?

Zip Mourning.

Moochie Eh?

Zip To put earth. On the head. Is a sign of mourning.

Moochie What's he mourning?
Zip (*thoughtful*) Maybe, he doesn't have a Mrs Giant.
Moochie He should be celebrating.

*Zip gives him a scathing look. The Giant gets to his feet
and lumbers off, still wailing dismally.*
*Zip whistles softly back to signal all clear, then he
and Moochie emerge, followed at a distance by the rest
of the Tribe, save for Cherokee, who has business
elsewhere. The Princess is with Skin, who now adores
her. Big Helen, who wears the snake scarf tied round
her, is with Reuben at the rear. They all look extremely
travel-worn. Zip squats down to examine the ground,
then speaks up to the Princess.*

Zip This is where I found you. (*to the rest*) Her.

*He looks up to the roof. They all follow suit. Silence.
Big Helen states the obvious.*

Helen Bugger all do I see. Of any poxy Golden Door.
Zip (*vague gesture*) She could've fallen . . . sideways.
Rolled. Or bounced –
Princess I don't remember –
Helen Bounced??
Zip (*to the Princess*) You don't remember?
Princess I was unconscious!
Zip I keep forgetting.
Reuben What about instinct?
Princess What?!
Reuben Everybody knows. Where they come from. Don't
they?

No one responds to this. Reuben gets upset.

They do – don't they!

*Again nothing. No one likes to contemplate this. No eye
contact, much shiftiness. Reuben grabs the Princess and*

hauls her up, so that her feet are off the ground.

Instinct! Where fell you from? Bouncing, sideways, falling, if not here, where fell you from?!

His desperation is expressed in violence and anger, and the Princess seems unafraid to find her face shoved up against his. She leans back, so that he has to support her, and closes her eyes in concentration – then she suddenly shoots out a pointing hand in an upwards diagonal.

Princess That way!

General consternation at the direction indicated. Reuben drops her hastily back to earth.

Reuben Oh, hell's teeth!
Skin That's the Hollow Land. Witchy land. Evil eye and hunch back –
Moochie (*hopefully*) Have another go.
Princess No. It's there. I feel it. Instinct.
Helen Puke your instinct! (*to the others*) We can go back. Leave her. Go back –

Since the Hollow Land was indicated, Zip has been running stuff through in his mind and has come to a hard decision. He cuts into Big Helen's words of retreat.

Zip No. (*Beat.*) We go on.

His matter-of-fact tone infuriates Big Helen. This is a difference that has been boiling many years. She moves in close to him.

Helen It's you, isn't it? You're the one, stinking stories, stinking dreams, stinking pukey dreams – you want this, don't you? You want this!
Zip Yes, I do.
Helen Why?

Zip Because I'm fed up. Living in slime. And darkness.

Helen It's not that bad . . .

Zip It's dying. The whole caboodle. The Mush harvest is dying on us, we eat leaches and drink insect piss.

Helen We're King Tribe –

Zip King of what?! Inside a rotting tooth, big deal. (*He squints into the direction of the Hollow Land.*) I want to find out . . . if there's something else. And if there isn't – then I'll die happy.

Helen But that's the Hollow Land. Uncharted. We don't know!

Zip doesn't answer. She gives up on him and looks round for support, but finds none. She looks at the Princess, then speaks to all of them:

Why d'you believe her – why?!

The rest of the Tribe look at her blankly. They want to believe and that's that.

Zip All right – Jagged Ones – move out!

General activity as they get ready to go. Helen moves away in disbelief and Moochie sidles up to Zip.

Moochie What about Cherokee?

There is a high-pitched scream out in the darkness as some predator meets its fate. Zip smiles a trifle grimly.

Zip That's my boy . . . (*to Moochie*). Come on, Mooch. Take a deep breath, close your eyes and step off the edge of the known world.

Moochie looks none too convinced by this travel itinerary. Zip turns to the Princess.

You lead. We follow. That's the deal with royalty, is it not?

The Princess hesitates for a moment and all eyes are on her, then she moves off into the darkness. A collective deep breath and the rest follow. Big Helen is left in terrible isolation. She falls on to her knees, clasping at the scarf, and lifts her face upwards.

Helen Rattler – why didn't you tell me? I would've saved you. From the dark. I would've saved you . . .

A sob of breath as she struggles for control. She bows her head. At that moment, Zip steps out back from the shadows.

Zip (*gently*) Come on, Helen . . .

Without looking up, she extends a hand. He crosses to help her up but, as their hands touch, she pulls him violently down to the ground and straddles him, hauling him back by the hair with her arm round his windpipe.

Helen Don't feel sorry for me – (*She jolts him back painfully.*) Ever – ever feel sorry for me!

She shoves him down and hurtles off to follow the rest into the Hollow Land. Zip shakes his head painfully.

Zip All right, then – I won't.

A laugh from the shadows and Cherokee steps out. There is a smear of blood round his mouth and Zip is perturbed by this.

Don't go native on me, Cherokee . . . I got enough balls to bounce.

A savage smile is his only response as the light changes to black.

SLOT 9   THE BAD EAT

Darkness. Menacing nightmare music/sound. A harsh light throws a shadow upon the wall. The figure has a humped back and long talons sprouting from each finger. It raises its hands high into the air as if to strike downwards.

A piercing scream. Lights up. The screamer/dreamer is Skin, keeping watch while the rest sleep. They awake in a state of total confusion, hearts beating wildly as they look around for a sign of enemy action, but there's nothing happening.

Skin I saw her. The Witch. I saw her! Aggggh –

As she starts to scream again Zip crosses swiftly and clamps his hand, none too kindly, over her face. Shock. Silence. Zip hisses like an angry snake.

Zip I give you first watch, the easy-peasy lemon-squeezy, and you – devastate my sleep! What – are – you – doing?!
Skin I saw her – Witch – the old Witchy bitch –
Zip You saw – the little bags of snot that run around your empty brainpan!

Nevertheless, he and the rest check the place out with a certain amount of fear. But no sign of the Witch. He turns back to Skin.

Where . . . did you see her?
Skin All around – all around us –
Zip Aghh. Grow some pubic hair or something . . . useful!

He throws her aside and stands up breathing heavily. His reaction has been fraught and out of character. It is obvious that he and the others are exhausted. They all look completely strung-out, except for the Princess, who seems the same as usual.

Reuben Wasn't sleeping anyway – too hungry.
Moochie I was dreaming Mush. Big fat fungaloids.
Zip Where's Cherokee?

He has suddenly noticed the absence of the hunter. No one knows, but Moochie is hopeful.

Moochie Maybe he'll get lucky out there . . .

Zip nods a weary head and looks out into the surrounding gloom. The Hollow Lands are like a black, sterile honeycomb of passages which they have been stumbling through for a long, arduous time. When he brings his attention back to the Tribe, he meets with a triumphant smile from Big Helen. A turn-away from that encounters only the cool, dispassionate gaze of the Princess.

Zip (*to Princess*) Your instincts . . . stink!!

No reaction. Moochie has a hacking cough. Zip tries to comfort the ragged band.

Get some . . . sleep. Rest. I'll – I'll keep watch . . .
Helen Thank you, great leader. Sleep. Rest. (*Beat.*) For what?

He bows his head, no response coming to mind. She answers her own question.

To look for what is not. Not there. Ever. Was. Or will be.
Princess We'll find it. You must have faith.

Big Helen nearly chokes with laughter on that one. She ignores the Princess and continues goading Zip.

Helen We look. Again. Then nothing. Again . . . then nothing. Again, then . . . what? What – great leader?

Moochie coughs painfully in the silence.

Moochie We go back.
Zip No.

Moochie All right – we *crawl* back –
Zip No!

He moves away and puts his hands up to his head, as if trying to keep it from falling off. The Princess pleads with Moochie.

Princess Moochie, you have to believe –
Moochie I did. I followed. But I have run out of . . . cred – ulosity. (*He coughs again in pain, then something strikes him.*) Mind you. I would like to look up your skirt . . . just the once.
Princess When we find it. I promise you.

A smile between them but nothing is settled. The Princess looks around. Skin, despite her inward terror, is hanging on in there, but Reuben will not meet her eye. Someone who will, with a vengeance, is Big Helen.

Helen You're running out of time, Goldilocks. This is the Hollow Land. Empty and dead. You led us here. To die hungry . . . and empty. (*mockingly*) Sing a little song, Princess – a lullaby – to ease our aching bellies. Be my guest.

Big Helen laughs, but the Princess takes her at her word. She stands erect, closes her eyes and sings in childlike fashion.

Princess
Hold my hand, don't be scared
Even though the cupboard's bare
You will find
Peace of mind
Behind the Golden Door.

Everbody wants to be
Underneath the willow tree
There you find

Peace of mind
Behind the Golden Door.

Close your eyes, so it seems
Like the fish that's in the stream
You will find
Peace of mind
Behind the Golden Door.

*The simple melody and words have a hypnotic effect,
lulling them all, even Big Helen, into closing their eyes.
Then the spell is broken as a thrown sack arcs through
the air and lands with a thump in the middle of them.*

   *The thrower is Cherokee. The Tribe all stare at the
sack, then Moochie steps forwards and gingerly picks it
up to empty it out. No one knows what to expect and
there are yells of delight when out of it tumbles a pile of
huge livid yellow mushrooms.*

Moochie Mush – big fat beautiful Mush – ahhh, come to
daddy!!

*They all pounce on the large fungi and are about to
cram them into their mouths when a scream from the
Princess stops them in mid-action.*

Princess No!! Don't touch – don't eat –
Moochie Don't eat? Down my gullet they will go –
Zip Wait a minute, she could be right, that's not a known
colour –
Moochie I don't care if it's pigment of the anal canal,
down my gullet –

*The Princess lets out a high, piercing shriek. The sound
is eerie, chilling . . . to freeze the blood and stop them
where they stand. In the frozen silence, she moves
towards Cherokee.*

Princess Cherokee . . . did you eat?

He nods. She bows her head for a moment, and when she looks up there are tears in her eyes.

Show me. Show me where you found . . .

He stares at her. For once, he does not smile.
Lights out.

SLOT 10   DEATH IS THE HUNTER

Lights up. A short time later.
The Tribe stand in front of a wall-surface section of the Hollow Land. High up on it are the yellow mushrooms, with a bare patch where Cherokee has prised them off. Total silence. They all watch the Princess as she looks up at the Mush. When she speaks, there is a tone in her voice not heard before.

Princess I thought I'd killed them off. But they made a come-back. Damnation.

She seems lost in deep reflection and regret. The Tribe still clutch the yellow growths but don't dare to eat them yet. Big Helen finally steps forward so that she is directly in the eyeline of the Princess. Big Helen raises a chunk of Mush to her lips. She does not bite in, but the challenge is there.

Helen Why not?!

For a moment the Princess hesitates, then she moves off to another part of the wall surface. She pulls at something and what appears to be part of the wall is revealed to be a black covering which falls to the floor. Behind it is a group of hanging figures which send a shock wave through the Tribe, who immediately adopt a fighting posture and howl out their war-cry.

315

Whole Tribe Pus Balls! We fight, we kill, we eat their guts!

The cry echoes then dies as the tribe register the curious stillness of the hanging figures. The Princess does not move and it is left to Moochie to step forward cautiously and sniff at the feet of the bodies in suspension. He then looks closely up at them.

Moochie They're just skin.
Skin I'm Skin!
Moochie So are they. Nothing but. Not even bone.
Princess They climbed up to eat the yellow Mush. Died instant. I covered them up. Didn't want to touch.

Moochie has been poking at a Pus Ball with his finger but at these words jerks hastily backwards.

Moochie Thanks for telling me!

Then his eye falls on Cherokee. As the import of the Princess's words strikes home, they all look at the hunter. Zip moves towards him.

Zip You ate?

Cherokee nods.

You sure?

Another nod, then Cherokee holds himself very still as if he senses poison in the blood. Reuben turns to the Princess, trying to cling on to a glimmer of hope.

Reuben (*to Princess*) But you said instant – instant means . . . like right away!
Princess Not him. Too tough. But . . . it will come.

Cherokee speaks his first words.

Cherokee Death. My friend. (*Beat.*) Good –

316

He bends over in agony as a spasm of pain hits him. Big Helen moves towards him, but he whips out his killing blade and keeps her at bay.

Cherokee Most welcome!

He doubles over again. It is a terrible sight to behold and, in his desperation, Zip turns to the mystery in ankle socks.

Zip Yellow Mush, Pus Balls, you find – you tell us you fall down, you – who the hell are you??

The Princess moves over to Cherokee, who straightens up despite his pain. They gaze deeply into each other's eyes, two equal powers of nature. The communication between them causes Cherokee to grin in savage recognition, then he grabs her hair and makes a scalping motion with his knife. The hair (a wig) comes off in his hand to reveal a crop of jet-black hair underneath. He throws back his head and roars with laughter, as she turns to the bewildered Tribe and answers Zip's question.

Princess I'm the Witch.

At these words, all hell breaks loose. The Grabbers swoop in from the sides and as the Tribe move to avoid them, they run into a vengeful Mamma Leech. They recoil from her only to find the other exit filled with the looming figure of the Giant. Panic. It seems as if they're doomed, but then the Witch/Princess hauls at a section of the wall to reveal a hidden opening.

Jagged Ones – let's go!

She runs off, followed by the rest, but in the panic Skin gets knocked to the ground and seized by the Grabbers. When Big Helen tries to go to her aid, she runs into the Giant, who bats her aside into the gaping maw of

Mamma Leech. Things look bad, but then Mamma Leech gives a high-pitched squeak of pain as a blade is plunged into her slimy flesh. The dying Cherokee pulls Big Helen away, then cuts Skin free. Skin runs off to safety, but at the escape-hole, Big Helen turns back to see Cherokee almost cut in two by a spasm of terrible pain. He is enmeshed by the Grabbers. The Giant stands back, but Mamma Leech does not. The hunter is now the hunted prey. Just before he is engulfed, Cherokee hauls himself up proudly and throws his killing blade over to Big Helen. A last sardonic smile. The monsters slobber and haul him down.

Black-out on Big Helen's scream.

SLOT 11 JACOB'S LADDER

The Tribe are now scattered every which way. A single spot picks out the Witch/Princess as she runs along. She drops to her hands and knees, gasping for breath. As she fights to recover herself, a knee thuds into her back and an arm grabs her windpipe as her head is jerked back. The assailant is Zip. He is in a mood to kill. They are both held in a small circle of light.

Zip Give me one good reason not to break your neck –
Witch Dream – I gave you a dream.
Zip You gave me a lie!!
Witch No – I saw it – world-over – a vision. I had a vision.
Zip Did you now??

He jerks her head back cruelly so that she is hardly able to breathe, but she forces the words out, despite the pain.

Witch I saw me. Climbing. It was there. Above. The

Golden Door, it was there. All of you. With me.
Climbing. The Jagged Ones.

Zip A bloody vision!!

*He throws her down in disgust, but she wheels round
like a cat and confronts him, face to face. They are both
now on their hands and knees.*

Witch Just like your stories, Zip – just as real. (*She closes
her eyes.*) I hate this world. Just like you. I hate it. The
slime. The darkness. Watching the darkness eat the
light! So . . . I fasted. I purified. I waited in the dark.
And it came to me. My vision . . . The Golden Door.

*Her intensity is powerful, and despite his every wish Zip
is affected by her words. Her eyes yet closed, she seems
locked into an inner world. He fights against his desire
to believe.*

Zip Did your . . . vision tell you to dress up pretty?

She opens her eyes and smiles.

Witch No – that was my idea. I knew you had a soft spot
for princesses.

Zip How come you knew?

Witch I'm a witch, remember?

*He almost responds, then recalls the ugly present and
decides to let her run.*

Zip Well, you better get going, Witchy –

Helen No – I think not.

*At these unexpected words, the lights snap back on to
reveal that the pair are surrounded by the rest of the
Tribe. How long they have been listening is anybody's
guess, but there are no friendly faces to be found. Big
Helen steps out, holding the blade before her. The
Witch/Princess gets warily to her feet.*

You killed Cherokee.
Witch No.
Helen You killed my love. Rattler. You killed her too.
Witch No. Mamma Leech got her –
Reuben Why didn't you leave us be?
Witch I had to. You were in my vision. I needed you. To make it work –

But while she has turned towards Reuben, the opportunity for attack is seized by Big Helen. She steps behind the Witch and jerks her back so that her throat is totally exposed, with the blade pressed up against it.

Helen When the blood jumps out of your neck – I'll sing you a little song, shall I? For Rattler and Cherokee – I'll sing a little song.

The Witch sees many emotions on the faces before her but no one can step outside the laws of the Tribe. She accepts her fate.

Witch So be it.
Helen Kiss it all goodbye, you black hag bitch!

A moment of shocking stillness, then as Big Helen prepares to draw blood with a savage slicing motion there is a weird chord of sound/music and they are caught in a radiant light as the roof above parts in rectangle shape. It is the golden door. They are all transfixed as they look up at the sight. The Witch wrenches herself free from Big Helen and again lets out that eerie shriek to chill the blood.

Witch That's it. What I saw. My vision – it's true! There. It does not lie. My vision. (*She bows her head.*) Oh my dark earth mother – my shadow, my dark demon – thank you – thank you for the gift of light . . .

*Her eyes swim with tears as she regards the Tribe,
frozen like statues in the golden beam. They are scarcely
able to believe what they see, something stirring in their
hearts.*

It's true. The light. Above. World-over. The land. Like I
saw it. My vision – it's true!

*Big Helen lets out a howl of frustration and pain, and
lunges to shut this voice from speaking any more, but
Reuben pins her from behind. He is possessed by a new
hope, as are the others.*

Reuben No! We're going to need her.
Helen What?!
Zip If we go. We'll need her.
Moochie We can always kill her later, once we're settled
in –
Skin Shut up, Moochie – (*to the Witch*) You did see . . .
fishes in the stream. You saw that?
Witch Yes. (*Beat.*) And other things.

*Something in her tone awakens immediate suspicions in
Zip.*

Zip What *other* things??

*A roar off interrupts them, as the Giant lumbers into
view.*

Moochie Christ, doesn't he ever give up?

*Big Helen uses the distraction to pull free, still aiming to
maim.*

Helen She killed. Rattler. Cherokee.
Zip This place killed them.
Witch It's dark, it's dying and it kills you, Helen –

*Another roar. No time to lose. Big Helen glances round
the faces of the Tribe and sees that once more she will*

have to accede to the majority, but she fixes the Witch
with an implacable stare.

Helen We're not finished, Witchy –
Witch So be it.
Zip Let's go, Jagged Ones – up and on!

Urgency as the menacing Giant moves towards them.
Zip uses himself as a human lift-up for the rest so that
they can reach a high ledge, and then climb upwards.
The Witch goes first and Reuben is about to follow
when Moochie steps in with a sly but determined look
on his face.

Moochie Cook's perks . . .

He finally gets to look up her skirt as he follows on.
Everyone scrambles and inches upwards towards the
glowing rectangle, but Zip's luck runs out as he hurls
Skin up to the ledge only to find himself with the
Giant's large figure looming over him. Reuben dangles
his hand down from the ledge, but Zip is a few
agonizing inches short when he jumps up. The Giant
moves ever closer so that there's no chance of a second
leap. It doesn't look good, as they all stare down at the
scene below.

Zip (*desperately*) Now – the story is – the Giant could
have killed –

An approving growl from the Giant.

easily, but – chose instead to help and lift the handsome
young prince to safety!

A sceptical grunt from the Giant.

And, in the land above, world-over . . . whenever the story
is told . . . the Giant's name lives on for ever – (*He*
suddenly produces his favourite toy windmill and blows

it so that the propellers whir round.) And I'll throw this in as well . . .

The Tribe gaze down helplessly as the Giant reaches for Zip. To help or to kill? Which will it be?
  Lights out.

SLOT 12   HERE BE DRAGONS

Blinding white light as they stumble out of the door-shape into the world-over. After a gap, Zip comes out last, so the Giant chose immortality and the windmill. The Tribe shrinks back, their eyes dazzled by this glaring, luminous world. The Witch at once hands each a set of sunglasses. (Don't ask me where she got them, she's a witch, remember?) They put them on and look around in one direction, but a terrifying primitive animal roar from prehistory brings their heads whipping round in the direction of the noise. What they see does not inspire a feeling of well-being.

Zip Other things?
Witch Other things.
Helen I knew it.
Skin That's not a fish.
Moochie (*coughs in pain, then*) That's . . . big.
Reuben Where do we go from here, Princess?

A wild, reckless grin spreads across her face and the diamond in her headband sparkles in the light as she points in the direction of the terrible noise.

Witch That way.

The Tribe don't flinch. They form a fighting unit with her in the middle. Another roar sounds. They still don't flinch. Suddenly they let out a defiant tribal

howl in reply. The Jagged Ones are here to stay.
  Freeze-frame.
  Final lights out.

Illuminating the Shadow-Side of Life

David Ashton interviewed by Jim Mulligan

For most of his adult life David Ashton has made a living as an actor. However, even as a child he was writing stories and he has always written songs, but it was not until 1984 that he wrote a radio play, which was followed in 1985 by the Radio Times Drama Award.

> I suppose there was an element of frustration. I felt there were more creative juices in me than were being squeezed out by acting. That award, the only thing in my entire life that I have ever won, incidentally, set me off. Then I wrote for *EastEnders* and *Casualty* and within the past four years I have written three full-length plays for the theatre.

David Ashton has no preference for any particular writing genre. For television the characters are already formed but the requirements of the 'soap' format can be a straitjacket to a writer who likes his characters to take off: 'I know I'm on to something when the characters start bossing me around.'

The Golden Door is the first writing David Ashton has done specifically for young people. More than half the text is narrative but he is adamant that he is not being prescriptive. He wants the actors to be aware of his vision of the 'world-under' but directors must be free to interpret the world to suit the needs of young people.

> I was conscious of not wanting to burden young actors with too much dialogue; at the same time you have to respect what a young person is at that age. I wanted to give them something physical with energy allied to

dialogue. I hope in a real sense it is an adventure. It was an adventure for me to write it. I felt let off some kind of leash; I just let my love of the theatre cut loose. I hope young people will respond to that energy.

Although the 'world-under' is the force that makes the characters what they are, the dialogue is very important in parts of the play. At the start of the play Zip uses the applied psychology of myths to flummox the Giant and he does the same at the end to save his life. And the Witch is constantly using language and imagery to persuade and manipulate the Tribe.

The Golden Door started from a single visual image. David Ashton was in California eating a meal when he saw in his mind's eye a vivid image of a young woman lying face down in a rectangle of light, with blond hair spread out. She was wearing a white dress and red shoes and everything was perfect except that she was surrounded by darkness.

I have always been interested in mythology and I wanted to explore a mythological tale set in a world young people could relate to. I wanted to invite them into the story and then I saw this image and I knew I wanted my play to be a discovery of why she was there surrounded by darkness. In a situation like this all kinds of things that I have absorbed are dredged up but I am not aware of any conscious influences except, perhaps as a starter, *Alice in Wonderland*. I looked at Jung and Robert Bly and an article I read about people who live below the New York subway – all those things are a fertile pasture for the play to grow on.

The Golden Door is before everything else a good story well told. But all of David Ashton's writing is informed by his attitudes and beliefs. The darkness is filled with misfits, rejects, slimy creatures, predators and, worst horror of all, a mamma leech that sucks people dry and grieves for her lost offspring.

> The darkness is a nightmare. It's interesting that I first thought of the play in California where all things are bright and beautiful and you are not allowed to acknowledge the 'shadow-side'. In Europe, corruption and darkness and evil have been our bed-companions for a long time but even we have difficulty acknowledging that many people are living in a nightmare. I think a lot of young people are living very dark lives, and I don't just mean the obvious despair that comes from poverty, abuse, drugs and homelessness. I am talking about people who have no spirituality or mythological culture that enables them to understand the psychological darkness they live with.

David Ashton believes that young people would cope better if they could have their myths restored by such visionaries as the Witch. For him, she is definitely not evil. She carries the line of wisdom and has to survive in a very tough world. She is a sorceress and a visionary. She has a dream of an alternative life but in order to get through the darkness she needs the strength and energy of the Tribe.

> The Druids would have seen her as a powerful priestess. In the Middle Ages she would have been burned as a witch. The Tribe is essential to her plans. After all, there is not much point in being a sorceress if there is no one to listen to your predictions. It also seems that she needs a sacrifice. Myths always demand the death of the warrior hero. Cherokee is almost a part of the land they are leaving. They can't take him. His doom is that his line of time must end as the Tribe escapes. It is inevitably so. Although there is mourning there is also a feeling of release as his physical energy goes into the whole tribe, enabling them to burst through into light.

The ending is ambiguous. The Witch and the Tribe emerge into a light but it is a dangerous light. They set off united to confront new dangers. It is possible that they will find peace but for David Ashton enlightenment does not mean comfort. On the contrary, unless the light enables you to see the shadow side then you are avoiding reality.

> I hope this is a positive play. I think life, for all its dark moments, is a very precious gift. All things are not bright and beautiful in the real world and I hope that in some small way this play will help young people to realize that they can seek the light. All a play like this can do is give young people the opportunity to break through from darkness. Once it's written all I can do is stand back and hope that they and the audience can share that possibility.

David Ashton's previous work for the London theatre includes *Passing By* at the Old Red Lion, *The Mark* at the Cockpit Theatre and *A Bright Light Shining*, *The Chinese Wolf* and *Buried Treasure* for the Bush Theatre. His plays have also been performed in Belfast, Dublin, Edinburgh, Isle of Mull and Glasgow. His writing career began in radio where he wrote the prizewinning *Old Ladies at the Zoo*. Television work includes early *EastEnders*, *Casualty* and original films *The Other Side* for BBC 2, and *God on the Rocks* for Channel 4. He co-wrote an animated full-length feature film, *Freddie*, and is presently working on a film script for Peter Chelsom, the director of *Hear My Song* and *Funny Bones*. The name of the script is . . . *Tale*.

Production Notes

STAGING AND SETTING

The challenge here is to create the strange and echoey
'world-under'. Finding floor and wall texture that
describes the underworld of caves need not be too
elaborate if you also use light, darkness and sound to
enhance it. These textures could be developed in the
costumes – for instance, for the Tribe blending into the
caves, perhaps the backs of their costumes are cave-like
and the front the Tribe characters. They could also carry
their own torches. Projected slides of changing abstract
patterns and different light sources to alter entrances, exits
and scale can be used on top of the cave walls to suggest
the journey along the tunnels, and great fun can be had
with the red clay stalactite and stalagmite formations
sprouting from odd angles.

Prerecorded and live sound effects will help to create the
dripping and echo in the intestinal tunnel and the
atmosphere of this decaying underworld.

The Golden Door offers enormous scope to a large cast
aged between eleven and nineteen. There are six members
of the Tribe, four boys (though Zip can be played by a
girl) and two girls plus a princess who is really a witch.
Any number of actors can make up the chorus which
creates the music and sound effects as well as the character
of the giant (who must be frightening and might be played
or operated by a number of performers), the grabbers,
Mamma Leech and the baby leeches.

QUESTIONS

1 How did the Tribe come to be?
2 What are the Tribe's greatest hopes and fears?
3 How will you show that the Tribe has travelled from place to place?
4 Why did the Witch pose as a princess?
5 What has the Witch got to offer the Tribe?
6 Why does Cherokee sacrifice his life?
7 At what points in the story does Helen find her leadership challenged?
8 Which aspects of the play are funny? There is, for instance, the grisly humour of the baby leeches contrasting with Big Helen's pain in Slot 5.
9 What dangers do the Tribe and the Witch find when they ascend into the light?

EXERCISES

1 This is a play with a lot of action which makes considerable demands on the actors. The cast, including the giant, is made up of characters who have great individuality. This can partly be expressed through the way they move. The following exercises can help the actors to establish a physicality for their character.
2 Walk around the space as you would normally, observing how other people move.
3 Now walk with your nose leading. Stop and think about how this affects your centre; then walk off with your nose announcing your whole being.
4 Walk with your buttocks leading; walk as yourself, and then quickly shift back into being a buttock person. Notice the difference.

5 Walk with your chin leading and then your groin. Feel how much weightier your movement has become when your groin is your centre.

6 Choose a centre for yourself. It might be that you have become your neck and you are protecting it with your chin. Parade your centre and have everyone guess what it is.

7 Make a mental note of how these movements have affected other parts of your body. Discover how light or heavy your movements become if you move on your stomach and your belly button is your centre.

8 Leading with your chest on a count from one to ten, gradually lighten your walk until you appear to be floating. Now slowly descend on a count of one to ten to normal.

9 See how space affects your movement first by moving as normal in a large circle then gradually, and without discussion, form a small circle. Now take in the whole room. Be open to everyone and everything. Move into a small space, reining in your concentration. Close in further until gradually your world becomes just you and your body space. Note how much space you take in with a small circle, where you need to focus your concentration tightly, and how much freer and more welcoming you can be when the circle is bigger.

10 Decide what animal your character reminds you of. Moochie, for instance, is sometimes slow but always has the capacity to move really fast. He might be a fox. Find a possible centre for him, it might be his eyes, an ear, knees or, if you go for sensuality, his mouth. Use a metronome to beat out different rhythms for his character. Discover how slow and fast rhythms affect him. He might move quickly if under stress or excited. Apply this exercise to the other characters.

11 Experiment with making sounds. Stand still and take a deep breath. As you start to hum, walk. When you

need to take a new breath, stop, breathe in and then start to walk again. Choose a new note each time. Avoid making this a sombre and monastic exercise – bounce the sounds off the walls.

12 Repeat this exercise with resonance in various parts of the body. Make the sound in your chest, throat, lips, nose and in the top of your head. Discover how this affects your vocal range.

13 Walk around the room. When a colour is shouted out – dark brown, bright yellow, grey – make any sound that comes to mind. Now, imagine you are in the world-under: black, disgusting lime green, swampy yellow/brown. Imagine you are in the world-over and make the sound you associate with white.

14 Form two lines. The first is instructed to create moist slurping sounds in a long intestinal tunnel. The second is asked to make the sound of the Mamma Leech and her babies. Put these two sounds together

Suzy Graham-Adriani
February 1997

Note: A recording of music and sound effects for the play can be acquired from: Tim Eden, Head of Music, Woolston High School, Warrington; tel. 01925 493349.

IN THE SWEAT

Naomi Wallace and Bruce McLeod

For David Gothard

Characters

Nazreen, seventeen-year-old South Asian girl
of Bengali parentage
Fitch, seventeen-year-old Afro-Caribbean boy
Scudder, sixteen-year-old white boy, homeless
Duncan, twenty-one-year-old white security guard
Antonio Rodriguez Gompass, an old Sephardi Jew

Time: now
Place: a disused synagogue in Spitalfields, London

A disused and almost empty synagogue. There is a large building stone covered with sackcloth. Lights up on a lone figure seated and covered by a blanket from head to toe. A sleeping bag and some books lie near an old pew. Scudder enters, performing slow and controlled cartwheels. This appears ritualistic, almost dream-like. Cartwheeling, he slowly circles the seated figure.

Scudder Princelet, Fournier, Wilkes, Fashion. Hanbury, Lamb, Heneage, Chicksand. (*He pauses in his cartwheeling.*) This is my place. You gotta draw a line somewhere. (*He begins cartwheels again.*) Fleur de Lis, Folgate, Elder, Calvin. Quaker, Deal, Woodseer, Buxton. It's not my 'patch', my bit of 'turf'. It's my ways and means. Commercial, Wentworth, Brune, Hunton. Streets are fine, but it's the lanes that count: Artillery, Brick, Bell and Petticoat.

Duncan moans. Scudder falls to a sitting position.

You're awake then.

Duncan makes another sound.

Sorry. (*Beat.*) Princelet, Fournier . . . (*He begins cartwheels again.*) Wilkes, Fashion. I know my way around. Got a brick 'cross my skull on Osborn. Dropped it from my list right then and there. You can't keep a street that's turned against you. (*He comes to a halt.*) Broke my heart to lose it. (*Beat.*) Princelet, Fournier. But it's how I know what's what, who I've got, who I got to get to know, and who hates me. You hate me.

Scudder hears a noise. Duncan grunts. Scudder slaps Duncan's head to shush him, stuffs some more of the blanket into Duncan's mouth.

Shut it.

Fitch and Nazreen enter. They are wearing school uniforms, though heavily tailored to their specific taste in fashion. Nazreen wears a long skirt that reaches to her ankles and an oversized leather jacket. They drag their book bags. They do not immediately see Duncan.

Fitch Butter Baby, talkin' to yourself again. A wank with a bit of dialogue, eh, Scudder?

Nazreen This where Scudder lives?

Scudder comes forward. He is both nervous and overly excited.

Scudder A room of one's own. No view to speak of. Just me.

Fitch And too much of you. You need a bath.

Nazreen But this is a synagogue.

Scudder Not a very popular one. I've been here a month and not a rabbi in sight. There've been some weird noises though. Might be haunted.

Fitch Scudder, Nazreen. Wall-to-wall brain cells. Can lay down the law without a kicker. And no carpet in the bathroom.

Nazreen What's that supposed to mean?

A small moan is audible.

Scudder Carpet business. Fitch's whole family's in it. Short, shag, curly. Though most of it synthetic now and on the brain.

Fitch Yeah, well. The thing is, me and Nazreen have been walking around for a bloody hour trying to find Berwards Lane.

Scudder How romantic. First time out together?

Fitch Yeah. Where is it?

Scudder Berwards Lane?

Nazreen Having a carnival there tonight. There'll be shire horses. Exotic songbirds. Punch and Judy. The Green Man.

Fitch A real phoenix, and a guy who's more than a hundred years old. And some kind of skeleton in a glass boat.

Scudder Right. And a leopard who juggles its spots. You paid in advance, didn't you, Fitch? How much they take you for?

Fitch Look. I've got the flyer right here. (*He searches his pockets. Can't find it.*) Naz?

Naz shakes her head.

Anyway, it's only today so we can't miss it. Where's it at?

Scudder Berwards Lane? (*He does a slow cartwheel as he repeats the word 'Berwards'. Then he stops abruptly.*) Nope.

Fitch What?

Scudder Never heard of it.

Fitch You know every big-as-your-finger, crack-in-the-road, can-piss-the-length-of-it street in Spitalfields. What do you mean you never heard of it?

Scudder Look. An orange is an orange, right? A thumb has got two bones. One, two. Easy. Berwards isn't a street. Fact. You must have read it wrong.

Nazreen No. It's Berwards. He showed me the flyer.

Fitch Maybe it's a new street. A few weeks old. That can happen.

Scudder Not without my being there. I said no. Simple. No.

Fitch Shit.

Nazreen Then I'm going home.

Fitch Wait, wait. Give it a chance. There *is* a carnival here

337

today. That means noise. Lots of it. If we walk, we'll hear it.

Nazreen There's going to be a child who eats fire. I've seen it done before. But not by a child. Do you think she wants to do it or they make her?

Scudder Who says it's a girl?

Nazreen I don't know. I just supposed. (*Beat.*) How come you know the names of all the streets?

Scudder I don't just know the names, I make the streets. Happen. What I walk, I make. You know, mark them, make sure they run on time, then double back and change direction before the light turns red. But I like crossing over best. Unpredictable. You cross a street like you cross a man's mind, without warning, and if you're good you leave no tracks behind. Right? And Spitalfields. It's *my* domain.

Nazreen Oh, it's yours, is it?

Scudder Well, if I could get rid of those who've wheedled their way in . . .

Fitch Names? Dates? Addresses?

Scudder The whole rattlebag of wheedlers. They know who they are.

Nazreen You're hilarious. I could die laughing.

Scudder (*teasing*) Die? No. But as they say, if you're not happy here, go on back to Bangra land.

Fitch Scudder, shut the fuck up.

Scudder Hopetown, Weaver, Crispen Street. (*Beat.*) But the trick about streets is, once you turn your back, they don't stand still. They lead somewhere.

Another moan from Duncan.

If I could find one single street that didn't have an attitude, that didn't have to lead. Well. I could die a happy bastard.

Nazreen (*indicating the blanketed figure*) What the hell is that?

Scudder That? Well, that is a rat. Exactly, I think. And I am the cheese. Only in this case the cheese took action. The cheese fought back. Shit. The street brought him in. What was I do to?

Fitch Fuck the cheese. Who the hell is this?

Nazreen Looks like Mr Scudder the Street Man is playing dirty with one of his fellow strollers. Let's go. (*She goes over to the pew to sit.*)

Fitch Scudder?!

Scudder Oh yeah, that's how we get off, don't we? Just tie ourselves up in blankets and then beat each other unconscious. Tell us how your kind does it, Miss Nazreen? Through a hole in the sheet?

Fitch Scudder!

More groans and struggling from Duncan.

He's suffocatin'. Get the blanket off him!

No one moves except Scudder.

Scudder OK, OK. Ladies and gentlemen, Scudder, the boy without a rudder, would like to present to you his very own, fresh from the street, this one without a Petticoat, it's true . . .

Scudder slowly pulls the blanket off Duncan. Duncan, dishevelled and disorientated stares at them. There's a patch of dried blood on his forehead.

Nazreen (*unfazed*) I've got a fire-eater to find. I'm not interested in what Scudder picked up in the gutter.

Fitch He's alive.

Scudder Of course he's alive.

Fitch But it's, it's, it's the fucking police.

Scudder Looks worse than it is. (*Scudder spits in his hand, smacks it on Duncan's wound and begins cleaning the blood away roughly.*) Just a bit of dried blood. He's got lots more where that came from. (*He* *stops his cleaning.*) He came into my house.

Fitch This is a synagogue.

Scudder He poked me while I was sleeping. With his foot, of course.

Nazreen This is private property.

Scudder Then he kicked me. One, two, three. Right at the corner, then a sharp left, and straight at the lights. So I hit him over the head with a bottle of beer. It was still half full. The bastard.

Fitch Jesus Christ, Scudder, he's a security guard.

Scudder See? Not so bad after all.

Fitch My dad's going to kill me.

Nazreen So Scudder likes a man in a uniform.

Scudder Well? What're we gonna do?

Nazreen WE? WE?

Fitch Kidnapping and, and everything. Oh shit.

There is a moment of quiet while their situation sinks in. Naz nears Duncan, calmly. She pulls the gag out of his mouth, drops it on the floor and looks at her fingers in mild disgust. Duncan takes a deep, ragged breath in, then lets it out slowly.

Duncan Finally. Bit of quiet. I've had my head yacked at and cartwheeled for three hours straight.

Nazreen Who are you?

Duncan Ladies and gents. (*He winks at Scudder.*) You are all fucked. No-holds-barred fucked.

No one responds.

As it stands now, neither of you is in for it but Scudder. Charges are trespassing, resisting arrest, assault with a deadly weapon –

Scudder That was a sacrifice – it was half full.

Duncan And kidnapping.

Scudder You see? You see? I stuffed his mouth 'cause he's been saying this since I smashed him. Won't close the hole. Won't shut it. What am I supposed to do?

Duncan If the two of you release me now, you'll be all right. That's a promise.

Fitch How long have you been tied up?

Duncan 'Bout three hours now.

Nazreen Does your head hurt?

Duncan It's not so bad, thanks.

Nazreen What did you do to him?

Scudder I told you. He came in here shouting –

Nazreen I'm talking to the man.

Duncan Me? Do to him? I told him to move on.

Nazreen He says you kicked him. Called him names.

Duncan I tripped over him while I was checking the premises. He went berserk. I tried to restrain him. Then whack and I was out.

Fitch Let him go, Scudder. Before it's too late.

Nazreen Before it's too late? You sound like television, Fitch.

Fitch Do I?

Duncan Untie me.

Nazreen What's your name?

Duncan Duncan. Now, please –

Nazreen How old are you, Dunk?

Duncan Twenty-one. I'm losing my patience.

Nazreen Got a girlfriend?

Scudder Security guards don't have girls.

Nazreen And why not?

Scudder They roam the streets. Hit people with clubs. Pretend they're police.

Nazreen Sounds like most boys I know.

Fitch Look, Scud. You're my mate. Best mate, really. I laid carpet in three of the past shit-holes you squatted in over the last year. They were remnants, sure, but carpet nevertheless –

Scudder (*to Fitch*) You pig. You're going to run for it.

Nazreen (*to Duncan*) Is all of Spitalfields your beat? Do you know the area well?

Duncan Yeah. And Berwards isn't a street. I'd know if it was.

Fitch Listen. Uh. I'm going to quietly get the hell out of here. Now. And pretend this never happened. Come on, Naz. We've got a street to find.

Nazreen Wait. Just a sec. We either let this man walk or we're part of this. I'm not sure I want to let him go.

Fitch What?

Nazreen This guy's a security guard. A security guard, Fitch.

Scudder In other words, he's not one of us.

Nazreen None of us is one of us, dear Scudder.

Fitch My family is respectable. None of us has got a record. I won't be the first.

Nazreen I'm just saying let's think this over. This could be an opportunity.

Fitch For what?

Nazreen I don't know. But he's tied up. Look at him. A security guard. And he's ours. Ours. At least for now. I mean, think about it.

Fitch Fucking hell!

Scudder Fitch. Listen to her. She's a street.

Nazreen Look. This man has got the right to whack you if you walk into a room that's not yours. If you're in the wrong place he can take that club of his and change the size of your skull. He can break our fingers one by one – snappity-snappity-snap. Make you smile from a new hole in your face. Take your teeth off at the gums. 'Cause he's a security guard and he's got the right.

Scudder The stop-and-go man.

Nazreen The move-along man.

Scudder The I-don't-like-the-look-of-your-type man.

Fitch The what-are-you-doing-in-this-part-of-town man. (*Beat.*) Yeah. Can you whack someone for just walking into a place you're guarding? Just bust their face for steppin' into your space?

Duncan I use words before I use force.

Fitch How many words?

Duncan What?

Fitch How many words do you use before you use force?

Duncan Depends on the situation.

Fitch Depends on the situation. Yeah? Well, let's say
you're checking on one of your pads. And you come
into this warehouse and well, there I am. What would
you do?

Duncan What are you doing in the warehouse?

Fitch Well, I'm cold. Yeah, cold. Run out of the carpet
business. Been standing on lino so long my feet are
green. My teeth are doing the tap. My gums are on ice.
But your warehouse, it's warm. I come in to soak it up
like sunlight through a straw.

Duncan Why don't you go to a pub or a café to warm up?

Fitch Got no money.

Duncan There's Salvation Army, government B and B,
Itchy Park.

Fitch They're full.

Duncan That's not my problem. My problem is you're in
the warehouse and my employers don't like it. So out
you go.

Fitch No.

Duncan You've got no choice.

Fitch I'm not going anywhere. I'm cold. Cold. That's all
I'm doing, just being cold.

Duncan That's it then.

Silence.

Fitch What do you mean, that's it then?

Duncan Well, you give me no choice but to use force. But
I'm not surprised it's turned out this way. I know your
kind.

Fitch My kind? What's that.

Duncan What I'm looking at. Another black bastard
sliding down that cold, slippery slope on his bare arse,

dropping right down into that hole to the dole and hookin' the arm of a Paki slut on his way down, hoping it will make the ride a little hotter.

Fitch slaps Duncan. Silence. No one moves. Then Duncan laughs quietly. Fitch looks at his hand, then at Duncan. He realizes what he's done. He backs away from Duncan, bewildered.

Now that was too easy. (*Beat.*) I wouldn't have cracked your skull, though. I don't aim for the head. Across the back, mostly.

Nazreen I don't think I like you.

Duncan Is that the line you give 'em? Before or after they've got you on your back?

Nazreen moves away, then stands up on the pew and faces the audience while Scudder puts his arm around Fitch. She sings in Bengali. For some moments they all listen.

Scudder So she's a star. What about Dickhead? (*He points to Duncan.*)

Nazreen (*She stops singing, abruptly.*) Why'd he choose me for the part?

Fitch What part?

Nazreen The part of the slut. I mean, he doesn't know. He can't. Is it how I speak? Something in my face? The way I smell?

Duncan Just another dark, deceitful girl in the land of opportunity.

Fitch Lay off her.

Nazreen And we're all the same when we sit on your little white faces, right?

Fitch Jesus wept.

Scudder Sure he did. But I'm with Dunk on this one. Just because you want to go fishin' with her, right, Fitchin'? Fish-fingerin'-lickin'-good. That's what some of them say about Naz-the-Razatas, right?

Fitch Hey. Hey! What the hell are we going to do about this, this, mess we're in?

Nazreen Scudder is *in*. You are *in*. Not me. And him? He's not going anywhere. He's a pre-pubescent queer's catch-'n'-carry. Last moment of glory. Before Scudder hits the dole queue and the glue. I'm not going to stand in his way.

Scudder You know, there's something about this chick. Chin in the air. Never sweats. Has both indoor and outdoor slippers. But I bet her Mom slops toilets for a living. Just like mine. How much you want to bet?

Nazreen My mother works in a jewellery store. My father's the manager.

Fitch Hey. Want to hear this dream I had last night?

Scudder Sure. Yeah. And that's why you need to be touched. And touched and touched. Just like a diamond. But sad to say, a fake one.

Fitch I was at the docks, but there weren't those yachts or ritzy flats, no Canary Wharf, just water and a cold wind.

Nazreen (*approaching Scudder closely, finishing his metaphor for him*) All cut and flash and shine. But up close, just small change. Like you?

Fitch And then I'm on this old boat, like something out of the Armada, only with no sails, nothing, and we're going down the Thames.

Scudder Yeah. So queers and Pakis should stick together, right?

Fitch And I know where I am, but I don't know the buildings and I get scared.

Nazreen Don't get your wayward cruising confused with hellholes for housing, sweatshops, deportation and –

Fitch (*interrupts*) So fucking scared I get sick.

Scudder (*mocking*) Oh yeah, you get my vote for most oppressed.

Fitch And I start throwin' up over the side of the boat.

Scudder But tell me, who runs the sweatshops then? The best of your bunch, right?

Fitch And I'm spewing up my dinner, hanging over the water, and I see London. The London I know. In the water.

Nazreen I'm not afraid of you.

Fitch Built, way down there, under the water. The Tower, St Paul's, Battersea, train tracks, squares.

Scudder I'll tell you why your family got the part playing middle class. 'Cause they toe the line.

Fitch But the problem is, I'm still getting sick. So while I'm trying to see where I live, the pork pie is misting up the picture.

Scudder And while you finger your jewels, I'll be looking for the last greasy job in this part of town.

Fitch And I'm leaning further and further and the boat is tipping over and now I can see Regent's Park through the bottom of the boat. But I still can't see where I live. And I can't swim.

Scudder Oh, that chin might go up when you walk, but the crowd's still smelling garbage when you pass.

Naz just looks at Scudder, then turns away.

Fitch I can't swim.

Scudder (*angry now*) Then drown, OK! Look, Fitch. She's a bitch who hates queers. Sorry. You might want to kiss her but I wouldn't touch her, even if she were a boy.

Fitch Maybe she just doesn't like you. Maybe it has nothing to do with who you do. Ever thought of that?

Scudder It always has to do with who you do. Right, Naz?

Duncan (*to Scudder*) Hey. Listen to me . . .

Scudder If you don't shut up I'm going to kick you really hard.

Duncan I need to piss.

There is an awful silence.

Nazreen Let him wet himself.

Fitch Untie him and let him have a piss.

Scudder No way. Might be a trick. She's right. Let him piss where he sits.

Fitch Wait a minute. We might not like the man but must we degrade him?

Nazreen If he does it in his pants, it'll run to his shoes. He'll smell nasty, get awful sores. I'd like that.

Scudder OK. Let's be humane. Get it out.

Fitch Get it out?

Nazreen Lovely.

Fitch But this is a synagogue. You can't just let him . . . let fly.

Nazreen Yeah, this is sacred ground. This could be turned into another Jamme Masjid.

Scudder Jamme who?

Nazreen The Great Mosque. (*looking around her*) Where do you piss, Scudder?

Duncan I'm gonna burst.

Fitch Anyone got a container or something?

They rummage through their bags.

Scudder We need something deep. Dunk's about to blow. There'll be splashin' and fizzin'. Enough to float a boat on.

Fitch (*holding it up triumphantly*) Sandwich box. Deep-dish model. Waterproof.

Nazreen A condom! (*displaying it*) Extra-large, never mind the ridges, etc. It'll work. We'll just put it over the tip and bingo.

Fitch Right. Scudder, you'll be the most experienced.

Nazreen Beg your pardon. I've no wish to do it, but who says Scudder's more in the know about the world of the phallus than me?

Scudder You gonna do it or am I? Right. Next question. Tip, you said? Is our man a Roundhead or a Cavalier?

Fitch / Nazreen (*simultaneously*) Cavalier / Roundhead.

Scudder Does it matter with a condom? It matters not one jot but we'll put 'flapper' down for the record. All right. Now listen up, troops. I'll get it out, Fitch, you aim, Naz, you seal, and I'll dispose. Right? Any questions?

Scudder unwraps the condom and stretches it, letting it snap back. They all take up their positions, surrounding Duncan. Scudder gingerly unzips Duncan's fly. After some moments, Duncan begins to laugh quietly at them. They back away, disturbed.

Duncan Schoolkids. One minute, fangs at each other's throats. The next, all banded together at the drop of a hat. Or, for a flash of dick. Very sweet. It's classic. Ha. The streetwise queer, the whore with the heart of gold, and (*to Fitch*) what's your part, Black Face?

Fitch James Bond with a black fist. And you're fucked.

He grabs the blanket and throws it over Duncan and roughs him up. In a rage, Duncan manages to fling himself, still tied to the chair, at Fitch. They both crash to the floor. Scudder pulls out a knife. Fitch and Duncan are motionless on the ground. Then Fitch stands, and with Scudder's help they pull Duncan's chair, with him still in it, into an upright position. Fitch speaks to Scudder:

What's that?

Scudder What's it look like. If the bastard tries that again, I'll cut him.

Nazreen steps up and takes the knife from Scudder. Scudder doesn't resist. Nazreen approaches Duncan.

Fitch Naz, take it easy.

Nazreen Take it easy. Take it easy. (*Nazreen speaks the following as she cuts a hole in the blanket, just large enough for Duncan's face to appear in.*) It gets easier

and easier all the time. To let those little words brush
past you, just like a breeze, and that little shove mean
next to nothing, that hand on your body be an accident.
There, a little window on to the world. All you have to
do is look out. My sister does that. She sits at the
window all day long and just. Looks out (*Beat.*) Well,
isn't he pretty? I like pretty men. Maybe because I'm not
pretty myself. Am I a whore? They don't give me money.
No. And I'd rather have a bag of chips then their
respect. So what is it they give me? Memories? Funny,
but I can hardly remember their faces. What I remember
is how they take off their pants. Slowly. Quickly.
Gracefully. Stupidly. Do they hop around? Do they try
to hide their erection? Do they have one? Or am I
pulling the trousers off? And they're looking
embarrassed, all exposed, legs raised, staring over their
dicks and up at me? Good times? Always over too
quick. Open the drawer, rummage around, find it, don't
find it, close the drawer. But I keep on with it. What is it
I get? Do you know, Duncan? You're a man. Tell little
Naz-on-her-back just what it is she's getting from all this
wetting.

Duncan You're part of it now. You know that? Holding
that knife.

Nazreen runs the knife across his lips, gently, carefully.

Nazreen I could make you smile. I've never been able to
make anybody do anything, unless it was to me. But I
could make you smile. (*She holds up the knife, looks at
it.*) Close your eyes. Close them! Now, what do you see
when you close your eyes?

Duncan closes his eyes.

What do you see when you close your eyes? Answer me!
Duncan Nothing, God damn it. I see nothing.
Nazreen Right. Duncan. I knew you knew. That's what I

get from a fuck. It's like closing my eyes. And I see. I see. Nothing. Just nothing. And most of the time that's the only thing I want.

There is a silence. Then Scudder begins to do slow cartwheels around the three of them.

Scudder Fournier, Princelet, Wilkes, Fashion.
Fitch Fleur de Lis, Folgate, Elder, Quaker.
Scudder Calvin. Not Quaker. Lamb, Hanbury, Heneage, Chicksand.
Duncan I didn't want this job.
Scudder Oh, oh, oh. (*He stops cartwheeling.*) Ladies and gents, buckle down your arses. Suck your sodas and relax. This is the moment we've been waiting for: the I'm-really-a-nice-guy-under-all-this-crap moment. I say cut, cut, cut. We're all servants – only some of us enjoy it in the bargain.
Fitch I'm nobody's servant. Nobody's fuckin' servant.
Nazreen Of course not, Fitch. But then how do you mix all your gangsta rap with your little carpet empire? Axminster, Wilton, Royal –
Scudder Snoop Doggy Dog –
Nazreen Brinton –
Scudder Ice T –
Nazreen Stoddard Templeton –
Scudder Tupac Shakur –
Nazreen Hugh Mackay. Carpets.
Fitch (*to Nazreen*) You know, I thought you were something else.
Nazreen Well. What something else did you think I was?
Fitch Somebody. Kind, maybe. Polite. Someone to take to a carnival.
Nazreen Somebody smart, but not too smart? Fuck you.
Fitch Nah. I was hoping you were young. New. You know what I mean? Like someone I could surprise. Someone who could laugh and say 'I didn't know that till

tonight.' But nothing could surprise you, Naz. You're
sweet, and you're not bad to look at on the outside.
But you're not really a girl on the inside. Pull back
that skin just a little and there's an old woman
underneath. You're not what I want. Nah. Not what
I'll ever want.

*Nazreen slaps him in the face. He gives her a violent
push which fails to push her over. She returns the push.
They face off.*

Duncan Now this! This is carnival!

Fitch You shut your mouth or I'll shut it.

Duncan Oh, sweet, sweet, sweet. But this girl's got some
class. And you? Just carpet on the loo. You'll always be
her shadow, Fitch. And just a few short yards from
getting the boot on to the boat back to Jamaica. Or
wherever your dad came from.

Fitch Oh, stop the trains. Stop the clocks. What's new? I
don't need a landlord's goon to tell me I can't shake the
street from my back. It's my sign. But goon squad,
you're in the hot seat now – Brain of Britain – and I've
got the final question, the make-it-or-break-your-face
question: how much shit did you eat for this dog's
'thank you' job, for your security-man mission?

Nazreen Just leave it.

Fitch No.

Nazreen He's not worth it. He's an under-educated bigot
who'll be pushing a night stick thirty years from now,
thinking his life is worth while 'cause he protects empty
buildings. Look at him. It should make you laugh. He
knows something, sure, but he doesn't know what that
something is. And he never will.

Scudder (*to Duncan*) Then why'd you take the job if you
didn't want it?

Duncan Why do most people take jobs they don't want?
Money.

Scudder But you could have taken another job you didn't want. Why this one?

Fitch The man likes the uniform. Makes him feel like a soldier in the jungle. (*He makes monkey sounds to mock Duncan.*)

Nazreen He took the job 'cause he likes the idea of legalized violence. He finds it sensual – touching the bodies of strangers, whispering orders in their ears. Maybe it's the stick. Do you like swinging your stick?

Duncan (*menacing*) You've no idea.

Fitch Really. I bet you came top of their list in your interview. But what made up their minds?

Scudder Maybe how he cleared his throat.

Fitch grabs a notebook and pen and begins to circle Duncan.

Nazreen Maybe how he swaggered in the room and popped the seat, legs spread, groin cocked.

Fitch Yeah, but what exactly was that mysterious quality that made them go 'click': short, shag or curly, here's our man, no two ways about it? (*He stops in front of Duncan and suddenly jerks hard on the blanket so Duncan's head pops through and he's wearing it poncho style.*) Name?

Duncan What?

Scudder is behind Duncan and smacks Duncan in the head.

Scudder Your name?

Duncan What is this bullshit?

Nazreen picks up the knife and calmly approaches Duncan. She holds up the knife but not too close.

Ah. The interview. The old breakdown. Go on then, Fitch. Give it all you got.

Nazreen Shut up. He's asking you your name.

Duncan All right. Duncan Tressle.

Fitch Age?

Duncan Twenty-one.

Fitch Present occupation?

Duncan None.

Fitch Experience?

Duncan Worked as a vendor off and on.

Fitch Been locked up?

Scudder And knocked up?

Duncan No.

Fitch Pity. That sort of experience is useful in the security business. Any sexually transmitted diseases?

Duncan You can't ask –

Nazreen (*grabbing Duncan's face*) Oh but we can and do and will. Have you been a slag, a box of chocolates? Sleeping with the whites and the blacks? Mixing-'n'-matching where the sun don't shine?

Scudder Answer, slut.

Duncan I mean –

Fitch Sexual orientation?

Duncan What?

Nazreen Cleanliness is next to securityness. Where dost thou stick it?

Fitch There can be no hanky-panky, wanky-wanky.

Scudder Or other nibblings and nobbings on the job.

Duncan Is this really necessary?

Scudder Need the job, shut the gob, right?

Duncan Yes, but –

Fitch Butt is exactly what's at issue here. Are you or have you ever been –

Scudder Fond of that word? (*He gently brushes Duncan's hair out of his face.*) If so, its OK.

Duncan just looks at Scudder.

Nazreen Dangerous.

Fitch This can be a dangerous job, Mr Tressle. Have you ever used violence before?

Duncan What? Yes.
Fitch Consistently?
Duncan Yes. But it was a few years back.
Fitch Against whom?

No answer.

Against whom? (*He smacks Duncan this time.*)
Duncan Pete.
Nazreen (*also like an interrogator*) Why?
Duncan He asked me to.
Nazreen Sure. We all ask for it.
Fitch What kind of violence?
Duncan What kind? Are their different kinds?

Scudder smacks him again.

Scudder Just answer the man, Dunk.

Duncan is still silent.

Nazreen Answer him, you son of a bitch. (*She puts the knife to his throat.*) Or you won't get the job.
Duncan I used to hit Pete. But only when he asked me to.
Fitch Tell us another.
Duncan Pete's own father used to hit him. Not all the time, but enough. But then only in the mornings, just before school. He was white but they called him Pete-the-Black, because his face would swell up black as the sole of your shoe. This embarrassed Pete. You know. Especially 'cause his father was a little man, didn't reach Pete's chin and he was so thin from the drink Pete could lift him with one arm. Pete was afraid his Dad would die from the sweat the beatings brought out of him. So one day he says to his dad, 'Dad, you're going to kill yourself hitting me so it's got to stop. Whenever you feel you got to do it, I'll call my friend Duncan over and he'll hit me for you.' And what do you know, the old man agreed to it. I lived just up the road. Between seven

and eight in the morning I'd get the call, couple times a week. I'd walk over and Pete's dad would be sitting in a chair and he'd hold up one finger and that meant I had to hit Pete once. Sometimes he'd hold up two fingers. Three. I don't think it was ever more than four fingers. And so I'd do it. I'd hit Pete. Well, one morning I just got so sick of it I said no. In all that time before, when his dad was still hitting Pete, I never saw Pete cry. Until that morning when I said no. Pete just stood there. And looked at me. And cried. You know what Pete said to me the first time he asked me to hit him? Pete was my best friend. He said. Well. He said, if you really love me, you'll hit me. Yeah. That's what he said.

There are some quiet moments.

Fitch You're hired.

Nazreen goes and stands behind Duncan. Then she slowly lifts the blanket from his shoulders, over his head and free, almost as though she were undressing him.

Scudder You've got to stay on your toes, let your guard down at the right moment. But sometimes there's a street that's off limits so you wait.

Duncan Osborn, Greatorex, Cheshire.

Scudder Bide your time. All the while imagining yourself in that street, travelling up and down it.

Duncan Sclater, Brushfield, Stewards.

Scudder Yeah. They keep good company, like this old synagogue and its night-noises –

Duncan There's a library on Alderney Road –

Scudder (*He moves close to Duncan and in one quick movement rips open Duncan's shirt. Then Scudder gently traces the streets out on Duncan's chest*) Fournier, Princelet, Wilkes, Fashion.

Duncan – where I spend my lunchtimes when it's cold.

Scudder Linking up, delivering you, meeting you, testing you –

Duncan There's nothing to read but back issues of the *Jewish Chronicle*.

Scudder Lamb, Hanbury, Heneage, Chicksand –

Duncan You'd be surprised.

Scudder Fleur de Lis, Folgate, Elder.

Fitch Calvin. Quaker.

Duncan Synagogues, theatres, charities, clubs, music halls, sweatshops –

Scudder Buxton, Deal, Woodseer – here? Is Woodseer here?

Duncan Clothing, brewing and furniture; Lenin, Chaplin and Mosely – yeah, it's there.

Scudder Ghosts in Brune, Wentworth, Hunton, Commercial.

Duncan Spitalfields was a meeting place then, a place that found us.

Nazreen Now it's a place that loses us.

Scudder Artillery, Bell, Petticoat, Brick –

Duncan And what about Osborn?

Scudder Never fancied him.

Duncan Immigrants and refugees galore.

Fitch Big fucking market-place.

Nazreen To sell and prosper.

Fitch Or be sweated and sold.

Duncan Huguenot, Jewish, Irish.

Scudder (*tracing Duncan's bellybutton with his finger*) And here. At the border, we go south?

Nazreen Somali, Bengali. They sell cheaper and live very –

Fitch Odd. The un-English.

Scudder And you?

Duncan (*looking intently into Scudder's face*) I'm from Luton.

There is a strange, unearthly sound and an old man in

robes enters. His robes are black but with glorious designs in colour on the front, which derive from the Sephardi tradition.

Antonio What an unholy racket, and I emphasize the unholy because, as you all know, since Señor Tressle informed you, this is a synagogue, and I, being one Antonio Rodriguez Gompas, nephew of, or so the family said, Antonio Rodriguez Robles, the wealthy importer, famous for the confiscation of all his stock, including two of his vessels anchored in the Thames – 1656, I believe – I, as I was saying, Antonio Rodriguez Gompas, Sephardi Jew, resident of London, though my heart yearns for the warmer climes of Portugal, am a congregant of this synagogue, and what a noisy afternoon it has been. Noisy and unholy.

Nazreen Who the bloody hell –

Antonio (*interrupts*) And Luton? Never heard of it.

Fitch You know, Exodus, raves, Ecstasy?

Antonio Exodus I know.

Nazreen Who is this?

Scudder Anthony something.

Duncan Gompas.

Antonio Still tied up, Señor Tressle? Ah well. Perhaps the streets have marked you too deep. But such foul language and violence. And in my synagogue, which, I may add before you think it has always had a rather absentee congregation, was once brimming over with congregants, so many in fact that we had to make some men of importance share their bench, which they, I can tell you, did not like one little bit, and complained loudly. Luckily they did not know, because they were dead by then, that Ashkenazim were also later permitted to be buried in Betahaim Velho, right alongside their august but rotting persons. (*He goes to the pew and sits, as peacefully as if he were asleep.*)

Scudder Told you this place was haunted.

Fitch There's something fishy about this guy.

Nazreen I'm tired of all of this.

Fitch But he wasn't in my dream. No.

Nazreen What dream?

Duncan Where London's drowned.

Nazreen I don't feel too well. (*She sits on the floor.*)

Fitch Nazreen, I'm sorry about . . .

Nazreen No, it's him (*indicating Antonio*), he's making my stomach churn.

Scudder You should cartwheel. It'll clear your head.

Antonio (*muttering to himself*) Whirligig boy; a spinning top, always.

Fitch Naw. He's got to be a nutter.

Antonio (*oblivious to any remarks*) It is hard to find, Betahaim Velho – few come to visit. It is on the way back to Portugal, of course. Not for the tourist, mind you. Tucked away, like you four, out of sight – 1,500 souls buried there, and London has risen up and away from it. 273 Mile End Road. It remains. (*suddenly turning on Naz*) Ever been there?

Nazreen No. No. I mean –

Antonio Well, you should. Take Fitch here with you.

Duncan Graveyard might be a little serious for them.

Scudder This is their first time out.

Fitch (*to Antonio*) You were talking about the Thames. And the boats. Do you know anything about them? What they looked like back then?

Scudder Fitch, does he look like a sailor? They're looking for a street that's not. I said –

Antonio (*interrupts*) We were the first lot hereabouts – Houndsditch actually – when it was mostly fields and cheap housing like mushrooms sprouting up here and there, and then the French arrived – Huguenots, a very orderly lot those weavers. That was when they said we Jews were out to buy St Paul's. There was a nasty

rumour spread about those weavers, if I remember
rightly, though most thought highly of them, even
calling them, and definitely not us, 'the profitable
strangers'. The weavers loved songbirds, birds in
general, and caught them to sell in London. They
supplied London with its singing birds. A rumour got
out that the weavers wanted to raise their prices and
were planning to blackmail all of London by threatening
to release a new variety of bird, some said a giant
singing pigeon, that would cover the city with plague-
causing droppings. The aerial bombardment didn't
happen, of course, but it caused quite a stir. When that
rumour quietened down, we Jews were at it again, of
course: planning to buy the monarchy *and* Oxford
University.

Scudder Sold! Help yourself.

Nazreen Scudder, *do* you know this guy?

Scudder I don't think so. (*Sniffs.*) But he smells like a
street.

Antonio Señor Scudder has been my house guest this past
month. I watched when a friend bound his wounds. He
was attacked by some, what did he call them?

Nazreen Gay-bashers.

Scudder Osborn Street.

Antonio Osborn?

Nazreen Leads to Brick Lane.

Antonio Of course, where else? And to the Great Mosque
which I used to inhabit when it was the Ashkenazim's
Great Synagogue, though not when it was a Methodist
Chapel, nor when it was, before that –

Duncan A French church.

Antonio You know. Good. We must know all the bits and
pieces. And that squat building is all bits and pieces.
The same building, allow me to emphasize, has been on
that corner embracing all those Spitalfields shadows.
Hundreds of years of the stuff. Usefulness. Holiness.

Though, listen, and I don't mind telling you because it was also useful, most in Spitalfields passed right by that building, whoever was setting the pace of prayer, and went for the free-thinking, like bees to the nectar. Between sweating, playing and free-thinking, there was not a great deal of anything else done. Of course.

Fitch Sounds like us.

Duncan No, it's somewhere else.

Scudder You gotta wheel and deal for free-thinking. (*He does one cartwheel, which takes him to where Naz is, whom he then embraces.*)

Nazreen (*She pushes Scudder off.*) This has got to stop. I mean, this is bloody weird.

Antonio A hotch-potch of free-thinking. What else can you expect with such a place, such a recipe? Add drinking and fighting over scraps of bread to religion, stir in an overcrowded space and, let me tell you, free-thinking blooms – and smells all the way up to the heavens.

Fitch Well, he knows how to talk. You don't need carpeting where you hang out, do you?

Scudder I never knew you were watching me.

Antonio (*He has now stood up on the pew.*) Ah. What a day. Just this kind of day exactly for a carnival.

Nazreen Do you know where it is then? Berwards Lane?

Antonio Oh yes. I cross it every time I head home.

Fitch There's a carnival there tonight.

Antonio I've already been.

Nazreen Did you see the child who eats fire?

Antonio Of course I did. And so did you.

Nazreen I haven't been there yet. Me and Fitch, we –

Antonio Such a small mouth and such a big flame. You can hardly imagine she survives. But she does.

Nazreen Then it's a girl, isn't it?

Antonio Of course it is. And such beautiful hair. Black, black. And the tiny flowers at her feet. Yes. What colour were they? I can't remember. Tell me.

Nazreen I don't – No. I never saw her.

Antonio That's it. Yellow. The flowers were yellow. She was older than you were then, but smaller.

Nazreen No. No, you stop it. You are – No. (*She turns her back to him.*) I don't want to talk to you.

Antonio *Umbra sumus*, Nazreen. We are shadows.

Nazreen (*Picking up the knife, she begins to circle them all. This circling eventually diminishes so that she is slowly circling Duncan.*) Yes. Shadows. It happened on Scudder's streets. One way or another. All of us out of sight, here – (*She stalls.*)

Antonio It was years ago.

Nazreen Yes. Seven years ago. Seven years. My sister, Mahfuza, and I, we went out to use the phone. To call for flowers. It was my mother's birthday and her favourite were – were. I don't remember the name of them. They're not easy to get, small yellow flowers on thin stalks. I waited on the corner to make sure my mother did not see us making the call as she walked home from work. Mahfuza was older than me but smaller and had to reach up high to put the coins in and dial the number. What was the name of those flowers? And then suddenly they were there, three of them, tall, fast boys, who moved quick, quick. Like white flames they sprung up from the stones of the pavement. (*She stops speaking and turns to Antonio.*) It makes no difference. It's done.

Antonio They sprung up from the stones of the pavement.

Nazreen No. It happened to her. Not me. It has nothing to do with the rest of this. No. And this? This? This is over.

She cuts the ropes from Duncan's hands. She drops the knife and walks away from it. There is a stunned silence. Duncan, finally, stretches arms and legs.

Scudder There's four of us.

Duncan One of me.

Fitch Sorry about hitting you. And everything. You know.

Duncan I'll go back to Luton, I think. I've lost this job – missed clocking off. I should go. This town's finished, as good as dead. Listen. How quiet it is.

Scudder In here. Out of the way.

Antonio Out of the way yes, but at the heart of things. Now we are moving along, so swiftly. And dead? Look at me, prime of life, so to speak, fresher than a daisy on old Spital Field and I've been dead ages and ages. I think. Who knows? We build with the dead; we should get to know them.

Nazreen Ashes to ashes into ashtrays.

Fitch Nazreen. You want to go?

Antonio An old story before you leave; way before Uncle Robles, evil King John and his barons were squabbling. These Barons exactly came to London to look for the king and money and trouble if it led to more money. They found the Jews.

Fitch Course they did.

Duncan I should go now. (*He makes no attempt to move.*)

Antonio Many died. They tore down their houses, stole their goods –

Fitch Put the loot in Swiss bank accounts.

Scudder No questions asked. Business as usual.

Antonio Our houses were strong – we pay attention to history, give it its due, but sometimes history becomes a monster so big that wealth and a strong house are not enough – these houses, as I said, were torn down and used to repair the city walls, and Ludgate – one of the gates to protect London from other historical monsters.

Nazreen Foreigners.

Fitch Beggars, burglars.

Scudder Bartenders.

Fitch And blacks.

Duncan And you? You a monster?

Scudder Fee, fie, foe, fum.

Scudder cartwheels so that Fitch catches his legs and holds him upside-down.

Fitch I smell the blood of an Englishman. (*He lets Scudder's legs go.*)

Antonio Alas, I am just an observer, a collector.

Scudder I collect streets.

Antonio A noble occupation. There is a stone, such a heavy stone, and I should know since it has accompanied me for a very long time, ever since it caught my eye at that carnival, and this stone comes from old Ludgate. They tore it down in 1586 or thereabouts – dates are slippery things – and they found engraved on one of the stones: 'This is the ward of Rabbi Moyses, the son of the honourable Rabbi Issac.' (*Beat.*) I do aspire to be a monster.

Nazreen Don't. It's unpleasant, to say the least. Leaves a bad taste in the mouth. Dirt, ashes. Well, this party is over. I think I'll be off.

Duncan No. Don't go. I mean. Just yet.

Scudder Yeah. Let her go. Stay. What's the difference. None of us is one of us, right, Naz? Then who are you, huh?

Nazreen Someone who needs to be alone. Then I'll know who I am. But Fitch, you're wrong. I can be surprised. I just can't find the thing to surprise me. (*to Antonio*) And you, sir, not even you could do that.

Nazreen begins to leave. The others watch her. Suddenly Antonio explodes.

Antonio Stay. Go. What's the difference! Be alone and then you'll know who you are!? In all the noise this, this is the loudest, the greatest blasphemy! A noise to send pigeons to their deaths. A noise to turn the streets to gold and turn us all into glass children spouting great plumes of smoke! A noise to stop the green man's carnival. *(He uncovers the large building-stone that has been there all along, unnoticed, perhaps covered by a dirty sackcloth. An old rope is tied around it.)* Let me tell you, and I have heard noises big and little in my time, this stone has more sense than all of you – and it is dead, dead, dead. Now, move it! Señor Scudder, move this stone. Move it! And then you can go out and away into your city. The lot of you. *(He shouts at them.)* Now move it or I'll turn you all into little stones and sell you as souvenirs to American tourists.

Taken aback by Antonio's sudden violence, Scudder moves to stand before the stone. He looks serious. Then laughs. Then looks serious again.

Scudder Well, Sure. It's not such a big stone.
Antonio That's right, Scudder my whirligig boy, into battle!
Scudder Yeah!
Fitch Lock up your sons, Scudder-with-the-rudder, who's out to stir your butter, is on the prowl.

Scudder gives a howl, then bends to move the stone, with great effort. He can't budge it.

Antonio Samson you are not exactly. *(commanding)* Fitch. You do it.
Fitch And what do I get if I do?
Antonio Shut your mouth, child, and do it, or you'll be dust before your time.
Fitch That sounds like a threat.
Antonio It is, my boy. But if you succeed, that glass boat at the carnival shall be yours!

Fitch looks at Antonio for a moment and then takes up Scudder's position. He's also uncertain whether to take this as a joke or not.

Scudder Lock up your whity daughters, here comes Fitch the Caribbean gang-banging, she-shagging, black-bouncing-Betty. Got for it. Fitchie!

Fitch performs a few lewd movements, then strains to move the stone. He cannot.

Fitch Dunk. You're our last hope. White hope to be sure, but hope nevertheless.
Scudder Onward, my stud. This battle will not be pretty.

Duncan stands at the stone. Then he looks at the others, waiting.

Duncan Well? What's my title?

No response from the others.

I can't move it without some intro.
Scudder (*to Antonio*) Who was it tore down those houses?
Antonio The barons of course.
Duncan I knew I'd be the baron. No, I'll be the Jew.
Antonio Well, I think I have that covered, perhaps a rowdy sailor, a weaver's apprentice, a brick burner . . .
Duncan Forget it. I'm not part of this game. Turn me into little rocks if you like. I'm not playing. (*He sits, turning his back on them.*)
Antonio (*Standing on Duncan's chair, he directs his orchestra.*) All right. Then you lose. But Pandora's box, my Spital box, is still open. Who else will appear and try to move the stone?
Nazreen I suppose it's my turn. But why should I try? You know I can't move it.
Antonio But you don't know that. Yet. Let us find out exactly.

Nazreen stands before the stone.

Scudder Lock up your shops, your sons, and your silver. Run up the Union Jack.
Fitch Coz Nazreen the Bengali Queen Boadicea is behind your back and ready to take up the slack.

365

*Nazreen adjusts her skirt and shirt and strikes a few
'sexy' poses. She then attempts to move the stone,
with as much effort as those before her. She cannot
budge it. She tries again. They silently watch her.
Duncan turns around where he sits and watches her
too. Again and again and again, Nazreen strains hard
to move the stone. Finally she collapses around it, her
face buried in her arms, her body shaking from her
previous efforts, as though weeping, but we hear no
sound. They all watch her still figure. Then Fitch
slowly moves towards her and crouches beside her, as
though to comfort her. After some moments, Scudder
does the same. The three of them are crouched over
the stone. Finally Duncan gets to his feet, and slowly,
hesitantly, joins the three of them. The four of them
crouch over the stone. There is no movement for some
moments, then suddenly, precisely and in unison, the
four of them lean into the stone and with tremendous
effort manage to push it a few inches in front of them.
Then they all collapse around the stone, breathing
heavily.*

Antonio This stone. It caught my eye at the carnival.
Pressed at my heart. It has followed me ever since. Or I
have followed it. It stood beside the child with her fire,
the acrobats, the bear-baiting. Berwards Lane? It is just
around the corner, the upper part of Brick Lane where,
like this old stone, there is a curious design on one
paving-stone – as if a child in sooty feet walked in a
circle, maybe three, before disappearing home. Nazreen,
do you know that place?

Nazreen Yes. I know it.

Antonio Like white flames they sprung up from the stones
on the pavement.

*Nazreen slowly gets to her feet. She and Antonio stare
at each other for some moments.*

Nazreen Seven years ago. Yes. Like. Seven hundred. My
sister, Mahfuza, and I, we went out to use the phone. To
call for flowers. It was my mother's birthday and her
favourites were – they were – yes. Mimosa. Small yellow
flowers, thin stalks. Mimosa. They smell like dust.
Almost sweet. I waited on the corner to make sure my
mother did not see us making the call as she walked
home from work. Mahfuza was older than me but
smaller and had to stand on her toes to put the coins in
and dial the number. And then suddenly they were there,
three of them, tall, fast boys, who moved quick, quick.
Like white flames they sprung up from the stone of the
pavement.

*Nazreen steps on to the old stone. While she relates the
rest of her story, Antonio quietly recites phrases in
Portuguese.**

One of them had a can and he circled the phone booth,
wetting it like a dog. Another wedged something against
the door so my sister could not get out. The third boy, I
remember he was laughing but his laugh was strange,
almost like crying. He lay broken pieces of wood against
the door of the booth and lit the match. And suddenly it
seemed the glass of the phone booth started to burn. My
sister still had the receiver to her ear, but she was no
longer speaking. Her mouth was open. So open. But no
sound. And I had started to run towards her. But by

* The following phrases in Portuguese are to be used by Antonio during
Nazreen's last monologue. They represent a prayer of sorts. They can be
used more than once (though with significant pauses between each
phrase), but always in this order and ending with the last:
Somos sombras.   We are shadows.
Somos barulhentos e profanos.   We are noisy and unholy.
Estamos escondidos fora de vista.   We are tucked away out of sight.
O livre pensamento floresce e cheira bem até os céus.   Free-thinking
blooms and smells all the way up to the heavens.

then the flames were high and someone grabbed me and held me back. And Mahfuza's mouth was still open behind the flames, as though she were going to eat them. As though she could swallow them whole. And there was smoke, lots of it, and after some moments I could only see the top of Mahfuza's head in the booth, her black hair blacker than the smoke.

The neighbours got her out. In time. What does that mean? In time? In time for what? For months and months after I came home from school I sat with Mahfuza by the window. I wondered if she was looking out for the three young men. Afraid they might come back. But the expression on her face was not one of fear. It was not one of anything. And no matter how many times we bathed her, for years afterwards, her hair still smelled of smoke. It wouldn't wash out. There's nothing wrong with her body but she doesn't walk. There's nothing wrong with her mouth but she doesn't speak. I look at her and I think: 'She is my England.' No, I say. But the hands in her lap, they are cold. 'She is my England.' I say no. Not for me.

Antonio finishes his recitation.

For Mahfuza. Perhaps. Yes, for Mahfuza, that silence. Sometimes that's how it happens. But not for me. (*Nazreen takes Antonio's hand in her hand.*) No, not that for me.

Silence some moments.

This is it. Here. Right here, isn't it? Under our feet?
Antonio Yes. All of this. Tonight. Right here. This is our carnival.

Antonio lifts his hand and they listen as the sounds of carnival begin to rise all around them. Laughter. Shrieks. Strange lights. Shadows. Shouting. Louder and louder the noise. Nazreen, Scudder, Duncan and Fitch look about them in wonder and surprise. They do not notice when Antonio takes hold of the rope of his stone and slowly continues on his way.

Uncrushed by the Monster of History

Naomi Wallace and Bruce McLeod interviewed by
Jim Mulligan

In the Sweat is the result of a collaboration between two
writers. Naomi Wallace was born in Kentucky. She has
written from about the age of nine and studied at the
University of Iowa writers' workshop and drama
department. Her poetry has been widely published and her
most recent play was performed by the Royal Shakespeare
Company. Her first feature film is just being completed.
Bruce McLeod was born in Scotland and studied at the
University of Hull. He teaches English Literature at the
University of Iowa. He writes literary criticism and drama.

> We discuss and debate whatever the other is working
> on; continual input, criticism and redrafting are intrinsic
> to our writing. So collaboration is something we put
> quite a bit of effort into and believe is tremendously
> important. Poetry or writing about literature can be a
> very private activity. But drama is all about production
> and that means collaborating with the director, actors
> and others and being public. That's exciting.

Naomi Wallace and Bruce McLeod spent about six
months in preparation before they started writing. They
were interested in writing a play about the issues, interests
and struggles that young people in England face every day.
They were familiar with London and had visited
Spitalfields several times but the play imaginatively
reworks their research.

> If we were writing the play about American youth it
> would be very different. Of course, young people in the

370

USA and Britain are confronted with many of the same issues: where power resides and who is outside and being written off as some hopeless Generation X. This is an identity we wanted to challenge. *In the Sweat*, however, is grounded in a specific place with a very specific history of immigration.

Scudder, the homeless sixteen-year-old, is almost defined by the streets of Spitalfields. He recites their names as a litany. He 'makes the streets happen' and his unpredictability is expressed in his observation that, 'When you cross a street without warning it is like crossing a man's mind without warning.' When Nazreen and Fitch come to the synagogue looking for a carnival at Berwards Lane, Scudder is absolutely convinced it does not exist.

The writers of *In the Sweat* have chosen to throw together characters whose lives invoke both Britain and that historical melting-pot of immigrant cultures, Spitalfields. Fitch is Afro-Caribbean, his family middle-class carpet dealers. He is terrified of being sucked into a situation that will criminalize him but when he is roused he is capable of behaviour as violent as that of Scudder or Nazreen. But what do we make of Nazreen? Again she is from a respectable family, a Muslim for whom the synagogue is sacred ground that might one day become a mosque. Her reputation might be in the imagination of racist males but she herself revels in the way she uses her sexuality. Naomi Wallace comments:

> I am interested in writing characters that are ambiguous or contradictory. I think there is an old school which believes that when you create characters you shouldn't write anything that is out of character for them. I am interested in having the characters transgress. Nazreen, for example, seems a mass of contradictions and I hope that is what makes her interesting. In this play we set

out to work against the notion of identities as being fixed and exclusive. Here they are volatile, shifting, constantly under construction and interactive. We wanted to make sure that these different cultural identities are not seen as mutually exclusive and that they defeat any attempt to stereotype them.

In the Sweat deals with an extreme situation: Scudder has been beaten by a homophobic gang; Nazreen's sister has been traumatized when racists petrol-bombed the telephone booth she was in; Duncan confesses to a bizarre pact in which he agreed to beat his best friend in order to save the boy's father from the guilt of beating his son; and Fitch struggles against the racism that would categorize him as a criminal. As their violent confrontation begins to reveal their ties to one another, an elderly Sephardic Jew comes in dragging a stone. It is almost as if their act of reciting the history of Spitalfields is a prayer that calls up Gompas.

As a representative of the first group to be persecuted, Antonio brings into focus the history of oppression and struggle of immigrant communities in Britain. He is the past rupturing the surface of the present. The stone he is dragging is this history, the commonality that links the different characters irrespective of their apparent differences. It represents the importance of historical consciousness. You need to know the history of the immigrant communities to see how similar they are. If you don't recognize and learn from the monster of history it can crush you.

In the Sweat is an uncompromising play. The language is fierce and direct, the behaviour is violent, the characters tell their life stories with brutal honesty. The play deals with physical violence, racism, homosexuality, physical abuse of children, a British-Asian woman who is promiscuous and that particular form of racism that seems beyond control – anti-Semitism.

We *did* put our heads on the block because these are the issues that young people are faced with every day. It would be irresponsible not to deal with these things. We did it to bring out the reality young people face, to be provocative, to initiate discussion and to get people to think about the system that creates such a reality. The play is about dismal and frightening situations but ultimately it strives to be positive. We have this small group who clarify their experiences and begin to see the links they have with each other. When that happens there is always hope and the possibility of building a different reality.

Naomi Wallace is a poet and playwright. Her previous plays include *The War Boys*, *In the Heart of America*, *One Flea Spare* and *Slaughter City*. Most recently, she adapted William Wharton's novel, *Birdy*, for the stage.

Bruce McLeod teaches English Literature at the University of Iowa. He has also written a children's play with Naomi Wallace, *The Girl Who Fell Through a Hole in Her Jumper* (London New Play Festival). He is now working on a play about architecture and politics in the seventeenth century.

Production Notes

STAGING AND SETTING

The play is set in a disused synagogue in Spitalfields; the
time is the present. Spitalfields is in the East End of
London, and since the eighteenth century has been an area
noted for its nonconformity. Foreigners in large numbers,
most notably Huguenot refugees from France around
1685, account for some of the street names. The Georgian
properties that remain were originally the homes of some
of the more prosperous French silk merchants and master
weavers. The area declined in the early eighteenth century
and became home to an impoverished and partly criminal
population, and a multitude of 'sweat shops' sprang up.
Later, Jack the Ripper was to terrorize the area. Jewish
immigrants settled in increasing numbers in the 1880s.
One building at the corner of Fournier Street and Brick
Lane reflects the dramatic social changes in the area. Built
as a Huguenot chapel in 1743, it later became a synagogue
and is now a mosque, catering for the latest immigrants to
settle there, the Bangladeshi.

The setting is simple and open. Lighting will help to
suggest the shadows and degrees of light and dark you
would find in a synagogue. An old pew is the only
necessary piece of furniture. This is a play which could
work extremely well in an unconventional theatre space.
Traditional proscenium or school stages would diffuse the
danger and edginess it evokes. Large basements,
warehouses, disused churches or better still synagogues,
if health and safety regulations permit, would be
stimulating both for actors and audiences. If you are
stuck with a hall take the action off the stage. Light
from the floor and catch uneasy angles on the actors.

Make the most of the shadows they create and dark places left unrevealed.

Sounds can help to evoke the atmosphere of a disused building. Towards the end of the play we hear the carnival outside filter in.

CASTING

In the Sweat looks at history, racism, sexism and homophobia. It is a demanding piece, best suited to a cast of five aged seventeen years or older (one female, four male). Nazreen (a girl of Bengali parentage) and Fitch (an Afro-Caribbean boy) go to the same school and are probably taking their A levels. Their interpretation of school uniform should reflect current fashion. Scudder (a slightly younger homeless white boy) must have the ability to cartwheel well. Duncan is a twenty-one-year-old white security guard from Luton in uniform and covered in a blanket. Antonio Rodriguez Gompas is an old Sephardic Jew dressed in black robes with glorious coloured designs on the front.

QUESTIONS

1 What effect does the very specific setting of the play have on the action of the individual characters?
2 How is it that the characters are so familiar with the area and its history?
3 Who is Antonio Rodriguez Gompas? Why does he know so much about the other characters?
4 What effect does Antonio's entrance have on the others and what do they subsequently learn about each other that they didn't know before?
5 What does the stone symbolize?

6 Who says 'none of us is one of us' and what do they mean by this?
7 Why does Duncan stay when he has been released?
8 Why does Antonio speak Portuguese at the end of the play?

EXERCISES

1 Look carefully at what the characters say about themselves and one another. Decide what is accurate and what is said to be provocative.
2 Create a history for each of the five characters. Base them on solid information from the play.
3 Agree on how Fitch, Naz and Scudder first got to know each other and how their relationship has developed.

Suzy Graham-Adriani
February 1997

MORE LIGHT

Bryony Lavery

Characters

The ladies of the Emperor:
More Light
Love's Gift
Young Friend
Fresh Morning
Many Treasures
Rapture
Sparkling Eyes
Moist Moss
Playful Kitten
Scent-of-Ginger
Shy Smile
Love Mouth
Pure Heart
Pure Mind
Pure Joy
Perfect Pleasure

Man, a convict
Modern Man
Modern Woman

Act One

There is darkness.
   *There is the sound of wooden chimes blowing in the
wind. A single, nearer sound, as of a tinder box struck.*
   A small light appears.
   We smell sandalwood incense.
   *The light picks out the face of a young woman. She is
dressed in an enveloping black cloak, but we cannot see
this. All we see is a whitened face, eyes, a red mouth. She
speaks.*

Woman
   In the twentieth year of his rule
   the all-powerful Emperor
   now in sight of Death's gates
   gave thought to the construction of his tomb . . .
   To the high-ceilinged palace
   were admitted
   mathematicians   astrologers   metalsmiths
   artists   architects   inventors.
   Each put the most splendid workings
   of his mind upon paper
   and rolled out the paper
   so that covering the Emperor's tables
   was the most splendid Art
   of the most splendid minds
   in The Empire.
   And soon, in his all-powerful mind,
   the Emperor saw his tomb.

379

A sound of galloping hoofs.

Leaving the palace at dawn
with only four soldiers
he mounted his horse and rode east.
At dusk,
having ridden all day, he stopped,
dismounted and said,
'Here is where my tomb shall be.'
And so it was
for the Empire was his
and the gentle hill on which he stood
was his
and the red sun which lit the hill
was his.
The four soldiers marked the place.

In the high-ceilinged palace
on his return
the all-powerful Emperor
summoned one of his Guard.
The Guard moved silently through
the sleeping palace.

She listens.
    Four screams fill the air.

As the sun rose
four soldiers in the palace did not.
The punishment for this infringement of
rules
is flogging.
This did not greatly trouble the four
soldiers,
now in Death's kingdom.

Some miles off from the gentle hill
a tunnel was started.

The tunnel,
dug day and night by the Emperor's
convicts,
approached the hill.

The Emperor,
his body now frail
but his all-powerful mind not,
entered the twenty-first year of his rule.
There were many celebrations.

Fireworks briefly illuminate the space.

The tunnel reached the hill.
It was wide and high.
The Emperor's convicts worked and slept
in the tunnel.
The smell of their bodies
was wide and high.

In the light of many lanterns
the hill was hollowed out.
Above spring turned to summer
autumn to winter
day to night.

Beneath the hill
it was always day
for the work was continuous
and it was always night
for it was always dark.

The cavern
they hollowed out
was enormous.

Mathematicians   astrologers   metalsmiths
architects   inventors
rode on horses along the wide high tunnel

into the hill.
They dismounted
and with their Art
began to prepare the tomb.

The tomb was like this.
Such Art!
The ceiling was the night sky
above the Empire.
Artists painted it the deepest blue.
Their arms ached with the work.
Every star was in its place,
a jewel cut and set by the most precise
of jewellers.
The floor was the map of the Empire,
fields, woods, houses, roads, the skill of
gold and silversmiths,
the three mighty rivers
made, in this tomb,
from quicksilver,
dry to the touch
and flowing from source to end
by the art of engineers.

Three gates there were to the tomb
set within three walls.
Mounted at each gate
was a pair of mechanical archers.
Anyone entering these gates
uninvited
into the tomb of the Emperor
would be shot with silver arrows.
Such Art!

In the centre
beyond the third gate
was the entire army of the Empire

cast in bronze
with which the Emperor
would fight his enemies
in the realms of Death.

In truth
the Emperor's tomb
was the most splendid
of all the wonders accomplished in his
rule.

The Emperor
now with one hand knocking at Death's door
said,
'So that my tomb
may be my final resting place
and so that my body
will not be disturbed,
let it be made clear
that all those who have worked on this
tomb
shall die with me.
They shall stay in the tomb,
the gates will be locked,
the entrance sealed
and no one on this earth
will know where my tomb is.
This Art will survive in perfection.
And I will be as inviolate in death
as I was in life.'

A bell starts tolling far away.

So it was
that at the outer wall
stood the Emperor's convicts,
at the middle wall
stood

architects   astrologers   metalsmiths
artists   architects   inventors,
the most special minds in the Empire.

The Emperor
now with both hands
pulled at Death's doors
and they parted.

'Take me to my tomb,'
he said.
And the ones so honoured to escort
the Emperor
on his last journey
were those of his ladies
who had borne him no son
and were to tend his body
within the inner gate.

The Emperor walked through Death's doors.
'More light,' he said,
and his ladies
held lanterns close to his body,
but he did not see,
for Death's doors had closed upon him.

And so it was,
walking beside a dead man,
my hands burning from the lantern,
I,
one of his ladies
who had borne him no sons,
entered the tomb.

Many lanterns provide more light.
   The woman takes off her dark cloak. She is wearing a magnificent eastern gown, lacquered wig, white powder, high platforms supporting bound feet. Her name is More Light.

More Light
    I have had a most wonderful life.
    I have known only the finest of food.
    I have slept on the softest sheets.
    I have known only the Emperor.
    My garden has been green.

    I walked the wide road to the tomb
    ready to serve my Emperor.

    Death is an honour
    in such company.

    The wide road came to an end.
    Our procession stood at the outer gate.
    It opened.

    She takes out a fan.

    Such heat.

    She opens her fan.

    Such a smell of unclean bodies.

    She uses her fan to waft the air. She is short of breath.

    I lower my eyes.

    She lowers her eyelids modestly. Her fan covers her face
    but not her eyes.

    Saw this way and this way
    shapes, men, eyes watching.
    The Convicts I think.

    Her eyes dart and sidle.
    We pass through the outer gate –
    it closes.

She is more breathless.

Our procession at the middle gate.
More heat still.
Men stand
looking.
I lower my eyes.
Put up my fan.
The most special minds of the Empire
mathematicians   astrologers   metalsmiths
artists   architects   inventors
eyes watching.
Men I think.
So
the middle gate
opens,
closes.

Her eyes fix on something ahead. It is horrible.

Our procession
at an end
at an end
at the inner gate.

It opens,
it closes
for ever.

She looks towards us. Her eyes are blank and dark.

My garden has been green.
My face is white.
Inside my head it is black, it is black,
it is black.
I am twenty years old.

*Everything goes black. She screams and screams and
screams.*

SCENE THREE   BEFORE DEATH'S DOORS

Light returns suddenly.

*A screen or curtain has been removed and sitting in a
row, in the inner gate, are the Emperor's ladies who have
borne him no sons. They are of all ages, from sixty down
to six. They are all dressed as concubines, ladies of the
court, wealthy whores . . . there are countless examples in
the different periods of art to choose from.*

*They are all painted with white paint. More Light sits
with them. They will sit quietly like this for as long as
possible. When it becomes unbearable, More Light speaks.*

More Light
No one has spoken
since the Emperor died.
All of us women sit in silence,
backs straight,

Some backs are straightened.

hands still.

One pair of hands flutters and is still.

What to do

Their faces express apathy.

but sit and die
with our Emperor?

They sit still for another long time.

We are hungry.
We are thirsty.
What shall we do?
We have known only the finest of food.
We have slept on the softest sheets.

Our garden has been green.
We have known only the Emperor

All eyes look modestly down.

and now his soul lives behind
Death's doors
and we sit before them,
our minds on his empty body.
What shall we do?

I look at them,
the Emperor's ladies
who have borne him no sons.

She names them. Each one makes a small, precise
acknowledgement of her name.

Love's Gift
Young Friend
Fresh Morning
Many Treasures
Rapture
Sparkling Eyes
Moist Moss
Playful Kitten
Scent-of-Ginger
Shy Smile
Love Mouth
Pure Heart
Pure Mind
Pure Joy
Perfect Pleasure

They all start to piteously rock

Piteously they rock.
What shall we do?

SCENE FOUR   A BIRD IDEA

More Light
   My mind washes.
   I am in fresh air.

   Wind blows. It is cold and fresh. More Light takes a
   sheet of paper. She proceeds to make an origami bird as
   she reveals the image in her mind.

   I see an egg
   in a nest
   on a cliff
   above the sea,
   although I have never in my short life seen
   a sea.
   I hear a 'chip chip'.
   A small hole appears in the brown-speckled
   shell.
   A beak.
   An ugly damp matty head appears.
   An ugly damp matty bird falls from the
   broken shell.
   It dries in the sun.
   It grooms itself.
   It is sleek, it has feathers, it has wings.
   It stretches and launches itself over the
   cliff.
   It drops.
   It steadies itself on the air
   and then it flies
   up into the wind,
   up into the sky.
   The sun warms it.

   The bird is now constructed.

I look at the ladies.
Piteously they wail . . .

The ladies wail.

Eat him
I say.

SCENE FIVE   MORE BIRDS MAKE A FLOCK

The ladies all stop wailing at once.

More Light
Eat him
I say.

The ladies' eyes go round. Their mouths open in an 'O'.

Each painted red mouth
in each white-painted face opens.
He is our Emperor.
He has always fed us.
He would not want us to go hungry.
Let us eat him.

*Each lady takes a sheet of paper and constructs an
origami bird. They are considering the proposition.*

If we leave him too long
he will not be fresh

and we have known only the
finest of food.

More Light is playing with her paper bird.

The most special of dishes.

The finest cuts of meat.

We have always eaten royally.

I am so hungry.

What else is there to eat?

There is silence. The ladies finish their birds. They contemplate them.

There is silence.
All eyes look down modestly.
Then
one red mouth opens.

A lady's mouth opens.

Love's Gift . . .?
Love's Gift Sister, how shall it be done?

A great sound of birds' wings flapping. If only the paper birds could fly away in a great white flock, this would be wonderful.

SCENE SIX   THE ROYAL ARMY PROTECTS AND
SUCCOURS ITS LADIES

More Light puts an elegant finger to her chin to ponder the question. She walks a little. The ladies watch with rapt interest.

More Light Ah!
Ladies Aaaaaah!
More Light
  Perhaps we can borrow some
  utensils
  from the Emperor's own bronze army
  of death?

Stirring, impressive, solemn martial music. The ladies

remove a screen, revealing the head of a phalanx of
bronze military figures.

Each bronze warrior stands
his bronze weapon in his bronze grip.
The entire army of the Emperor,
each face individual,
each belt fastening,
each link of chain mail lovingly wrought.
Such Art!
I take a bronze sword.

She does.

Pure Heart takes a bronze dagger.

Pure Heart does.

Pure Mind takes a bronze axe.

Pure Mind does.

Pure Joy takes a bronze helmet.

Pure Joy does.
   They return the screen. As they do, they hear the
sound of men's voices.
   More Light continues in a whisper.

At the wall we hear
   a voice, many voices . . .
Voices
   Who is that?
   What is happening?
   What is going on?
   Have you food?

The ladies freeze.

More Light (*still in a whisper, this time informative*)
the mathematicians   astrologers
 metalsmiths   artists   architects   inventors
 the most special minds in the Empire.

The ladies are impressed.

We say nothing.
We, the Emperor's ladies,
speak to no man but
the Emperor.

All ladies are in full agreement here.

SCENE SEVEN THE EMPEROR

*The ladies remove another screen and there, lying in state
on a bed, is the Emperor.*

More Light
 The Emperor lies asleep
 in Death's arms.
 The ladies of the Emperor
 remark on his deathly form.
Rapture How still he is!
More Light Rapture gazes.
Moist Moss How blue-white his skin.
More Light Moist Moss touches his cheek.
Shy Smile How cold he is.
More Light Shy Smile touches his hand.
Perfect Pleasure How fat he is.
More Light
 Perfect Pleasure lays both hands
  upon his richly embroidered chest.
Perfect Pleasure Sister . . . how is it to be done?

More Light
All eyes, all white faces, all round
red mouths turn to me.

They do.

Take off his clothes.

As they do, More Light contemplates.

We have undressed for our Emperor
many times.
He sat on cushions of silk
as we unwound our sashes,
opened our robes,
stepped down from our shoes,
rolled our white stockings down past
our knees, over our ankles, off our toes,
one by one
unpinned our hair
and combed it with our fingers
down over our marble breasts.
His eyes followed our every move.
Now we undress him.
Fresh Morning unfastens the row of
pearl buttons
on his embroidered coat.
She works from neckband to hem.
Her fabled fingers fly.
Moist Moss and Scent-of-Ginger shell the
Emperor of his coat.
He is very stiff.
Their celebrated strength succeeds.
Little Friend takes off his jewelled shoes,
his white socks off his toes,
one by one.
Pure Heart, Pure Mind, Pure Joy

ease off his silk trousers.
The Emperor lies naked
but for his golden war helmet.

*The ladies put up their fans to hide their faces. More
Light stares at the Emperor.*

I have never
looked at him like this.
He has always looked at me!

*She puts up her fan. The ladies simultaneously bring
theirs down.*

Ladies

I have had no joy of
the Emperor.
He lay on his bed.
I stood at the foot.
He stared at my face.
Two girls,
thirteen years old,
pour oil on to their hands,

Dance with their hands.

Anoint his loins.
Such art.
Mould with the hands,
shape with the hands,
the soft, soft clay there
into something,
caressing, kneading, moving, shaping,
sculpturing,
turning soft clay
firing soft clay,
into hard, firm, erect Male Figure Sculpture.
I crawl from the foot of the bed
on hands and knees,

Round Female Sculpture.
The two girls help me,
help the two sculpture figures,
become one.
I am hard dry clay.
Ah Ah Ah.
Art is Pain.
I feel a hand over my face,
the hand of the Emperor.
It turns my head,
turns the Female Sculpture
through ninety degrees.
Ah Ah Ah
Art again   Pain again.
I make no sound.
My face shows pleasure.

Many Treasures Sister . . . we have taken off his clothes . . .

Playful Kitten Apart from his golden helmet . . .

Rapture Dead as dead . . .

Love Mouth In his huge golden war helmet . . .

Sparkling Eyes Naked as naked . . .

Playful Kitten With his small white love-member . . .

They put up their fans. We hear a giggle. Fans start to shake. One by one the fans come down and everyone is grinning, then giggling, then chortling, then laughing . . . They try to show respect for a while. They fail. They fall about, hit each other, cry with laughter. More Lights lowers her fan and watches.

More Light
This is what they fear . . .
those who hold empires
that we will look and really see.
The Emperor is dead.

396

More Light I lift up the bronze sword.

She does.
  The ladies fall back.

The ladies melt back into the gloom.
I stand before my Emperor.
I use all my strength.
The sword goes 'clish' in the air
and I slice through his left shoulder
clear to the bone.

The ladies gasp and ululate.

A thick line appears in the skin,
the flesh parts.
My mouth is dry.
Rapture
  Sister,
  the limb is not cut through . . .
  Perhaps if we bend back the arm
  we might sever the tendons
  as one might snap off a chicken wing . . .
More Light
  Fresh Morning and Many Treasures
  take the arm.
  They twist it.
  Then there is a sound worse than any
  I have heard . . .

The ladies keen.

It is the shoulder socket dislocating.
I lift the sword again,
'clish' the blade arcs down,
and the Emperor's arm drops to the floor.

Moist Moss Oh, sister . . . it is done.

She pats More Light's sword arm.

Many Treasures Hard work . . . butchering.
Playful Kitten What a lot of flesh on a man's arm . . .

She examines the shoulder.

Perfect Pleasure I am so hungry!

She kneels on the floor.

Love Mouth (*pouting*)
But . . . raw meat . . . my
  stomach is too delicate for raw meat . . .
Shy Smile
Look . . . the lanterns . . . they still
burn . . . perhaps . . . if we made a fire . . .
we might roast the Emperor's arm . . .

A sound of a fire crackling. It roars. The area is suffused with flame red. Then darkness.

SCENE NINE MANY TREASURES

Light up on Many Treasures.

Many Treasures
The Emperor's arm tastes
of venison.

This is all very new and interesting. Many Treasures is interested in the art of cooking.

Slightly gamy with a suggestion of salt.
I think we roasted the arm too quickly . . .
the outside was scorched
and the meat nearest the bone too raw.

Our cooking improved.
The ladies of the Emperor are noted for
their quickness.
Their brains are not softened by
child-bearing.
His legs tasted of roast pork!
His ribs of beef.
His feet of duck.
His innards made a fine stew,
thick, good gravy, with many tasty lumps.
His member was soft and tasted of cheese,
but we all knew that,
for many of us
had tasted it before.
The Emperor
with his fine strong body
shields us from death for many days.
The Emperor protects us
in death
as he did in life.

SCENE TEN   MORE LIGHT EXAMINES
SCULPTURE

*Lights up on More Light, alone among the bronze army. She
is contemplating the figure of a soldier. She looks at its
forthright stance, its open face, and compares it with herself.*

More Light
The inner gate is strewn with bones.
The air smells of cooked meat and
tallow grease.
The ladies' faces are no longer white.
The red paint is gone from the mouths.
The skin is dank, yellow and smutted.

Our bellies are round and full
as if we bear sons.

She strokes the face of the warrior. Then his chest, then
his legs, then his feet.
Various ladies appear.

Love Mouth Sister . . . the Emperor is almost gone.

She nibbles a fingerbone.

Smell-of-Ginger Sister . . . the Emperor is almost used up.

She scrapes a piece of skin.

Pure Mind Sister, the Emperor can no longer
Pure Heart Provide for us.
Pure Joy What is to be done?

More Light thinks.
The various ladies think.

More Light
Our brains are small,

This is demonstrable from the bronze warrior.

unused but for pleasure pastimes.
For help in this most difficult
problem we must look to the most special
workings
of the most special minds in
the Empire . . .
Love Mouth the mathematicians
Scent-of-Ginger astrologers
Pure Mind metalsmiths
Pure Heart artists   architects
Pure Joy inventors
More Light Who occupy the middle gate.

All faces turn to the wall. They listen.

Love Mouth (*quietly*) We have heard voices,
Scent-of-Ginger the sounds of motion,
Pure Mind cries even,
Pure Heart but it is not our practice to talk with other
   men.
Pure Joy We ladies talk only to the Emperor!

> *They tiptoe to the wall screen. They listen.*
>   *All is silent.*
>   *They all whisper.*

Love Mouth Nothing.
Scent-of-Ginger Perhaps they are all asleep.
Pure Mind Perhaps they are all weak with hunger!
Pure Heart Perhaps they are all dead . . .
Pure Joy For they have not had the protection of the
   Emperor!

> *They listen.*

More Light There is no sound beyond the wall.

> *More whispered conference.*

Love Mouth
   If they are all dead
   we must collect them and cook them.
Scent-of-Ginger Pickle them!
Love Mouth Before they go off!
Scent-of-Ginger Ay . . . what a waste of meat!
Pure Mind
   We must find out the state of matters
   beyond the middle wall!
Pure Heart Sister . . .

> *They all turn to More Light.*

Pure Joy What is to be done?
More Light We must prepare!

The ladies watch as she starts to remove her high-heeled shoes. She makes her clothes comfortable.

The ladies understand. They remove restricting garments – corsets, restraining bodices, tight unbendable sleeves.

They borrow pieces as needed from the bronze army. They start to move, then almost dance, in a much freer, more open way.

They hear chinking and clanking. It is their jewellery – bangles, necklaces, earrings and rings. They remove them.

Pure Joy How well we move!
Pure Heart How free!
Pure Mind How light!!!
All three Sister, what is to be done?
More Light
    We must open the door
    and take a peep!
Ladies Yes!
Pure Joy
    Ayee . . . but the mechanical archers!
    They will fire on us!
Ladies Ayee!
More Light
    No . . . no!
    The mechanical archers
    fire out
    not in!
Love Mouth They will fire upon the mathematicians
Scent-of-Ginger astrologers
Pure Mind metalsmiths   artists
Pure Heart architects   inventors
Pure Joy all the most special minds in the Empire . . .
More Light who Built This Tomb!

SCENE ELEVEN   OPENING THE GATES OF KNOWLEDGE

More Light
  Take hold of the left handle,
  Pure Mind.
Pure Mind Yes.
More Light
  Take hold of the right,
  Pure Heart.
Pure Heart Yes.
Pure Joy Now!

*They open the gates. There is the sound of mighty
doors opening in a vast building.*
  *All the present ladies follow More Light through the
gates.*
  *Pure Joy remains with us. She is well mannered and
loves beauty, so she describes the gate screen to us.*

The gates in the middle wall
are exquisite,
of beaten gold and silver.
They bear pictures of the triumphs
of the Emperor's rule.

*A sound rends the air. Two arrows travelling at speed.
Then silence.*
  *Pure Joy gasps with fear and clutches her heart. She
listens. Nothing. She continues to entertain us.*

Of beaten gold and silver,
they bear pictures of the triumphs
of the Emperor's rule.

She loves detail.

Here is his army victorious in battle,

403

here are his road-builders reaching the
farthest outposts of the Empire,
here are his tax collectors in a small
village collecting corn,
here is a thief, having his hand cut off,
here are his stonemasons building a
great wall in the north.
Around the gate handles
choirs sing praises
and hosts pray.

There is a knocking at the gate.

Who is it?

From behind the gates.

More Light Open the gates, Fool!

*Pure Joy abases herself for us at More Light's rudeness
as she opens the gates.*
    *Another sound of two arrows travelling at speed. The
sound of muffled screams from behind the gates.*
    *The party of ladies appears, dragging or carrying two
men sitting bound and cross-legged, their mouths oddly
full and each with staring eyes and arrows embedded in
their hearts.*

Shut the gates, Fool!

*More abasement from Pure Joy for More Light's
rudeness as she shuts the gates.*

Scent-of-Ginger My heart pounds!
Love Mouth My mouth! Dry!
Pure Mind My palms! Moist!
Pure Heart I have wet myself!

    Pure Joy abases herself.

Ladies Oh oh oh oh oh!!!!

They scream.

More Light
Quiet, fools!
My head is full with your wailing.
I need to think!

They are silent at her fierceness.
  She kneels down before one of the corpses.

This was Clever Hands
the inventor.
He it was who made the water flow
upwards to the higher fields.
He it was who made the device which
turned the ox carcass so that it
roasted evenly.
He it was who made the mechanical
singing linnet for the Emperor's
third son.
He it was who made the mechanical
archer which has now shot him
through the heart.
Love Mouth Sister . . . we are all hungry . . .
Scent-of-Ginger
Sister . . . we must attend to him
before he goes off . . .
More Light
Who bound his arms and legs?

She feels in his mouth, takes out rags.

Who gagged him?
Love Mouth (*to Pure Joy*) Make sure the gates are secure.
Scent-of-Ginger The important thing is to eat!

Pure Mind, Pure Heart, Love Mouth and Scent-of-Ginger take the bodies away to the other ladies.

See what we have found!

Many Treasures Ayee!

Love Mouth An inventor!

Playful Kitten This is Sees Future, the astrologer!

Many Treasures
Thinner than the Emperor
leaner flesh
tougher
more consistent of texture . . .
Careful braising I think . . .

They take the corpses behind a screen. There are the
shadows of swords raised, the sound of dismembering.

SCENE TWELVE   THE MIDDLE GATE

Pure Joy
It is written
in works of astrology
that the astrologer can foretell
everyone's future
but his own.

More Light
Beyond the gates there
we peered into the blackness.
All is silent.
But no . . . we hear breathing.
Love Mouth lifts the lantern.

Everywhere
eyes
low
staring up at us,
row upon row of eyes
staring out from the most special minds

of the Empire.
Their feet and hands
are bound.
Their mouths stuffed with rags.
Two move not at all.
Arrows in their hearts.
'Take these two,'
I hear a voice say.
The ladies look at me.
It is my voice.
They move along the seated trussed men
the most special minds of the Empire
and drag away the two carcasses
across the floor
and through the gate
to eat.
What of our future?
Pure Joy Sister, we are in a tomb.

SCENE THIRTEEN   A MEAL

Many Treasures brings on a steaming cauldron. The ladies coo and flutter with pleasure. They line up, each with a bronze helmet. Many Treasures ladles steaming stew into each one.

Love's Gift I have a little more than my sister.
Fresh Morning Ah no. I am happy.
Rapture
  Little Friend is still growing . . .
  Perhaps another spoonful?
Sparkling Eyes How carefully cut is the meat!
Many Treasures
  The size of a walnut.
  The best size.

Rapture
  Little Friend . . . Playful Kitten . . .
  take the soft place.
Scent-of-Ginger Heaven in the mouth!
Many Treasures Not too melting?
Ladies
  No, no.
  Not too melting at all!

Pure Joy and More Light enter.

Many Treasures Casserole, dear sisters?
Pure Joy Aaah!

*Playful Kitten gives her helmet of stew to More Light,
then goes and lays her head in Rapture's lap. Playful
Kitten is very young.*

More Light This is yours, Playful Kitten.
Rapture You must eat, little sister.
Many Treasures
  Perhaps cut up the pieces to
  pistachio size, sister?
Playful Kitten It makes me dream.
Rapture What does it make you dream, little one?
Playful Kitten Bad things.
Rapture What bad things, little one?
Playful Kitten
  I become a big bad thing
  and I roar
  and I stand in the dark
  and my chin is hair
  and my eyes look at me
  and want to watch me all
  the while
  and I hurt between my legs.

She puts her face to Rapture's lap.

The ladies have stopped eating.

Rapture I have this dream too, little sister.

She strokes her head.

Love Mouth I too.

The other ladies nod.
Love Mouth addresses Many Treasures.

It is no criticism of your cooking!
Ladies No! Oh no, no!
Love Mouth We are simply doing wrong.
Ladies Yes! Oh yes!
More Light (*laughs*)
Yes!
We are the ladies of the Emperor!
We are here on this earth to serve
the Emperor...
to please him
to amuse him
to bear him sons!
But we have not borne him sons ...
So we must serve him in other ways!
How?
Let us go with him through Death's doors!
Yes!
Let us walk with him!
But wait!
Where is he?
Where is he, Playful Kitten?
Playful Kitten We ate him, More Light.
More Light
We ate him!
He was good to us, Playful Kitten ...
better than he knew!
For he is now in us!

He occupies our bellies
as if he had given us sons!
We have his dreams!
Ladies, we are now all . . . all . . .
Emperor of all we survey!

The ladies ponder this.

Pure Joy
It is written
in studies of other religions
of a religion whose devotees
eat of the body of their god
and drink of his blood
and their god lives in them.
More Light
I am Emperor here.
I believe this is possible.
Playful Kitten, do you believe
this also?
Little Goddess.
Child Emperor.

More Light abases herself before Playful Kitten.

Playful Kitten Yes!
(*imperiously*) Hand me my helmet!
Many Treasures (*equally imperiously*) More casserole!

The ladies resume eating.

Pure Joy (*thoughtfully contemplating her casserole*)
If it is true that we are all now
the Emperor
for he is now one with us

All ladies nod.

by the same token
we must all be

She takes a mouthful.

inventors

She takes another mouthful.

astrologers
for they too
are now one with us.
More Light What of our future, sister?
Pure Joy
Let us have one, sister!
Let us be Emperors of our world.
Let us be its
mathematicians   astrologers   metalsmiths
artists   inventors
architects.
As the Emperor constructed his tomb
so let us construct our world!

*The ladies dress Playful Kitten in the dead Emperor's
clothes.*

Playful Kitten It's a game?
Pure Joy It's a game!
Playful Kitten I'm an Emperor!

SCENE FOURTEEN   THE EARLY RENAISSANCE

More Light
In the first year of her rule
the all-powerful Emperor
now in sight of Death's gates
gave thought to the construction of her
world . . .
to the high-ceilinged tomb
were admitted

mathematicians   astrologers   metalsmiths
artists   inventors   architects.
Each put the most splendid workings
of her mind upon paper
and rolled out the paper
so that covering the Emperor's tables
was the most splendid Art
of the most splendid minds
in the Empire.
And soon, in her all-powerful mind,
the Emperor saw her world.

The ladies, who have adopted new attitudes as the Emperors and the most splendid minds in the Empire, contemplate their world.

SCENE FIFTEEN   THE EMPEROR LEAVES HIS PALACE

Pure Joy Such Art, sister.
More Light What else have we?
Many Treasures
   Sister . . . a word.
   The inventor is on his last legs . . .
   Someone must go beyond the gate.
More Light Why me?
Many Treasures
   The ladies are occupied.
   constructing . . . inventing . . .
Pure Joy
   You are our Empire's sword.
   Without this our world is threatened.
More Light
   I have had a most wonderful life.

I have known only the finest of food.
I have slept on the softest of sheets.
I have known only the Emperor.
My garden has been green.
Pure Joy I will open the gate.
More Light
My voice is no longer low and melodious.
It is harsh as a sword stroke.

More Light takes a sword.
  The gates are opened by Pure Joy.
  We hear the sound of two arrows through the air.
  More Light walks into blackness.

I can see nothing!
Fool!
I search with my hand out in front
of me for dead men.

A sharp intake of breath.

I smell a wide, high smell!
There is something here.

We hear women's voices ululating.

I light my lamp.

She lights her lamp. Light reveals her standing with her back to us. Projected is the shadow of a huge man.

Aaagh!

The man's arm rises. It holds an axe.
  More Light turns round.

Aaagh!
Standing before me,
an axe in his hand,
is a man.

The axe is raised.
It is made of bone!

The light comes up to reveal exactly that.
Furious drumming. Women wailing. Then darkness.

Act Two

SCENE ONE   PURE JOY OF ART

A sound of something musical, between a xylophone and a celeste. The notes are tentative, exploratory.

   The lights reveal Scent-of-Ginger among the bronze army. She tries out notes on various bits of the bronze soldiers.

Scent-of-Ginger
   Tsk!
   Ah!
   Bah!
   They are so out of tune!

She takes out a percussion instrument composed of hung helmets, daggers, belt buckles etc. She plays a melody on them.

   Hmm.
   Yes.
   I see . . .
   It all needs rearranging!

Nearer, lights reveal some of the ladies posing. Above them is a mobile of origami birds.

   Love Mouth is sketching them.

Pure Joy
   Love Mouth draws us all for a
   composite group portrait.
Love Mouth Don't move.
Pure Joy
   None of us is moving.
   Trained only for politeness,

respect and servitude,
we struggle like crawling toddlers
towards the skills of creation.
Love Mouth Daaghhh!
Pure Joy
I find myself the stillest of us
all for I am thinking.
What art?
Hundreds of years hence
people will penetrate this tomb
and they will see the painted sky
studded with jewelled stars,
the rivers of quicksilver,
the mechanical archers,
the gates,
the bronze army,
and say,
'Look, it is the sky,
the stars, the rivers, archers,
the gates, and that must be
the army!
What Art!
And look, in this middle section here,
these skeletons, wrapped in fine clothes,
these must the women!
What were they doing here?'
Love Mouth Keep still!
Pure Joy
And one of them, keener-eyed than
the rest, may find, among the dust,
the shape of a bird,
and he will touch it
and the old old paper bird will
fall to dust,
and he will say,
'No, I was mistaken.

it is nothing,'
and will turn back to the beautiful
gold and silver gate.

Love Mouth
Hold your heads a little more . . .

They all hold their heads a little more . . .

Yes, that's pretty, yes.

Pure Joy
So I keep still,
while my eyes and mind scamper and
scrape like a rat about this monument,
looking,
looking for the post and lintel
on which to rest the architecture
of my dis-ease,
for the arch to take the weight
of my fear,
for the rib vaults and flying buttresses
to hurl my hope stone-like
into the ether.

Love Mouth
If you want to be part of my
picture, sister . . .
you must Keep Still!

Pure Joy keeps still.
Love Mouth sketches.

I am going to put us all
in the palace garden.
With the sun coming through the trees.
Flowers in the grass in the foreground.
A table with food.
Dew-dropped fruit.

Red wine in a glass flagon.
In the background the village
of my childhood just under
the mountains.
An early evening sky.
And we will all be smiling
in delight!

Phhh!
Well . . . rest a while.

Love Mouth contemplates her work furiously.
    Pure Joy rises.

Pure Joy
There are no flowers here.
No sun.
But I remember.
Do I make flowers?
We are in a tomb?
Do I show Death?
We are in a hell.
Do I create hell?
We construct a world.
Do I show hope?
What colour is hope?

*Playful Kitten and Little Friend run on. They have tied
long ribbons to the end of bronze daggers. They play
with them, slashing the air with random trickles and
blazes of colour. They run off.*
    *Pure Joy starts moving in time with the melody of
Many Treasures. She adopts a strong pose.*

You remember that statue in the
Great Hall?

She slightly alters her pose.

The beautiful young man?
Walking forward.
into the future.
The Kouros.
Feet planted firmly on the earth.
Strong limbs.
Striding forward.
Head high and proud!

All the women adopt the strong pose.

We thought him splendid!

Love Mouth
Oh, that is new!
I need *more light*!

The lights fade.

SCENE TWO   ADAM AND EVE

*Lights up on the second gate. More Light, bound and
gagged, is hurled in by a Man, wild and hairy, who sports
a recent sword gash. He carries an axe of bone and a
bronze sword.*

Man
Can't run much, Royal Shag!
Can't run at all now!
Can't screech now, Palace Parrot!
Nice piece o' work this!

Indicates sword.

Nice piece o' work this!

Indicates sword gash.

Do it ta you now, eh?
Bleed blue, willya?
Cut off a wing, eh?
Taste of parrot, willya?
I've ett of the smart boys thought up this cage.
Tasted of paper and books.
Gotta taste for bird.
Eaten raw fowl before.
How I got penned in this hutch
For that big misdemeanour,
stealing food.
Mebbe make a big fire
Have
Sunday roast.
Right royal feast you'd be
Parrot.
Na . . . gonna take the stuffing outta
your crop, Polly . . .
an' ya gonna say who's a Pretty
Boy then to me
an' no screeching or your blue
parrot tongue's Pretty Boy's
first bite, am I clear?
Nod your head if you're a
talking bird!

More Light nods her head.
   He takes out the gag.
   She chokes and gags.

Too much dry corn, Poll.

He gives her water to drink from his hip flagon.

'Ave some pure fresh rainwater.
Courtesy the lads on the outer
gate.

Comes through the walls.
Very tasty tomb with running water
we got.
'Spect you're sipping purified silver
in the middle there?
Let's you and me talk, Parrot.
Emperor dead yet?

More Light Yes.

Man Yessss!

He smites the air.

And maggots forever bite and chew
his fat carcass!
Yessss!
Fat bastard took along a flock
of you parrots.
Wass happened to them?

More Light
Dead.
Every one.

Man
Every one but you, Poll.
How comes you still fluttering?

More Light Same way as you, convict.

Man You ett bird?

More Light I ate bird.

Man
Yessss!
What it taste like?
Sweet?
Soft?
Chicken?

More Light
Sweet.
Soft.
Chicken.

Yes.
Man
Like that, me.
Like a taste of that.
More Light
But you can't taste that, convict.
It is all gone.
Man Part from this, Poll.

He touches her.

More Light
Apart from this, convict.
Emperor's Parrot.
Whose voice sung him melodies.
Whose tongue caressed his ear.
Only the best for the Emperor.
Finest, softest of voices
talking to him only of pleasure
in his ear,
lips murmuring on his ear
of pleasure.
Man
Emperor's woman.
Say what you did.

He puts his ear to her mouth.

More Light (*in a whisper*)
I gave him pleasure.
Only the best for the Emperor.
The most practised of touches.
The most elegant of movements.
The deepest of knowledge in how
to show the Emperor love.
Man
Show me, woman.
I'm Emperor here now.

More Light Unbind me then, my lord.
Man What am I, a fool?
More Light Yes.
Man You're dead.
More Light You also, Fool.
Man

Then I'll go like an Emperor.
Die of pleasure from a
bird of paradise pecking
and feathers.

He unties her.

Show me the art of love,
Parrot.
I'm the Emperor.
More Light

He lies in his bed.
I stand at the foot.
He looks into my face.
I lower my eyes modestly
behind my fan.
Two girls,
thirteen years old,
pour oil on to their hands,

She performs all this for him.

anoint his body,

She begins to stroke him.

take away all his cares,

She places the bronze sword and bone axe carefully,
usefully for her. He watches.

anoints his head, his neck,
his shoulders stiff from battle,

423

She puts her hand inside his shirt.

his manly chest.
He has no breasts.
Anoints his thighs, his loins.
Such Art.
Mould with the hands,
shape with the hands,
the soft, soft clay there
into something
caressing, kneading, moving, shaping,
sculpturing,
turning soft clay,
firing soft clay,
into hard, firm, erect Male Figure Sculpture.
I crawl from the foot of the bed
on hands and knees,
Round Female Sculpture.

She begins to open his trousers.

Ah Ah Ah.
Art is Pain.
I feel a hand over my face.

The man takes her chin and directs her down to his lap.
   She looks at his lap.

Aaaaaagh!
Man
   Squawking, Parrot?
   Seen nothing like it, Parrot?
   Different diet, Poll?
   How will you eat this chopped-about delicacy?
   What Art is needed here!
More Light Who did this to you?
Man (*takes hold of her*) Who did this to you?

424

SCENE THREE   RIBBONS OF COLOUR

*A lantern appears in the darkness. Lightens to reveal
Playful Kitten and Young Friend carrying their ribboned
sticks.*

Playful Kitten Down here.
Young Friend It's dark.
Playful Kitten I'm the one who holds the light.

> *They would both prefer to be the one who holds the
> light.*

That's the river.
It's poisonous but you can drink it
if you like.
Young Friend No!
Playful Kitten Drink it!
Young Friend
No!
I drink blood!

> *This makes them laugh. Then scares them. They both
> would prefer to hold the lantern.*

Playful Kitten
No!
I'm the one who holds the light!
We lie down here.

> *They lie down on their backs.*

It happens when the lantern warms them.
It takes a while.
Young Friend All right.
Playful Kitten (*pointing left*)
There's where it's darkest.
That's where Paa lives.

Young Friend
   Oh.
   Who's Paa?
Playful Kitten
   My friend.
   He's an animal really but he can talk.
   I won't let him hurt you.
Young Friend What does he eat?
Playful Kitten
   Dark.
   He eats dark.
   He chews it up and swallows it
   and then he belches
   and it makes light.

   They giggle.

   And then he farts
   and it makes light.

   They giggle some more.

   And when he shits
   he shits candles
   and they're lit!

   This is very funny.

   And once he was sick
   and it was a lantern!

   This is even funnier.

   You can kiss me.
Young Friend All right.

   She does.

Playful Kitten You can touch me if you like.
Young Friend No, I don't want to.
Playful Kitten

All right.
You can hold my hand if you like.
Young Friend
All right.

They hold hands.

I don't like being touched.
Playful Kitten
I don't either really.
Not like that.
It's horrible really.
Young Friend
It's horrible.
Sister.
Playful Kitten
Sister.
Here they come.

Stars appear.

They're jewels really.
But they look like stars.
Young Friend I once found a star.
Playful Kitten Where?
Young Friend
In the grass.
It was green and sparkly.
Playful Kitten Did you keep it.
Young Friend
Yes.
But a robber stole it when I
was asleep.

They both play with their ribbons, swirling them in the air.

There's someone in the dark.
It's probably Paa.
Playful Kitten Probably.

She is not so sure.

Young Friend
He might have woken up and be
hungry.
Playful Kitten Yes.
Young Friend He might belch some light.

*A voice whispers from the dark: 'Playful Kitten . . .
Young Friend . . .'*

Playful Kitten Help . . .
Voice (*whispers*) Are you there?
Young Friend Yes, Paa . . .
Voice (*whispers*)
Come over here.
Bring the lantern.

*They go into the darkness with the lantern. It lights the
face of Rapture.*

Rapture (*hugging them and smacking them*)
Foolish! Foolish!
We thought we'd lost you!
Our sister is still behind the gates!
We are lost!
Bring the lantern!
How much light do you think we have!

She hurries them away.

SCENE FOUR   PERSPECTIVE

*Rapture arrives with Playful Kitten and Young Friend
among the ladies.*

Rapture
Here they are!

In the dark!
These two at least are here!

Scent-of-Ginger
Foolish girls!
Did you hear anything?
Did you see anyone?

Playful Kitten and **Young Friend**
No.
Nothing.
No one.

Playful Kitten Just the dark.
Sparkling Eyes Oh, misery!

She bursts into tears.

Love Mouth
More Light has not returned!
What has happened to her?
Oh, it is all awful!

Many Treasures
We are so low on . . . ingredients!
What is to be done?

Pure Joy A fine world!
Many Treasures
You were with her at the gates!
What happened, sister?

Pure Joy
She walked through the gates.
I closed them.

Silence.

I heard a scream.

Silence.

I came back to pose for Love Mouth.

There is nothing we can do!

There is nothing we can do!

Love's Gift We could go after her . . .

Pure Joy Why? Why? Why?

Shy Smile To save her, sister . . .

Many Treasures
And there is the matter of
eating . . .

Love's Gift We should go after her . . .

Pure Heart It would be only fair . . .

Pure Mind It would be only polite.

Scent-of-Ginger It would be dangerous . . .

Pure Joy
Dangerous?
Polite?
Fair?
We are in a tomb!
It is not the Emperor's any more!
It is ours!
We are dead already!
This is the world of Death!

Love Mouth
No! No! No!
I am painting!
We are all . . . making!
For the first time in my life . . .
it is . . . my life!
I am . . . creating!
Not Death!
No!
No!

Many Treasures
And we eat, sister.
We eat.
We are alive still.
We are alive!

Pure Joy

We are eating human flesh!
What will we *not* do?
Many Treasures
Nothing.
There is nothing we will not do now!
Nothing!

(*to others*) . . . Now, let us think
sensibly . . . What is to be done?

Shy Smile
It seems to me . . . excuse me . . .
there are three tasks to be accomplished.
Many Treasures Yes?
Shy Smile There is the getting of food.
Ladies Yes.
Shy Smile And the getting of our sister.
Ladies Yes.
Shy Smile And the getting on as normal . . .
Love Mouth Yes. Creating.
Pure Joy
As normal! Hahaha!
As normal!
Love's Gift
Some of us should see about the
getting of food and the getting
of our sister . . .
Shy Smile
The two tasks . . .
may be . . . may be one.
Ladies Ayeeee!

They contemplate this.

Many Treasures
So be it.
Who will go?

Show of hands.

Who will stay?

Show of hands.

So be it.

They look to Pure Joy. She has not raised her hand.

Pure Joy
Love Mouth paints.
Many Treasures cooks.
Makes music.
Playful Kitten dances.
I have made nothing yet.
Let me make a gesture.

She takes a bronze dagger and puts it to her heart.

Let me make a sacrifice.
Here I am. Meat.
Many Treasures
Sister, you have been meat long enough.
Be a woman with us.
Pure Joy
There is nothing worse than this!
Many Treasures Let us find out.
Pure Joy I'm frightened!

She drops the dagger.

Many Treasures You're hungry!

SCENE FIVE   FAUVISM

The middle gate. More Light and the Man.
    They sit facing each other. Between them lie the sword and the axe. They are playing scissors, paper, stone. She is

scissors, he is scissors. He has never played before.

Man More Light?
More Light Yes.
Man More Light?

She is scissors, he is stone. He blunts her.

More Light
I was named for my quality.
The Emperor felt
when I entered a room
it became brighter.

He is paper, she is scissors. She cuts him.

Man And you played his games?
More Light He liked competitions.
Man Emperor's favourite?
More Light
At first.
But I read, listened.
My mind grew.
More light in it.
He turned to softer, more
flattering flames.

He is stone, she is paper. She wraps him.

Man You were sad?
More Light
I was glad.
My love for him was all Art.

She is paper, he is stone. She wraps him.

Man
Art don't work on me.
Practical me.
More Light Three. I win.

433

Man Then choose, More Light.

She takes the sword.
    She is stone, he is scissors. She blunts him.
    She is scissors, he is paper. She cuts him.
    She is paper, he is stone. She wraps him.

More Light Three.
Man Choose, More Light.

She puts the sword to his throat.

More Light Your Death.
    I choose your death.
Man
    Got hungry.
    Stole.
    Got caught.
    Got me balls chopped off.
    Dug a tomb.
    Got banged up in it.
    Whore stuck a sword in me gizzard.
    Did I live well!
    One last request.
More Light
    Of course.
    It would be only polite.
Man Make me happy.
More Light
    I can do nothing
    I say.
Man You can do this

He takes her hand, puts it to his cheek.

More Light
    He says
    and touches me so

He puts his hand to her cheek.

and so

She puts her other hand to his face

and so.

He puts his hand to her face.
    They look at each other.

I can do nothing for you
I say.
Man You can do this

He caresses her.

More Light
    he says
    and I touch him so
    and so and so.

She strokes his face, his hair.

Man Hurts . . . happiness,
More Light he says.
Man Worst pain . . . happiness,
More Light he says.
Man
    Makes ya think of the life
    ya wasted,
More Light he says.

She kisses him.

Man You using Art?
More Light I don't know.
Man Doesn't matter.
More Light
    It does
    I say.

435

He kisses her.
    From the darkness come Scent-of-Ginger, Pure Mind and Pure Heart. They leap upon him.

Ladies Excuse us . . . so sorry!

They hurl him to the ground.

Scent-of-Ginger Forgive us . . . we must hold you down!

They bind him fast.

Pure Mind and Pure Heart A thousand pardons . . . we
    must bind you tight!
Scent-of-Ginger Gag him! Excuse us . . . you must
    make   no sound!!!
Pure Heart
    What have you caught here, sister . . .
    a philosopher?
More Light Yes. A philosopher. Yes.
Pure Mind
    Our sisters guard the gates!
    We are hungry!
    Hurry!

They hurry the convict and More Light through the gates.

SCENE SIX   SCULPTURE

*Love Mouth among the bronze army. She is alight with
excitement.*

Love Mouth
    I see it all now!
    The light had to be in my head!
    We must observe what has gone before!
    How things were done!
    We must see how the light in the

heads of our past masters struck
their space!
Of course!
By chipping and painting our friends
here . . . I destroy.
I take them into my head . . . transform
them with the light there . . .
the magnificent
correct
and knowledgeable play of
objects in light!
Yes?
Yes!
Yes! yes! yes!
I need something to make with!

The ambush party enters.

Scent-of-Ginger
Here . . . here!
If we bind him to this warrior he
will be held fast!

They bind him.

Pure Mind and **Pure Heart**
Excuse us . . . so sorry . . . just a little
tighter. There!
Scent-of-Ginger More Light has lit our world again!
Pure Heart
Scent-of-Ginger will make such
music over this!

They hurry off.

Love Mouth
More Light . . .
I have got all the other ladies'
likenesses in rough working form . . .

Would you be so kind . . . so gracious
as to spare me a short time for a
sitting?
More Light
I am to be painted?
Again?
Love Mouth
Sculptured!
Three-dimensional!
Beautiful object!
More Light
Of what material,
Love Mouth?
Love Mouth
Of clay!

She hurries her off.

SCENE SEVEN   PAA

The convict is chained to the bronze warrior. He hears a noise. A whispering.
Playful Kitten and Young Friend appear.

Playful Kitten Greetings, Paa.
Young Friend Greetings, Paa.
Playful Kitten
We have to touch him, or he can
escape.
Young Friend
All right.
You first.
Playful Kitten All right.

She goes to touch him. Runs back.

It's not frightening at all.

It is.

Now you.
Young Friend All right.

She goes to touch him. Runs back.

Now he can't get us.
Playful Kitten
No.
Never.
He's dead.
Young Friend Good.
Playful Kitten I'm hungry!

She runs out.

Young Friend
Bad Paa.
Don't . . .

She goes to stand right before him.

Don't ever do that again!

She smacks him.

Ever ever again!

She smacks him again and runs off.

SCENE EIGHT   A FEAST AT THE HOUSE OF LEVI

The ladies sit, thinking.
Many Treasures It is our world.
Ladies It is. Yes.
Many Treasures
No one but us can say what is right

and what is wrong.

Ladies No. No, they cannot.

Many Treasures
Therefore the decision is ours
alone.

Scent-of-Ginger We are all Emperors here!

Ladies Yes. Yes we are all Emperors
here.

Many Treasures So.

They think.

Shy Smile It is but a short step . . .

Love's Gift But a very short step . . .

Shy Smile
From eating the dead . . .
to . . . making someone dead . . .
in order to eat them.

Ladies Yes. Yes, a very short step.

Many Treasures And we are hungry.

Ladies
We are. Indeed we are.
Starving.

Pure Joy
I have never been so hungry
in all my life.
I am sick with it.

Ladies
Yes. Yes, indeed.
We are all sick with it.

Playful Kitten runs in.

Playful Kitten I am hungry.

Rapture Shush now. Shush.

Young Friend runs in.

Young Friend We should have a party!

Rapture Shush now. Shush.
Pure Joy
We should have a party.
Celebrate this . . . Empire
we find ourselves in!
Ladies We should. Yes.
Shy Smile What else have we on?
Ladies Exactly!
Many Treasures
We are back to the problem of . . .
provisions.
Rapture
We have just the one . . .
source.
Shy Smile Which requires . . .
Ladies Attention.
Many Treasures Sisters, what is to be done?

More Light and Love Mouth enter.

Pure Joy Sister, is your sword sharp?
Many Treasures We are preparing for a party!
Shy Smile
Sister, the guest you brought back
needs attention.
Love's Gift He must be prepared for the feast.
Ladies Our most important guest!
Many Treasures
Here . . .

She hands More Light the sword.

prepare him, Sister.
More Light Why me?
Scent-of-Ginger
When we came to help you, sister,
You were in great danger
for your lips touched his

and you were not bound.
A test.
We need this so.

More Light takes the sword and goes to leave. Pure Joy catches her.

Pure Joy
Sister . . . if I may . . . I would be
pleased to perform this task
for you . . .
More Light
He has been cut about all
his life!
He is a man
but he is not a man!
Pure Joy
No one but you or I shall
know of this.
Give me the sword.
The deed is done.
More Light
How will you do this deed,
Pure Joy?
Pure Joy
I will take the sword so . . .
Find his heart so . . .
and with all my strength . . .
push.
More Light
You will leave him bound?
Leave in his gag?
Tied to a piece of the Emperor's Art?
Pure Joy
I am a lady of the Emperor, sister!
I cannot fence with him until he
drops!

More Light
    Why do you want to do this deed,
    Pure Joy?
Pure Joy
    I have done nothing.
    Ever.
    I am without Art!
More Light
    Pure Joy.
    You give pleasure.
    You are justly named.
    It is enough.
Pure Joy
    It has no heirs.
    It leaves no fortune.
    It does not survive.
More Light
    You remember Laughter . . .
    who died in childbirth . . .
    at the palace . . .
Pure Joy Yes.
More Light Her jokes?
Pure Joy Yes.
More Light When she dressed up as the Emperor?
Pure Joy Yes.
More Light
    Your face lights up.
    Your heart warms.
    She is dead.
    It is enough.
    Give me the sword.

*More Light goes to the bronze army. She takes the gag out
of the convict's mouth. He spits in her face. She nods.*

Man Bitch.

More Light nods.

Bastard.

More Light
That, too.
Shall I cover your eyes?

Man
No, bitch.
I want to watch you at your work.

More Light So be it.

She lays the sword at his breast.

Any last requests?

Man
Listen to my song, Parrot.
We're digging out,
us lads.
We dug in . . . we can dig out.
Got the clever boys telling us where
to dig . . . using their most special minds to
fashion tools for us.
We're going to get out, Cage Bird,
What do you say to that?

More Light You're sure?

Man
I'm sure.
We're men.
We got brawn, we got brain.
Be out in the open very soon.

444

Going to be free.
Breathing fresh air.
Not this meat-filthy soup.
What do you say to that?
More Light Not you though.
Man
Less you let me go.
Less you and me slip away in the
dark like thieves in the night.
Take you with me.
Outside.
Fresh air.
Free.
Empire.
Gentle hill.
Red sun.
What do you say?
More Light I say . . .

She plunges the sword into him.

Die!
Man
Aaaaaagh!
Bitch!
Fool!
Bitch!
Why?
More Light
It would be no different!
For the Empire was his
and the gentle hill on which he stood
was his
and the red sun which lit the hill
was his!

He slumps.
    She holds him.

It is too late for us.
There would be no change.
Man
    You daft bitch.
    You'll never know.
    Kiss me.

She does. He dies. She cradles him.
    The ladies come and take him away. More Light cries
pitifully.

CHAPTER TEN   AN OBJECT PLACED IN ITS
ENVIRONMENT

Love Mouth enters carrying something covered in cloth.
Playful Kitten and Young Friend carry lanterns.

Love Mouth
    Sister?
    Sister . . . I have something to show you.
    Put the lantern . . . there.
    And that one . . . here.
    And this . . . THE OBJECT . . . here.
    I
    More Light . . . look what I have made!

She takes off the cloth. It is a paper sculpture . . . quite
small . . . of the ladies of the emperor.

    See . . . it is us!
    A bit rough . . . an early piece . . . but . . .
    here is Playful Kitten . . .
    and Young Friend . . .
Playful Kitten We're dancing!

Love Mouth
Here is Many Treasures . . .
stirring a pot of . . .
Here's Rapture . . . Love's Gift . . .
Fresh Morning . . . Sparkling Eyes . . .
Scent-of-Ginger . . . Pure Joy, Pure Heart,
Pure Mind arms about each other . . .
Perfect Pleasure . . .
Me . . . hands making . . .
and look . . . look . . . who is this
holding up a lantern?
More Light More Light?
Love Mouth More Light.
Young Friend I'm dancing!
More Light So you are.
Love Mouth
I place it here,
close to the bronze army
but not of it, do you see?
When, many years hence,
people of the future gaze on this place
they will say,
'Aaah,
Aaah . . . this is to do with this
and this is to do with this.
How very interesting Art is!'

SCENE ELEVEN   A FESTIVAL OF ARTS

Music plays. Playful Kitten and Young Friend run off.
*A procession of the ladies enters, some playing. Playful
Kitten and Young Friend are dancing. Other ladies bring
on a steaming pot that smells of cooked meat.*
They take up the exact position of the small sculpture.

Love Mouth
> You see!
> You see?
> Exactly as we are!
> But for me with my hands in clay
> and you, More Light,
> holding the lantern!

Many Treasures Sisters . . . our feast.

Ladies
> We are hungry
> We are starving
> We are ravenous!

Scent-of-Ginger How good it smells!

Young Friend I'm so hungry!

Love Mouth
> I have deserved this!
> All this . . . creativity!

Pure Heart Have my seat, sister.

Pure Mind No, no, take mine!

Pure Joy My headache has quite gone!

Shy Smile
> I am getting quite used to this
> darkness.
> I see quite clearly!

Ladies
> Yes, yes!
> The eyes get used to it.
> One adjusts.

Rapture
> And one adjusts to the amount
> of air.
> It is quite fresh.

Ladies
> Yes, yes!
> It feels quite fresh!
> It feels like fresh air!

More Light looks up.

Shy Smile
   One adjusts.
   How miraculous the human body!

More Light stands.

More Light It is lighter.
Ladies One adjusts.
More Light It is cooler.
Ladies It feels like fresh air.
More Light
   It is fresh air.
   Listen!

Silence. Then a sound of digging.

TWELVE   THE TRANSFIGURATION

The ladies all become quite still.
   *The light grows and grows from a central source high
above. For the first time, natural daylight floods the tomb.
A modern rope ladder drops into the centre of the space.*
   *A man, dressed in modern dress, descends. He looks
around.*

Modern Man (*soundlessly*) Christ!

   *A Woman in modern dress comes down the ladder. She
stands with the Man. They look around.*

Don't touch anything.

   The Woman looks at him wordlessly.
      He goes to the bronze army.

Christ!

She kneels to look at the paper sculpture.

Modern Woman What's this?
Modern Man Don't touch anything.
Modern Woman This is falling to pieces . . . We must
  be . . .

The Man finds the women of the court.

Modern Man Christ! Look at these!

The Woman goes to the ladies of the court.

Don't touch anything!
Modern Woman
  Poor bastards!

*She reaches out to gently touch the face of More Light,
as the Man calls up the ladder.*

Modern Man
  Get down here and have a look
  at this lot!

*There is a sound of rustling and movement of old layers
of dust. From the ceiling flutter and drop millions and
millions of origami birds. The Modern Man and
Woman watch them silently as the lights fade.*
  Music.

A Million Birds, a Million Forgotten Artists

Bryony Lavery interviewed by Jim Mulligan

When Bryony Lavery was at college playing the part of the left arm of a sofa in a surrealist play best forgotten, she realized she could write better plays herself but it never occurred to her that she could make a living from it. However, over the years, as she had a succession of jobs including teaching and theatre administration, she gradually built up her expertise and became a writer.

I have often written specifically for children and I have learned that you have to free your mind from thinking that, because they are young, they won't understand complex ideas. You certainly have to be entertaining and cut out any flab from your work. Young people are very obvious critics. They will tell you directly what is not working. But, after all, they are open to ideas, excitement and magic.

More Light is based on a real historical event that Bryony Lavery had read about, a tomb that was opened in the twentieth century. That was as much as she knew and she invented the rest, but later she found that many of the ideas she had incorporated had been present in the real tomb.

The play is obviously about despotism, but this is taken as a historical fact. The Emperor in *More Light* has absolute power and learns nothing; the women are totally subjugated, but they are able to learn. Bryony Lavery did not set out to explore this phenomenon, rather she was interested in examining how our society regards art.

When experts talk about art they are usually male

experts talking about male art whereas women's art is frequently not solid or monumental and therefore it is not considered. When More Light says, 'Such art!' she is sometimes being ironic and sometimes commenting on an observable fact. The artefacts in the tomb are wonderful. But the irony is the importance given to that art as opposed to the art of the women which is released in the play.

All the women in the tomb 'had not borne sons' so that, presumably, those who had were left outside to carry on with life in an unchanged empire. The play deals with many aspects of sexuality: courtesans, oral sex, faking pleasure, castration – strong stuff for young people, some playing six-year-olds.

I don't know how young people are going to cope with it. That depends on how the companies deal with these issues. I made some changes in the second draft to make the sexuality more covert as I imagine it would have been in that society. But it is, after all, a play about courtesans and it is their job to pleasure men. In this sense it is a play about sex without love but finally there is sex with love. I think More Light and the Prisoner fall in love. Until they met they had only experienced loveless sex. What I present is the hideous imbalance of a power relationship between the Emperor and a concubine and between the Emperor and someone he can castrate. They start to communicate in a way that seems to me to be with love and understanding but More Light is faced with a frightful decision. She chose to support her sisters and to sacrifice the relationship with the man and a possible life outside the tomb. She probably thinks that, once they left the tomb, those men would set up the same constructions. Whether she's right or not – who knows?

A second moral issue in this play is cannibalism. In order to live, the women choose to eat the Emperor and then to kill men in order to continue living. In so doing they acquire part of the personalities of the people they eat. In some societies that practised cannibalism it was considered a compliment to eat an ancestor but in our society it is probably the ultimate taboo.

> When a person is dead it doesn't harm them to eat them but for me to do that is the ultimately evil thing. It unhinges you morally and from then on you will be capable of anything. In the play I have explored the fact that they have got over that hurdle in the most extreme of circumstances and it has kept them alive. This act releases them to do other things. I don't think they become immoral. I think they started to operate in a different morality. Remember, there are children there and they justify it for the children who are having horrible nightmares because they have become part of the people they have eaten. So, when a leader says, 'That's all right,' it puts a new construction on what is permitted.

In *More Light* Bryony Lavery has deliberately made her women very similar. She intended that they would start as a crowd of identical-looking women. Each had only one distinguishing quality which was the one the Emperor gave her when he named her. Once they have broken the taboo of eating human flesh they are able to become themselves. The exception to this is More Light who, from the start, is clearly different from the other women.

> She is a very clever young woman who has been allowed only a very narrow band of excellences. The many qualities she has are only realized when she is put in an extreme situation. In each scene she discovers something new: how to lead, the problems of leading, how to look

after her society, the hideous choices you have to make if you are protecting your society. The person who plays More Light will have to pay clear attention to what she says and feels. Why does she keep saying, 'I have had a most wonderful life'? It could be a very sensible option to count your blessings if you are going to die. But then she realizes she doesn't have to die. The people taking part in this play will have to think. This is hard but like More Light it gets you along. Play this well and you can learn a lot.

The climax of the play is when the twentieth century breaks into the tomb. For the first time a shaft of daylight penetrates the darkness to reveal dust and the shadows of what had been. As the archaeologists exclaim in wonder at what they have found, 'From the ceiling flutter and drop millions and millions of origami birds.'

In my experience the theatrical moments that people remember have hardly ever been when actors have made beautiful speeches but moments when something surreal has happened. I put the birds in because it felt right. Perhaps when they see them people will think of the hundreds of millions of artistic endeavours that have been forgotten and the people that have been forgotten. Every bird is a person.

Bryony Lavery is a playwright, director, performer and teacher of playwriting. Her plays include *Bag, Flight, Two Marias, Wicked, Origin of the Species, Witchcraze, Calamity, Kitchen Matters* and the award-winning, *Her Aching Heart*. She has been writer in residence at The Unicorn Theatre for Children and was one of the Artistic Directors for Gay Sweatshop.

Production Notes

The play is set in the tomb of a recently deceased far
eastern emperor. Sixteen of his concubines who have borne
him no sons, his bronze army, astrologers,
mathematicians, inventors, artists – those who represent
the finest achievements and mastery of the civilization are
immured alive with his body. Three screens or curtains
open in turn to reveal the Emperor's ladies, the Emperor in
death and the bronze army. The women determine to
survive by first eating his corpse and then resorting to
murder. They are led by the narrator of the piece, More
Light.

Lighting will need to suggest the darkness of the tomb,
which is occasionally lit by red lanterns. There are
moments requiring the shadow of an arm being raised and
the projection of the shadow of a huge man. Stars appear
at one point and natural daylight needs to flood the set
towards the end.

Sound effects include wooden chimes blowing in the
wind, galloping horses, the Emperor's arm being
dislocated, fire crackling then roaring, arrows travelling at
speed, furious drumming, men being dismembered and the
sound of digging. There is a burst of stirring and
impressive, solemn martial music, a sound somewhere
between that of a xylophone and a celesta. Scent-of-Ginger
uses the belts, swords and other appliances used by the
bronze army as percussion instruments.

There is the smell of sandalwood incense in the air at the
start of the play. The women make paper origami birds
which should fly away in a white flock and later become a
mobile. At the end scores of origami birds are dropped

and a ladder from the outside world needs to be lowered. The women use fans, bronze swords and daggers, bronze helmets as bowls and a steaming cauldron. They also create a small paper sculpture of themselves. A decision will need to be reached as to whether it is simply the sculpture that the man and woman discover at the end or the ladies.

The women are dressed in magnificent eastern gowns and wear lacquered wigs. Their names might suggest details in the costumes that will make them more individual, Many Treasures might wear more than her fair share of jewellery, for instance. High wooden platform shoes support bound feet and will make a great sound. Some of the items of clothing are later removed when the women become more active. At first their faces are whitened and their mouths are red. More Light wears a dark cloak at the beginning. The Emperor is dressed in a richly embroidered coat, jewelled shoes and white socks. The design for the bronze army, architects, inventors and so on can be as creative as desired because this is a fiction and not based on any particular culture.

CASTING

This play is suitable for a large mature group. The sixteen women are aged between six and sixty. It is perfectly possible for them to be played by boys but, ideally, the group should be the same sex. There is a bronze army that might be made up of actors or shadow puppets, the Emperor might be a dummy or never revealed. There is a wild and hairy man sporting a recent sword gash and a man and woman who appear briefly at the end in modern dress.

QUESTIONS

1 The women are proud of their art. What types of art do they practise in the play?
2 At the beginning of the play the women are what the Emperor would have wanted them to be, gradually they become themselves. How does this happen?
3 Playful Kitten and Little Friend use three ribbons attached to daggers. What does this symbolize?
4 What do the origami birds symbolize?
5 More Light and the Prisoner have been abused in different ways. How has this coloured their views of the world?
6 What happens to the women at the end?

EXERCISES

1 Have the actors playing the women make fans and explore their uses and the images they make. The fans will be different shapes and designs according to each character's individual taste.
2 Create the following tableaux:
– The moment the ladies walk into the tomb.
– Ladies sitting in a line.
– The bronze army.
– The men trussed up waiting to die with a few dead already.
– A glorious feast, everyone bloated and gorging.
– The moment when the Prisoner and More Light touch each other.
– The women attacking the Prisoner.
– What the modern man and modern woman discover.
3 Create a soundless moving image where the women are transformed from the ladies with fans to liberated women.

Suzy Graham-Adriani
February 1997

SHELTER

Simon Bent

Characters

Carly
Wally
Lesley
Anna
Niki
Gary
Darren
John
Dougie
Angela
Alf
Big Lad
Man offstage
Dan
Wayne

The play is set in the present. The action takes place in London and the location of the youth theatre presenting the play: where Scarborough and Yorkshire appears in the text, read the name of your town and county.

The characters in London are from different parts of the country; actors should only adopt accents that they feel comfortable with.

The play does not need an elaborate set, the less the better: for example, where the play indicates the need for a bench use an ordinary school bench, something very simple. There should be no black-outs between scenes; allow the scene to end and then for the actors to leave the stage, while the actors for the next scene take their place. Music may be used to cover the actor/scene changes if necessary.

SCENE ONE

London. Night. The Strand. A shop doorway. Gary, Dan and Niki wrapped in blankets and sleeping bags.

Niki sits upright, eyes closed, listening to a Walkman. Dan holds a cardboard sign saying I'M HOMELESS AND HUNGRY. PLEASE HELP ME IF YOU CAN. GOD BLESS. *A smiley face is drawn at the bottom.*

A commuter walks past.

Dan (*to commuter*) Can you spare us some change please, ten pence please, anything please for a cup of tea please?

Niki sings out loud a phrase from the song she is listening to. Gary looks at Dan's sign.

Gary Did you write that?

A commuter walks past.

Dan (*to commuter*) Have you got twenty pence please?
Gary It looks stupid. What's the smiley face for?
Dan A laugh.
Gary I saw a smiley face like that I wouldn't give you anything. I wouldn't.
Dan You wouldn't give anyone anything.
Gary Yeah, I would.
Dan Yeah, a cold. (*He looks at Niki, who is in a world of her own, and speaks loudly to her.*) How are you doing, Niki?

Niki doesn't respond. Dan nudges her. Niki opens her eyes.

Niki What?

Dan sticks both his thumbs up at her.

461

Yeah, great. (*She shuts her eyes and continues listening to her music.*)
Gary I'm cold.

Dan inhales deeply through his nose.

It's going to rain.
Dan I love that smell.
Gary That copper'll be back.
Dan Just smell it.
Gary I'm going up Piccadilly Circus later.
Dan I love the smell of beefburgers.

Niki takes off headphones.

Niki London is shit.
Dan Yeah.
Gary So go home then.

Enter Dougie and Anna.

Hey, Dougie.
Dougie Gary.
Gary Dougie, my man.
Dougie Gary.
Gary How's it going, man?
Dougie Cool.
Gary Yeah, cool.

They embrace. A lot of hand-slapping, etc.

Dan Hi, Anna.
Anna Hi, Dan. Niki.
Niki Yeah.

Gary and Dougie have finished embracing. Dougie does a flying kung-fu kick.

Dougie Yah!

He imitates Bruce Lee fighting, chopping and slashing

with arms and fists and kicking with feet. They all laugh.

Anna We're getting married.

Dougie Yeah. If I had some money we could score some draw.

Gary Yeah.

Dougie Yeah.

Dan Not me, I wouldn't. I don't like it.

Dougie What about you?

Gary What?

Dan Well, I don't.

Dougie Have you got any money?

Gary No.

Niki Me neither.

Dougie So we can't get no draw?

Gary No.

Niki No.

Dougie Oh well.

Gary Yeah.

Niki Yeah.

Silence.

Anna I've got some chocolate.

Dan (*to passer-by*) Can you spare us some change please, mate?

Niki So when are you getting married?

Anna It's not decided yet – Dougie only just asked me.

Dougie Yeah, coming over Waterloo Bridge, down on one knee, the works.

Gary Romantic, man.

Niki (*looks at Dougie*) Yeah, dead romantic.

Dougie I'm speeding, man. I can't keep still, I'm going over Leicester Square to see if there's anything doing.

Anna You said you were taking me home.

Dougie Oh yeah, after, yeah, after.

Niki Still at Bina Gardens?

Dan What's it like?

Anna Yeah, all right.

Dan D'you get your own room and that? So it's not like a hostel?

Anna It's only for another week.

Dan Then what?

Anna I don't know.

Niki You're getting married.

Dougie Yeah.

Anna Yeah. I thought you were in Cardiff.

Niki I was. I was going to stay but I got bored. London is shit. (*She exits.*)

Silence.

Dougie The coppers round here are pigs.

Gary, Dan and Dougie laugh.

Maybe see you later then.

Gary Over the square.

Dougie Yeah.

Anna You don't have to take me home.

Dougie I want to.

Anna No you don't.

Dougie Yeah I do.

Anna You don't.

Dougie I do.

Anna You said it was finished.

Dougie What – it is.

Anna So why did she walk off like that?

Dougie I don't know.

Anna You could hardly look her in the face.

Dougie It is, it's over, it's over between me and Niki.

Anna Yeah. (*She exits.*)

Dougie What? What have I done?

Gary Women.

Dougie Yeah, women. Anna – wait – Anna! (*He exits.*)

Gary and Dan sit. Gary wraps himself up and Dan picks up his sign. A commuter walks past.

Dan (*to commuter*) Can you spare some change please, mister. Ten pence, that's all, anything – I haven't eaten all day.

SCENE TWO

John's story, addressed to the audience.

John My mam and dad don't live together. I don't get on with my stepdad, he hits my mother. I can't live with my mam and I don't know where my dad is – so I left.

SCENE THREE

Scarborough, the park. Enter Carly carrying an old doll.

Carly (*shouts off*) Lesley.

Enter Wally running backwards straight into Carly. They collide and fall over. A tennis ball flies across the stage, over their heads and off.

Wally Watch it, you.
Carly Get lost.

Exit Wally. Carly shouts off.

Lesley.

Enter Wally with tennis ball.

Wally (*to offstage*) I was born here, Sparky. I've lived in Scarborough all my life. I belong here, you don't.

Boys offstage Wally. Chuck it. Chuck it, will you? Wally. Just chuck it. Chuck us the ball.

Wally throws the ball offstage and then takes up a fielding position.

Carly (*shouts off*) Lesley.
Wally (*looks at doll*) You're too old for that.
Carly What do you want?
Wally Nothing.
Carly (*shouts off*) Lesley.
Wally Is that your sister?
Carly Yeah.
Wally She's all right is your sister.

Enter Lesley, *her arm in a sling.*

Lesley That's my doll. What have you got my doll for?
Carly I want you to come home.
Lesley I'm not coming.
Carly I've come to take you home.
Wally Mind out the way, will you?

Carly and Lesley look at Wally.

Carly He fancies you.
Wally No I don't.
Carly He said.
Wally No I never. I'm playing cricket. (*He concentrates on his game.*)
Carly I want you to come home.
Lesley Carly.
Carly It gets lonely without you.
Wally (*referring to Lesley's arm*) How did you do that?
Lesley I fell on it.
Wally My mam says your mam's boyfriend gave it you.
Lesley And what does your mam know?
Wally Nothing. You don't look like sisters – one of you's big and the other's little. (*Pause.*) So, what

466

colour knickers have you got on?

Enter Big Lad upstage.

Big Lad (*to Wally*) You, yeah you.

Wally goes over to Big Lad.

Lesley I'm not coming home.
Carly Where are you staying?
Lesley With a friend.
Carly He's changed the locks so you can't get in.

Big Lad thumps Wally.

Big Lad Next time you can kiss my shoes. (*He exits.*)
Boys offstage Howzatt!

Clapping, cheering and whistling offstage. Exit Wally.

Carly I get lonely without you.
Lesley You'll be all right.
Carly You wouldn't just go away without saying?
Lesley No.
Carly You'd say?
Lesley Yeah.
Carly You'll be here for my birthday?
Lesley You'll be all right – he touches you and she won't
stand for it.
Carly I've used some of your make-up.
Lesley You can have it if you like.
Carly What, all of it? Really? Cool. Wait till I tell Tracey
Jackson. How's your arm?
Lesley It's all right. I'm all right.

Carly gives Lesley money.

Carly One pound thirteen pence. Get yourself a bag of
chips or something.
Lesley How's mam?
Carly I don't know. She's been out.

Lesley near to tears.

Lesley He had no right . . . no right . . . and she just . . .

Carly takes out a lolly and sucks it.

She's frightened he'll run off like all the others. He hasn't touched you?

Carly No.

Carly gives lolly to Lesley. Lesley sucks on it.

Lesley You haven't told anyone? I fell going up the stairs, right?

Carly Right.

Lesley You haven't told?

Carly No.

Lesley They'll take you away. They will.

Carly I don't want to go away.

Lesley He touches you, you tell me, you hear? You tell me.

Carly I haven't told anyone. Honest. I've told Arnie. Then I picked him up, but he didn't like it and scratched me.

Lesley Yeah.

Carly Yeah.

Lesley He's mental, that cat.

Carly Yeah.

Lesley Like the rest of the house.

Carly I'm not mental. They won't take me away.

Lesley No. I'm going to London.

Carly When? Can I come?

Lesley No.

Carly But I want to.

Lesley You can't.

Carly I want to.

Lesley You can't.

Carly I want to.

Lesley You can't – wah, wah, wah going on in my ear all

the time! I'll get a job, I'll get a flat, you can come and
stay – you'll see.

Carly I want to come.

Lesley Carly.

Carly How will you know where to go?

Lesley I'll know.

Carly Yeah, but how?

Lesley I just will.

Carly But how?

Lesley Shut up, will you? Come on, I'll buy you a bag of
chips.

Carly And I can come and visit?

Lesley We've got enough for onion rings.

Carly Nobody in our class has been to London.

Lesley D'you want onion rings or not.

Carly I'll have chips.

Exit Lesley.

Then I'm going round Tracey Jackson's.

Exit Carly.

SCENE FOUR

Gary's story, addressed to the audience.

Gary He's all right when he's sober – it's when he's had a
few. I mean, we really get on, me and my dad, he used
to take me fishing – but then when my mam died he
went to pieces. That's when he really started on the
drink. See, he didn't know what he was doing – one
minute he's crying and I'm trying to say come on, Dad,
and the next he's really laying into me, and he used to
be a boxer, you know. And then in the morning he'd be
really sorry and he'd start crying again. He loves me, my

dad, he taught me how to swim, but it just got like I was his punchbag. I went to stay with my gran, but she doesn't like me, I remind her too much of my mam, she hates my mam – says she ruined her son.

SCENE FIVE

London, Leicester Square.

Downstage right a bench. Lesley sits on it, a small backpack at her feet. Centrestage left Dougie and John lying flat on their backs, on a blanket. Between them a plastic bag, around them several empty beer cans. They are not drunk.

Dougie Let's swap places.

John I can't be bothered.

Dougie You'll feel better.

John Will I?

Dougie We'll stay where we are then.

John I'm not sick.

Dougie It doesn't matter. It'll just be the same wherever we go.

John I'm having the day off.

Dougie You don't work.

John I work.

Dougie You've never worked.

John I've worked. I had a job washing up.

Dougie You couldn't even do that.

John How long have you been in London?

Dougie turns away.

Come on, how long have you been here?

Dougie See that girl?

John And you're still sleeping rough.

Dougie She can't take her eye off me.

470

John Oh yeah.

Dougie I'm going to take her for a drink.

John No you're not, you're getting married.

Dougie So?

John So you can cut all that out for a start.

Dougie Not married now, am I?

John No.

Dougie So I can do what I want – if I can't do it now, when can I do it? After I'm married?

John No!

Both look away.
    Enter Alf. Sits on bench at other end from Lesley and reads a paper.

Dougie Let's have another drink.

John (*sulking*) Yeah.

Dougie What do you want?

John I don't know.

Dougie (*looking at the can John already has*) What's that?

John Beer.

Dougie You want beer?

John Do I?

Dougie What do you want?

John I don't know.

Dougie I'll have lager.

John You like lager?

Dougie I don't like beer, I've never liked beer.

Dougie throws can to John. They both open cans and drink. As they do so, Gary enters, chased by Niki. He is swinging a duffle bag round.

Niki You'll have to pay.

Gary Oh yeah?

Niki Just give it me.

Gary I'll give it you all right.

She lunges for bag.

Niki (*misses bag*) Anything happens to that bag and you'll pay.
Gary Oh yeah?
Niki Yeah.

She goes for Gary. He catches hold of her and they fall to the floor, rolling about on top of each other.

Alf (*to Lesley*) That statue's Charlie Chaplin.
Lesley Yeah, I know.
Alf I don't like Charlie Chaplin.
Lesley Oh.
Alf What about you?
Lesley I don't know.

Lesley looks away from Alf and he goes back to reading the paper.
    Gary is now on top of Niki and has her pinned to the ground.

Gary Give in.
Niki Never.
Gary I'll spit in your face.
Niki No.
Gary Give in.
Niki No.
Gary I will.
Niki No.
Gary I'll spit in your face.
Niki Never.
Gary Say it.
Niki No.

Gary spits in her face and rolls off, remaining by her side.
    Enter Darren, who goes straight over to Dougie and John.

Darren Give us a drink?
Dougie No.
Niki You spat in my face.
Gary I said, didn't I?
Darren I've lost my ring, my favourite ring.
John So.
Darren It's my favourite ring.
Dougie You're not getting a drink.
Alf (*to Lesley*) What's your name?
Lesley Lesley.
Alf Alf, Alfie – you can call me Alfie if you like.
Lesley Thanks.

Niki joins Dougie, John and Darren. She now has her bag.

Darren I've lost my ring.
Dougie Belt up, Darren.
Darren Don't tell me to belt up.
Niki He spat in my face.
Darren Silver skull and crossbones, I won it in Brighton.

Gary joins them. He sits next to Niki and playfully ruffles her hair.

Niki Get off.
Gary I spat in her face.
John (*to Niki*) Here, have a drink.

She takes can and drinks.

Gary What about me.
John You spat in her face.
Darren I'll never get another ring like that.

Niki gives can back to John.

Dougie Here, have you seen that advert for jeans with the old man in it?
John No.

Dougie Yes you have.

John I haven't.

Darren What advert?

Dougie I'm not talking to you, am I?

Darren Why, what have I done?

Dougie Nothing.

Niki (*looking at bag*) You've broke my bag.

Gary That's not broke.

Niki It's broke.

Dougie An old man standing next to a young woman.

John And they're wearing jeans.

Dougie Yeah.

John And he's got a tattoo on his arm.

Dougie Yeah. I don't understand it.

John Me neither.

Niki It's broke.

Gary It's not broke.

Niki You've broken the strap.

Gary I'll fix it then.

Niki You'll get me another.

Gary (*taking bag off her*) I'll fix it.

Dougie Maybe he's her dad, maybe they're family.

John No, no – definitely not – she's a supermodel.

Darren I've lost my ring and you don't care. Not one of you gives a toss.

Alf (*to Lesley*) Are you waiting for someone?

Lesley No – yeah.

Alf I'm not. Would you like a cup of tea?

Lesley No, thanks.

Alf Where d'you come from?

Lesley Scarborough.

Alf Nice, very nice. Have you been down here long?

Lesley No. I'm looking for a job.

Alf Come on, let me get you a cup of tea.

Lesley All right.

Alf exits and Anna enters.

Anna (*to Dougie*) Where have you been?

Dougie Nowhere.

Anna I've been looking all over for you.

Gary (*to Niki*) Give us a kiss.

Niki (*pushing him away*) Get off.

Darren (*picks up Dougie's can of beer*) Whose beer is this?

Anna You said the Embankment.

Dougie No I never.

John Yes you did.

Dougie I never.

Darren drinks beer.

That's my beer. You're drinking my beer. Who said you could drink my beer? (*He swipes can off Darren, then speaks to Anna.*)

Come on, give us a smile. You're here now – we're taking the day off.

Anna From what?

Enter Alf with tea. Gives one to Lesley.

Alf There you go.

Lesley Ta.

He sits next to her.

Alf Careful, it's hot.

Darren (*quoting*) 'Choose the bed of your dreams.' I saw that on the tube – it's an advert for beds. Who's bed would you choose?

John That woman sells flowers at London Bridge.

Gary Yeah.

Dougie Yeah.

Darren Yeah.

Anna You don't like her, do you?

Dougie Why not?

Anna She's old enough to be your mother.

John Yeah.

Darren Oh yeah.

Gary Yes, yes, yes!

Alf (*to Lesley*) So, what sort of work are you looking for?

Lesley I dunno, anything.

Alf Yeah. It was the same when I came to London – no job, nowhere to live. I like your bag.

Lesley Thanks.

Niki (*to Anna*) I don't mind, you know.

Anna What?

Niki You and Dougie, you know.

Anna D'you want some chocolate?

Niki Yeah, all right.

> *She takes some chocolate.*
> *Gary throws her bag at her.*

Gary There you go, all fixed. Now give us a kiss.

Niki No thanks, I don't want to catch anything. Has he bought you a ring?

Anna No, not yet.

Dougie (*quoting*) 'We shape the things we build, thereafter they shape us.'

John Look over there.

Gary What's that from?

Dougie An advert for shoes.

John Just look over there, will you?

Dougie Stop poking us, will you?

Darren I don't like the sound of that.

Gary Don't buy the shoes then.

Darren No, I won't.

John Alfie's chatting up your bird.

Anna Who's Alfie chatting up?

John No one.

Anna Who is she?

Dougie How should I know.

Niki One of us should go over.

Gary I like that one where she's hanging out the washing, you know?

Dougie You go over then.

Niki You go over.

Dougie I'm not going over.

Anna Why, what have you done?

Dougie Nothing.

Gary She's hanging out the washing in her bra and jeans, nothing else, her head half turned and she's smiling – blonde hair and a ponytail.

Darren Oh yeah.

John Gypsy Rose Lee – the Genes that built America.

Gary Spelt with a G.

Darren Yeah.

Dougie Yeah, she can do my washing any time.

Anna You don't wash.

Dougie I would for her.

Alf (*to Lesley*) I work in the entertainment business.

Lesley What, on the telly?

Alf No, not on the telly, but I know a lot of people that are.

Anna comes over to them.

Anna Now then Alfie, who's the friend?

Alfie Oh, this is Lesley. Lesley, I'd like you to meet Anna.

Anna Nice to meet you.

Alfie Hey, Dougie.

Dougie (*waves back*) Yeah, great.

Alfie How's the planet going?

Dougie Yeah.

Alfie Dougie's looking after the planet for us all. What do you think, Lesley.

Lesley I'm a vegetarian.

Anna Right, so am I.

Alf Dougie! (*He exits.*)
John (*to Dougie*) See you in hell, man.

> *Dougie exits after Alf.*
> *Niki, Gary, John and Darren gather round Lesley.*

Anna Got any fags?
Lesley I don't smoke.
Anna This is Niki, Darren, Gary and he's John.
John Like John Wayne.
Niki Yeah, right.
Anna How d'you know Alfie then?
Lesley I don't.
Niki Have you got anywhere to stay?
Lesley No.
Anna (*to Darren*) Stop picking your nose, you.
Darren I like picking my nose.
Anna Where are you sleeping?
Lesley Nowhere.

> *Darren smashes his fist on the bench.*

Gary Darren, behave.
Darren I've lost my ring. I can't believe I've lost my ring.
John He's always losing everything.
Darren No I'm not.
John What do you call it then?
Darren I just forgot, that's all.

> *Enter Alf and Dougie.*

Alf I'll see you round then, Lesley.
Lesley Yeah.
Alf Yeah.
Anna Yeah.
Lesley Thanks for the tea.
Alf Any time.

> *Exit Alf.*

Anna So what were you talking to Alf for?
Dougie Nothing.
John No, come on out with it.
Dougie I'm telling you, it was nothing.
Niki What d'you come to London for?
Gary Leave her alone.
Niki You broke my bag.
Gary So?
Niki You're going to pay for it.
John (*to Lesley*) They're always arguing, those two.
Lesley I'm looking for a job.
John That bloke you were talking to, he can get you anything, whatever you want.
Anna Whatever it takes.
Darren Alf's more for the tourists.
Niki Darren knows Alf, don't you, Darren?
Darren So, I do a bit of work for him, so what?
Niki Like what?
Darren You know, this and that.
Niki Oh yeah.
Darren Yeah. (*He exits.*)
Anna Have you got a sleeping bag?
Lesley No.
Anna Come on.
Dougie Where are you going?
Anna I'm taking Lesley to get a sleeping bag, all right.
Dougie I'll see you later.
Niki I'll come with you.

The girls go to exit.

John Here, Lesley – you want to keep away from Alf, doesn't she, Gary?
Gary Yeah.
John He's bad.
Gary Yeah.
John Like really bad – he does everything, drugs and

everything, you know, the lot.

Exit Niki, Lesley and Anna.

Dougie (*to a passer-by*) Got any spare change, mate – just ten pence, that's all – Your wife's screwing the milkman.
John I thought we were having the day off.

Exit Dougie.

Gary I like that poster over there.
John Where.
Gary There.
John Oh yeah.
Gary Tells you exactly what you're going to get – explosions, guns, helicopters, fast cars and pretty girls.
John Brilliant.
Gary Yeah, brilliant.

SCENE SIX

Anna's story, addressed to the audience.

Anna I had this one job, through an agency like, working in a hotel as a cleaner. Anyway, the manager sent me down to clean the toilets and I couldn't do it – I just stood there looking at these toilets and all the time I could hear this voice, this teacher we had at school, saying to me, 'You'll end up nothing, Glover, you'll end up a toilet cleaner,' and I kept looking at these toilets and I kept thinking, 'This is it, this is the rest of my life' – I couldn't do it, and the manager went ape, he threatened to sack us, so I told him where to stick his rotten job. I'd rather be out on the street. The money's not much worse and you haven't got some fascist shouting in your face if you don't like it.

SCENE SEVEN

Scarborough, the park.
  Carly with doll, crying. Enter Wally.

Wally Here, have a goodie. (*He offers her a sweet.*)
Carly Have you got any bubbly?
Wally Cherry Cola.

  He gives her some and has a bit himself. They chew
  gum.

Right, I'm going to throw some bricks at my house.
Carly It's my birthday.
Wally Happy birthday. Are you coming or what?
Carly No.

  Exit Wally.
  Carly alone on stage, chewing bubbly.
  Enter Wally.

Wally It's no fun on your own. (*He looks at doll.*) You're
  too old for that.
Carly It's not mine.
Wally Have some more Cherry Cola.

  Carly takes another piece. Both unwrap bubbly and put
  in mouths.
  Silence.

She'll come back.
Carly No she won't.
Wally Yes she will.

  Pause.

Carly You think so?
Wally Yeah.
Carly How do you know?

Wally Come on, let's go and throw some bricks at my house.
Carly All right.

Exit Carly and Wally.

SCENE EIGHT

Angela's story, addressed to the audience.

Angela This afternoon I just sat and cried. I couldn't stop. I don't want to die, but I wish I was dead.

SCENE NINE

London, Charing Cross tube.
  John eating a sandwich. Enter Dougie.

John You're wet.
Dougie It's raining. What's that then?
John A sandwich.
Dougie What is it?
John Egg summat.
Dougie Egg what?
John I dunno.
Dougie Go and get us one, will you? I'm soaking.
John It's raining.
Dougie Go on. I'd do it for you.
John Would you?
Dougie Yeah.
John No you wouldn't.
Dougie I would.
John You bloody wouldn't.

A commuter walks past them.

Dougie Can you spare us some change, mate? Just ten pence, that's all. I haven't eaten all day. I hope your bloody house burns down.

John They won't have any left by the time you get there.

Dougie Go on, go an' get us one, will you? I'm knackered.

John Why, what you been doin'?

Dougie Nothing.

John Where have you been?

Dougie Nowhere. Just around, you know – sleeping.

John You're always sleeping, you are.

Dougie Not asleep now, am I?

John No.

Dougie I was sleeping.

John Don't give us that.

Dougie Give over, will you, for Chrissakes. You're worse than me mam, you are.

John What did Alfie want then?

Dougie Nothing.

John So he didn't want anything?

Dougie What would he want? (*Pause.*) Enjoy your sandwich?

John Yeah.

Dougie Go on.

John It's raining.

A commuter walks past.

Can you spare us some change, mate? Just twenty pence, that's all.

The commuter gives.

Cheers, mate.

Enter Anna, limping, supported by Lesley.

Dougie What's the matter with you?

Anna What's it look like?

John You're wet.

Lesley Yeah, it's raining.
John And you look lovely.
Anna Drop dead.

Anna sits and tries to take off her shoe. Dougie helps her.

John You do, you look like Princess Di.
Lesley Oh yeah?
Anna I've been run over – flippin' shoe. I'm standing on the pavement and this bike just runs me over –

John smiles at Lesley.

Think it's funny, do you?
John No – honest, Anna.
Dougie Sit still, will you?
Anna What's so funny then?
John Nothing.
Dougie Do you want this shoe off or not?
Anna No.
John You should stick it in a bucket of water.
Anna Yeah?
John Yeah – stops the swelling.
Anna Why don't I use your mouth instead, do us all a favour.
Dougie Here, have a fag. Go on, calm your nerves – go on, I'll get some more.
John So, how are you?
Lesley Yeah, all right.
Anna I'll need a light an' all.
Dougie Oh yeah.

Dougie lights Anna's cigarette. Her shoe is now off.

John They're getting married.
Lesley Yeah.
Anna I was standing on the corner of Warren Street, talking to Lesley and Niki –

484

A commuter walks past.

John Can you spare us some change, mate – for a cuppa tea like . . .

The commuter gives.

Ta.

Anna Are you listening to me?

John Yeah – go on.

Anna No.

John I'm listening, aren't I?

Dougie Just ignore him, he's thick as pig shit.

John Heard about Darren? This fella smashed a bottle over his head –

Anna So I'm stood there talking to Niki and Lesley, right – when all of a sudden something hits me from behind and I'm not standing any more. I'm flat out on the pavement and it feels like someone's just punched me in the ribs, like I've been hit by a sledgehammer – and I can see my bag in the road and a bus runs over it and all I can hear is Niki shouting and screaming, and I don't know what's happening and I'm lying there thinking I could've been my bag and no one cares – I get run over in broad daylight and no one cares.

John When was this?

Lesley Four o'clock.

John What you been doin' since then?

Anna Recovering. I'm in a state of shock – I'll kill the pig that did it and if I can't find him I'll go round London and slash every bike tyre in sight.

Dougie Just calm down, will you?

Anna I could've been killed, for all the difference it'd make to you two – 'Where's Anna? . . . Dead, got knocked over by a bike . . . Oh, got any fags?'

Dougie Ah, don't say that, I wouldn't say that, I'd be dead upset me.

Lesley Yeah.
John Yeah.

A commuter walks past.

Got any spare change, mate?

The commuter gives.

Thanks. C'mon, we'll take you up the hospital.
Anna Would you really be upset?
Dougie Yeah.
Lesley Here, John, have you read this week's *Viz.*
John No.

Lesley takes a copy of Viz *out of her bag and throws it to John.*

Lesley Keep it if you want.
John What don't you want it?
Lesley No, I'm throwin' it away.
John You didn't buy it for us, did you?
Lesley No.
John Brilliant, this is brilliant. Thanks, Lesley.

Dougie snatches comic off John.

Ah, that's not fair. She give it me, not you.
Dougie Come and get it then.

John tries to get comic off Dougie. Anna joins in the chase. Dougie and Anna pass the comic between them, dodging Lesley and John.

Anna Over here.
John Just give it back.
Dougie Here.
Lesley Go on, give it him back.
Anna Dougie.
John Just act your age, will you, and give it back. What d'you want me to do, thump you?

Dougie stops.

Dougie You couldn't knock the skin off a rice pudding.
John No.
Dougie No.

Dougie throws the comic on the floor and John picks it up.
  Dougie lies down on his back, looking up at the sky. Anna lies next to him.

John She give it me, not you. (*He reads the comic.*)
Dougie We're killing the planet, the planet's dying.
Anna You're mad, you.
Dougie Yeah. (*He kisses Anna.*)
John (*reading*) 'I can drink fifteen pints of lager, eat three curries and still give the missus a good seeing-to when I get home. Can any of your readers beat that?' (*He laughs.*) Get it, eh? 'Can any of your readers beat that.'
Lesley Yeah.
John Man, this is funny.
Anna It's my last night at Bina Gardens.

Dougie gets up.

Dougie We'd better make the most of it then.
Anna No, I'm serious, Dougie.
Dougie We'll find something, all right. (*He pulls her up.*) So, where do you want to get married?
Anna Chelsea.
Dougie Yeah.

He puts his arm round her. Exit Dougie and Anna. Silence.

Lesley They've gone.

John looks up.

John Yeah.

He goes back to reading Viz.
    Silence.

Here, we should go up Oxford Street, you and me, do some
    thieving, get some jeans. You get good money for jeans.
Lesley No thanks.

    Lesley goes to exit. Enter Alf.

Alf Where's Dougie?
John I dunno. Honest, Alf, I don't.
Alf Are you all right?
Lesley Yeah.
John I'll tell him you're looking for him.
Alf Yeah.
John He said he'd seen you.
Alf What's your name again?
Lesley Lesley.
Alf Yeah, Lesley, great, great. (*Pause.*) You're doing all
    right?
Lesley Yeah.
Alf Good, good – If ever you need any help.

    Exit Lesley.

John What do you want Dougie for?
Alf What's it to you?
John No reason.

    Exit Alf.

SCENE TEN

London, a phone box.

Lesley Hello – mam? It's me – me, Lesley. London, I'm in
    London. Yeah, great, I'm great, everything's great.
    How's Carly . . . Look, I was thinking of coming – . . .

488

Who's paying? You, you're paying – you're paying for
him to go to Spain with you – What about Carly . . .
Because – because he – . . . That's not true – It's not,
that's not true – I never – I never – He's a liar. No, no,
no, I don't want your money, I don't need it – I don't
need fifty quid. I'm fine, everything's fine, I've got a job,
I've got a flat, I've got friends, I don't need you to send
anything.

SCENE ELEVEN

London, a room in a squat.

*Darren, Gary, John and Dougie stage left. Niki, Lesley
and Anna downstage centre. Dan and Wayne stage right.
They are all lying down on or half in sleeping bags, in
various stages of recline.*

*Centrestage, Angela sat on an upright chair, a large
suitcase at her side. She stares out front.*

Alfie stands upstage and watches.

Dan Got any fags?
Wayne No.
Dan Give us a fag.
Wayne Get off, will you?
Dan I never touched you.

Niki coughs violently.

Darren One person dies after taking E and it's all over the
papers. Ten people die of mad cow and they're not sure
you can get it from eating a hamburger.
Niki My head hurts.
Dougie We'll go down Heathrow tomorrow, nick some
aftershave, then go up the West End and flog it, right?
John I like watching the planes take off.
Gary I'm going to get a job as a dispatch rider.

Darren More people are dying of mad cow than they are of E.

Dan Go on, give us a smoke.

Anna I need chocolate, I can't live without chocolate.

Gary There's this firm I know, Hornets, they lend you the bike. I'm going up there tomorrow, see if they need any dispatch riders.

Dougie You can't drive.

Gary I can drive.

Dougie You need a licence.

Gary I'm seventeen.

John Yeah, but –

Dougie You haven't got a licence.

Gary I'll buy one then.

Niki I'm sick in the stomach, sick in the throat and sick in the head.

Lesley Yeah.

Darren I don't believe in God. Do you believe in God?

John I dunno.

Gary What does it matter?

Dougie We're all part of the planet, we are the planet, the planet is us.

Darren I never did really – I just thought there was something, but I didn't know what, but now I know for definite.

Gary No money, no home, no job.

Darren There's nothing.

Gary No job, no money, no home.

Darren Ecstasy is the best thing that's happened to me, the best – I don't care. I don't care if I'm dead in six months.

Dan (*to Wayne*) Do you like model aeroplanes?

Darren I'm so happy, I don't care if it kills me.

Dan takes out a model aeroplane from his bag.

It's the best. You should do some E.

Gary No thanks.

Darren Go on.

Dan (*to Wayne*) It's a Spitfire.

Darren Just half an E.

Gary You don't know what's in it.

Darren Yeah I do – E.

Gary You'll drop that but you won't eat a hamburger because of mad cow.

Darren Yeah.

Gary Mental.

John Everyone in London is mental. You have to be to live here.

Dan (*looking at Spitfire*) They won the Battle of Britain. I love model aeroplanes. I've got loads. Mosquito, Lancaster Bomber, Hurricane, Tornado, Lightning, Messerschmitt, Camel, Mig, B-52, F-11, Tiger Moth, and an Avro Vulcan B Mark 2 – all hanging off the ceiling, like they're flying.

Wayne Shut your face, will you?

Dan I'm only saying.

Wayne Go on, bugger off.

Niki coughs violently and Lesley wraps a blanket round her.

Dan I like painting them.

Dougie Get this right – if God made the world in seven days, then man didn't get here till ten o'clock Sunday night and in the last sixty seconds we've raped the earth.

Niki (*to Lesley*) Thanks.

Dougie We've made hundreds of species extinct, destroyed rain forests, burned up nearly all the oil and made a hole in the ozone layer. Sixty seconds, man, groovy.

Anna Fab.

Darren I've lost my jacket. This isn't my jacket.

Gary Where d'you get that from?

Dougie Greenpeace.

Darren I don't know how I ended up wearing this jacket.

Gary I'm gonna join Greenpeace.

Darren I woke up and I was wearing it, I don't know how it got on my back.

Dougie That one looks warmer.

Darren I've lost my jacket.

Dougie That looks better, I'm telling you.

Darren I don't care, I've lost my jacket. I can't find my jacket. I love that jacket.

Dougie All right, so I'll have that one.

Darren Like yeah – I'm going to look for my jacket. (*He exits.*)

Gary Where's he gone?

Dougie Do some E.

Gary Soft bugger.

Anna Fruit and nut chocolate.

Niki I'm burning up.

Lesley Who's that girl sat on the chair?

Anna She's Irish.

Dan sits with Dougie, Gary and John.

Dougie Danny.

John Danny Boy.

Gary Dan-o.

Dougie How are you, mate?

Dan Great.

Dougie Great.

John Yeah.

Gary Yeah.

Dougie Yeah, great. So how did you get the black eye?

Dan I got thumped.

Gary What for?

Dan Nothing. I didn't do anything.

John You must've done something.

Dan Nothing. This bloke just hit me.

Dougie Maybe he didn't like the look of your face.

Wayne Yeah, you're an ugly pig.

Dan I was sitting in Leicester Square and this bloke comes up to us with a little kid and shouts, 'Why don't you get a job?' so I says, 'Show me a bloody job and I'll take it,' and he thumps me, like that. I couldn't believe it.

John So what did you do?

Dan Nothing. I couldn't believe it. I says, 'Why did you do that?' and he picks the little kid up and tells us to fuck off.

Lesley What's she doing here?

Niki She's Irish.

Wayne Yeah, that or she's just fat.

Niki She's pregnant.

John (*looks at Angela*) I wouldn't touch it with a barge pole.

Dan He picked up the kid so I couldn't hit him.

Wayne Don't mind us, love, you just sit there. We're English.

Dan I mean, how can you hit someone carrying a kid?

Wayne What's in the suitcase then?

John A bomb.

Wayne You a terrorist?

Gary She's going to blow us all up.

Dougie Somebody blew her up all right.

Wayne Go home and blow your own lot up, Paddy.

Dan Yeah.

John clips Dan over the head.

Wayne She's on a kamikaze mission to blow us all up. Thick Irish Paddy.

Dan Yeah.

John clips Dan over the head again.

Gerroff, will you?

Wayne (*to Angela*) Don't let me bother you, love, I'm English.

Lesley Leave her alone.

Wayne What for?

Lesley Just leave her.

Wayne (*to Angela*) Blow up your own buses and office blocks.

Lesley I said don't.

Wayne Why, what's it to you?

Lesley Just leave her.

Wayne Irish cow.

Lesley Leave her alone. I said leave her, leave her alone. It's not her that's thick, it's you. You're stupid, thick and stupid.

Dougie Yeah, you're prejudiced.

Wayne I'm not prejudiced.

John You're prejudiced.

Wayne I'm not.

Dan You don't like black people.

Wayne Don't let me bother you, I'm English – I'm nothing. (*He gets back down in his sleeping bag.*)

Lesley Are you all right? Is there anything you need?

Angela I'm looking for Hammersmith. I can't find Hammersmith, I've got to get to Hammersmith.

Lesley I don't know where it is.

Wayne Don't let me bother you.

Angela I've got a friend lives in Hammersmith.

Wayne I'm English, I'm nothing.

Anna It's over the river.

Dougie We can do it, man, we can do it. We can save the planet.

Dan Yeah.

Wayne throws a boot at Dan.

Wayne Go to sleep.

They all settle down into their sleeping bags.
Silence.

Dan Night then.

SCENE TWELVE

Niki's story, addressed to the audience.

Niki I was in this squat in Kennington and we all just got out of our heads and raved – you just slept where you dropped – for six weeks. It was great. Then these heavies moved in and started asking for money, so I left. This one lad didn't pay and they found his body in the bins out back a couple of weeks later.

SCENE THIRTEEN

Scarborough, night. The woods.
Wally and Carly. Wally is trying to light a fire. He sits up and looks round.

Carly What?
Wally Nothing.
Carly I can't hear anything.
Wally No. (*He goes back to lighting fire. Noise off. He looks up.*)
Carly What?
Wally Listen. Over there. Behind that tree.

Both listen. Silence.
Wally kicks the fire to bits.

Carly What did you do that for?
Wally A laugh.
Carly What about the sausages?
Wally They were your idea.
Carly So you kick the fire out.
Wally It wasn't going. I couldn't get it to go – the matches are wet. Anyway, we haven't got anything to cook them in.

Carly holds up a stick with a sausage on.

Think you're clever don't you.
Carly Yeah.
Wally Dead clever, I bet.

She stands.

What?
Carly Sssh.
Wally What, what, what is it?
Carly Sssh.
Wally Stop it, will you?

Exit Carly.
  Silence.

Carly! Carly! Where are you, Carly? Stop playing games, Carly.

Noise off.

Carly!

Loud sound of wood hitting something hard.
  Silence.
  Wally picks up a stick.
  Noise of wood striking hard several times against the ground.

Come on, then – come on, you bugger – come on out.
  Come on – I'll kill you, I'll kill you, I'll kill you I will.
  Come on.

Silence.

Carly.

Silence.
  He sits.
  She runs up behind him and tags him on the shoulder.

Carly Gotcha!

Wally Arrrgh! What – what you laughing at?

Carly You.

Wally I knew it was you. I was just playing.

Carly Oh yeah?

Wally Yeah. I knew it was all a game, I was playing. I would have killed you if I wasn't.

Carly makes up the fire.

Now what do we do?

Carly Anything. Chuck us the matches.

Wally They're wet.

Carly Give them here, will you?

He throws them to her.

Go to sleep.

Wally I don't want to go to sleep.

Carly Go home then.

Wally You go home, I'm not going home. I'm hungry.

Carly I'll cook the sausages.

Wally Great.

Carly They're wet.

Wally So, I said.

Carly What are we going to light the fire with?

Wally How should I know.

Carly Great.

Wally Where's your mam gone on holiday?

Carly Spain.

Wally Why didn't they take you?

Carly I didn't want to go.

Wally Can I stay at your house tonight?

Carly We're sleeping out.

Wally Yeah.

Carly What's wrong with your house?

Wally I could come round and look after you.

Carly I can look after myself.

Wally They're fighting again.

Carly What for?

Wally I don't know. I keep getting in fights.

Carly What for?

Wally I dunno. Paul Pickering called my mam a slag, so I told him his mam was a prostitute and he hit me.

Carly Well, he would.

Wally Well, she is. And then when I got home my dad laid into us with a broom.

Carly What for?

Wally I don't know. Here, do you believe in ghosts.

Carly No.

Wally Me neither. I saw one when I was young – by my bed, an evil-looking pixie with straw hair, grinning, holding this dirty great big knife, bigger than a bread knife – up here like this. (*He raises his hand in the air.*) If I hadn't turned on the light, he'd have killed me.

Carly You were just dreaming.

Wally Yeah.

Carly Yeah.

Noise off.

We've got a frying pan at home. You can come back and stop over.

Wally All right.

Exit Wally and Carly.

SCENE FOURTEEN

Darren's story, addressed to the audience.

Darren I don't have to be here. I can go home any time I want, you know. Like at Christmas, it got really bad, it was cold and I had nowhere, there wasn't anyone,

nothing – so I rang my mam, just to have someone to
talk to – and she was like really pleased to hear me. She
was so pleased she says when am I coming home and
how much a week I'd have to pay to stay and I says I'll
be home in a week. That was four weeks ago but I'm
not going. It's got warmer, I got some cash and a few
mates have turned up. I reckon I'm all right for the
moment – I do what I want. I just want to have a bit of
fun, you know, fun, before I get old and settle down and
die.

SCENE FIFTEEN

London, St James's Park.
  Dan, Anna, Niki, Lesley and John.

Dan They have a military band here in the summer.
Niki He hasn't got a mam, I'm telling you.
Lesley How do you know?
Niki Because he hasn't. He was in care.
Lesley That doesn't mean he hasn't got a mam.
Niki He hasn't.
Lesley So why does he say he has?
Dan D'you think the Queen's ever gone hungry?
John I saw Darren working up Piccadilly Circus last night.
  He's working for Alf.
Dan He wants to watch that.
John He'll be all right.
Lesley What does Darren do for Alf?

  They all laugh but Lesley.

John He does a bit on the side for Alf.

  Anna and Niki laugh.

Dan I couldn't do it.

John You've done it.

Dan Not for Alf I haven't, not for anyone.

John Alf's all right.

Dan You don't like Alf.

John No, I don't.

Dan You're mad, you.

John Yeah. (*He exits.*)

Anna I'm fat.

Niki You're not fat.

Anna I'm fat. I'm getting fat.

Niki How can you be fat when you eat nothing?

Dan I'm going to look at the ducks. (*He exits.*)

Anna D'you like my ring? (*She shows them her ring, made of coloured string.*) It's only till he can afford a proper one. Dougie's got one as well.

Lesley Oh, it's lovely.

Niki Yeah, smashing.

Anna (*to Niki*) You haven't heard anything, have you?

Niki About what?

Anna Dougie.

Niki What's to hear?

Anna Nothing.

Niki So why d'you want to know if I've heard anything?

Anna No reason.

Lesley It's romantic.

Anna I think he's fooling around.

Niki No.

Lesley Never.

Anna I don't know.

Niki What makes you think that?

Anna He's been acting a bit funny, a bit odd like – detached. If you hear anything, you'll tell us?

Lesley and Niki Yeah.

Niki It gets cold when the sun goes in. Are you coming to the party tonight?

Lesley No.

Niki Come on.
Lesley No.
Niki It's easy.
Lesley I'm not coming.
Niki It's a party.
Lesley I can't do it.
Niki All you have to do is get drunk.
Anna And the rest.
Niki It's good money.
Lesley I don't care.
Niki There'll be food. It's warm.
Lesley I can't.
Niki So what are you going to do?
Lesley I'll find something.
Niki Oh yeah?
Lesley Yeah.
Niki I'm not staying out tonight.
Lesley No.
Niki I don't want to spend another night out on the street.
Lesley No.
Niki No.

> *Niki exits.*
> *Lesley swings her bad arm round, loosening it up.*

Anna What's wrong with your arm?
Lesley Nothing. I fell on it going up some stairs.
Anna Oh.
Lesley I did.
Anna I never said you didn't, did I?
Lesley No.
Anna Did you?
Lesley Yes.

SCENE SIXTEEN

The following are all addressed to the audience.

Angela I want to go home but my mum won't have me.

Wayne We shaved this kid's head. He was drunk, he passed out, so we shaved off all his hair.

Niki I'm getting used to it now, the things that happen, the fights and things.

Dan I don't want to go home. I can't go home. There isn't any room.

Gary I'd do all right in London me, if I had a job, if I had somewhere to live.

Alfie I kept running away. I did it so often, even the police gave up bothering. So when I left they didn't really help much. You were either adopted, got foster parents or had to look after yourself. I was sleeping rough and I met this girl, Carol, nice girl – she had a flat. I had nothing and she paid for everything. Then one day this mate says she's working King's Cross and I couldn't believe it. So I went up. She was scared I'd leave her if she said. But I didn't mind, not as long as I got half her money. I don't approve of children, that's sick – they should hang people like that, it's disgusting.

SCENE SEVENTEEN

London, Embankment tube.
Dougie and John begging. Dougie is eating a sandwich.

John You could've got us one an' all.

Dougie She wouldn't let us have another, all right?

John I'd have got you one.

Dougie Would you?

John Yeah.

Dougie Yeah. Look, I wasn't gonna get into a scrap with a
nun over a spam sandwich on your account, right?
What d'you want me to do – mug one of them?

John You could've just taken one when they weren't
looking.

Dougie Seen Lesley?

John No.

Dougie takes a bite of sandwich.

Dougie Ah, what. (*He throws sandwich away.*)

John I would've had that.

Dougie I thought she was with you.

John Look at the face on that.

Dougie So you haven't seen her.

John What does it matter where she is? (*Pause.*) When's
the wedding then?

Dougie Gary's looking for you.

John Can I be your best man?

Dougie He wants his sleeping bag back.

John Well, he can't have it. I've lost it.

Enter Lesley.

Dougie How's your arm?

John Hasn't dropped off then yet?

Lesley hits him with her bag.

What was that for?

Dougie They're giving out sandwiches round the back.

Lesley What have they got?

Dougie Spam.

Lesley I'm a vegetarian.

John looks at the sandwich Dougie threw away.

John I would've had that.

Dougie Go and get one then, will you?

John I don't want to.

Dougie What you going on about then?

John I'm not.

Lesley Stop going on, will you? You're not married to him, are you?

John No – I'm his best man.

A commuter walks past.

Dougie Can you spare us some change, mate. Just ten pence for a cup of tea like – Ah, go screw your grandma. (*Pause.*) Why don't you go and get a sandwich, John?

John Because I don't want to.

Dougie Go and get a sandwich, John.

John I don't want to.

Lesley What have you been doing?

John This and that, you know.

Lesley See you later then. (*She goes to leave.*)

Dougie Hang on, I'll come with you.

John What about me?

Lesley What about you?

John Oh, that's right, just piss off and leave me.

A commuter walks past.

Dougie Got any spare change, mate?

John What's going on?

Dougie Nothing.

John Don't give us that.

Lesley There's nothing going on.

John So why are you two running off together?

Lesley We're not.

She makes to go and Dougie follows.

John Hang on. Where are you going?

Lesley The Bullring.

John I don't want to go down there.

Dougie Don't come then.

John I like it here.

Lesley Well stay here then. You're old enough to look after yourself, aren't you?

John There's something going on.

Dougie Pack it in, will you?

John Don't talk to me like that. You're not me dad, you know.

Dougie Just grow up, will you?

John All right, there's no need to get like that. So how come you want to be alone with her all of a sudden?

Lesley throws her bag on the floor.

Lesley I don't care, I don't care whether he comes with me or not – all right! I've had enough, I've just about . . . What is it with you? There's nothing, right, nothing, nobody . . . Well, piss off, leave off, the lot of you – I'm going, I'm pissing off and going for good and I don't care, I don't care.

She falls to her knees and clutches her bag. Dougie puts his arm round her and cradles her.
A commuter walks past.

John Got any spare change, mate? I take credit cards an' all, you know.

Dougie kisses Lesley. She kisses back, then pushes him away.

Lesley No.

Dougie Why not?

Lesley I don't want to.

Dougie Come on.

Lesley Get off.

Dougie All right, all right – I was only being friendly.

He goes over to John.

John Alfie's looking for you.

Dougie What's he say?

John He'll have you, he'll bloody have you.

Dougie No he won't.

John You owe him, don't you?

Dougie No.

John Yeah you do. What do you owe him for?

Dougie Nothing, all right.

John That's not what Darren said.

Dougie What does Darren know, eh?

John So what's he want you for then?

Dougie Nothing.

Pause.

John You shouldn't have kissed her.

Dougie Grow up, the pair of you. (*He exits.*)

John You're not really thinkin' of goin', are you?

Lesley No. I love it here.

John Yeah. You'd say though, wouldn't you, if you were?

Lesley Yeah.

John So you're not going?

Lesley I might.

John I'm not going. I'm here for good, me.

Lesley I know this millionaire keeps offering to pay for me to go anywhere in the world I want – all I have to do is look after his kids.

John Why don't you do it then?

Lesley I don't like children.

John You don't really know a millionaire, do you?

Lesley Yeah.

John No you don't.

Lesley I do.

John Honest?

Lesley Yeah.

John Bloody hell.

Lesley Believe everything anyone tells you, do you?

506

John No. (*Pause.*) I've got second sight, me, honest – saw
a ghost once. You ever seen a ghost? It was stood in our
hall laughing – this old woman, a witch. (*Pause.*) D'you
like football?

Lesley No.

John D'you like dogs?

Lesley No.

John What do you like?

Lesley Nothing.

John I've got a dog.

Lesley Don't you know any jokes?

John I'll go and see if I can get us a cup of tea.

He exits.
   A commuter walks past.

Lesley Got any spare change, mister – Shit, just fifty quid.
I'm pregnant and I need an abortion . . . Don't bloody
look then – all right, two pounds for a bottle of meths.
Shit.

Other commuters walk past.

Got any spare change, sir. Please, sir.

They give.

Thank you, sir. Thank you.

Man offstage You.

Lesley looks offstage.

Yeah, you. You hungry? Come on, I'll buy you something
to eat. I'll get you something to eat if you want. What
do you want?

Lesley A burger.

Man offstage You can have what you want, anything.

Lesley I want a burger.

Man offstage What sort of burger.

Lesley A veggie burger.

Man offstage Have two veggie burgers.

Lesley No thanks, just the one please.

Man offstage You're sure you don't want two veggie burgers?

Lesley Yeah, I couldn't eat them.

Man offstage You probably couldn't eat one. Bugger off.

> *Laughter offstage.*
> *Lesley sits and cries.*
> *Enter Anna.*

Anna I'm looking for Dougie. (*Pause.*) Have you seen Dougie?

Lesley No.

Anna Come on, I'll buy you a bag of chips.

Lesley I don't want a bag of chips.

Anna I'm going to have a baby. (*Pause.*) I'm pregnant.

> *Enter John with tea.*
> *Enter Gary from opposite side.*

Gary Where's my sleeping bag?

John I dunno, honest I don't.

Gary You've lost it.

John No I haven't.

Gary Where is it then?

John I don't know.

Gary You've lost it?

John No – no – I just –

> *Enter Wayne.*

Hey, Wayne – how's it going?

Wayne It's all over, finished, mate.

Gary He's lost my sleeping bag.

Wayne Yeah?

Gary Yeah.

John No I haven't.

Wayne I've given up. I'm off the gambling for good. Dogs, horses, fruit machines, scratch cards, the lot – just the lottery.

Enter Dougie.

It's all over. Alfie's looking for you.

Exit Wayne.

Gary I want my sleeping bag, right?
John Right.

Exit Gary.

Anna What's Alfie want you for?
Dougie I don't know, all right.

John gives tea to Lesley.

John I think it's gone cold.
Anna Dougie?
Dougie Yeah.
Anna I'm going to have a baby.
Dougie Good for you. When?
Anna Don't be stupid – I'm pregnant, four months pregnant.
Dougie How do you know?
Anna I read it on the back of a cornflakes packet.
Dougie You're sure?
Anna Yeah.
Dougie Great, that's great.
John You don't look pregnant.
Dougie Whose is it?
Anna What do you mean, 'Whose is it?' We're engaged to be married.
Dougie I know, I know – only joking.
Anna You don't want a baby.
Dougie No, no – I love kids – I do.

Enter Alf. He runs up behind Dougie, swings him round

509

*and punches him in the stomach. Dougie doubles up
and Alf knees him in the face, then knocks him to the
floor. Alf kicks Dougie several times while he's down,
then takes out a knife and holds it to his face.*

Alf You leave my girls alone, right? You want one, you
pay for it like everyone else. They're my girls, they work
for me – Right? Right? You don't get it free. You've got
her for that. Right? Right?
Dougie Right.
Alf So now you owe me, right?
Dougie Yeah.
Alf Say it.
Dougie I owe you.

*Alf lets go of Dougie.
Exit Anna.*

Alf What are you looking at?
John Nothing.
Alf Are you trying to be funny?
John No, Alf. Honest, Alf, I'm not.
Alf Have you been fooling around with my girls?
John No.
Alf Good. (*He exits.*)

SCENE EIGHTEEN

Lesley's story, addressed to the audience.

Lesley He called me a slag, he said I was asking for it the
way I dressed and went mad, thumping me. My mother
tried to stop him but he pushed her away and kicked me
down the stairs, yelling and punching, and my mam's
trying to pull him off and he's kicking and I can feel
blood in my eye and she gets between us and she's
holding my head and kissing me and he's shouting, 'Get

her out, get her out, it's me or her, it's your choice,
woman.' And she's kissing me and says it's best for
everyone, how I've gone too far – and he's throwing my
stuff out on the street and she's kissing me and I wanted
to say fuck off, go away and die, kiss yourself awake,
kiss yourself awake – but I didn't, I couldn't say
anything. He broke my nose and did this arm in and
she's still living with him.

SCENE NINETEEN

London.
   *Niki and Anna begging at the end of Hungerford
Footbridge, downstage left.*
   *Lesley is sitting on a bench in Leicester Square, upstage
right.*

Anna I can't feel my feet.
Niki My sister's got blonde hair.
Anna That big church, it's St Paul's.
Niki (*to passer-by*) Have you got any spare change
   please?
Anna I can't feel my feet.
Niki Jump up and down.
Anna I want chocolate.
Niki (*to passer-by*) Ten pence for a cup of tea, that's all.
Anna It's ugly.
Niki How much money have you got?
Anna You've got all the money.
Niki Have I?
Anna Yeah, you have.
Niki Oh.
Anna I hate St Paul's.
Niki (*to passer-by*) Got any spare change please, miss?

   The passer-by gives.

Thank you, miss. Thank you.

Anna Yeah, happy Christmas.

Niki It's not Christmas.

Anna I can't feel my feet.

Niki What's wrong with St Paul's?

Anna It's ugly. How much money have we got?

Niki empties her pockets.
    Enter Alf upstage right. Sits at opposite end of bench from Lesley.

Niki Sixty-seven pence and a Polo.

Anna Where did you get the Polo?

Niki Out of a packet.

Anna Give us the Polo?

Anna breaks it in half and gives half to Niki.

Niki Ta.

They eat Polo.

Anna It's because I've got big feet.

Niki You'll be in bed and breakfast soon.

Anna He's not coming anywhere near this baby.

Niki But he's the dad.

Anna I've got bad circulation. There's not enough blood to go all the way round.

Niki Stop going on, will you?

Anna He's not interested.

Niki Have you got a sister?

Anna No.

Niki I've got a sister.

Anna It's the same with my ears.

Alf (*to Lesley*) Hello.

Lesley Oh, hello.

Alf You're still here? You haven't gone home?

Lesley No.

Alf My dad's a millionaire – he's from another planet.

(*Pause.*) D'you get on with your dad?

Lesley Yeah.

Alf He came round once, packed all my things in a suitcase and said he was taking me away if my mum didn't stop drinking, taking me away and they'd put me in care. Yeah, like he's the big man – big house, big car and I have to go into care. (*He offers Lesley a fiver.*) Go on. Get yourself something to eat.

She takes it.

I'll take you for a drink if you like.

Lesley No, thanks.

Niki (*to passer-by*) Got any spare change please, sir? I'm HIV-positive and I can't get a job.

Anna Let's get some chocolate.

Niki No.

Anna I need chocolate.

Niki That's because you're pregnant.

Anna No it's not. I like chocolate. I'm not having it christened. I don't believe in all that.

Niki You'll be in bed and breakfast soon.

Anna You can come and visit.

Niki Yeah.

Anna I might call it Clint.

Niki You can't call it Clint.

Anna Why not?

Niki It might be a girl. My sister's name is Harley Rose.

Anna Let's get some chocolate.

Niki She was four the last time I saw her.

Exit Anna and Niki.

Lesley I've got a place in a night shelter.

Alf How is it?

Lesley All right. It's only for two weeks.

Alf Yeah.

Lesley Yeah.

Alf It makes you feel bad, doesn't it?
Lesley Thanks for the money.
Alf Come on, I'll buy you a drink.
Lesley All right.
Alf That's it, let yourself go.
Lesley Just the one.
Alf You need a bit of looking after.
Lesley Yeah.
Alf Come on.

Exit Alf and Lesley.

SCENE TWENTY

Angela's story, addressed to the audience.

Angela I was wearing big woolly jumpers in summer and throwing up. The look on my mother's face. She knew all right, but she wasn't saying, she was hoping, praying that it would just go away so she wouldn't have to say. My dad would have killed me. I should go to church. I can't go to church. I thought you could just walk in off the street – I had the money. I rang my mother, I was drunk, she was crying, I wanted to go home – She called me a slut then cut me off. I'll have to get some maternity clothes.

SCENE TWENTY-ONE

Scarborough, the swimming pool.
Enter Carly and Wally, with wet hair and towels.

Carly D'you want crisps?
Wally The machine's broke. Does your mam take tablets?
Carly What for?

Wally I dunno. The doctor gives my mam tablets.
Carly What flavour do you want?
Wally The machine's broke. They're for her nerves.

Carly looks in a wall mirror and combs her hair.

I might be gone soon.
Carly Where are you going?
Wally Anywhere.
Carly You're not going.
Wally I'm going.
Carly You won't go.
Wally I might go to London and stop with your sister. How is she?
Carly I got a card.

She takes a card from her swimming bag and gives it to Wally. He looks at the picture.

Buckingham Palace.
Wally I know, I can read. (*He turns it over and reads:*) 'Love, Lesley.' Doesn't say much, does it?
Carly She's got a job, she's got a flat, she's got loads of new friends and – and I'm going to see her.
Wally When?
Carly When I go.
Wally You're going to London?
Carly Yeah.
Wally Can I come?
Carly Maybe.
Wally I'd like to live in London. I hate this place.
Carly You like swimming.
Wally Yeah, I like swimming. I don't like school.
Carly You don't go to school.
Wally Yeah, I don't like it.
Carly I like school.
Wally I wouldn't get thumped in London. They've got everything in London.

Carly What flavour crisps do you want?
Wally The machine's broke.
Carly We'll have to go to the shop then.
Wally Yeah.

Exit Carly and Wally.

SCENE TWENTY-TWO

London, a shop doorway. The Strand.
Dougie lying half asleep and John sitting up. John shakes Dougie by the shoulder.

Dougie No.

John shakes him again.

Don't, I said don't.
John We can't sleep here the copper said.
Dougie He would. It's his job.
John He'll have us.
Dougie Stop it, will you? I'm trying to sleep.
John He'll be back and he'll 'ave us.
Dougie Give over, will you?
John Well, that's what he said. I don't want to spend the night locked up.
Dougie Are you gonna let me sleep or what?
John No.
Dougie Why do I put up with you?
John Dunno – 'cos you like me, I suppose. (*He takes out a fiver.*)
Dougie Where d'you get that from?
John This German bloke – he give us it for standing outside a restaurant while he took a photo of it. Said it were for the papers.
Dougie Which one?

John Dunno – be in Germany somewhere. I've never been
to Germany.

Dougie You've never been anywhere.

John I come here, didn't I?

Dougie That's breakfast taken care of then.

John My breakfast, yeah.

Dougie What about me?

John What about you?

Dougie You said we'd split it.

John No I never.

Dougie We split everything.

John Oh yeah?

Dougie Yeah.

John I'll think about it.

Dougie Go to sleep.

(Pause.)

John Have you seen Anna?

Dougie No, and I don't want to.

John She's having your baby.

Dougie It's not my baby!

John All right. (*Pause.*) Have you seen Lesley? Nobody's
seen Lesley. Where d'you think Lesley's got to? I saw
Darren today, he hasn't seen her neither, no one has.

Dougie Stop going on.

John She's gone.

Dougie So, she's not your mam, is she?

John You'd have thought she'd say goodbye.

Dougie Give it a rest, eh.

John Well, she said she would. D'you think she's gone
home?

Dougie How should I know.

Enter Gary.

John Here, Gary, have you seen Lesley?

Gary No.

John I haven't forgot about your sleeping bag, honest.

Gary Keep it. I don't need it. I moved into the Camberwell Foyer this morning – my own room and everything.

John Really? You hear that, Dougie?

Dougie Yeah, yeah.

John How long's that for then?

Gary Two years.

John Two years?

Gary I've been waiting months. It's great. They've got everything – a café, workshops and everything. I rang my dad and he's really pleased, you know – He's coming down. You should meet my dad, you'll like my dad. (*Pause.*) I'm learning to drive.

John Yeah?

Gary Yeah. See you around then.

John Yeah.

Exit Gary.

Here, can you ride a motorbike?

Dougie Yeah, 'course I can.

John I mean a proper one.

Dougie So do I.

John When?

Dougie I had this mate.

John Oh aye.

Dougie He had a Honda 125 and he let us go on it now and again.

John Bloody moped – You couldn't go scrambling on that.

Dougie He didn't want to.

John I do.

Dougie What you doin' in London then?

John I'm gonna get a motorbike.

Dougie What with?

John I'll nick one. You can teach us to drive it.

Dougie Yeah. Now go to sleep, will you?

John We can't sleep here.

Dougie We'll go down the Arches then, shall we?

John Oh, I'm not going down there.

Dougie Shut up then, will you, and go to sleep.

John All right (*Pause.*) Here, you don't think anything's happened to Lesley, do you?

Dougie No.

John Where's she come from?

Dougie Dunno. Yorkshire.

John He'll 'ave us, that copper'll 'ave us.

Dougie She's probably gone home.

John Yeah.

Dougie turns away and curls into a ball. John pulls his blanket up over himself, turns away and curls into a ball. They are sleeping back to back. John turns and curls up into Dougie.

From *Wigan Kiss* to *Sugar Sugar*

Simon Bent interviewed by Jim Mulligan

Simon Bent studied drama at Birmingham University and spent his formative years as a writer at the Royal National Theatre Studio under the direction of Peter Gill. He started work in the theatre as an actor/ASM for Caricature Theatre, Cardiff. Then he and a colleague formed a small touring company, Frank 'n' Sime, for which he wrote a play called *Wigan Kiss*. They toured this round youth clubs, community centres and studio theatres.

> It was when I became writer in residence at Essex University that I decided to stop acting and to write full time. I had an office on the campus and anybody could drop in to discuss their ideas. I did a few workshops for MA students and I did some workshops in local prisons and remand centres.

Shelter is written for young people to act their own ages. He did not want a seventeen-year-old playing a fifty-year-old. He welcomed the challenge of writing for a large cast and he wanted a subject that was relevant to them and one that he felt strongly about. Originally the play, ten minutes long in three acts, was written for the National Theatre Writers' Workshop.

> I did a lot of research and went to see people at Centre Point and spent nights in housing shelters. They knew I was a writer but they didn't mind. I don't think I ever penetrated into their world. To a point they volunteered their stories but not in detail. It would have been an intrusion if I had asked them about their life-stories. In the play, of course, I know all the life-stories because I

520

have invented the characters but that doesn't mean to
say I have to reveal everything. It is my way of writing
to drop hints and make the audience work hard to fill in
the gaps.

At the start of writing Simon Bent knew that there was a
girl called Lesley who had a younger sister. Lesley is going
to leave home for London where she will meet other
young people living on the streets. At the end of the play
she will disappear. After that he did not know for certain
what would happen. In fact the play explores the lives of
fifteen young people and in so doing touches on physical
abuse, bullying, drug-taking, low-paid jobs, prostitution,
begging and racism.

I found *Shelter* a very upsetting play to write because I
kept on being drawn into situations where things were
intolerable. Young people leave home because they are
being beaten or sexually abused or there is not enough
room for them at home. And all the time legislation is
making it more difficult for them to survive. The
problems for the homeless include the cold, sickness,
their vulnerability, the loss of dignity. But I think the
worst thing must be the sheer terror inside, the fact that
anybody can come up and give them a severe beating
and no one would care.

The play is structured with scenes interspersed with
monologues when characters reveal themselves, not in a
didactic way, but in order for the audience to be pulled up
abruptly and for a new emotional level to be reached. The
play starts with a scene in London and then cuts to a scene
in a provincial town where Lesley says she is going to
London. From then on, as we follow her until her
disappearance, we go back to her home town to find out
the effect of her leaving.

The monologues were an experiment to break into the

action. When you are writing something I don't think you're always aware of what is happening. It is an adventure. The characters I was working with were good material and I let them work for me. Rather than me deciding a structure, sometimes the monologues declared themselves to me. Some issues I chose not to deal with. For example, Lesley's step-father has beaten her, knocked her downstairs and forced her to leave home and her mother has not protected her daughter. I do not allocate blame here. I do not condone their behaviour but it is not an issue in this play.

Simon Bent makes a distinction between what a character says and what he would say about a situation. He rarely allows his characters to pass moral judgements, although in *Shelter* he allows one character to call Darren a 'soft bugger' because he is taking ecstasy. He also allows characters to comment mildly on Wayne's virulent racism.

Shelter is a play with aimless characters wandering around trying to make sense of an absurd situation. One of the counterpoints to the central dialogue is the way these destitute young people discuss the potency of the advertising images that surround them, images of things there is no possibility of them buying, images of great sensuality and beauty.

The fragmented dialogue should work like music. If I've structured it properly, what looks difficult on the page will appear very accurate with natural rhythms of speech. And there are some carefully constructed contrasts that should help. For example, in one scene Lesley is in a squat. She is totally adrift with nothing to hang on to. The next scene shows Lesley's sister and Wally in a dark wood. Both scenes are dark and frightening like a fairy story. And throughout you have the deliberate and unconscious humour of unrelated conversations being interwoven.

Shelter is a political play but it is not the agitprop of the seventies. The anger is understated. A fragment of society is portrayed without comment and the audience is left to make up its mind about how our society causes homelessness and deals with it.

I find it totally unacceptable that there should be homeless people sleeping on the pavements of our towns and I have written a play about it, probably to draw attention to it, but I can't see that this play will make a big difference. The most I can hope for is that the young people who take part in the productions and their families will become more aware.

At the time of this interview, Simon Bent was in the final stages of finishing a new play called *Sugar Sugar*.

Simon Bent graduated in drama and worked as an actor before spells as a writer in residence at Essex University and the Guildhall. His previous plays include *Wasted*, *Bad Company* and *Goldhawk Road*, a Bush Theatre commission in 1996.

Production Notes

STAGING AND SETTING

The play is set in the present in London, and another
location which can be the company's home town. The play
is broken up into twenty-two short scenes which should be
seamless. The London outdoor locations are the Strand,
Leicester Square, the Embankment, Charing Cross Tube
Station and Saint James's Park – in other words, areas well
known to be hang-outs for the homeless. One scene takes
place in a squatters' flat. The scenes out of London take
place in a wood and in the foyer of an indoor swimming
pool. This is an impressionistic play and locations should
be suggested or hinted at as simply as possible: it is
important to create a flexible space that enables the action
of the play to flow quickly from scene to scene.

There is a series of monologues which should not hold
up the action of the play. The audience should be in
close proximity to the actors, rather like the sort of
crowd you would find at Leicester Square, who will
observe ugly arguments and scenes of violence and will
not intervene.

CASTING

Shelter offers great scope to a company aged between
twelve and eighteen with a capacity to work as a strong
ensemble. There are fourteen main characters (nine male,
five female) who can double up as a crowd and
commuters, and there is a man's voice offstage. The
characters in London are from different parts of the
country, but actors should only adopt an accent they feel

comfortable with. Avoid spoiling the rhythm of the
language or throwing away words such as 'yeh'.

QUESTIONS

1 What help and advice are young homeless people
   entitled to?
2 Bina Gardens is a local authority centre referred to in
   the play. Which characters are reluctant to take
   advantage of the help it offers and why?
3 In what circumstances would you give money to
   someone who is begging?
4 What strategies for survival have the various characters
   adopted and with what varying degrees of success?
5 Which characters do you have the most/least sympathy
   for?
6 What do you think has become of Lesley?

EXERCISES

1 Interview homeless people, find out at first hand what
   it's like to sleep rough.
2 Make a prop list for each of the characters which takes
   into account their various obsessions. What does it tell
   you about them?
3 Often we enter a scene mid-conversation. Take Scene 5,
   for instance, and improvise what has gone on between
   Dougie and John immediately before the scene begins.
4 Rehearse the play at speed with none of the actors
   permitted to sit down when not directly involved in the
   dialogue. Recycle characters so their roles are constantly
   changing to become the crowd, commuters, scene
   movers and so on.
5 Look at Lesley's monologue in Scene 10. Improvise her

mother's side of the telephone conversation.

6 Create a monologue for Dougie.

7 Choose a few of the monologues and improvise the scene that is described.

8 Imagine that Carly and Wally do come to London in search of Lesley and meet up with Dougie, John and the others. Improvise the scene that might take place.

Suzy Graham-Adriani
February 1997

SPARKLESHARK

Philip Ridley

'We won't use guns,
we won't use bombs,
we'll use the one thing we've got more of –
that's our minds.'

from 'Mis-shapes' by Pulp

Characters

Jake
Polly
Natasha
Carol
Russell
Buzz
Speed
Shane
Finn

*The rooftop of a tower block in the East End of London.
Many TV aerials and satellite dishes, a large puddle,
discarded household furniture, piles of rubbish and
various scattered detritus.*

*Some metal steps lead from the main larger area of roof
up to a tiny platform. There's a doorway here, leading to
the emergency stairs. This is the only entrance to the roof.*

*It is about 4.30 in the afternoon. Mid-September. The
weather is overcast.*

*Jake enters. He is fourteen years old, slightly built and
clutching a satchel. He is wearing a well-worn, but still
clean and tidy, school uniform and glasses (the left lens is
cracked and the bridge held together by sticky tape). His
hair is neatly cut.*

*Jake makes his way down to main area of roof and sits
in an old armchair. He is familiar and comfortable with
these surroundings. It's a place he's been many times
before – his secret hideaway.*

*Jake takes notebook from satchel and reads, nodding
and murmuring thoughtfully. Then he takes a pen from
inside pocket and writes.*

Jake Big . . . fish! Bigfish! . . . No, no.

*Tears page from notebook, screws it up and throws it
aside. Starts pacing the roof and continues to write –*

Glitter! Glitterpiranha! . . . No, no.

*Polly enters. She is fourteen years old and wearing the
same school uniform as Jake, although hers is brand
new (and has a skirt instead of trousers). Her hair is*

longish, but held primly in place by an elastic band. She is clutching a tiny tool box.
     Polly watches Jake from the raised platform.

Jake Shark! Yes! Shark . . . glitter –

Jake turns and sees Polly. He lets out a yelp of surprise and drops his notebook. Loose pages flutter everywhere.

Polly Oh, I'm sorry.

Jake starts picking up pages.
     Polly climbs down metal steps and starts helping him.

Jake Don't bother.
Polly No bother.

Picks page from puddle.

This one's a bit soggy. Can't quite read –
Jake (*snatching it from her*) Don't! This is . . . it's personal stuff. You can't just stroll up here and start reading things willy-nilly! Watch out! You're treading on one now! You should be in a circus with feet this size. What you doing here anyway? This is *my* place! Go away!

Pause.

Polly I've only got three things to say to you. One: what I'm doing up here is none of your business. Two: the roof is not your private property – unless, of course, you have a special clause in your rent book, which I doubt. And three: I find it strange that someone who can write such magical words has such a spiteful tongue in his head . . . Now, I've got something I need to do, then I'll be gone. In the interim, I'd be grateful if you didn't speak to me again.

Goes to satellite dish that's positioned on the edge of the roof. She opens tool box, removes screwdriver and –

none too convincingly – starts fiddling.
  Pause.

Jake Is it really magical?
Polly . . . What?
Jake My writing.
Polly Bits.

Pause.

Jake I . . . I was wondering whose dish that was.

Pause.

I'm Jake.
Polly I know.
Jake How?
Polly Oh, please – Your eyes! Use them!

Indicates her school uniform.

Jake You go to my school!
Polly Started last week.
Jake Haven't seen you.
Polly Not surprised. All you do is hide between those two
  big dustbins at the back of the playground.
Jake I like it there.
Polly But, surely, they're a bit . . . well, smelly?
Jake Don't notice after a few deep breaths.
Finn (*off stage*) AAARGHHNAAAHHH!

Polly leans over ledge.

Polly All right, Finn! Tell me when it gets better.
Finn (*off stage*) AAARGHHNAAAHH!

Polly continues fiddling with satellite dish.

Jake That . . . that voice! I've seen it – I mean, I've seen
  who it belongs to. He joined my class last week.
Polly That's my baby brother.

Jake Baby! But . . . but he's huge! He grabbed two desks. One in each hand. And lifted them up. Above his head.

Polly I suppose even you would have to notice that.

Jake The teachers want him expelled already. All the boys are scared of him. They call him the Monster –

Polly He's not a monster! Everyone calls him that! Everywhere he goes! But he's not! He's very gentle! Cries easily, if you must know.

Finn (*off stage*) AARGHHNAAAH!

Polly (*calling*) OK, Finn! (*at Jake*) It's getting better.

Jake You understand him?

Polly It might sound like a meaningless groan to you but – believe me – once you grasp the nuances, it's a very subtle form of communication.

Finn (*off stage*) AARRGHHNAAAHHH!

Jake Subtle? That?

Polly Well, he's in a bad mood. Missing his favourite programme. The one with real-life accidents. You know? Housewives setting themselves on fire with dodgy hair-dryers –

Finn (*off stage*) AAAH!

Polly All right, Finn! – And everyone watches these programmes because they're supposed to be educational –

Jake But all they really want to see is someone's head getting sliced off by helicopter blades.

Polly Precisely.

Finn (*off stage*) AAAH!

Polly Thanks, Finn! – That's it! He'll quieten now. Picture's perfect. Well, perfect as it'll ever be with this equipment.

Starts packing up tools etc.

Dad got it cheap somewhere. I'm sure there's bits missing. And there was no instruction manual. Haven't a clue what I'm doing really – You know anything about this sort of thing?

Jake All I know for sure is you've got to aim the dish at a
satellite up there.

Polly Perhaps I should put it higher – Oh!

Jake What?

Polly A dead bird . . . Poor thing. Only a baby. Must have
fallen from one of the nests.

Peers closer at dead bird.

All mauve and scarlet. Little yellow beak. Come and have
a look.

Jake . . . Rather not.

Polly Can't hurt you.

Jake Not that . . . I can be seen up there. By people in the
football pitch.

Polly There's no one in the football pitch.

Jake But there might be. Any minute now. If he sees me –
oh, you won't understand.

Polly Try me.

Pause.

Jake It's Russell –

Polly The turbo-dreambabe?

Jake Turbo *what*?

Polly That's what's written all over the toilets. TICK HERE
IF YOU THINK RUSSELL'S A TURBO-DREAMBABE.

Jake Bet the wall's covered.

Polly Everyone loves him –

Jake Love! I'll show you what your precious turbo-
whatever has done . . . Come here! Come on!

Polly goes to Jake.

Feel!

Jake points at top of his head.
    Gingerly, Polly feels.

Polly Oooo . . .

Jake An elbow did that. (*Rolling trouser leg up*) And here!

Polly Very colourful.

Jake A foot! – And look in my eyes. Does the left one look a little bloodshot?

Polly . . . Yes.

Jake A fist!

Slight pause.

Polly The turbo-dreambabe?

Jake Bingo! – Hang on! You ticked! You like him!

Polly I don't know if I *like* him –

Jake You ticked!

Polly Yes, I ticked! The other day he took his shirt off in the playground and – yes, I admit – I felt a tingle.

Jake Animal!

Pause.

Polly I'm sorry you're bullied. Russell is a nasty piece of work. It's like my mum said about Dad, 'Sometimes the worst presents come in the nicest wrapping paper.'

Slight pause.

Jake Muscles! Who needs 'em? I don't want to do six thousand sit-ups a day. I don't care if I don't make people tingle –

Polly But you do! At least . . . you do me.

Jake . . . How?

Polly Your stories.

Jake How do you know about my stories?

Polly The other day . . . when I was fixing up the satellite dish – totally wrongly, I bet – I noticed . . .

Takes several folded sheets from pocket.

I'm sorry, I'm sorry. I know I shouldn't have. But . . . oh, Jake, there's such wonderful things here. When I read

534

them I . . . I tingle as if a thousand Russells had revealed a thousand six-pack stomachs.

Pause.

Jake You see the tower blocks? Over there! I imagine they're mountains! And other blocks – like this one – they can be castles. Or mountains. Depending on the story. And . . . those television aerials. They're a forest. I'm . . . I'm working on this new story. Don't know what it's about yet. But it'll have a dragon in it. A dragon with a head like . . . like a giant piranha. Or shark. And its skin is all shiny. It sparkles –
Polly Like sequins!
Jake Exactly! I'm trying to work out the dragon's name. I was thinking of something like . . . Glittershark.
Polly Not quite right.

Slight pause.

Sharktwinkle!
Jake No.

Natasha enters. She's fifteen years old and, although she's wearing the same school uniform as Polly, her skirt is much shorter, the shirt is bright pink and unbuttoned to reveal some cleavage and her shoes are stilettos. Her make-up is heavy and her hair, though not long, screams for attention. In place of a satchel, she has a handbag covered with gold sequins.
    Natasha watches Jake and Polly.

Polly Fishtwinkle – oh, no! That's terrible!

Polly and Jake turn and see Natasha. They let out a yelp of surprise.

Natasha! How did you get up here?
Natasha How did I? – Oh, just my usual after-school abseiling. What d'ya mean, how did I get here, you silly

535

cow? I walked up the bloody stairs. The last two flights need a bloody government health warning. Thought the boys' toilets at school were bad enough.

Takes perfume from handbag and sprays herself.

Polly How did you know I was up here, Natasha?

Natasha Your brother told me – Well, told's a bit of an exaggeration. 'Where's Polly, Finn?' 'Uggghh!' (*pointing up*) 'What? She's in her bedroom?' 'Uggghh!' (*pointing up*) Finally, I work out it's either heaven or the roof.

Takes lipstick and face compact from handbag and starts to retouch make-up.

And, Polly – please don't take this the wrong way – but your brother stinks. The state of his hair should be punishable by law. And as for his breath! Phew! It could strip nail varnish at twenty paces.

Starts to climb down stairs.

Polly What you doing, Natasha?

Natasha Oh, don't start that again! Give us a hand, Pol.

Polly helps Natasha down.

Polly You should wear sensible shoes.

Natasha No girl wears shoes to be sensible.

Polly They wear them to get blisters, do they?

Natasha Beauty knows no pain – Now, Pol, quick. A word –

Natasha pulls Polly to one side.

Looks like we've got a yellow alert situation here.

Polly Yellow alert?

Natasha Don't play dumb, Little Missy. Cast your mind back. Your first day at school. You're standing alone in the playground. You're close to tears –

Polly I was not!

Natasha Who saved you from total cred oblivion?

Polly You made friends with me, if that's what you mean.

Natasha And you know why? Because under your totally naff surface, I detected the *real* you. The one who, by half-term, with my help and a make-over –

Polly I don't want a make-over –

Natasha Park your lips! What did I tell you on that first day? Be careful who you talk to. Ask me who's in, who's out. Did I say that?

Polly Yes.

Natasha So why the geek?

Polly He's not a geek! He's very nice.

Natasha Orange alert! Niceness has nothing to do with it. It's like saying someone with measles is nice. It don't matter. Geekiness is contagious! Now, let's get away from here pronto –

Polly I like Jake.

Natasha Red alert! Pol, you'll be hiding between the dustbins before the term's out.

Polly I don't care! He's my friend. And if you can't accept that, then . . . well, you're not the deep, warm, sensitive, mature person I thought you were. Someone who's as beautiful inside as she is out.

Pause.

Natasha . . . Hiya, Jake.

Pause.

I'm doing my hair different now. Had it cut since last term.

Polly Don't talk about yourself. Be interested in *him*.

Slight pause.

Natasha So, Jake . . . What do *you* think about my hair –

Polly I didn't mean that!

Natasha Oh, I give up!

Jake Looked better before.

Slight pause.

Your hair. When it was longer. Really suited you.
Polly Jake, I don't think –
Natasha Let him finish.

Slight pause.

Jake Everyday you'd do it slightly different. Sometimes
swept this way. Sometimes that. And no matter what
style it always looked . . . oh, so perfect. A real work of
art. The effort that went into that.
Natasha Hours, believe me.
Jake And you wore hairclips – My favourite! The one
with yellow flowers.
Natasha My favourite too, Jake. I've still got it.

Searches in handbag.

Jake But shorter . . . it's like you've lost part of you. Even
your make-up looks different –
Polly Stop flirting.
Natasha He ain't flirting. He's talking like one of the girls.
What's more, he's the only one who's had the guts to be
honest. My hair was better longer –

Finds hairclip.

Jake?
Jake That's the one.
Natasha Won't suit me now.

Slight pause.

You have it, Pol.
Polly . . . Me?
Jake It'd suit you.
Natasha The voice of an expert.
Polly (*taking hairclip*) Tasha, you know I can't . . .

Natasha There's nothing wrong with making the most of yourself, Pol.

Slight pause.

You've got to . . . express yourself now and then. Not bottle everything up. Otherwise . . . you're gonna explode.

Jake It's just a hairclip.

Polly Try telling my dad that.

Natasha Dads! Dads! Dads! What've I told you, Pol? You mustn't let it bother you. Water off a duck's back. Just like mine.

Jake What's wrong with your dad?

Slight pause.

Natasha . . . Hardly says a word to me.

Jake Why?

Natasha Just doesn't . . . like me any more, I guess. If I walk in the room he looks right through me. Or worse – like I've got a dog turd smeared across my forehead. Oh, I know what he's thinking. What he thinks of me – You know, I was in hospital last term. Just before the summer holidays. A whole week. Guess how many times Dad visited . . .

Slight pause.

Spilt milk. Been there. Seen it. Boohooed that!

Carol enters. She is fourteen years old and, although she's wearing her school uniform in the same way as Natasha – short skirt, coloured shirt (lemon), stilettos, gold handbag etc. – she can't quite pull it off. Nothing seems to fit her properly and, even if it did, the awkwardness and self-consciousness would still remain.

Carol's a little breathless and clings to the rail for support.

539

Carol! I thought I told you to wait downstairs, Little
    Missy.
Carol Didn't say. Wait a million. Years though. Did you?
    Honestly, Pol, I can put up. With your brother breathing
    last night's curry. I can even put up with his Richter
    scale seven farts. But when he starts setting fire to them
    – well, I'm outa there. What you doing up here anyway?
    (*She sees Jake.*) Yellow alert! – Geek!
Polly Don't call him that!
Carol Orange alert!
Polly He's my friend!
Carol Red alert!
Natasha And mine!

    Pause.
       Carol starts to negotiate descending the steps.

Leave us alone, Carol.
Polly Perhaps we should all go.
Natasha Don't you dare, Polly. I was just beginning to
    enjoy myself – Carol, sling your bloody hook!
Carol I was your friend first! Before her! Help me down.

    Slight pause.

Don't leave me out.
Natasha Clear off!

    Carol starts to cry.
       Pause.
       Jake goes to Carol. He helps her down.

On your head be it, Jake.

    *Carol has now reached the roof. She smiles briefly at
    Jake, then starts strolling round roof.*

The level of conversation's gonna drop faster than Carol's
    knickers in the boys' toilets.
Carol Why you such a bloody bitch all the time?

Natasha You make me! Bloody following me everywhere. Everything I do, you copy. You bloody wannabe. I buy stilettos, so do you –

Carol You didn't bloody invent stilettos!

Natasha (*indicating handbag*) I buy this. The very next day – Oh, surprise, surprise –

Carol They were in a sale!

Natasha I wear a coloured shirt –

Carol Mine's citrus lemon!

Natasha Because they ran out of frosty pink. You even cut your hair 'cos I did.

Carol I was thinking of this for ages!

Natasha Liar!

Carol is by Polly's satellite dish now.

Polly Mind the dish there, Carol.

Carol Tell me this, Miss All That. If you're so bloody special, why did Shane dump you?

Slight pause.

Natasha Shane didn't dump me.

Polly Who's Shane?

Jake He left school last year. Why did Shane dump you?

Natasha He didn't. I dumped him.

Carol Then why the Richter scale eight boohoos?

Natasha The boohoos weren't for him.

Carol Not what you told me.

Natasha Think I'd tell you the truth, Little Miss Internet?

Jake Why would you dump someone like Shane? He's so . . . you know.

Natasha Oh, yes, I know. Shane the Brooding. Shane the Cool. Shane the Let's-Paint-My-Bedroom-Black. Shane the Let's-Stick-A-Compass-in-My-Palm-Whenever-I'm-Fed-Up. Oh, honestly! Sound like me?

Carol You said you loved it.

Natasha Boyfriend stuff is complicated. You won't
understand till you get one.

Carol I've got a boyfriend!

Natasha Tonsil hockey with Russell is not having a
boyfriend.

Carol He can't take his eyes off me.

Natasha For chrissakes, Carol, don't you know anything?
Listen, if you go to a party, you wanna know what boy
fancies you? I mean, really, really fancies you? It's the
one *not* looking at you. 'Can't keep his eyes off me!' –
Jesus! Shall I tell you what your precious Russell told
wonderful, brooding Shane kissing you was? Charity!

Carol Liar!

Natasha Ask him yourself.

Carol I will!

Leans over edge of roof.

Russell!

Jake Don't!

Natasha She's joking.

Carol (*calling*) Up here! With Natasha!

Jake She's not! He plays down there!

Polly The football pitch!

Carol He's coming!

Polly Hide, Jake.

Carol (*at Natasha*) And he's not alone.

Jake starts looking for a hiding place.

Natasha Buzz and Speed are always with him.

Carol Not just Buzz and Speed.

Natasha . . . Shane?

Carol laughs excitedly.
Jake is unable to find hiding place.

Polly Behind me! Quick!

Jake gets behind Polly.

Natasha Oh, my God! Polly! It's Shane!
Polly Tasha, we need your help. Quick!
Natasha . . . What?
Polly We need to hide Jake. Russell will –
Jake Kill me!
Natasha (*at Carol*) This is all your bloody fault, Little
  Missy.
Polly Quick!

Natasha runs to stand beside Polly.

Carol What's going on??
Polly Closer, Tasha – Carol, we need you too. Quick! Or
  do you want to see Jake hurt?
Carol Hurt? . . . No.
Polly Hurry!

*Carol rushes to join Polly and Natasha.
  Jake hides behind them.*

Close up, Carol. No gaps!

*Russell enters. He is fifteen years old, glossily good-
looking, with a defined, hard body, created to flaunt.
His school uniform (which would have been the same as
Jake's) has been reduced to trousers and shirt, the latter
being worn untucked, unbuttoned to reveal chest and
with the sleeves rolled up. Instead of shoes, he's wearing
trainers.*

Russell (*in a voice of a sports commentator*) 'The winner!
  Russell the Love Muscle adds Gold Medal for Tower
  Block Climbing to his long list of trophies. Is there any
  stopping this sex-machine, babe-magnet?' (*Calls down
  stairs.*) Come on, you two. Hear them panting down
  there? Pathetic. But, girls, feast your eyes! Am I
  breathless?

Girls . . . No.

Russell Sweating?

Girls . . . No.

Russell Tired?

Girls . . . No.

Russell Do not adjust your sets, girls, you are witnessing perfection. Look at you! Too dazzled to move. 'The crowd cheers at this spunky, funky, hard-bod hunky. Women are throwing flowers. He blows one a kiss! She faints –'

Buzz and Speed enter. They are fourteen years old and wearing the reduced school uniform favoured by Russell, although their shirts are not unbuttoned. They are both shorter than Russell and, while not unattractive, lack the arrogant dazzle that makes Russell the natural leader.

Both Buzz and Speed are carrying sports bags instead of satchels. (Buzz is carrying an extra one which, presumably, belongs to Russell.) This extra weight has no doubt contributed to their breathless condition.

Talk about fainting! Pathetic or what? Ha!

Buzz He kept pushing me, Russ.

Speed He got in the way, Russ.

Buzz I'm carrying your bag, Russ.

Speed He used it to trip me, Russ.

Russell Out of the way, losers – time to greet the fans.

Jumps to main area of roof.

I know what you're thinking, girls. Why can't my hair shine like his? And as for his eyelashes – they're wasted on a bloke! Don't blame me. I was born with these gifts . . . Others – I worked at!

Lifts shirt to reveal stomach.
Carol lets out an involuntary squeal.

544

Know what these muscles are called?

Slight pause.

Horny as hell!

Buzz and Speed go to descend the metal stairs.

You two! Jump like me! A man!

Buzz and Speed stand on edge of raised area, psyching themselves to jump. They are teetering on the edge, visibly wary and nervous.

Wotchya, Natasha. All right?
Natasha Fine.
Russell Avoiding us lately?
Natasha Why should I?
Russell Our Shane-boy.
Natasha Ancient history.
Russell Exactly what I just said. When Shane heard what's-her-face call you were up here. 'Come up,' I said. 'Let bygones be bygones. So you split up! No big deal. What's it mean – not twiddling with each other's rude bits any more?' (*at Buzz and Speed*) Jump, you two!
Buzz Stop calling us 'you two'!
Speed We've got names.

Shane enters and, without missing a beat, pushes Buzz and Speed. They fall awkwardly to the lower level.
   Polly, Natasha and Carol gasp.
   Russell burst out laughing.
   Shane is sixteen years old and wearing black leather trousers, boots, red silk shirt – unbuttoned to reveal a razor-blade necklace – black jacket and sunglasses. His hair is longish and well groomed.

Russell Nice one, Shane!
Buzz Bloody stupid, that!
Speed Could have broken my neck!

Russell Shut up, you two!

Shane sits at top of metal steps.
Pause.

Natasha Hiya, Shane.

Pause.

How's it going?

Pause.

. . . Have a good summer?

Shane still doesn't respond.
Pause.

Carol Russell! When you kissed me. Remember?
Russell No.
Carol Yes, you do.
Russell If you say so.
Carol Natasha said that . . . well, said you said. Said you
said to Shane –
Russell Said what, for chrissakes?
Carol Said . . . it was charity.

Buzz and Speed start laughing.

Stop it! Stop it!
Natasha Belt up, you scrotums!

Buzz and Speed stop laughing.

Russell Well, to be honest with you – what's your name
again?
Natasha Carol. Her name's Carol.
Russell Well, Carol, it's probably true. But let me explain!
I am a dreamboat. You are not. Now, when a
dreamboat kisses a dreamboat-challenged person – it's
always charity. This ain't a bad thing. I'm giving you
something that – in normal circumstances – you

546

wouldn't stand a hope in hell of getting. Don't tell me you didn't like the kiss.

Carol . . . No. I mean, yes!

Russell Would you like another smackeroonie?

Natasha Control yourself. Carol.

Russell Come here.

Polly Don't move.

Carol is whimpering at the back of her throat.

Russell Oh, Carol! My tongue! It'll go deep enough to taste your cornflakes.

Suddenly, Carol can resist no more and rushes at Russell.
Immediately, Buzz and Speed get a glimpse of Jake.

Buzz Geek alert!

Speed Geek alert!

Russell What? Where? – Well, well, well, hiding behind the girls. How pathetic. How . . . one hundred per cent geek!

Carol Where's my kiss?

Russell Get him, you two.

Buzz and Speed go to grab Jake.
Jake runs.
Buzz and Speed chase.

Jake Help!

Polly Leave him!

Natasha Don't, Russ!

Carol Where's my bloody kiss?

Buzz and Speed catch Jake.

Jake Help!

Buzz Kick him, Russ!

Speed Punch him, Russ!

Russell I've got a better idea. Let's dangle him over the edge.

Buzz Wicked!
Speed Awesome!
Jake Polly!

Buzz and Speed take Jake to edge of roof.

Polly He's done nothing to you!
Jake Natasha! Help!
Natasha Stop it, Russ! Stop! Shane – tell him!
Carol My kiss!
Russell Shut up about your bloody kiss! Who'd kiss you anyway? Like dangling your tongue in a dustbin – Right, Shane?
Carol You bloody . . . git! You! You're . . . A liar! You –
Jake Carol!
Carol Let him go!
Russell Hey, Shane! You should see his face! All scared and – He's pulling Buzz's hair! Ha! A geek with cheek!
Speed He's pulling *my* hair!
Buzz I'm Buzz.
Speed I'm Speed.
Russell Don't get touchy now, you two – Lift him!
Jake Nooooo!
Polly Stop!
Carol Stop!
Natasha You're gonna really hurt him.
Russell Trying my best.
Natasha Shane!
Polly But you can't! Please! He . . . he was telling us a story. Wasn't he, Tasha?
Natasha . . . What? Oh . . . yeah! A good story.
Polly And we want to know how it ends.
Russell I hate stories.
Jake Help! Help!
Natasha Shane! Tell him! Please!

Slight pause.

548

Russell What's it to be, Shane? Dangle or story?

Pause.

Shane . . . Story.
Russell But, Shane –
Natasha You heard!

Slight pause.
    Buzz and Speed let go of Jake.
    Pause.

Russell So?

Pause.

Polly It . . . It was about this Princess, wasn't it, Jake? Am
I right? Yes? This Princess. What happened, Jake?

Slight pause.

That's right! Yes! She lived in a Castle. Well, I suppose all
Princesses live in Castles, don't they?
Natasha Wouldn't be seen without one.
Carol No way.

Slight pause.

Polly And this Princess . . . she lived in a Castle with her
father.
Natasha The King, right.
Polly Exactly, Natasha! Thank you for reminding me. The
Princess lived in a Castle with her father. Who was
indeed the King.
Russell Bloody riveting this! – Now, don't tell me. Her
mother was, indeed, the Queen.
Polly No. The Princess didn't have a mother. She died –
Russell At childbirth! Boring! – Shane! Let's dangle the
geek! He's not even telling it.
Natasha The Queen had been murdered, if you must
know.

Pause.

Very nastily.

Slight pause.

Horribly.

Buzz . . . How?

Polly One day . . . the Castle was attacked. By the King's enemies. The kingdom had been at war for a long time.

Speed The King should have been prepared then.

Polly Well . . . yes. He was. Usually. The King was a great soldier.

Buzz So how come the enemy surprised him?

Natasha . . . The baby Princess.

Carol The Castle was celebrating. Right?

Polly Exactly right, Carol. It was the day for celebrating the birth of the Princess! A holiday for everyone. The Castle was full of food and music and flowers.

Buzz A good ol' booze-up.

Speed Peanuts and sausages on sticks.

Carol Everyone strutting their funky stuff.

Natasha And that's when the enemy attacked!

Buzz Bet the Castle was slaughtered.

Polly The King was too good a soldier for that. In fact, the King defeated the enemy that day!

Buzz But the Queen!

Speed What happened to her?

Polly She was shot in the heart with a single arrow.

Pause.

And then . . . her head was chopped off.

Pause.

And then . . . her head was eaten by a hungry pig.

Buzz Wicked!

Speed Awesome.

Carol I feel a bit sick.

Polly After that . . . the King never let his defences down again. Am I getting this right, Jake? The King banned pleasure from the Castle.

Buzz What? No telly?

Russell Wouldn't be telly in those days.

Polly No dancing. No singing. No flowers. Nothing pretty or frivolous at all. He thought these things would turn the Princess weak.

Russell (*to Buzz and Speed*) Like you two!

Polly And, as she had to rule after him one day, and possibly fight many battles, he had to train her to be strong. Right, Jake?

Jake nods and murmurs.
  Slight pause.

The King made the Princess wear a simple dress. And only one colour . . . black!

Carol Not even citrus lemon?

Polly No.

Natasha Bet her shoes were sensible too.

Polly Very sensible. And guess what she had to drink . . . Vinegar!

Buzz Disgusting!

Polly And eat . . . Plain bread!

Speed No butter?

Polly No.

Buzz What about margarine?

Polly No! Nothing! The King forbade it! And then, one night . . . Yes! That's it! I remember now! The Princess heard something thump against her window.

Buzz What is it?

Polly A bird.

Speed Is it dead?

Polly Its neck's broken.

Carol She buries it!

Polly In a secret corner of the Castle.
Buzz Why do girls bury things?
Speed Instead of cutting them up?
Jake . . . There's something inside the bird.
Polly What, Jake?
Buzz Yeah, what?
Speed What?
Carol What?

Slight pause.

Jake . . . A flower seed.
Polly Of course. The bird's dinner! So, when the bird is buried – the seed grows! And next summer –

Takes hairclip from pocket.

Look! I'm going to wear it in my hair.
Buzz Don't let the King see.
Polly Too late!
Carol Yellow alert.
Polly The Princess says, 'I'm sorry, Dad! Please! It's just a flower. Please – Ahhh!'
Speed What's happened?
Polly He's . . . he's hit me.
Russell Bully!

Pause.

Polly 'What's that, Dad? Oh, no! No!'
Carol What's he say?
Buzz What?
Speed What?
Polly . . . He doesn't want a daughter like me.
Natasha No!
Jake You're banished!

Slight pause.

Polly I leave the Castle. (*She walks around roof.*) And for a while . . . there's nothing. I don't know where I'm going. Just . . . a wasteland. I walk and walk. And then – yes! – I find a forest!

Jake She plants her flower.
Polly It's full of seeds.

Buries hairclip beneath some rubbish.

Jake And one year later . . .
Polly Hundreds of flowers!
Jake The following year!
Polly Thousands!
Jake The next!
Polly Millions! Look at them! Millions of yellow flowers! As far as the eye can see! So beautiful. And I'm . . . I'm so happy here in the forest of a million yellow flowers. Smell them! And, what's that? There! Look! In the lake!

Points at puddle.

Dolphins! Splashing and playing together. Oh, yes! Oh, yes! Yes!

Pause.

Jake And then, one day, a Prince arrives.
Buzz Me!
Speed No! Me!
Jake The Prince is the most handsome man in all the land.
Russell Someone call my name?
Buzz I said it first.
Speed No! I did!
Russell Shut it, you two!

Jake gets the supermarket trolley and wheels it in front of Russell.

Jake The Prince rode a chariot –
Russell You must be bloody joking!
Jake Said the Prince. Because he was strong and proud.

He thought he should walk everywhere. But he also knew that riding in . . . the solid gold chariot was an honour. An honour only given to true heroes.

Slight pause.
    Russell gets in supermarket trolley.

Russell Where's my horses then?

Everyone looks at Buzz and Speed.

Buzz No way!
Speed No way!
Russell Shane?

Slight pause.
    Shane points at supermarket trolley.
    Buzz and Speed grab hold of it.

Gee up, Lightning! Gee up, Ned!
Buzz Hang on a bloody minute! Who's Ned?
Russell You are.
Buzz Oh, no! If he's Lightning, I ain't going to be called Ned. You can stuff that up your –
Jake Thunder!

Slight pause.

Russell Gee up, Thunder and Lightning!

Buzz and Speed pull supermarket trolley.

Faster! Faster! Come on, you two!

Buzz and Speed pull supermarket trolley round and round.

Faster! Faster!

Buzz and Speed pull supermarket trolley faster.

Faster!
Speed That's it! I've had enough!

Jake The horses were exhausted so the Prince – who was as kind and understanding as he was handsome – let them rest by a lake in the middle of a forest.

Slight pause.
    Buzz and Speed pull supermarket trolley to puddle.

Polly Who are you?
Speed Lightning!
Russell She's talking to me, you pillock! You're a bloody horse! – Wotchya! I'm a Prince.
Polly Beautiful.
Russell I work out.
Polly Not you. My forest. Look! A million yellow flowers.
Jake But, as far as the Prince was concerned, the Princess was more beautiful than all the flowers put together.

Slight pause.

Polly Why are you looking at me like that?
Russell . . . Like what?
Polly Like there's something you want to say.

Pause.

Oh, I know it's difficult. For a Prince like you, I mean. To say things . . . gentle things. You've had to be strong and brave all your life. As hard as your horny-as-hell stomach. But you can say them to me, you know.

Slight pause.

Do you think I'm beautiful.
Russell . . . Not bad.
Polly Do you want me to leave my forest and live with you in your Castle?
Russell . . . I'm easy.

Slight pause.

All right. Yeah. I wouldn't mind.

555

Polly But, Prince, my forest is so beautiful. How can I leave it? Even for a Love Muscle like you?

Russell You're . . . you're playing bloody games with me! I never liked you in the first place – Shane!

Polly Don't go!

Jake The Princess could see the Prince was upset. She knew he didn't mean what he was saying –

Russell Bloody do!

Jake So she offered him a challenge.

Slight pause.

Polly Prince! There is . . . something inside me that tingles for you. Honestly. I can't explain it. I'd like to give you a chance – or me a chance.

Russell What?

Polly Find me something more beautiful than a million yellow flowers. If you can do that, I will follow you anywhere.

Jake So the Prince searched.

Slight pause.

The Prince looks!

Russell looks at Shane.
   Shane nods.
   Russell searches roof. He finds an old shoe and takes it to Polly.

Polly The most beautiful shoe ever made. Decorated with rubies and diamonds and stitched with gold thread . . . Beautiful. But not beautiful enough.

Slight pause.
   Russell throws shoe aside. He searches roof once more. He finds an old baseball cap and takes it to Polly.

Russell This is a crown! Right? It's made of platinum. It's decorated with a trillion bloody diamonds. Beautiful or what?

Polly Beautiful. But not beautiful enough.

Russell (*throwing cap aside*) Bloody hell –

Buzz Go to a Witch.

Speed Yeah! Wicked! Ask a Witch.

All look at Natasha.

Natasha Well, that's bloody typical!

Slight pause.

Come on, then. What you waiting for?

Russell goes to Natasha.
Slight pause.

Natasha Hiya, Prince. So you've got to find –

Russell I haven't told you yet!

Natasha I'm a bloody Witch, dickhead!

Pause.

So . . . Little Miss Flower Power wants you to find something more beautiful than a million yellow flowers. I can do that. But first . . . you gotta pay.

Russell How much?

Natasha Not money, you turbo-dreambabe. A kiss. A big smakeroo. Mouth open. Tongue in lung.

Russell What? Here? In front of . . . everyone?

Natasha But we're in my own witchy hovel.

Russell looks at Shane, then back at Natasha.

I'm waiting.

Russell kisses Natasha. It grows increasingly passionate.
Carol slaps at Russell.

Carol Stop it! You sod! Why her?

Russell Hey! What's your problem?

Carol It's not fair –
Natasha Calm down! Jesus! Get a grip!

Carol calms.

You make yourself look a bloody idiot sometimes. Then wonder why everyone's laughing at you. It's humiliating. You should be bloody ashamed. Hear me? Ashamed.

Slight pause.

You'll have to forgive my little creature, Prince.
Russell Little creature?
Natasha . . . My pet frog.

Slight pause.

Carol . . . Croak, croak.
Natasha And now, Prince. I'll grant your wish.

Takes spray from handbag.

This is my most magic potion. One spray of this and the Princess will quiver and swoon.
Russell What you think I am?

Russell turns to face Shane.

Shane?

Natasha sprays perfume on Russell.

Stop!
Natasha Done now!

Buzz and Speed laugh.

Russell It's the knacker's yard for you two!

Pause.

Polly Mmmm . . . what's that smell?

Slight pause.

Russell goes to Polly.

Very, very beautiful. But . . . a bit too fruity for my taste.
Russell That's it! Enough!
Shane You shouldn't have trusted the Witch.
Russell *You* did!
Shane Her magic potion worked then –
Jake Said the Wizard.

Pause.

Shane . . . Let me tell you about the Witch.

Slight pause.

A million years ago I met her. On a planet far away. She
was a powerful sorceress then. Her magic potion was
the most potent in the universe. Savage monsters could
be tamed with one whiff. I was tamed.

Slight pause.

And then, one day, she refused to answer when I called her
name. I screamed so loud stars became supernova.

Slight pause.

She has spent a million years avoiding me. Fleeing each
planet as I arrive. I never worked out why she loved me
so much one day . . . then, the next, not at all.

Slight pause.

An egg.
Natasha What?

Slight pause.

Jake A Dragon's egg.
Polly A Dragon's egg, yes!
Buzz Wicked!
Speed Awesome!

Carol What about it?

Slight pause.

Jake . . . The Wizard told the Prince about this Dragon. It lives in the mountain –

Polly I've heard about this Dragon. It's got jaws like a shark.

Jake And scales like sequins.

Polly And this Dragon – yes, of course! – it lays eggs.

Jake (*with Polly*) Eggs more beautiful than a million yellow flowers!

Polly (*with Jake*) Eggs more beautiful than a million yellow flowers!

Pause.

Shane Go to the mountains. Find the Dragon's egg. The Princess will be yours.

Buzz But . . . won't there be two Dragons.

Speed A Mummy and a Daddy?

Jake It's an hermaphrodite Dragon.

Slight pause.

Half boy, half girl.

Russell Relative of yours, Jake?

Jake It's a ferocious Dragon. It might be covered with sequins. But each sequin is as sharp as a razor blade.

Slight pause.

Be careful, Prince.

Pause.

Russell (*in sports commentator voice*) 'The Prince faces the challenge without fear. Is this the bravest man on earth or what? In a few incredible strides he scales the heights of the mountain.'

Climbs metal stairs.

'It's freezing cold, but is the Prince shivering? No! He's not even wearing protective clothing. Is this man mortal? we have to ask ourselves. And there . . . Is it? Yes! I believe it is! He's found it! Easy!'

Takes football from his sports bag.

The Dragon's egg!
Shane The cold must be making the Prince hallucinate.

Pause.

Russell 'Undeterred, the turbo-dreamboat of a Prince searches again! What stamina! What grit! And now – Yes!'

Lifts an old lampshade in air.

The Dragon's egg!
Shane Hallucination.
Russell What then, for chrissakes?
Carol I'll help you! Yeah, me, the frog! You see, ever since you came to visit the Witch . . . I've been thinking about you. Richter scale eight crush. Can't help it. Don't understand it – Before you say anything, I don't want a kiss. You don't fancy frogs. That's your problem. No reason to hate you. I'll find a frog of my own to snog when this is over. In the meantime, there's the egg.

She points.

Russell Where?
Carol There!
Russell But what? Where?

Pause.

Ah! I get it! Hallucination and all that. Imagination. Nice

one. Yeah, yeah . . . Yes! I see it! There! More beautiful
than anything I ever thought I'd find.

Shane Describe it.

Slight pause.

Russell It's in a nest. A huge nest. Trees instead of twigs.
All twisted and broken together. Bushes instead of
leaves . . .

Slight pause.

The egg's in the middle. Very big! Sparkling with a million
colours . . . I'm climbing into the nest now . . . Insects
buzz all round me . . . Wood cracks at my feet . . .

Mimics picking up the egg and descends metal steps.

The Princess will be mine!

Natasha You helped him, you frog!

Carol You made me a frog! With the last Witch I served I
was a cat! A sleek, graceful cat with big green eyes. Yes, I
change depending on who I'm with. But it's the Witch that
changes me. You hear that? I don't change myself. I hate
you for changing me into a frog. I hate you for laughing
because someone . . . someone I love thinks I'm ugly.

Russell I don't think you're ugly.

Carol Then why didn't you kiss me?

Russell Because I don't feel . . . like that towards you.
Doesn't mean I think you're ugly. We can be, you
know . . .

Carol What?

Russell You know.

Carol No. What?

Russell . . . Well, we don't have to be enemies?

Slight pause.

Jake And look! You're not a frog any more. You're a
beautiful nightingale.

Carol A nightingale! – Princess! Look what the Prince has found!
Russell The Dragon's egg!
Polly Take me to your Castle.
Jake And the Prince and Princess were married!

Polly and Russell parade hand in hand.
   Everyone, except Natasha, cheers and claps.
   Buzz and Speed tear bits of paper up and throw them as confetti.

Natasha It's not over!

The celebration dies down.

What? You think it's that bloody easy. Find a beautiful egg and all live happily ever after – You make me puke!
Shane . . . What you going to do?

Slight pause.

Natasha Curse the egg!
Russell What curse?
Natasha The egg's beauty! It'll be too much for the Princess! It'll . . . hypnotize her. Possess her! Yes!

Pause.

Do it!

Slight pause.

Do it!

Slight pause.
   Polly sits in armchair and stares in front of her.

Polly Oh, the colours! The lights! The shapes!

Russell goes to Shane.

Russell I've got a feeling that Witch has cursed the egg.
Shane Spot on.

Russell You're a bloody Wizard. Break the spell.
Shane It's too powerful for me.
Russell What now?
Shane Does the Princess love you?
Russell Who knows?
Shane Do you love her?
Russell I . . . well . . .
Shane *Could* you love her?
Russell . . . Probably.
Shane Then you must go to her. Every day. Tell her how much she means to you. Perhaps, in time, she will love you back. Who knows? This love might break the spell.
Russell You don't sound too sure.
Shane I'm not.

Slight pause.
   Russell goes to Polly.

Russell Wotchya, Princess. you know, I've been thinking about you . . . a lot. You know? In my mind! You pop into it.

Pause.

I've never spoken to anyone like this before –

Buzz and Speed giggle.

Shut up, you two. This is important. Help or clear off!
Buzz Sorry.
Speed Sorry.

Slight pause.

Russell I've seen lots of nasty things, Princess. In battles. You know? It's hard out there. Tough. I've seen friends really hurt. You know what I'm saying? Out there – I've done what . . . what a Prince had to do. Otherwise . . . well, he'll never be King.

564

Pause.

Princess . . . please . . . listen to me. I'm trying . . .
Polly Oh, Prince.
Jake It's cracking!
Shane The egg!
Polly It mustn't hatch! No! No!

Polly picks up imaginary egg and starts to run.
Russell, Buzz and Speed chase after her. Everyone is
crying out, adding to the general pandemonium.

Jake Catch her!
Russell Stop!
Shane Don't panic!
Buzz It's all right!
Speed Don't worry!
Polly The egg mustn't break!
Buzz She's lost it!
Speed Going doolally.
Carol Princess!
Jake Mind the edge!

Polly is standing by her satellite dish now.

Polly I hate you! Hate what you've done to my beautiful
egg! You monster! Hate you!
Buzz Who's she talking to?
Speed The baby Dragon.
Carol It's hatched.
Buzz It's at her feet.
Shane She's going to kill it!
Natasha No!
Russell No!
Carol No!
Buzz No!
Speed No!

Natasha rushes to Shane.

Natasha Shane! Don't let her! Please! I never meant this to happen!

Polly screams out and violently stamps her foot.
Silence.
Long pause.

Wh . . . what have you done?

Slight pause.
Slowly, Natasha goes to Polly. She sees the dead bird.

It's dead!

Natasha falls against satellite dish.
Shane rushes to Natasha.

Shane Tasha!
Finn (*off stage*) AHHHHHHHHGHH!

Everyone freezes
Slight pause.

Russell What's that?
Buzz That noise.
Speed I think it's –
Buzz It is!
Russell Can't be!
Carol It is!
Speed (*with Buzz*) Him!
Buzz (*with Speed*) Him!
Russell Run!

Russell, Buzz and Speed explode in activity and scarper for stairs.

Finn enters. He is fifteen years old and very large, in all directions, for his age. He is wearing well-worn black jeans, boots and a T-shirt emblazoned with some heavy-metal logo, many silver rings and studded wristbands.

His hair is extremely long and – like the rest of him – in need of a wash.

Finn WAAAAAGOOOOOAAAH!

Russell, Buzz and Speed yelp and scarper.

Russell The Monster!
Buzz The Monster!
Speed The Monster!

Russell, Buzz and Speed hide.

Polly Don't call him that! You'll upset him! – It's all right, Finn.
Finn WAAAAGOOOOOAAAH!
Polly Shhh! Don't worry, Finn. I'll explain.

Polly whispers in Finn's ear.
    She points at Jake.
    Jake gasps.
    Finn murmurs and nods.

Polly continues whispering in Finn's ear.
    She points at Natasha.
    Natasha gasps.
    Finn murmurs and nods.

Polly continues whispering in Finn's ear.
    She points at Carol.
    Carol gasps.
    Finn murmurs and nods.

Polly continues whispering in Finn's ear.
    She points at Russell.
    Russell cries out.
    Finn murmurs and nods.

Polly continues whispering in Finn's ear.
    She points at Buzz and Speed.
    They both yell.

Finn murmurs and nods.

Polly continues whispering in Finn's ear.
She points at Shane.
Finn murmurs and nods.

Polly points at herself.
Finn's nodding and murmuring get more emphatic.
Polly points at dead bird.
Finn's nodding and murmuring get even more
emphatic.

Polly points at Finn.
Finn nods and cries out gleefully and grabs hold of
Polly.

Polly The Dragon! Help!
Russell The Dragon?
Buzz Him!
Speed He's the Dragon?
Polly Show them, Finn?

Finn claws his hands and roars.

Finn RAAAAAGGGHHHHH!
All The Dragon!
Russell He's gonna do it!
Finn RAAAAAGGGHHHHH!
Polly Help! Help! I've killed what was in the egg. Now the
Dragon's kidnapped me for revenge. He's taken me to
the top of the mountain. Help! Help!
Natasha It's all my fault!
Russell No mine!
Carol No mine!
Jake Mine!
Buzz How's it your fault?
Speed Who are you in all this anyway?
Jake I'm . . . her father.

Slight pause.

Russell The King!
Carol The one who wouldn't let her grow a flower.
Buzz The one told her to clear off.
Jake That's me!
Speed Then it *is* your fault!
Russell Where you been all this bloody time?
Jake After what I did to my daughter . . . I realized I was
wrong. I . . . I was so upset. I hid. Wouldn't show my
face. Thought no one would want to see my face
anyway. But then . . . then I realized. That wasn't the
answer. It just made the problem worse. So now . . .
now I'm not hiding any more. I'm here to save my
daughter. Save her from the Dragon. Is there anyone
brave enough to help me?
Russell I will.
Buzz Me too.
Speed And me.
Natasha And me.
Shane And me.
Carol . . . And me!
Buzz What can you do?
Speed You're a bloody nightingale.
Natasha Not any more she's not! Like the King, I'm sorry
for what I've done. I've been a bit of a cow really. Let's
be friends again – I make you human!
Buzz What about me?
Speed And me.
Shane You too! Human! Human!
Polly Any chance of a bloody rescue!
Jake Arm yourselves!

*They rush around finding dustbin lids and other detritus
to use as shields and weapons, etc.*
 Jake finds an old umbrella to use as a sword.
 Much noise and activity.

569

Jake stands on an old milk crate. The others gather round him and cheer. They continue to cheer at key moments throughout the following speech.

Today we do battle! Battle with a terrible Dragon. A ferocious Dragon. A Dragon with jaws like a shark. A Dragon with scales sharp as razors. A Dragon who glitters bright enough to blind! But a Dragon we must fight! And it's a fight we will win! We'll win because we'll fight it together. Individually – we don't stand a chance. But together – oh, look at us! We are invincible! Are we together?

All Yes!

Jake (*louder*) Are we united?

All (*louder*) Yes!

Jake Then the Dragon is doomed. This Dragon called . . . Sparkleshark!

All (*chanting*) Sparkleshark! Sparkleshark! Sparkleshark! Sparkleshark!

Everything explodes into action.
The chanting is loud and vigorous.
Various bits of detritus are used as drums.

Jake, Natasha, Carol, Russell, Buzz, Speed and Shane pursue the fleeing Polly and Finn around the roof.

Polly is screaming.
Finn is roaring.

The chanting and general clamour get louder and louder.
Everyone, although taking their various roles very seriously, is thoroughly enjoying themselves.

Buzz, Speed and Carol help each other over various obstacles etc.
Likewise, Shane helps Natasha, and Russell helps Jake.

Finally, Finn is surrounded.
  He lashes out with his clawed hands.

Polly watches from one side.

Finn RAAAAAGGGHHHHH!!!
Buzz Get him!
Speed Kill him!
Carol Save the Princess!

Slight pause.
  Tentatively, Russell approaches Finn.

Jake No, Prince! This is my job! I'm the one who started it all. I must be the one to end.
Russell But I'm stronger than you!
Finn RAAAAAGGGHHHHH!!!
Russell (*at Jake*) You're right! You do it!

Jake – his umbrella raised – approaches Finn.
  Finn is roaring and clawing at him.
  Polly is screaming.
  The others are avidly cheering Jake on.

Suddenly, Finn lashes out at Jake.
  Jake cries out and falls to the floor.

Russell rushes forward and pulls Jake away from Finn.

Jake Wh . . . what are you doing?
Russell The Dragon's broken your arm. You can't carry on. Let me take your sword. Please.

Jake gives Russell the umbrella.

Jake Thank you, Prince.
Carol Save the Princess!
Buzz Do it, Prince!
Speed Do it!
Natasha Kill the Dragon.
All (*chanting*) Kill! Kill! Kill! Kill! Kill!

Russell approaches Finn.
  They circle each other for a while.
  Everyone cheers, claps, stamps their feet, chants, etc.

Finn is clawing at Russell.
  Russell is swinging the umbrella. They do this in
slow motion, playfully exaggerating every sound and
gesture.

In the course of the ensuing fight, Russell's umbrella
touches Finn's arm.
  Finn lets out a roar.

Then Finn touches Russell's chest.
  Russell lets out a roar.

The crowd continues cheering etc.

Finally, Finn is beaten to the ground.
  Russell raises his umbrella.

All Kill! Kill! Kill! Kill! Kill!
Russell Die, Sparkleshark! Die!

Then just as Russell is about to strike –

Polly STOP!

Polly rushes to Finn and cradles his head in her lap.
  Everyone is still and silent.
  Pause.

This is a good Dragon! A kind Dragon! Yes, I know it
  kidnapped me. But look what I did. I destroyed its egg!
  The egg more beautiful than a million yellow flowers.

Pause.

And while I've been on this mountain the Dragon has
  looked after me. Kept me warm at night. Given me
  food. And I've learned to understand what it's saying.
Finn (*softly*) Raaagghhhaaa.

Polly Yes, my kind Dragon. I'll tell them – Everyone is afraid of him because of what he looks like.

Finn (*softly*) Raaaghhhaaa.

Polly At night, the Dragon spreads its magnificent wings and there's no one there to marvel how they sparkle by moonlight.

Finn starts to weep.
    Slight pause.

Natasha The Dragon's crying.

Carol Poor Dragon.

Buzz Don't cry.

Speed Don't.

Shane What can we do to stop him crying?

Slight pause.

Polly You must lay your hand on the Dragon and say . . . Oh, tell the Dragon you're his friend.

Pause.

Slowly, Natasha approaches Finn.
    She kneels beside him.
    Lays her hand on him.

Natasha I'm your friend, Sparkleshark.

Slight pause.
    Carol approaches Finn.
    She kneels beside him.
    Lays her hand on him.

Carol I'm your friend, Sparkleshark.

Slight pause.
    Buzz approaches Finn.
    He kneels beside him.
    Lays his hand on him.

Buzz I'm your friend, Sparkleshark.

> *Slight pause.*
>> *Speed approaches Finn.*
>> *He kneels beside him.*
>> *Lays his hand on him.*

Speed I'm your friend, Sparkleshark.

> *Slight pause.*
>> *Shane approaches Finn.*
>> *He kneels beside him.*
>> *Lays his hand on him.*

Shane I'm your friend, Sparkleshark.

> *Slight pause.*
>> *Russell approaches Finn.*
>> *He kneels beside him.*
>> *Lays his hand on him.*

Russell I'm your friend, Sparkleshark.

> *Slight pause.*
>> *Jake approaches Finn.*
>> *He kneels beside him.*
>> *Lays his hand on him.*

Jake I'm your friend, Sparkleshark.

> *Slight pause.*

Finn Raaahhh.
Polly Sparkleshark is your friend too.

> *Pause.*
>> *Jake stands.*

Jake And, from that moment on, the land lived in perfect peace. The Prince and Princess lived happily in their Castle. The Wizard and the Witch created planets together. The one-time horses, Thunder and Lightning, became best friends with the one-time frog and nightingale. I – the King – was forgiven. And, at night, if children saw a strange light in the sky, their parents would say, 'Don't worry, my love. That's just moonlight on the Dragon's wings.'

Long, silent pause.
Polly begins to applaud Jake.
Then Russell begins to applaud.
Then all the others join in.
They all cheer and congratulate him.

But it wasn't just me! It was all of us! Together! The story belongs to all of us.

Russell Let's do another one! Jake! Another story! Another story!

Jake I can't! Not now! I've got to get home for tea.

Everyone nods and murmurs assent.
Slight pause.

Russell But . . . we can't just stop there!

Shane We should meet again.

All Yeah.

Russell Next week!

All Yeah!

Buzz Same time!

Speed Same place!

All Yeah!

Natasha And we'll tell another story!

Russell All of us together!

All Yeah!

Russell We should call ourselves something!

Buzz The Storytelling Group!

All Nah.

Speed Secret Storytelling Association!

All Nah!

Finn . . . Sparkleshark!

575

Slight pause.

Polly Yes, Finn! That's it! We'll call ourselves
'Sparkleshark'!
All Yeah! Sparkleshark!
Russell And we'll have a salute! Our secret sign when we
meet each other – the Dragon's claw.

Claws his fist as Finn had done.

Jake (*punching air with salute*) Sparkleshark!
All (*punching air with salute*) Sparkleshark!

Slight pause.
*They start making their way up the metal staircase to
the raised platform.*
*Jake collects his notebook etc. together. He is the last
to climb. Russell helps Jake on to the raised platform.*
Slight pause.
*They all smile at each other, then look at the roof
around them. Then, suddenly and simultaneously, they
all punch the air with the clawed salute and –*

All (*triumphantly*) SPARKLESHARK!

*Then, one by one, they leave the roof until only Jake
and Polly remain.*
Slight pause.

Polly Sparkleshark, Jake.

Slight pause.
Polly exits.
Jake looks around the roof.

Jake (*softly*) Sparkleshark.

Slowly, almost reluctantly, Jake leaves the roof.
Fade to black-out.

Dreaming the Sparkling Monster

Philip Ridley interviewed by Jim Mulligan

From his earliest years Philip Ridley has told stories and drawn pictures. When it came to higher education he chose art college where, refusing to be constrained by the tradition of specializing in a single discipline, he insisted on working in many different media. As well as painting he wrote stories, performed poetry, experimented with photography and film and set up his own theatre company for which he wrote, directed, acted and composed music. His first published work, *Crocodilia*, was written when he was eighteen. Ostensibly an academic treatise which was part of his course, it was a story in which he reflected the images he was engaged with in his visual art. Creatively, Philip Ridley has made many journeys, but all of them seem rooted in Bethnal Green, the heart of London's East End.

I still live in the block of flats where I was brought up. My grandparents, all my aunts and uncles, cousins and second cousins, we all lived down the same street and all my parents' friends were called 'aunt' or 'uncle'. So I grew up in this extended family where everyone knew each other. One of my earliest memories is of a street party to celebrate England's football team winning the World Cup. Everyone was dancing and singing along to 'Shout' by Lulu. As childhood memories go that must rate a ten. Pure magic. But, of course, living in that part of London there was plenty of menace too.

Menace and magic seem to be major components in all of Philip Ridley's work and, in particular, *Sparkleshark*. For, although the play eventually deals with an imaginary

577

world of enchantment, it has its roots in violence. The play starts with Jake taking refuge on the roof of a tower block. He is a victim, the classroom 'geek' who is bullied by the boys and avoided by the girls. Before long seven other young people join him and an eighth, Finn, can be heard offstage. As soon as they discover Jake, the taunting begins and leads to a life-threatening incident, the outcome of which is decided on the whim of Shane.

In many ways Jake is me. Or rather, an aspect of me at a certain stage in my life. I was always very different from other kids. To start with I was chronically ill with asthma. I couldn't do sports or run around and play. Also, probably as a result of being bedridden for weeks at a time, I was a bit of a loner. I read a lot – superhero comics mainly – and wrote my own fantasy stories. My interior world was always more real than what was going on around me. My nickname, by the way, was 'Alien', which gives you some idea of what my classmates thought of me. Needless to say, I was bullied mercilessly. I can honestly say that on at least three occasions I was lucky to get out alive. And this, in a way, is the menacing viciousness at the heart of the play. What you do as a writer is to take this single aspect and magnify it into everything. You concentrate on the micro until it becomes the cosmic.

In contrast to this 'menacing viciousness', the magical aspect of the play – and the most surprising – is the way in which the tower-block teenagers become enmeshed in a fantasy about a princess, a dragon, a forest and a suitor in search of impossible gifts.

At first glance it might seem that the teenagers would find no meaning in this story at all. Certainly, there's an initial resistance to it. But Jake, Polly and Natasha gradually persuade – seduce, if you like – the others into taking part. By the end, all of them have roles in this fairy story. But you see, in a way, this is perfectly natural for them. After all, they are playing roles when the drama begins. They're playing the stereotypical roles that their immediate social structure – in this case the school – has forced them into. They are, if you like, the natural stereotypes that any group of people, especially in a school, tends to produce: the Bully, the Geek, the Mr Cool, the Victim, the Wannabees, the Swot. In *Sparkleshark* all the characters realize they can shake off these roles by playing other roles. And they do it through the ritual of storytelling. And, in these new roles, they attempt to communicate their true emotions for the first time.

Communication is one of the main themes of the play: how we do it, how we fail to do it, how difficult it is, how easy it is to send the wrong signals. Thus the satellite dish is more than a device to get Polly on the roof. It is the overriding symbol of the drama: it has to be angled precisely if it is to receive a clear, undistorted picture from the satellite. And so it is with the characters in the play. Until now their images of each other – and themselves – have been distorted. During the course of the play they discover a way of channelling the energy – themselves – honestly and clearly.

All of the characters, during the course of the fairy tale, learn to feel something. They have a revelation about themselves. They exorcise some of their fear. The fairy tale gives them the courage to do this. In order to feel something it has to have a ritual.

Even Finn, who is an extreme example of non-communication, shares in this ritual by the end. Like the others, he is immersed in all the things that prevent young people from expressing their true feelings. But in Finn's case it is heightened by the fact that, even by his peers, he is perceived as a stupid, violent thug, to be avoided at all costs. As a result, Finn has retreated into a world of television and loud music, where even speaking has lost its relevance. But Finn can speak if he wants to – as the end of the play demonstrates. Ironically enough, it is Finn who gives the play its title, and he is seen in an entirely new light by the others.

It takes a lot of courage to break out of the stereotypical roles we're forced into. It takes a lot of courage to feel something and then express that feeling. Particularly these days – and particularly for the young – where the whole culture seems to be one of don't feel anything, don't care about anything, violence is cool, there is no tragedy, just mildly amusing irony. The young people in *Sparkleshark* find the courage to break out of this trap. Now, I know the end of the play can be considered ambiguous. And I think that's right. After all, they have to leave the roof. Who knows what will happen? Perhaps Jake will be hiding between the dustbins again the next morning. Perhaps the bullying and stereotypes will surface once more. But, for the moment – one afternoon on the top of a tower block – these characters realized another truth.

Philip Ridley sees the artist as the one who is shrieking out against apathy. In today's cultural desert the storyteller is someone who can help people to understand the terrors of life.

Storytelling has always been a way to exorcize fear. In some tribal cultures the role of the storyteller was taken by the Witch-Doctor. For example, if you were a member of a jungle tribe and your village was being threatened by a tiger, the Witch-Doctor would sit the whole tribe around a fire. He would give everyone a mildly hallucinogenic drug. As the drug slowly takes effect, you stare into the flickering light of the fire and, as you stare, the Witch-Doctor tells a story. It's about a monster threatening a tribe and members of the tribe have to go into the jungle to kill the monster. The Witch-Doctor describes the monster in great detail – every claw and every tooth. The Witch-Doctor's story is so vivid, the mixture of drug and fire so hypnotic, that you're there killing the monster. In this dream-time of storytelling you vanquish your fear. The next morning you sharpen your weapons and go out into the jungle. And you say, 'In the dream of my story-time I faced this monster. I am not afraid.'

Philip Ridley is a playwright, novelist, screenwriter, director and painter. His stage plays include *The Pitchfork Disney*, the multi-award-winning *The Fastest Clock in the Universe*, and *Ghost from a Perfect Place*. His bestselling and award-winning children's novels include *Krindlkrax*, *Kasper in the Glitter*, *Meteorite Spoon* and *Scribbleboy*. His highly acclaimed screenplay for *The Krays* and his directoral debut *The Reflecting Skin* earnt him the accolade of Most Promising Newcomer to British Film at the Evening Standard Film Awards.

Production Notes

STAGING AND SETTING

The entire action of the play takes place on the rooftop of a tower block in the East End of London during the course of one late afternoon. The satellite dishes, TV aerials and scattered detritus, including dustbin lids, an old umbrella, a milk crate, and so on, set the scene and are used as props during the play. Some metal steps lead from the larger main area of the roof up to a tiny platform and a doorway that leads to the emergency stairs. This is the only way on to the roof through which all but one of the characters make an entrance.

We know that it's around 4.30 p.m. and that the weather is overcast. The lighting should take this into account. Another consideration will be the transition from the characters' normal interaction to their collective storytelling, which must be believable. There might be a slow build-up of colour as the characters' collective imagination takes over and the audience suspends its disbelief to enter the fairy tale before returning sharply to the reality of the situation. Finn's voice is heard offstage and sound might help to create the rooftop illusion through the spillage of sounds associated with life in the various flats in the tower block, the playing field and traffic below, and the wind that whistles around high buildings. There is very clear guidance in the text on the way the characters interpret their school uniform and establish their varying street cred.

The play needs to move at a good pace. The last twenty minutes in particular need to be energized and must not be allowed to become sentimentalized.

CASTING

There are nine characters (three female, six male). Most are aged between fourteen and fifteen, though Shane is older and has the distinction of having left school already. Buzz and Speed are Russell's sidekicks. There are lots of clues within the play to each individual's status within the group.

QUESTIONS

1 Jake has created his own world in the rooftop hideaway, he has found a way of protecting himself through his ability to tell stories. To what extent can we compare him to a modern day Scheherazade from *The Book of a Thousand and One Nights*?

2 How do the characters arrive on the roof and what do their entrances tell us about them?

3 The satellite dish has a practical function because it brings Finn on stage. But it also works as a metaphor for the play – each character aims their dish hoping for a return signal. Many of the initial encounters start badly. How does the play allow hostility to be transformed into friendship?

4 As the characters warm up with their storytelling they become more adept at using it to 'get back' at each other. Russell, for instance, is tricked into becoming the Prince. He rises to the bait thinking he's being clever then falls into Jake's trap. Natasha undermines him by spraying him with girlie perfume. Where else does the power shift in the group through the enacting of the tale?

5 The most powerful character is Shane. As the Wizard he manipulates the story to unlock the secret between himself and Natasha. How does he do this and what has gone on between them?

6 What might Natasha stamping on the egg symbolize?
7 When Polly saves Sparkleshark she translates the central metaphor as 'We've got to find a way of communicating with each other.' Where else are there moments of discovery?

EXERCISES

1 Find out from the play what the characters say about themselves and one another which gives us clues about their self-image and the way they are viewed by the others. For example, Natasha, when asked by Jake about her dad, says that she feels he doesn't like her any more: 'If I walk into the room he looks straight through me. Or worse – like I've got a dog turd smeared across my forehead.'
2 'Hot seat' the various characters by having the actors sustaining their roles and imagining that it is the day after the action of the play. Question them closely to find out if the rooftop encounter has changed them in any way.
3 Rehearse *Sparkleshark* on the roof of a tall building (but be careful!).
4 The dialogue gives us a good indication of the characters' status at a given moment. In this extract Natasha scores high:

Carol (*sees Jake*) Yellow alert – Geek!
Polly Don't call him that!
Carol Orange alert!
Polly He's my friend!
Carol Red alert!
Natasha And mine!

Pause.

Natasha stops Carol in her tracks by asserting her right

584

to be friends with a 'geek' without losing her credibility. In role as the nine characters in the play, form a line from left to right, with the character with highest status on the left and the others in descending order to the right. This illustrates which character has highest status in the play at the beginning. Find a point in the play where these positions are challenged, and revise the line up. Decide if any of the characters hold their positions and why.

5 The play can be described as a journey from isolation to community, and a journey from violence to harmony for the characters. In pairs, improvise a scene that starts badly for the two characters and ends well.

6 In pairs, one partner (A) describes a life-changing event helped by prompting and questions about detail from their opposite (B). Bs then retell the stories as if it were their own, embellishing the story and exaggerating where necessary to make it more interesting. The audience is permitted to question, interrupt and lead the story in another direction.

7 In a group of five, collectively tell a story lasting no longer than five minute. It must include two objects and two animals. The challenge is to appear to have worked it out thoroughly beforehand and for it to seem scripted.

Suzy Graham-Adriani
February 1997

TRAVEL CLUB AND BOY SOLDIER

Wole Soyinka

Characters

Ground Hostess
Vashni
Sally
Donald
Benjy
Saunders   } all school pupils
Pesa
Fabori
Danny
Sean
Commandante
Guard

The school pupils are aged between fourteen and sixteen and a half, with the exception of Sean, who is thirteen.

An airport lounge somewhere among the South Sea islands, a favourite holiday resort. Enter a group of secondary school pupils, in school uniform, the blazers slung over their arms or shoulders. They are aged between thirteen and sixteen and are ushered into the room by a uniformed Ground Hostess. They have with them their carry-on luggage, shopping bags and odd souvenirs and gifts. They look tired, nervous and somewhat unkempt. Two or three wilted floral wreaths suggest a vacationing idyll reluctantly abandoned.

Ground Hostess Here we are. I shall try and get you some blankets.

Vashni Thank you, miss. But please, just do this for us if you can. Find out where they've taken our teachers. We'd like to be sure that they're all right.

Ground Hostess They'll be all right. You stay here and don't worry your heads.

Sally I saw one of the guards shove Miss Roberts. All she did was try to look back and wave to us, try to reassure us.

Donald And the other poked Mr Bailey in the back with his gun. He didn't have to do that.

Ground Hostess (*sighs*) You've seen for yourself. They are so . . . excitable. Most of them are too young to be involved in this sort of thing. But your teachers are all right. They'll be all right. (*She smiles.*) After all, they have some experience handling young people. I'm going to see them now and will tell them you are being taken care of.

589

Donald But why separate us? What are they going to do with them?

Ground Hostess Someone gives the orders and . . . (*She casts a quick look over her shoulder.*) Just keep reminding yourselves that they are a rather erratic lot. And they seem frightened. Some of them even look lost. Anyway, it's best to do as they say, and in turn, say little. From the little I've heard, their leader is a former ambassador to England, but I would never have guessed that, considering the manners of his ragtag soldiers.

Benjy No, it's clear they are no diplomats.

Saunders I don't like it. I think things have taken a turn for the worse. Why the sudden decision to keep us separate? Why?

Ground Hostess I've told you all I know. We are all in the same boat.

Sally The women with babies – well, children. There are children no older than four or five. Even three. What are they going to do – separate them also from their mothers?

Ground Hostess No, of course not. Listen, I mustn't stay any longer. I've got to take care of the others . . .

Pesa Will you be looking after us, like you told Mr Bailey?

Ground Hostess Yes. I've been assigned to you, but also to some other young groups. I'll be back. I'll also bring you some food once we've settled the other passengers in the remaining rooms.

The Ground Hostess leaves and there is silence.
    The pupils look around the room. One by one they drift to a spot – a corner, table or chair – where they let drop their bags, slide down a wall, squat, or simply stretch out on the floor or table. Pesa slowly takes off her wreath and arranges it on a table.

Pesa So this is what it's like. One reads about it. It's in the papers and on television. I had always wondered what it was like.

Fabori It begins like a joke . . .

Benjy More like a dream, don't you agree, Vashni?

Vashni We'll be rescued.

Danny Or killed in the attempt.

Vashni Oh yes, do look on the cheerful side.

Sally Good ol' Danny. Always good for a cheerful note.

Danny I am only being realistic.

Sean (*He's never stopped exploring and opens a flush door, revealing a cupboard.*) Oh look, there's a sink.

They gather round, not excited, just curious.

Fabori Any fridge?

Sean Nothing that looks like it.

Fabori I've had it then. Two more days without some cool storage . . .

Benjy I warned you not to splash out on perishables, Fab.

Fabori I couldn't resist the fruits. They reminded me of home, even though I've never seen the like. (*He takes out one or two.*) Just look at these. If for nothing else that travel agent was right – it's the original Garden of Eden.

Donald My offer still stands. I'll eat them for you.

Fabori I'll wait it out, Donald. When they start to rot, you can have them.

Donald In this heat, that won't be too long. They're not called same-day fruits for nothing.

Benjy You're just envious 'cause you didn't think of taking some home with you.

Donald You heard the fruit vendor – eat them same day you pluck them. Second day they go soggy and sour. Third day they start fermenting.

Fabori (*Feels one and sniffs it.*) The skin is holding up, nothing soggy about it. Those islanders exaggerate everything.

Benjy That was sales talk. How else would he get you going back for fresh ones day after day? He had you hooked.

Saunders Hm. Garden of Eden. Tropical paradise. And see where we end up.

Sally Here's a small stove . . . and an electric kettle.

Pesa (*looking around*) Maybe there's a bathroom somewhere. A shower – anything. Aren't airports supposed to have what they call day-rooms? It's been three days now – steamy and hot. I stink.

Donald Don't we all?

Sean It's only an office kitchenette. There isn't anything else.

Sally (*rummaging in a cupboard*) Then there'll be some tea around. Or instant coffee. Help me look around, Sean.

Sean (*Jumps down from the desk.*) All right.

Danny (*Flicks a switch and looks at the lighting.*) And what use would that be? There's no current in here.

Donald Hear that, Fabori? A fridge still wouldn't be much use to you.

Benjy Dogged Donald, daunted never.

Donald I'm only trying to be helpful. I'm sacrificing myself for a friend in distress.

Fabori Your offer is still rejected.

Sally I wonder what Nescafé is like when prepared with cold water.

Danny Mix instant with cold water? You nit. You'll give yourself the tremblies for ten days at least. That would be like licking up caffeine, neat. Don't you remember your chemistry? As for drinking the local water, unboiled . . . much less painful to die of thirst.

Sally (*flushing out a tin of Nescafé*) Well, here it is anyway. And here's sugar. And some condensed milk. (*She sniffs it.*) Ugh.

Benjy (*Swipes his finger across a table and holds it up.*) What do you expect? Anyone can see that this office hasn't been used in ages. (*He brushes off the dust.*)

Danny They are simply dirty, that's all. The entire airport is dirty. I noticed it as soon as we arrived. The school should never have brought us here.

Donald There was a vote, Danny. Don't you start shifting the blame on the school.

Danny I don't care. What did we know about the natives? You can't expect the travel agent to mention the open gutters and stench or whatever. Just the exotic parts, not the slums or bad habits. Once you left the beaches and the souvenir shops, what do you get? What are teachers for it they don't dig deeper into that side of things we can't know about?

Pesa Whine, whine, whine . . .

Danny It's a lot of money to pay just to end up in this end-hole of the world.

Donald Wait a minute.

Others also react.

What lot of money exactly?

Saunders Yes, how much is the trip costing you this time, Danny? Or your parents, to be more accurate?

Pesa That's right. By just how much are you out of pocket? Compare it to last year in Guadeloupe.

Benjy Where the little French we thought we had was no use to anyone except ourselves.

They all laugh.

Danny Sure, we had cut-rate prices on this one, but so what? My parents still had to fork out something. We haven't been living on air. And it was a separate charge for the excursion trips.

Donald But nothing like the usual whack, so stop complaining.

Benjy What is he talking about anyway? Wasn't that why the club voted to vacation here in the first place? One-third the usual fare – who could resist that kind of bargain?

Danny It's not been much of a bargain, has it? See where we've ended up, and we don't even know what's yet to come.

Saunders You enjoyed the sightseeing while it lasted.

Danny I did not. I hated every moment of it.

Donald Well, you certainly fooled me.

Sally Me too.

Pesa (*Snatches up his bag.*) Just feel the weight of that. Bursting with souvenirs.

Danny (*Leaps after her.*) You leave that alone!

Pesa throws it to Donald. Danny makes for him.

Donald (*tosses it to Saunders*) Here, Saunders!

Saunders catches it and passes it on to Fabori, who tosses it to Sally. She tosses it to Benjy, who then passes it to Sean. Sean hesitates.

Benjy Over here, Sean, over here.

Danny makes his leap at the hesitant Sean, bears him down, but Sean's tossed the bag behind his back to Benjy. Danny raises his hand to hit Sean, but Vashni rushes forward and stops the arm.

Danny Let go!

Vashni That's just like you. The one person who would have given it back to you and you want to hit him.

Danny I want my bag.

Benjy (*Slides it towards him.*) Here, Dan Dare.

Danny (*Snatches it up and turns on Pesa.*) And you! The next time you dare touch any of my things . . .

Pesa sticks out her tongue at him.

Vashni You too, leave him alone. Look everybody, just calm down. Let's take stock of our situation.

Danny What is there to talk about? They're savages. We've fallen among savages and it's going to get worse.

Vashni They haven't treated us too badly so far.

Danny You are just about ready to put up with anything. You're used to it. No difference from what it is like at home, eh, Vashni?

Vashni I wouldn't know, you know. I've never been home.

Danny (*under his breath, but the others hear him*) Bloody foreigners!

Fabori And just what do you think you are out here? Native son?

Sally Are you wasting your breath on that one?

Danny I'm a tourist here, that's what I am. A tourist. I pay to come here. They live off my money, don't they? If people like me didn't come here, they couldn't balance their budget.

Fabori Thank God for you, Danny. But for knowing you, I would have sworn your kind was totally extinct.

Vashni Hey, everyone, take it easy. We mustn't go to pieces under stress.

Danny turns his back to them.
   Pause, while Vashni looks round each one.

All right. Let's look at the situation. At least before now we had the teachers to do the thinking . . .

Danny And now we've got you? God help us!

Saunders Shut up Danny! Just you shut up!

Vashni I was going to say, now we've all got to do our own thinking. If they've taken the step of taking the adults away, it means they have decided on something – either release the children, keeping the adults, or . . .

Sally Or bargain with us, keeping us to the very last.

Benjy What makes you think that?

Sally Something I overheard. In the other lounge, when I went to the toilet with Pesa. Some of the guards were talking. I overheard them.

Vashni What did you hear exactly?

Sally It was all about not wanting their leaders to give up too easily. I heard them say – if we keep the children, we could strike a really hard bargain. They accused their leaders of beginning to act like politicians.

Benjy Well, if they are ex-ambassadors and the like, like the air hostess said . . .

Vashni You think there is disagreement . . . you think there is division in their ranks?

Sally That's what it sounded like.

Fabori In any movement, there'll be different factions. You can't help having some extremists. Those are the ones to watch out for. And that's why you can't go by anything you hear.

Saunders Why didn't you tell us?

Sally I told Miss Roberts. She told me to keep it to myself, not to alarm everyone unnecessarily. Pesa . . .

Pesa shakes her head. They look at each other.
    Vashni catches them at it.

Vashni What is it? Was there something else?

Pesa again shakes her head, moves away.
    Vashni watches them.

Danny What a thing to do? Why keep it from us? It's us it concerns directly, not so?

Benjy And what difference would it have made? What could you have done about it?

Danny (*hotly*) At least we would know what to expect. We wouldn't be taken by surprise – like this.

Benjy Taken by surprise? And prevented from doing what? Escape? What master plan did you have in mind?

Danny Did I say I was planning anything? But out there, we had all those facilities we could have used. The telephone, for instance. This one here is just an intercom – useless. (*He holds it to his ear.*) Dead. I was waiting till night to use the one in that lobby. I have my phone

card – I could have telephoned home . . . or
someone . . .

Saunders To say what? To tell them what the whole world
knows already? That we are being kept prisoners?

Danny I could have spoken to my family. Just to let them
know I'm all right.

Donald All the lines have been disabled, fool.

Danny Then why was the guard screaming at us each time
anyone moved near the phone?

Vashni They are young. And jittery. Anyone can see that.
They need to scream at people, that way they hide their
fear. The hostess was right.

Pesa He screamed at me when I went near the games
machine.

Fabori Maybe he'd never seen one before. Did you see the
way some of them examined everything, like they'd
found themselves in wonderland. I don't think they had
ever been inside an airport before. That one probably
thought the games machine was a space rocket and you
were going to try and escape in it.

Benjy They're nervous. Pesa, you acted excited as you
went towards it, so he screamed at you. With some you
have to ask permission to scratch yourself. That's how
they're trained.

Danny And what do you know about it?

Benjy (*gravely*) You learn a lot from watching films.

*They laugh. The atmosphere lightens somewhat. Then
they grow sober again, in an uneasy silence.*

Vashni It's quieter in here. It's bare, but it's better than
that big lounge. We don't have a nervous guard
glowering over us, watching every move we make.

Sean (*He's never stopped investigating the room and turns
on a switch.*) The air-conditioner is not working – oh, I
forgot, no electricity.

Danny You expect a lot, don't you? Even the conveyor

belts weren't working in the luggage hall when we arrived.

Fabori I think I'll propose my home for the next excursion. For Danny, you know. His education is lacking. He needs a really strong dose of culture shock. Then he'll agree this place is paradise and wish himself back here.

Sean (*Climbs on a chair to reach the grille up on the wall and puts his hand against the vent.*) The central system isn't working either.

Danny Will someone teach this Irish lad he is far away from civilization?

Sean It was working in the lounge, but it's so hot and stuffy in here.

Benjy This room has been disused a long time. They must be desperate with this idea of splitting us people into small groups. They'll end up putting some others in the toilets.

A brief pause.

Pesa I wonder how he's feeling.

Vashni Who?

Pesa That sleek travel agent. The one who sold us on the super cut-rate excursion fares to the dream island. That's what decided us in the end. The vote was going for Mauritius until he came into the picture.

Saunders Maybe he doesn't even know.

Donald He must know by now. It would be all over the papers . . . television, the lot.

Saunders But he may not know we are involved in all this. We are just one more group of school tourists. So many flights come here on excursion.

Benjy Taking over the whole bloody airport. Just one plane doesn't satisfy this lot. They have to seize the entire airport.

Pesa You think the government will pay our ransom?

Saunders What ransom?

Pesa It always boils down to a ransom, doesn't it?

Danny What's she been reading?

Sally They usually ask for prisoners to be released, that sort of thing. They don't go for ransom. It's all politics.

Pesa Our case may be different. Sally was right, you know.

She hesitates, then she and Sally exchange glances. Sally shrugs.

We may as well tell you. There was a bit more . . . I heard more than she did – when she went in and I waited outside.

Vashni I thought so. What else did you hear?

Pesa (*frowning*) I'm trying to remember the very words they used . . .

Danny Nothing that matters, I'm sure. Stop trying to make yourself important.

Vashni Look, ignore him. Try and remember what else you heard.

Pesa Well, I heard one say . . . (*She hesitates and looks at Sally.*) You think I should really tell them?

Sally Can't do any harm. We are on our own now.

Benjy What on earth have you two been keeping from us?

Vashni Go on. Spill it.

Pesa All right. It was the one who appeared senior to the others.

Saunders Yes, yes.

Pesa He said . . . Look, what it boils down to is this – I don't think we got here by accident. I don't think we chose this place for our annual excursion, the way we normally do.

They all sit up at this. There is a brief silence.

That's what I'm trying to say. For instance, one said, 'Well, we got them exactly where we want them.' And the other said, 'It took some planning. It's taken nearly a year.' It's like they've been planning it for a long time, you see – just to get us here. To trap us on this island. To get us to choose it for this year's excursion.

Vashni Are you sure? Do you know what you're saying?

Benjy That can't be. It doesn't sound possible!

Pesa Well, that's what I heard. They were feeling very pleased with themselves. Smoking and laughing. They said the operation had been very neat, that their overseas network deserved all the credit. Then there was something about . . . an . . . identification parade. But he didn't actually use the word 'identification'. He did say 'parade' though. They're waiting for someone they kept calling the commandante. I think he's the one coming here to conduct the parade. I told it all to Miss Roberts and Mr Bailey.

Vashni (*frowning, obviously worried*) An identification parade or . . . a selection parade? You can't remember the exact word?

Pesa (*Thinks hard.*) No. Does it matter? Anyway, they're all waiting on this man they call the commandante.

Danny (*exploding*) What's keeping him then? Why doesn't this bloody commandante or whatever come and hold his parade so we can all go home. (*sneering*) Isn't that just typical – commandante! They love giving themselves these grandiose names.

Benjy What are you thinking of, Vashni? What do you mean – selection parade?

Vashni We mustn't jump to conclusions. We simply don't know anything.

The Ground Hostess re-enters with two shopping bags.

Ground Hostess I brought you some snacks. It's not much. The food stock in the airport is running low, and no new delivery is being allowed. They've already shot the tyres off two supply trucks which tried to approach

– and that was after they had earlier given them permission to drive up. I bet they're going to empty them and keep the contents for themselves. That's how bad it is. We – the airport staff – we're having a meeting to decide on some way of rationing what's left. Right down to the junk stuff in the vending machines. Anyway, this will keep you going for now. And I managed to get you something to drink.

Danny See what I mean? We could have stocked up out there if those two had passed on their warning.

Sally Oh, be quiet, Danny! (*to Ground Hostess*) No news at all?

Ground Hostess (*handing round sandwiches*) Something seems to be happening. Someone has arrived. He seems to be quite important. I haven't seen him but the report is that he's come to take charge. He'll be addressing everyone over the public address system before long. You'll be able to hear for yourselves what he has in mind . . . Oh. (*She looks up at the ceiling.*) Oh, I forgot, not in here you won't. This was just a spare office space, not part of the passenger system.

Vashni What has he said so far?

Danny Did he say when we'll be released?

Ground Hostess He's given his first orders – I have to collect all your passports.

General consternation.

Vashni Is that good news or bad?

Ground Hostess We don't know. I can't tell why they need the passports. Maybe when they've checked them, they'll get round to releasing the people who are not involved in their problems. But then . . .

Pesa Yes?

Ground Hostess There are . . . cases where . . . You see, we don't really know what they want. They're not saying. A few more soldiers have arrived. They accompanied someone who looked like their big shot – maybe the ambassador I spoke of earlier. He walked around – like he was on a tour of inspection. Then he went away, leaving us to the tender mercies of this commandante. At first we thought the whole thing was a coup – You know, that soldiers had actually taken over government. But it's turned out that isn't the case. It looks like a hit-and-run operation.

Danny A hit-and-run job lasting three days? Some rebel army!

Vashni But the passports, miss. Why do they want our passports?

Sally (*with deliberate emphasis*) They want to look at the names, don't they? They want to pick their hostages – see whose names are Jewish or something like that. Isn't that what they usually do?

Benjy They did that at Entebbe, you know. They took all the Jews to one side – that is, all those with Jewish-sounding names – and herded them into one hall. It always begins with the passports.

Ground Hostess Now, now, don't let's start setting off our imaginations.

Sean (*He's still standing on the table, resting against the wall below the grille.*) But you have to collect our passports. You have to carry out those orders, don't you? Sally is right . . . when they start collecting passports . . .

Danny (*rummaging in his bag*) Here, miss. You can have mine. Anything to get us out of here.

Vashni No, wait. Let's think this over carefully. We don't want to hand them over just like that. It isn't smart.

Danny Why not? The sooner we do what they say, the sooner we'll get out of here.

Donald That's right. There is nothing we can do about it anyway. (*He hands his over.*)

Ground Hostess (*Collects both and stretches out her hand* *to the others*.) Please, the rest. None of us likes this, but we have to do it.

Saunders (*reluctantly*) I suppose so. Come on, fellows, let's get this over with.

Sally I am not very sure . . . that I want to give up my passport.

Benjy Nor I. In fact, I am damned near sure I do *not* want to hand it over.

Pesa That's how it starts. First they separate the adults from the children. The next thing is, they'll separate the boys from the girls. Then the blacks from the whites and the yellows from the reds . . .

Benjy And Muslims from the rest? Like in Bosnia.

Danny Have you all gone mad? You're letting your imaginations run loose instead of facing reality. What are you going to do when they burst in here and demand the damned things at gunpoint?

Benjy I expect I can wait till then.

Donald And to what purpose, Benjy? That would just be a gesture. You'd be forced to give it up in the end anyway.

Sean I don't think we should give them our passports.

Danny You don't think . . . ? You don't think, full stop. You're too bloody young to think, so shut up. And none of you is using your head. What on earth has got into you? Vashni, you started this . . .

Vashni I didn't start anything. I just don't want us to get separated any more, that's all. I prefer that we all stay together.

Danny None of you can prove anything you're suggesting! You're simply being alarmist.

Vashni Why do they want the passports? What are they looking for?

Danny Not us, that's for sure. What would they want with us? We're just students on our annual excursion . . .

Benjy In Bosnia, it didn't matter if you were an infant or a toothless grandmother. All you had to be was a Muslim, and they took you away. Those mass graves they've been digging up – it wasn't just the bodies of adults they found.

Danny We are not in Bosnia, for God's sake. This is a miserable South Sea island, a tourist resort, and we are just tourists caught in the midst of something.

Pesa Yes, but in the midst of what? And what has it got to do with our passports?

Vashni (*quietly*) There's a scene that continues to haunt me. I wasn't there but my uncle wrote me about it. You know, back home, on a lonely road – a passenger bus, it could have been any passenger bus. When the ambush came, they boarded the bus. They separated the Hindus from the Muslims, they told the Muslims to get out, then they locked the doors and threw in grenades through the windows. They sprayed the bus with machine-gun fire, then set it on fire. They didn't spare the children. They killed every Hindu in there.

A brief silence.

He even sent me a photograph of the scene, the mere skeleton of the bus and the charred bodies . . . It happened in his state.

Danny (*Looks around.*) Well, go on. Is the catalogue finished? Isn't someone going to remind us of the Hutus and the Tutsis? What of you, Fabori? You all come from the same Africa after all. We read all about their butchering sprees, but so what?

Fabori I don't need other people's lessons, Danny Boy. We had our own share of that business you know. The Biafran War, remember? My cousin was only a child then, no more than four. He told me of the day they came into the Midwest. They went from house to house, flushing out the Igbo. Marched them away. He was not

604

Igbo, though it took a while for his guardian to
persuade them that he was simply a ward of the family.
His parents had died in a motor accident and these old
family friends had adopted him. His guardian was
determined that my cousin should be spared, even
though he knew he was going to his own death. He
forced my cousin to speak a few words in our own
language – at four years, you understand? Still, he
managed to convince them . . .

Danny Lucky for him.

Fabori Later of course, the relations found their bodies in
a mass grave. And even before the war itself began . . .
in the northern parts, it was not good to be an Igbo. But
I do agree with you – for once. There is no point
fighting this.

Danny Thank goodness someone is using his head.

Fabori There is no point jumping to conclusions. And you
don't argue with a man with a gun, especially in a
business you know nothing about. Why should I stick
my head out of the window when there's a hailstorm
pounding the roof? That is a very wise proverb from my
part of the world.

Vashni Your cousin's guardian stuck his head out, you
said. Didn't he?

Fabori He was a doomed man. He did his duty by the
child of an old friend. For whom am I supposed to be
performing this duty? And what duty? I don't know
what the hell is going on, only that we are trapped here
and our gaolers have demanded something that is of no
use whatever to me. Why should I make an issue of it?

Ground Hostess I think that's a sensible way to look at it.
Please, I really must go now. Let me have the rest of the
passports.

Pesa still hesitates, then hands hers over.
Sean stares, surprised. Suddenly he wraps his scarf

over half of his face, leaps down from the table and brandishes an imaginary gun which he swivels around.

Sean Trick or treat?

They stare at him, surprised.

Saunders What's wrong with you? Is this a time for clowning?

Danny (*superciliously*) Stop being naughty, Sean.

Vashni (*Sighs.*) OK. I know what you're getting at.

Sean (*Gives a passing imitation of a machine-gun firing.*) Happy hallowe'en.

Sally Oh. (*She shudders.*) That.

Saunders For a moment, I didn't catch on.

Benjy You've made our point, Sean. Thank you.

Danny What point? What's he on about?

Vashni Come on, Danny. It wasn't that long ago.

Danny What wasn't? I don't know what on earth you're talking about.

Vashni Neither did the Roman Catholics who got slaughtered in that pub. They didn't know anything. (*There is disgust in his voice.*) Christ! How could anyone possibly fail to remember that? *I* remember. And it's far more your country than mine – as you never stop reminding me.

Danny Will you simply tell me . . . Saunders, what is he going on about?

Saunders The massacre in Northern Ireland, in that village outside Derry, in that pub that was used only by Roman Catholics. The men who burst in, wearing Hallowe'en masks. The customers all thought it was the usual Hallowe'en fun, until they opened fire, shooting at random. How many did they kill, Vashni?

Vashni Does it matter?

Danny Yeah, I remember now. But that just goes to show, doesn't it? They don't need to ask for your passport if they mean to kill you anyway. But your chances are better if you do as they say. That's the same as saying don't ask for trouble.

Fabori And don't argue with the man with a gun.

Vashni Passport. Passport! Don't you understand anything. That pub was their passport. Identity card – whatever you want. Being a Roman Catholic was their passport, and their death warrant. We're not just talking about a piece of paper. They were all at risk beforehand, simply for being who they were, but entering that pub confirmed their identity. After that . . .

An uneasy silence. The Ground Hostess tries to study their faces.

Ground Hostess Look, kids. I know you get taught all kinds of things in school, and I am not about to question the way you've come out of it, learning to think things out for yourselves, but if I may just bring you down to earth for one moment . . .

Saunders Sorry, miss, I think maybe I'll retain mine.

Danny makes a disgusted sound and turns his back. Donald retrieves his from the Ground Hostess before she can stop him.

Donald Me too. I think. I'll keep mine after all.

Ground Hostess But . . . this is . . . childish.

Danny (*his back turned to the scene*) Tell them, miss. You tell them. They think they are being high-minded, but maybe you can tell them.

Ground Hostess I do have to go. For the last time . . . They'll come looking for me any moment.

No one makes a move.

All right. I don't know how they'll react . . .

The Ground Hostess leaves.

For some moments, everyone remains where they are, in silence. Then one by one they open up their sandwich packs and begin to eat.

Sally rummages in the bag.

Sally She forgot the bottle opener.

Sean I saw one in the kitchenette.

Sean gets the opener and passes it to Sally. She opens the bottles while he hands them round.

They are all young-looking, but that doesn't fool me. They can prove rough, you know.

Saunders What do you know about it, Rambo?

Vashni I am sorry. I had no intention of provoking a dilemma.

Danny The trouble with you, Mr Dalai Lama or whatever, is that you do not distinguish between the debating hall and real life. This is not the school debating society tackling the subject 'This House is of the opinion that . . .' There are no pros and no cons, just guns and hostages.

Benjy You are entitled to your decision, but don't try to rationalize anything after the event.

Donald He's not altogether wrong, you know.

Sally Having second thoughts, Donald?

Donald No-o, not really. I am looking at it this way . . . I mean, why are we doing this? What got into me? Why did I take back my passport?

Benjy You thought it was right.

Danny Sentiment, Benjy, pure sentiment.

Donald If it's no worse than that, I don't mind. I don't mind being sentimental. I just don't want anyone to think I am trying to be . . . you know . . . morally superior.

Danny O-oh, I am glad that's occurred to you.

Donald Well, it troubles me. And anyway, you do have a

point. We can't help the situation we're in. But one couldn't ignore all those things that happen all over the world, once Vashni got us thinking about them.

Danny And to prove what? You are all meddling in something you don't understand. See? Meddlers. Bumbling, bungling meddlers. Trying to be special. Behaving like the pukka sahibs – you should know all about the pukka sahibs, shouldn't you, Vashni? But then all Indians secretly envy the sahibs, don't they? My dad used to be a civil servant in India. He told me how you all made yourselves ridiculous trying to ape the manners of the sahibs. Nothing has changed.

Saunders Watch it, Danny Boy! If you go too far, remember we'll all be writing our reports. In fact, you *have* gone too far. I'm going to put it in my report, even if the others don't.

Danny And I'll put all yours in mine. We were warned how not to behave among the natives. Don't go provoking them. Respect their customs. Watch how they do things and don't make yourselves conspicuous. Don't act superior . . . and so on and so forth. What have you just done but try to act superior?

Benjy How do you make that out?

Danny Moral superiority – Donald said it. And that's what it's all about, isn't it? You're all trying to act morally superior.

Sally To whom, Danny, to whom? To the man who wants to seize my passport? It's mine. *MINE!* My property! What's so superior about refusing to hand it over?

Danny That's not what the preacher said. He said it has nothing to do with passports. It's all trick or treat, not so? You take your chances.

Benjy Christ! Is that the way you understood it?

Sally Maybe he wasn't listening, Benjy. Let me put it this way to you: it's my identity. It is guarding my right to say who I am, and to keep that to myself, if that's what I wish. And not allowing someone to use that for his own ends. I refuse to be used, even indirectly!

Benjy Understand, Danny? That's what it's all about. Refusing to be used, even by a process of elimination.

Saunders Ugh. Don't use that word.

Benjy What? Oh. (*soberly*) What a terrible choice of a word – but appropriate in the circumstances. In the possible circumstances.

Danny Don't you both try and get clever with me. Vashni, you began the preaching. And the rest of you followed up with one sob story after another. Since when did school pupils try to become the conscience of the world? We have enough problems just getting to know it.

Saunders All Vashni did was remind us to be ourselves. That's all.

Donald Yes, he made it a moral issue. (*almost dolefully*) And I wish he hadn't. He didn't need to. I really wish you hadn't, Vashni. Especially as it's all so speculative. We don't *know*. We don't really know why they want the passports.

Benjy Don't take on so, Donald. Look, we are not adults. If we can't make gestures like that, when shall we ever? Soon it will be too late. (*chuckling*) For now, we are not supposed to be responsible for our actions.

Sally Well, we've done it anyway. Each one made his or her own choice. I don't care.

Danny There'll be some fall-out for the rest of us. You haven't thought of that now, have you? You took your decision, but it's going to affect the rest of us, one way or the other. We've made ourselves conspicuous – *you* have made us conspicuous. You've singled us out from the rest. And that's dangerous!

Footsteps returning. Enter the Ground Hostess, accompanied by a soldier.

Ground Hostess Those who submitted their passports, please follow me.

Danny (*scrambling up*) What's happening?

Ground Hostess And bring your things with you. The commandante has ordered that you be taken to a different room – to the business-class lounge.

Danny smirks at the others.

It is rather crowded, you know – very crowded – but the commandante doesn't know that.

Danny (*looking round*) I'm sure it is still an improvement. And it's the thought that counts, isn't it?

Fabori Actually, I would rather stay with the others.

Pesa Me too. I . . . I wasn't expecting this. Why take us away from the rest?

Ground Hostess Please, don't be difficult. That new commandante, he's taken charge of the listing of all the passports and he has someone enter the precise location of the holder. If for any reason they want to see you and you are not where they expect you to be . . .

Fabori (*He hesitates, then picks up his bag. He takes out the polythene bag of fruits and throws it to Donald, then looks round the room.*) I am sorry. (*He moves towards the door.*)

Pesa (*as she moves to join the Ground Hostess*) I am sorry too. I wish I had known this would be the . . . (*She hurriedly wipes away a tear.*)

Danny (*Turns as they leave and speaks to Vashni.*) You didn't want us separated, but what have you got now? Passport holders on one side, the rest on the other. Life doesn't offer much choice, does it?

They leave, the guard at the rear. He stops at the door and closes it slowly.

Vashni, Benjy and Saunders look at one another. Vashni nods. Benjy tiptoes to the door, listens, then tries to peep through the keyhole. The door is yanked open suddenly and Benjy finds himself confronted by the soldier. He gives a weak smile.

Benjy (*backing into the room*) Oh, hello, er . . . yes, I thought you might be around somewhere. No harm intended – sir.

The soldier slams the door viciously.

Saunders Well, I think that signifies a change in our status. They didn't think we needed a guard before.
Sally It's silly. As if it made the slightest difference.
Vashni You think they are trying to tell us we are now prisoners?
Donald What else have we been for the past three days?
Sally And we still – don't – know – exactly – what is happening.

Footsteps approach. Stamp of boot as the guard salutes.

Guard's voice Welcome, commandante.
Commandante Open.

The door is opened and in strolls a soldier in camouflage top and casual slacks. Of slight build, he stands and surveys his prisoners impassively. He jerks his head towards a chair. The guard runs to pick it up. The officer indicates where it is to be placed. He fetches the chair and remains holding it for his superior. The officer changes his mind as he is about to sit, but then strolls towards the table where the bags and school blazers have been placed. He stands looking at a blazer for some time, then picks it up and slowly puts it on. The soldier rushes to help him. The jacket will not go over his camouflage, however, so he contents himself with draping it over his shoulders. All this he does with a totally impassive expression. Then he smoothes down the lapels and front of the jacket, and slowly takes his

seat. He takes off his hat and lays it on the table. Only
then do we see that he is no more than fifteen. The
pupils gasp, staring in astonishment.

Commandante And what are you all staring at?
Benjy What? Oh . . . we . . . we meant no offence.
Commandante I was taught in school that it is rude to
  stare. But that was a long time ago. Have things
  changed that much in school? Perhaps no one taught
  you not to stare?
Vashni Of course, yes. Do excuse our . . . it wasn't
  rudeness. Really. It's just that . . .
Commandante And if not at school, then at home. By
  your parents. Were you not taught the same thing at
  home?
Sally Excuse me. If you are trying to say something rude
  about our parents . . .
Commandante No, I am not. You do have parents?
Sally Yes.
Commandante Both living?
Sally Both of them.
Commandante And the others? You, sir?
Donald I have just one. My mother is dead.

The soldier turns his head to one after the other.

Benjy Both of mine are alive.
Saunders Me too.
Sean My father is dead. Killed in the Irish troubles.
Commandante Really. He was a soldier?
Sean No. He kept a shop, that's all. A grocery store.
Commandante I see. And you?
Vashni I can't say if my father is alive. He's in India
  somewhere. Mother doesn't talk about him.
Commandante I congratulate you all. I have neither one
  nor the other. In fact, I have no family.
Vashni I am sorry about that.

Commandante Or rather, I have a new family. And I like
my new family.

*He holds out his hand, two fingers pointing out. The
guard rushes to place a cigarette in it and lights it. He
gives a brief smile.*

Now I suppose I am giving you even greater cause to stare.

Sally (*curtly*) There is nothing to stare at.

Commandante If you're rude, I shall teach you a lesson.

Sally I suppose you enjoy frightening people. You came
here to intimidate us.

Vashni Easy, Sally. (*to the soldier*) I think you know
quite well why we were staring. We were taken by
surprise.

Commandante By my smoking? Don't you sneak off in
school sometimes to have a drag round the corner? Yes,
I believe that's the expression. A quick drag.

Benjy You know it had nothing to do with the smoking.
You look so young. You're not older than any of us here
– except Sean.

Commandante Yes, I should be in a school uniform, not
in this camouflage. But you saw it yourselves, I tried
one. Only it didn't fit.

Benjy Because you didn't want to take off your jacket.

Commandante No. Even if I'd got my body into it, it still
wouldn't fit. What would a soldier be doing in a school
blazer?

Sally There are military cadets in schools. My brother is a
cadet.

Commandante Ah, how quickly one forgets. Of course
there are cadets. But being a cadet is not the same as
being a soldier. A warrior.

Vashni Excuse me, er . . . er . . . can we call you . . . I
mean, how do we address you? I'm Vashni. This is
Donald, Sally, Saunders, Benjy, Sean. Now you know
who we are. What's your own name?

Commandante You can address me 'Commandante'. I am the airport commandante.

The pupils look at one another.

Vashni You are in charge?

Commandante Yes, I am in charge.

Vashni Of the airport? Of the entire airport?

Commandante I have just taken over. I arrived a short while ago. I was summoned from the front – quite some distance from here. That's why I took so long getting here to take over the command.

Saunders Then, Commandante, are you about to tell us why we are being held?

Sally And how soon we can leave.

Commandante You refused to hand over your passports. You made me come down from my command post. You have interfered with my duties.

Vashni (*stepping forward*) I take full responsibility for that. It was my idea.

Commandante The air hostess came to me to ask permission to call in your teachers. She thought they might persuade you to change your mind. Naturally, I refused. I ordered that you be taken to the cells. There are cells here at the airport. Mostly for smugglers, especially drug runners – at least that's what the government tells the world. The hostess pleaded on your behalf. She asked that you be given another chance, she would guarantee to bring back the passports. She was very tiresome – I told her I would think about it, anything to get rid of her. Well . . . suddenly, I decided to come myself – just on a whim. I haven't set my eyes on school pupils for a number of years – you know, real school pupils, in school uniforms. (*He caresses the lapels again.*) They are smart. Do you have to wear them, even on vacation?

Benjy (*giggling*) We don't like it much but – rules are rules.

Commandante You wore them throughout your stay here?

Donald Oh no, they've been neatly folded away since we arrived. We only put them on for the flight home.

Commandante Uniforms are good things. They instil a culture of discipline. Unlike you (*nodding towards Benjy*) I never have objected to uniforms.

Vashni You've attended school?

Commandante Why? Do I sound uneducated?

Vashni I didn't mean that. I, er . . . I was just wondering how early you left school. I mean, to have risen in the ranks so quickly . . . Commandante. Excuse me, but you can't be more than fifteen.

Commandante I schooled like you – until five years ago. Then I left. It was time to continue my schooling elsewhere – in the bush. (*He rises abruptly, taking off the blazer.*) Now that I have indulged my curiosity, I must get back to my post.

Sally Excuse me, but don't you think you could indulge our own curiosity a little?

Benjy Yes, please!

Commandante How do you mean?

Benjy The question we asked when you came in. What is going on? Why are we being held? The country was peaceful all the time we were here, then suddenly . . .

Commandante The country was peaceful – is that what you were told?

Saunders Nobody said any different.

Commandante This country was peaceful? Peaceful?

Saunders And all the time we were here, we saw no sign of any unrest. We went virtually anywhere we pleased.

Commandante Is that really what you believed? You think you went everywhere you pleased?

Donald Well, we had an itinerary made out for us, and we followed it pretty closely.

Commandante Naturally. The government would make

sure you didn't go in any of the so-called rebel-held areas. But this island is not peaceful. It hasn't been for over ten years.

Donald It doesn't show.

Commandante You are tourists. You are here to have a good time. Others are not having so good a time.

Sally All right. And now you've taken the airport . . .

Commandante Indeed we have. The government wasn't quite expecting us.

Sally And what has it got to do with us? Why are we being held?

Commandante Maybe you were in the wrong place at the wrong time. Isn't that how these things usually happen? I must get back to my post. I shall send that lady back to collect your passports. This time, don't delay her.

Vashni You can take them with you if you wish – I think some may be . . . ready for collection.

The others glance at him, surprised.

Commandante (*Gives him a withering glance.*) Count yourselves lucky I haven't thrown you in the cells. And be careful not to tempt me. You think my job here is to run after your papers?

Vashni I'm sorry. I didn't think that would give offence.

Benjy Can I ask just one more question? Or rather, well, just ask for an assurance.

Commandante Hurry up.

Benjy Why are you taking the passports? You are not selecting people just to do away with them, are you?

Commandante You seriously expect me to answer that?

Benjy Because if you are, I still don't think I want to give up my passport.

The Commandante looks long and hard at him. Slowly, he resumes his seat.

Commandante Is your friend quite sane?

Saunders As sane as the rest of us – I think.

He looks round. They all nod.

Because we all feel the same. Even Vashni. What he said just now, it was just to let us know that we were free to act as we pleased. Nothing has changed. All we are doing is asking for an assurance.

Commandante (*He chuckles nastily.*) For school pupils of what I presume must be your grades, you don't seem to be very smart. Do you know what my position is here? I am in charge of the entire airport. I have the power of life and death over everyone here at this moment. Or maybe you are permitting the fact that I am . . . more or less of the same age as you . . . to lull you into a false sense of security?

Vashni No, it's true we are meeting someone like you for the first time, but I think we all know about you already. We've read all about boy soldiers, most of them forcibly recruited – Liberia, Uganda, Surinam, Afghanistan . . .

Sally We take courses on the United Nations, especially Unicef.

Commandante What's that?

Sally That's its agency for children – and youth. So we do know something about the subject. Once, we debated with another school over the issue of conscripting children into armies. You know, whether or not the UN should outlaw the practice below a certain age.

Commandante And your conclusion?

Sally We won.

Donald The other side never stood a chance, once we laid out the facts. We'd come across some shocking things. Some of those boys – as young as ten or eleven have done terrible things, even worse than adults.

Commandante And some of them have had terrible things done to them. (*A suppressed rage begins to surface as he proceeds.*) Some of them have had their parents, their brothers and sisters killed before their eyes. Not neatly, cleanly, but hacked to death, piecemeal, with machetes. Some of them have watched their baby sisters held by the legs, their brains dashed against a wall. Some have seen their grandfather flung into a blazing hut while the killers jeered. They said things like – you're just a bundle of twigs anyway, you'll make good firewood. Yes, and others have witnessed rapes, disembowelment, mutilation, they've seen innocent peasants on their way to farm, blown up in such tiny fragments by land-mines you couldn't tell if it was an animal or a human. (*He stops, slowly recovers.*) No, I was not conscripted. Yes, some were, but I was not forced into anything. I lost a family, and found another. And our family code is that you are either killing or getting killed. Giving orders or carrying out orders. (*Again, he rises abruptly.*) I have work to do. (*At the door, he turns.*) I am glad I yielded to a certain – well, curiosity I suppose, and came to see you. It brings back memories – both good and bad. And hopes, perhaps. That the future may return to something like – yours.

Sally We . . . overheard that you are actually looking for someone. Or some people. We heard some of your soldiers talking. You're here to find some people, aren't you? Is there going to be an identification parade?

Commandante (*A wistful smile.*) How wonderful it all is. I had forgotten how to ask questions, I had forgotten that being of a certain age makes you naturally curious. Oh yes, it's all coming back. There was also a time when all I did was ask questions, questions upon questions, keeping at it as if that was what life was all about.

Sally You no longer ask questions?

Commandante I've told you, orders have replaced questions. You either give orders or you carry them out.

Sally Well, is there anything in your code that says you cannot *answer* questions? You are, after all, the most senior – member of the family – at the airport. The most authoritative – from what you've said.

Commandante (*Pauses, then gives a brief smile.*) All right. If you must know – yes – my immediate task is to identify someone. A boy, about your age and mine, travelling on a false passport. We don't know his identity precisely, but we have information that he is here now, within this airport. We could have taken this place weeks ago. Our men had been infiltrated into strategic positions awaiting their orders. Our intelligence slipped up a bit – that is, the crucial information was late in getting to us. Otherwise, it was an excellent operation. Four days ago, we received information that our quarry was already in the country, travelling with his school group, and would be leaving any moment. We made our move.

Vashni A school group?

They exchange glances.

Commandante Yes. For all we know, it may be yours.

Vashni You actually did not know which school?

Commandante Only the town where the school is. And a few clues that made it possible to draw up a short list. We were able to target a limited number of schools within that city.

Sally But why? What's he done?

Commandante Not him. His father. He's our enemy – the chief of police. Brutal and corrupt. He's responsible for most of the atrocities against our side. The boy was born and raised abroad – the fruit of an illicit affair – but that's not our business. He comes home from time to time, always on a different passport. We learned of his existence only two years ago. If we take him hostage, we can negotiate the release of some of our own people. Some of them have been in prison ten, twelve years. All, without exception, have been tortured.

Saunders And you'll hold on to the airport until you find him.

Commandante It won't be long now. We can't hang on to the airport for ever. The government's overseas friends and partners – its masters in reality – are already amassing their paratroops to come to the aid of their friend. Defence pact – the usual thing. But we'll be finished and gone before they even lift off.

Vashni But suppose you're wrong. Suppose he's not here.

Commandante Oh, he's here. You didn't come here by accident, you know. We have friends abroad. (*Smug smile.*) Did your school get a good bargain off the travel agency?

Vashni What . . . travel agent?

Commandante The one who arranged your excursion?

Sally What do you know about that?

Commandante I believe he made your school a most irresistible offer. A keen travel club like yours, with a preference for interesting geological sites . . .

Donald But, we . . .

Commandante Yes?

Donald Nothing.

Commandante It will all be over soon. The passports will give us the main clues to the boy we want. We know where he spent his last vacation. If it is the same passport he used, we'll find the stamp in it. If not, I shall need to speak to you all, one by one.

Sally You're going to interrogate us?

Commandante That's my job. I sometimes work for intelligence. We receive our training on the job, but we're good. We've learned the ropes. And we have supporters in the most unexpected places – lots of exiles doing different things – taxi drivers, clerical workers, hotels, supermarkets and so on. That's how headquarters became sure of the city where this boy was schooling. One of our exiled comrades works for a travel agency. So, our commander set up a special task force. By the way, our commander used to be an ambassador in your country, before he broke with the regime. He's quite a match for the enemy, and sooner or later . . . Well, I must go now. I have enjoyed talking to you. In fact, I enjoyed our meeting so much, I hope the boy we want belongs to one of the other schools, not yours.

He leaves.
They remain silent, looking at one another.

Sally (*Signs to the others to come to the far corner of the room, away from the door.*) You really think it possible? You think it could be us – one of us?

Donald The odds are against. (*He shakes his head in bewilderment.*) What a network they must have built up! That travel agent – suddenly all those seductive brochures flooding the school.

Benjy We had virtually settled for Mauritius before he came on the scene. Then it all changed. Everything was going for this new resort – the climate, volcanic origins, ancient fossils, rare plants, unusual marine life and what else?

Donald More discos per square mile than any other tropical island resort.

Sally And, of course, the entire package deal – dirt cheap, just as he promised.

Vashni How many other school groups came with us on the charter flight?

Donald I counted eleven.

Benjy That travel agent really did some campaigning. But the whole business – what kind of single-mindedness is that! They actually bagged eleven schools?

Vashni And if it turns out to be ours?

Benjy What are you thinking?

Vashni Are we going to agree to leave him behind?

Some moments' silence, as the possibility sinks in.

Benjy We shall have to talk to Commandante. He's of our own age, after all. There must be a common language between us.

Vashni (*Shakes his head.*) I am not sure. Experience ages people, and terrible ones . . . he's not a boy any more. And I don't think he is a full-grown man either. But he is not a young person – not like you and me.

Sally Benjy is right. We can only try. Did you see the way he seemed to long for . . . even yearn for something? Something we reminded him of.

Saunders Oh yes. His vanished youth. And if we're not careful, he'll take his revenge on us for that loss. Deep down, I think he resents us.

Footsteps. Enter the Ground Hostess.

Ground Hostess You could have saved me and you all this trouble in the first place.

Vashni I am really sorry, miss. It was all my fault.

Ground Hostess Oh, never mind. Just let me have them now.

They look at one another, still hesitant. The Ground Hostess turns to Sean.

You're the youngest. Let's show the grown-ups you have more sense than they do.

Sean I can't do it.

Ground Hostess Plea-ease!

Sean It's just something I can't do. My father wouldn't have wanted me to – I just know it. He would never forgive me for doing it.

Ground Hostess I've done my best. He's going to pack you all off to the cells.

Sean How can he do that to everyone? He said he was only looking for a boy. Then why is he not letting the girls go? Why are they seizing everybody's passport?

Ground Hostess Who said? Who are you talking about?

Saunders The Commandante was here.

Ground Hostess He came here himself?

Saunders Yes. And he said it's a boy they want to take hostage.

Ground Hostess Which boy?

Donald The son of the chief of police.

Ground Hostess (*Shakes her head in disbelief.*) How the story keeps changing. I can no longer keep up with the latest.

Vashni What do you mean, miss?

Ground Hostess They've got the boy they want. The poor boy was seized the moment his group got to the airport.

Saunders Maybe the Commandante doesn't know that. He says he's only just arrived to take over operations.

Ground Hostess For one so young, he sure tells a lot of lies. The soldiers took the boy to him the moment he arrived. They took him to his office and I understand that the commandante had even begun to question him.

Benjy So why do they still want our passports?

Ground Hostess Look, stop asking why they do these things. Just do what they want.

Sean I wonder if it's someone we know. We've made many friends in the other groups. Just imagine if . . .

Ground Hostess (*becoming really anxious*) Listen to me, you kids – all the others have submitted theirs. Were they thinking of you when they did? And half of your group have obeyed the orders. Where does that leave you?

Saunders Come on, Sean. Vashni? (*He picks up his passport.*) Well, the game is over, isn't it? If the others have caved in, there is no point trying to be a hero.

Sally Why does he still insist on taking our passports?

Sean In my own case, I no longer have a passport, miss.

624

Ground Hostess Now you're really being childish.

Sean Honestly, I haven't.

Ground Hostess I don't know exactly what you're trying to say, but I hope you don't expect the Commandante to believe you.

Sean (*Points to the ventilation grille.*) I slipped it through there. So no one could force it out of me.

Sally Sean, you're not making a joke are you?

Sean shakes his head.

No, I suppose you would never make a joke of this.

Ground Hostess You silly boy, what have you done? Who taught you to make such pointless gestures?

Vashni You actually did that? You slipped it through the grille.

Sean I couldn't think of a better place to dispose of it.

Ground Hostess To think I virtually had to go on my knees, begging that arrogant boy not to send you to the cells.

Benjy You don't think he would actually go as far as shooting us, do you?

Vashni There is only one way to find out.

Vashni tosses his passport to Sean and nods towards the vent. Sean catches it and jumps on to the table.

Donald (*walking towards Sean, passport held out*) I still think this is pure madness.

Ground Hostess In God's name, what do you think you're doing?

Sally (*throwing hers*) Maybe it's a form of sunstroke.

Saunders hesitates, absent-mindedly caressing the document. Then he follows suit. Carefully, Sean feeds them one by one through the grille.

Saunders What now?

Vashni We wait.

A Sad Parable of Serpents Lurking in the Garden of Eden

Wole Soyinka interviewed by Jim Mulligan

The Nobel Prize-winner for Literature Wole Soyinka was born in a small Nigerian town where his father was the headmaster of a primary school and his mother 'a petty trader'. As a child he spent holidays in his grandfather's village, immersed in the oral tradition of storytelling, riddles and songs. Wole Soyinka was a voracious reader and started writing early, embellishing the stories he heard to make them his own.

> Before I left home I had already written a few things: stories and radio plays for the very young Nigerian broadcasting station which was a kind of branch of the BBC. This was in the fifties when Nigeria was still a British protectorate. We didn't get independence until 1960. After I had been through primary school where my father was headmaster I progressed through the different levels of Nigerian education and then went to Leeds to study literature. Somewhere along the road I realized that I wanted to write more than anything else. Most of my writing is for adults but I have tried writing for children and I find it one of the toughest things in the world. It requires total commitment to capture their intellectual and emotional level.

Travel Club and Boy Soldier takes a brief look at a group of teenage school students who are on holiday somewhere among the South Sea islands. The place is a holiday venue for foreigners. It is a playground for certain people but can be life and death for the people who live there.

> I have myself been a tourist and I've always wondered

about the impoverished, horrendous ghettos in India or Italy and even Paris and what would happen if they erupted and enmeshed the people who had just gone there for the beauties and pleasures of the place. These places are like paradise but in any Garden of Eden there are serpents lurking. It always seemed to me to be a precarious balance, a kind of contradiction between a place of pleasure and a place with some form of social agony. I don't know how you resolve that kind of moral dilemma. It's part of the contradiction of life. *Travel Club and Boy Soldier* calls this contradiction up to the surface without making a comment about it. I take the view that only those who run such countries can do anything about this kind of exploitation and the even worse 'original sin' of multinational corporations which exploit without putting anything back.

The play shows us the young people trapped in the airport after an insurrection has taken place. During their discussions we learn that Sean's father has been killed by terrorists in Northern Ireland, Vashni has an account of how a bus in India was ambushed and the Hindus savagely murdered and Fabori tells of the massacre of the Igbo in the Biafran War. It is clear that extremism is not confined to any one place.

I don't allow myself to feel anything about the terrorists in the play. I am content to expose the political and social background that led to this event. And what term should you use: terrorist, freedom fighter, revolutionary? The morality of the revolutionary is always different from the morality of the rest of the world. Even violence has its ethics. There is a difference between a target-directed bomb and one let off in a market-place irrespective of who is hurt. That shows a contempt for innocence and the perpetrator arrogates power to himself. That, for me, equates with fascism, whatever

the causes. On the other hand, there are certain forms of
violence which for me can be justified, depending on the
context and depending on the strategy of violence. I
don't allow myself to take on any blanket moral stand
in this area.

As they wait in the airport, the young people are asked to
make a moral choice, either to hand over their passports
and be relatively safe or to refuse because handing them
over is probably the start of segregation which could have
fatal consequences. At this point Fabori states, 'You don't
argue with a man with a gun.' And three of the young
people leave. The others are confronted by the
Commandante and an armed guard.

Many of the things I say in my plays I say within a
specific context. It doesn't mean I agree with it. It is a
fact that many people say and believe it is foolish to
argue with the man with a gun. There are others who
say absolutely that we must make a stand because, if we
don't, the man with the gun becomes our terror and
controls our lives. Some might call this heroism and
dismiss it as a futile gesture, others will praise the act.
But, for me heroism is a temper of the mind. Those who
are heroic will act in that way and the others will stand
back. I am not trying to put a value on the act. It seems
a pointless exercise.

For the past two years Wole Soyinka has been a member
of the United Nations Scientific Committee on the Impact
of War on Children. It is easy to see, therefore, why this
preoccupation should find expression in *Travel Club and
Boy Soldier*. The Commandante of the airport is a young
person no older than the school students. In what might
seem a despairing speech he describes the violence he has
witnessed and claims that he has now replaced questions
with orders. But he finishes by hoping that perhaps the

future may return to something like that of the school students.

> The issue of boy soldiers is something that has been uppermost in my mind. I've seen photographs and film footage and newsreels of these children who have aged before their time, whose humanity has become warped. They have become immune to violence and the most awful kind of viciousness. Watch the faces of these children. They have become old before their time.

For Wole Soyinka, extremism is a virus that is sweeping the world. With the development of technology, the shrinking world, the global community and the interpenetration of cultures, he sees nationalism becoming irrelevant in a couple of decades. He is not so sanguine about religious fundamentalism.

> I believe in religious sensibility, where people feel a genuine spirituality, but the extremist religious virus is like a plague. It is going to run riot for some time and I cannot predict when the fever will run its course. On the positive side there are some people who can influence the world. Nelson Mandela is one remarkable example with saintly qualities. But for the leadership of Mandela and Desmond Tutu you would have a cycle of unending revenge in South Africa. My play is a very sad parable about what is happening all over the world, but my immediate motivation comes from Africa. South Africa is unique. Let's hope it does not remain unique.

Poet, playwright and novelist, Wole Soyinka became the first African to receive the Nobel Prize for Literature in 1986. His work includes a collection of five plays: *A Dance of the Forests, The Swamp Dwellers, The Strong Breed, The Road* and *The Bacchae of Euripides*. Soyinka has been censored, prosecuted, and imprisoned under successive military regimes in Nigeria and has been forced into exile on three occasions since 1986.

Production Notes

STAGING AND SETTING

The entire action of the play takes place in an airport lounge somewhere among the South Sea islands. Two or three wilted floral wreaths suggest a vacationing idyll recently abandoned. There is the usual type of seating, plus a cupboard revealing a small stove and kettle. There is also a wall grille, through which passports will be fed towards the end of the play.

The lighting should be hard-edged, or even fluorescent. It is very hot, but the air conditioning and fans aren't working. A coup has recently taken place, and so gunfire, army trucks, helicopters and voices issuing commands in the distance will help to establish the setting. There is the sound of echoing footsteps as the Commandante enters, and the slamming of a door.

All the schoolchildren are in the same formal school uniform, but all will wear it differently according to their character. There is also a Ground Hostess, a Guard and the Commandante who wears a camouflage top and casual slacks.

CASTING

The school party of nine is aged between fourteen and sixteen and a half, with the exception of Sean who is thirteen. The Commandante is fifteen. Ideally the Guard and Hostess should appear slightly older. The students form the school's debating society and have mixed origins. Race shouldn't be a major issue when casting, likewise gender. Although only two of the nine students are girls, the play would not be compromised if this were altered.

QUESTIONS

1 Do the schoolchildren believe that they will be released? At what points do they feel their lives are in danger?
2 Whose side is the Hostess on? Do the pupils trust her?
3 Do any of the pupils suspect one of their members to be the boy the Commandante is looking for?
4 The play deliberately ends on a cliffhanger, what do you think happens next?

EXERCISES

1 The pupils have the school debating society as a common interest. They are articulate and fast-witted. Investigate the rules of debating or, better still, go and watch a debate. Set up the debate that is referred to in the play on the issue of conscripting children under the age of fourteen into the army. Which of the students is the best debater?
2 The students are being held against their will by soldiers, many of whom are their own age. Their rules must seem unreasonable. Play the following control game which is a version of the Court of the Holy Dido. In a circle, one of the players becomes the Commandante. None of the other players is allowed to smile, move, sniff, sneeze, avert their eyes from the circle, or whatever, without the Commandante's permission, which can be gained by raising the hand and asking as politely as possible if they can stand then speak. The Commandante isn't obliged to grant requests and can hand out punishments such as 'Stand on one leg with your nose pressed to the wall until further notice.' The other players can report one another for breaking the rules and suggest non-violent punishments,

and they can offer to test the strength of will of the other players by trying to make them laugh. Now improvise the situation referred to in the play where Pesa and the others are under guard, and are shouted at for appearing to be about to touch the phone and the games machine. How do the guards enforce their control over the schoolchildren?

3 Have each of the nine schoolchildren present their passport to the rest of the group. It needs to contain essential information about their character – a photograph, country of origin, place of birth, date of birth, parentage and visas, places visited and so on. Have each character put together their history based on facts in the play.

Suzy Graham-Adriani
February 1997

THE ULTIMATE FUDGE

Jane Coles

Characters

Holly
Kimberley Golden
Neil
Jodie
Brandon } at FAB TV
Shaun
Amy
Laura
Hayley

Lovell
Tomkins
Stavely
Emmett } in the Fox and Goose pub
Donna
Janet
Dora Biffen

Crawshaw
Lord David Docherty } at the stately home

Day. Open-plan office at Fast Action Broadcasting
Television (FAB TV). Desks, chairs.
   A blackboard is chalked with a chart scheduling the
company's weekly news magazine, Teleport. *This is a late-*
night programme and is sold to a network. It is the
company's only output. Ratings are dropping and to keep
the company alive items must become ever more audience-
grabbing.
   Staff members are sitting on desks, the floor and even
chairs. They are drinking Coke or coffee. Some are sharing
pizza pieces torn from giant margheritas. Others are
reading. Nobody is working.
   Everyone is awaiting the arrival of the editor, Kimberley
Golden, who will kick things into action and start the
weekly production meeting.
   Holly is in a pizza-eating group with Jodie, Neil,
Brandon and Shaun.
   Amy, Laura and Hayley are working out. (A simple
exercise routine that they are checking in a book.)
   Music comes from a system somewhere submerged.

Holly Kimberley said don't write –
Jodie Let FAB TV surprise them!
Shaun Don't even whisper *Teleport*!
Brandon They'd put the phone down!
Neil (*as Kimberley*) Don't *phone* them, darling!
Brandon and Shaun (*high-pitched*) Just go in with the crew!
Jodie Steven?
Holly Six foot seven Steven. This poor woman opened the
   door and Steven said I'm running, Holly. She'd never

seen a Camcorder. She thought it was an AK-47. She
fainted. Out cold on the floor.

Brandon I bet Steven kept on running.

Holly Got it for you, darling, he said, reloading in the car.
He got the woman's dirty slippers. Big hole in her tights.
He went in really tight on the eye make-up from hell.
He was still there when the dog arrived to lick her face –

Neil I won't work with Steven.

Brandon Why?

Neil Cheats on his expenses. Patronizes women. Smells a
bit. And overshoots.

Shaun He gets *good* wallpaper.

Jodie That sort of rubbish can save a story, Neil.

Brandon Kimberley will do the voice-over. (*as Kimberley*)
'This woman once had dignity, a PC and a proper job.
Teleport is here to tell her story, the story that the others
were too scared to tell.'

Holly Steven got two minutes of her husband's tears –

Jodie The husband!

Neil Two minutes is too much.

Brandon You got the husband?!

Jodie The tabloids only got a pic of him in nappies from
some auntie in Australia! You're a genius, Holly! You're
wicked, man.

Shaun Do you think he did it?!

Holly No, actually.

Jodie Kimberley will take you out to lunch.

Shaun Where's her watering-hole these days?

Brandon She goes Italian. I've been there. All white.

Neil Just like a morgue. But not so cheerful.

Holly I don't think I can use the tears.

Neil I don't think stranglers cry.

Brandon If she takes you to the Italian it could be your
moment, Holly. Pitch your Middle East idea while
you're topping up her Soave. You could be in Beirut by
Saturday. Wow, eh?!

Holly I'm having lunch with Neil.

Jodie No, you've got to go for it, Holly. If you don't go to lunch with her, you'll be letting women down!

Holly Kimberley Golden is a woman, Jodie. Some role model. She starts a war whenever she picks up that mobile. She makes big men cry like babies.

Shaun (*calling across to the other group*) Hey, girls! Do you think that stranglers cry?

Amy, Laura and Hayley come across and tuck into the pizza.

Amy Exercise just leaves me starving.

Laura There's this book! Kimberley wanted to do it! *The Sleeping Diet*! It was scheduled! Really! The week of the massacre! The week we lost everything, including my first trip to Belfast.

Hayley (*putting down a slice*) I'm giving up tomatoes. They're from the deadly nightshade family. Killers.

Amy Why are there still Italians then?

Shaun Well?

Amy Of course stranglers bloody cry.

Laura Particularly on television.

Hayley Particularly on FAB TV.

Amy Most particularly on *Teleport*, where they know that Kimberley Golden's on their side.

Neil On their side if there's fifteen million watching.

Kimberley Golden comes in, power-dressed and in a panic. She carries all the daily papers. She notices that nobody is working.

Kimberley (*sarcastic*) These leisure centres are springing up everywhere.

Staff quickly return to their workbases but are not over-respectful. Amy checks her make-up. Neil takes a piece of pizza with him.

Brandon Morning, gorgeous.

Amy and Laura Hi, Kimberley.

Shaun Want a bit of pizza, Kimberley?

Kimberley I want a programme, darling. And I want it now.

Hayley Would you like a coffee?

Kimberley I get my own.

Jodie Hayley. How long have you been here?

> *Kimberley sits at a desk and begins to glance swiftly at the papers.*

Kimberley For God's sake, that Muzak really pisses me off. I feel as if I'm trapped in a lift. Or even worse. In Laura Ashley's.

> *Music goes.*

Neil You're not a heavy-metal girl.

Kimberley Neil. You've joined Fast Action Broadcasting Television.

Neil FAB TV.

Kimberley Jokes stick, sweetheart. It's a damn good name. And the show we produce is *Teleport*. Hard news, my lovely. (*abandoning papers and getting angry*) Not some arty-farty slot with child musicians hot from art school! We don't feature kids who hit guitars because they're scared to touch the girls!

Holly I'll get a tape of distant gunfire.

Kimberley (*to Holly*) While you've been sitting here, darling, painting your nails and planning meals, I've been in the editing suite with lovely Steven. You got a tasty item and you turned it into comfort food. We go out at 11.30 p.m. Our audience is drunk and desperate and hungry for instruction. If you can't deliver the right story, perhaps you'd like to cut your contract? But remember, you'd lose your lovely flat and your cat would be so hungry. Also, work experience for the unemployed is *very dirty work* these days.

Holly (*after a silence*) I'm trapped.

Kimberley comes over and puts her arms around Holly and kisses her. Holly flinches.

Kimberley Only four million watched the show last night. That's why I'm edgy. We're slipping. If *Teleport* goes, no FAB TV. I *need* a pretty little reporter who can make a strangler cry. But give the story shape next time. Find a point of view. Say this man's a bastard. Tell the audience who to hate. That's what we have to do.

Hayley (*referring to Kimberley's outfit*) You bought it! It's lovely, Kimberley.

Kimberley (*breaking away from Holly*) An arm and a leg. (*She twirls to show off dress.*)

Amy How do you keep so thin?

Kimberley (sotto voce *to Amy*) It's very cleverly cut, darling. (*changing gear*) But it's goodbye shopping unless *Teleport* gets extra viewers. Goodbye clubbing, girls and boys. Goodbye designer trainers. Goodye pizza margheritas if it comes to that. Take it from one who knows. These days you're either buying an air ticket for the Virgin Islands or you're wrapped in paper underneath a bridge. So I need ideas and fast. (*She weaves among her staff, clicking her fingers. She then goes to the blackboard and stands poised with a piece of chalk.*) I'm waiting –

Brandon What we need is a running gag.

Jodie A running gag. Yes.

Kimberley A theme –

Brandon A theme. Something that sucks them in and keeps them going for weeks.

Jodie A theme. Yes.

Kimberley Nice. What?

Brandon (*after a pause*) Dunno.

Kimberley There are people out there not working who have ten languages and scars from Sarajevo.

Brandon Every week.
Kimberley Yes –
Brandon We could feature a story –
Kimberley Yes –
Brandon That once was hot.
Kimberley And now is cold?
Brandon Stories don't go cold. For a while they wipe the wars off the BBC and people buy papers who can't even read. Then the editors drop them. But the public's still interested.
Shaun Right, like that guy who ate people! What happened to him?

Kimberley writes 'The Cannibal' on the board.

Kimberley The Cannibal.
Jodie Yes! The guy who ate people! God!
Kimberley I'm listening.
Amy That old lady who bombed building societies and banks? Where is she now?

Kimberley writes 'Killer Grannie' on the board.

Kimberley Killer Grannie.
Laura I've never forgotten that man who got pregnant. Was it twins that he had? His poor wife.
Jodie Martin the mother!

Kimberley writes 'Martin the Mother' on the board.

Kimberley Martin the Mother. They never got to the bottom of that.
Hayley That nurse who killed children –
Jodie Mercy!

Kimberley writes 'Mercy the Nursie' on the board.

Kimberley Mercy the Nursie. She got life, the poor sweetheart.
Neil I hate prison-visiting.

Brandon We visit the *families*, old *friends*, the *victims*. See how they're doing now the fuss has died down.

Kimberley (*walking around, suddenly inspired*) Stories go away. The papers lose interest. The public forgets. The police and the social workers close all their files. But *Teleport* remembers. And *Teleport* cares. Where are they now? The mothers? The victims? The children? (*changing gear from near tears to smiling*) I like it. It's sexy.

Holly It's crap.

Kimberley That poor nurse, Holly. Mercy the Nursie! Sorry. Come on, Holly, smile. I mean, *why* did she kill? Social interest. Compassion. Going deep.

Holly It's not news.

Kimberley (*after a silence*) It's not what?!

Holly News.

Kimberley Are you saying I can't do my job?

Holly I'm saying the whole world is unstable. There are famines and wars. There's corruption in the City and chaos in Parliament. We should report on issues that are really important. You're only interested in the ratings. You've lost touch with what's news.

Kimberley (*after a silence*) I've dodged bullets, you know. I've stroked the heads of dead men. Don't you tell me what is news. (*She takes the floor.*) News is a marriage between the moment and history. News is a bomb going off in a car. News is the songs that the bomber sings. News is the blood that is spilling now. News is the laughter of living men. And news is the death of Robin Hood.

Everyone is silent for a bit and then they all applaud (except Holly).

Jodie Wow, Kimberley!

Kimberley (*very pleased with herself*) They don't give you late-night slots if you can't speak at meetings.

Holly (*sarcastic*) Just leave it with me, Kimberley. I'll get on to the agencies. See what they have on Robin Hood's death.

Everyone laughs, which annoys Kimberley.

Neil (*with a smile, to Holly*) You send the spin doctors straight into casualty!

Kimberley writes 'Robin Hood' on the board and 'Holly' in brackets beside it, causing more laughter.

Brandon (*to Holly, in threatening Hollywood tones*) Who killed Robin Hood, baby? You tell us. Come on.

Kimberley (*seeming now to join in with the joke*) Yes. Robin Hood. Holly. Up the M1 you go. Hire a good car. FAB TV looks after its staff. Get one with fog lights. At this time of year it's so murky up north. Those pile-ups! Such carnage! Be careful.

Holly (*bored with this joke*) OK, I'll try and come up with something else.

Kimberley (*suddenly very serious*) No. Robin Hood died in a brothel. It's a good one. I don't waste anything, Holly. Not film stock. Not words. Not chalk on a blackboard.

Holly (*seriously*) I'm reading you, Kimberley.

Holly and Kimberley regard each other in silence. The others watch, as if expecting a shoot-out, but Kimberley turns once again to the blackboard. General relief with the return of Kimberley's bonhomie, but Holly stays serious.

Kimberley (*chalking in 'Shaun'*) Shaun, you do the Cannibal. (*Chalks 'Amy'.*) Amy, the Grannie. (*Chalks 'Laura'.*) Laura, do Martin. (*Chalks 'Hayley'.*) Hayley, Mercy the Nursie. (*Pause.*) Brandon, my angel? Got an idea?

Brandon That man in New York who went mad on the subway?

Kimberley (*writing on board*) Schwarz's Corpses. Well, we can afford it. Bring me something from Bloomingdale's mind.

Brandon Thanks, Kimberley!

Shaun You've *been* to New York!

Jodie Brandon, how brilliant! *Two* trips! You can do a book now! *Brandon's Big Apple*! Go for it! I would!

Kimberley Jodie?

Jodie God. Well. It might be too nasty –

Kimberley Try me.

Jodie The heads in the bath?

Kimberley (*writing 'Brian's Brains, Jodie'*) I remember. Brian's Brains. Jodie. You were right. It is nasty. But try and dig up his friends. (*turning to Neil*) Neil?

Neil Do you remember that girl who stayed in a cage? She was starving for prisoners of conscience?

Kimberley Get real.

Neil The nun and the Rottweiler?

Chalks 'Nun and Rottweiler' and 'Neil' up on board.

Kimberley The Nun and the Rottweiler. Neil. Lunch everybody!

Staff gather up their things to go, except Neil and Holly.

Come on, my darlings. Kimberley is buying bubbly today.

Ignoring Holly and Neil, everyone leaves.

Neil Hungry?

Holly She's a cow.

Neil We won't eat her.

Holly This is serious. She knows what she's doing.

Neil Robin Hood did die in a brothel, you know. He escaped from Sherwood after an affray with the Sheriff of Nottingham. He was wounded and had a high fever. He took refuge in a priory. In those days they used to bleed people with fevers and the prioress bled him to

death. Were those medieval priories all brothels? That's
what they said. But you can't trust history any more
than the *Sun*.

Holly Neil. I'm the only one who's been to Beirut. Israel.
Afghanistan. Moscow.

Neil Kimberley knows that. She likes your name on the
screen.

Holly I went to those countries by plane, Neil. Internal
connections were mostly by chopper. I'm at home inside
a Chinook.

Neil Robin Hood's grave and the priory remains are on
the estate of Lord David Docherty.

Holly I *flew* to Edinburgh to pick up the strangler.

Neil No one gets past the Earl's henchman. You could
succeed with Lord David Docherty where other
researchers have failed.

Holly Neil?

Neil How do I know this? I read medieval history at
university. Don't tell Kimberley. I told her I got my whole
education going round America on a Greyhound bus.

Holly Neil, this isn't easy for me –

Neil (*after a pause*) Holly?

Holly (*after a silence*) Kimberley knows that I'm scared of
the road.

Neil The road?

Holly I could manage a rope bridge slung across a gorge.
Send me up K2, I'll get there. But the M1? At midnight?
In fog?

Neil I thought you were frightened of nothing.

Holly I'm frightened of driving.

Neil Driving?

Holly Don't tell the others.

Neil They wouldn't believe me.

Holly I know.

Neil (*after a pause*) Take the Nun and the Rottweiler! The
convent is just round the corner!

Holly No.

Neil Swap!

Holly No. That's not my style, Neil. You know that. Once I'm given a story I go.

Neil I just haven't got your dedication.

Holly You get up every morning at five to write poetry. That's dedication.

Neil Don't tell the others. I know what would happen. They'd write stuff on the blackboard. I couldn't handle it.

Holly (*reassuring him*) Neil. (*She takes out a notebook.*) Robin Hood. The grave. Lord David Docherty. What do you know?

Neil Well, the estate's not far from Nottingham and near Sherwood Forest. But it's right off the beaten track. Heavily wooded. Hard to find. I went there when I was doing my thesis. Docherty has a museum. Medieval weapons. A rack that works. Displays of thumbscrews. That sort of thing. I just wanted to see the priory remains! To look at Robin Hood's grave! I couldn't get in! He employs armed guards. Killer dogs at the gates. Sometimes he speaks in the house –

Holly (*realizing who Docherty is*) He wants to bring back hanging –

Neil You've got him!

Holly Perhaps I could find a pub in the area? Chat to the locals?

Neil Go carefully. He's hated.

Holly I'll get them to talk. I'll get inside the estate. I'll find the grave. I'll discover who killed Robin Hood.

Neil You'll be the first one to do so in five hundred years.

Holly And I'll interview Lord David Docherty. I'll make him cry.

Neil Like Kimberley said, use one of FAB TV's bigger cars. You'll have to drive all over the North.

Holly I'm not scared any more.

Neil Finding forests and castles is more lonely work than chatting with hacks in a Holiday Inn.

Holly I've got that feeling I get when I'm after the truth. Whatever the dangers, I know I'm invincible.

Neil Can I buy you a drink?

Holly You sure can! (*She hangs back.*)

Neil Come on or we'll never get to the bar.

Holly Neil?

Neil Yes?

Holly In case something happens while I'm away –

Neil Holly! Don't say that!

Holly There's something I want you to know.

Neil Yes?

Holly (*after a pause*) I think your poetry's brilliant.

Neil Really?

Holly Yes.

Neil I'm going to buy you the biggest gin in the world.

They leave.

SCENE TWO

The Fox and Goose pub (not far from Nottingham and somewhere near Sherwood). Night
Locals (Dora, Lovell, Tomkins, Stavely, Emmett, Donna and Janet) enter.
Dora goes to blackboard, cleans it and chalks up menu.

Dora (*shouting to locals as she enters*) Dish of day is same as always in Fox and Goose. Roast beef and Yorkshire pudding. Something to make your belly forget that chilly wind out there. Oh! Dearie me, it is an ugly night! I mustn't forget there's mushy peas! Extra vitamins to combat cold! Boiled carrots too! Help you to see way home in dark!

As Dora speaks, others move the office paraphernalia away as necessary. They arrange chairs and place beer mugs on tables.

Stavely and Emmett stand up at the bar with their pints.

Dora and Janet sit close together.

Lovell and Tomkins are armed with dominoes and start to play.

Janet (*shouting in immediate reply*) Lasagne off again?

Dora (*shouting back*) Yes, love. Gone to Filey for her holidays.

Janet (*shouting*) Dora! I was making a joke!

Dora (*shouting back*) No joke. She's gone. In middle of winter and no brolly neither, never mind a man!

Donna (*to Janet*) Leave her be, she's barkin'.

Dora (*writing 'parkin' on blackboard*) Thanks for reminding me, my love. (*To all*) I've always got a slice of parkin nestling up my sleeve.

Lovell (*calling out*) Wish I were a slice o' parkin!

Tomkins Come on, Lovell. Eyes on game, now.

Lovell (*looking at dominoes*) Jammy devil, Tomkins!

Tomkins Told you, Lovell. This game takes concentration. If you think on women once, happen you'll cry all night.

Lovell and Tomkins concentrate on game. Stavely and Emmett sip their beer in silence. Dora sits.

Janet (*in close cahoots with Donna*) He said who are you going out with?

Donna You must have nearly died!

Janet I said not you.

Donna You didn't?!

Janet Did.

Donna What did he say?

Janet He said why not?

Donna What did you say?

Janet I said because I don't like you.
Donna You do like him!
Janet Wasn't going to tell him that though, was I?

Janet and Donna giggle together.

Emmett (*to Stavely*) Same again?
Stavely Shouldn't.
Emmett (*to Dora*) Same again, darlin'.
Dora (*filling glasses*) Same again.
Emmett (*to Stavely*) Rubbish.
Stavely Rubbish game.
Emmett Rubbish team.
Stavely Nowt we can do.
Emmett Should sack manager.
Stavely Some say he's OK.
Emmett He's rubbish 'n' all.
Stavely If you were manager – ?
Emmett I'd not be so fawning over some kid from South.
Stavely On transfer list?
Emmett Against some bloody wall.
Stavely You'd shoot him?

Emmett points both fingers in a single line and, miming a shotgun, seriously lines up on one fellow customer after another. All observe this threatening behaviour.

Emmett (*pointing towards door*) Gun him down like a rabbit. Pow!

Emmett puts down imaginary gun and smiles.
   Silence.

Dora (*interrupting silence and releasing tension, to Emmett*) How's your mum?
Emmett I took her up to Moors in wheelchair last week. Carried her to where we used to picnic as kids. Cried, she felt that happy to be out under sky.
Dora You've always been such a good boy.

Stavely Mrs Biffin, could I try your parkin?

Dora My love, you can try anything that I've got.

This remark is overheard and causes general mayhem and riotous laughter.

Lovell (*shouting*) Young Stavely knows nowt about parkin!

Tomkins (*shouting*) Bernard Biffin will come back to haunt you, young Stavely. He were big man 'n' all!

Janet (*shouting*) You'll make a lovely couple!

Stavely Piss off!

Donna (*shouting*) If you want a toy boy, Dora, I wouldn't choose him!

Dora comes round and grabs Stavely and tries to get him to dance.

Dora Why not? (*stroking Stavely's arms*) These are my sort of arms all right!

Donna Wouldn't touch him if you knew what I knew!

Dora (*to Donna*) You're just jealous. (*to Stavely*) Come here, my love. (*She puts her arms around Stavely.*) I'll teach you to waltz. It's more fun than waving your arms in the air and not touching partner. One, two, three. One, two, three – That's it, my lovely.

Emmett Turn up, eh, Stavely? You didn't know you were going to get sorted tonight.

Everyone cheers and whistles. Stavely looks like he'd rather be dead. Dora, like she's never had so much fun in her life.

All (*with quickening pace and a fierce enthusiasm that immediately gets out of hand and becomes mob rule*) One, two, three! One, two, three! One, two, three!

Holly enters, a little windswept. She carries a briefcase and a mobile phone.

The pub locals freeze and go silent.
Holly sits.

Dora (*breaking away from Stavely*) Yes?
Holly I'd like a gin and tonic please. And, if it's not too much trouble, a packet of crisps.
Emmett Orders here are placed up at bar.
Dora (*to Holly*) He's in bad mood 'cos I fancy his friend. Prawn cocktail? Chicken tikka? Bombay duck?
Holly Have you got any plain?
Emmett Plain crisps in Fox and Goose pub! We're not rubbish, you know. We've a toaster. And microwave.

The silence in the pub continues.

Dora Nuts.
Holly (*not hearing*) I'm sorry?

Everyone laughs loudly.

Emmett Don't speak to the lady like that, Dora. We don't often get strangers in here. Mustn't insult them or they might go away.
Dora I've nuts, love.

More laughter.

Stavely Peanuts in packets, that's what she means.
Holly Yes. That would be lovely. Thank you.

Dora brings stuff to Holly. The silence continues. Locals sip drinks but keep watching Holly.
   Donna and Janet put their chairs very close and whisper together.
   Holly opens her briefcase and takes out a file. She starts reading.

Dora (*to Stavely*) I'll go for your parkin.
Emmett Don't leave your post.
Dora Why?

Emmett (*nodding in Holly's direction*) You'll be needed.

Stavely Can only be honest, Mrs Biffin. Had tea back home. Don't really need parkin. Forget it.

Dora Aye. Keep room for a nice dish o' stew before you hit road.

Stavely (*looking at Holly*) She'll drink fast.

Emmett They do everything fast in the South.

Dora (*shouting to Holly*) Can I get you another, my dear?

Holly Good heavens, no. I've hardly touched this one.

Dora Well, shout when you're ready. I'll be waiting up here.

Holly Oh, I won't have another. I'm a one-gin girl. But later I'd love some of your roast beef and Yorkshire. And the peas too. I just love mushy peas. Your food smells delicious! So good to find somewhere that does meals in the evening. I'm absolutely starving. I've been all day on the road.

Donna and Janet exchange glances, push their chairs back from each other and stare at Holly. Lovell and Tomkins stop playing dominoes and stare as well.

Emmett (*taking a glance towards a window, to Holly*) Miss? That your Mercedes out there?

Stavely (*taking a look*) M-y G-o-d!

Holly Pleased with it actually. It's been a dear little friend.

Emmett (*to Holly*) Drive, do you?

Holly And I can park! In very small spaces. It's got power steering, you see. Lucky me!

Emmett I mean for a living?

Holly A living?

Emmett Deliver stuff, do you? Spare parts? (*ominously*) Blood.

Stavely No! She's a rep. You're a rep, aren't you?

Emmett (*suspiciously*) What are you selling?

Janet (*to Emmett*) She's selling cosmetics.

Donna Show us! Come on! Let's see what you have!

Lovell When I were a lad women had children. They gave them a good breakfast and brought them up right.

Tomkins Aye. And there were no muggings in them days!

Lovell No terrorist bombs.

Tomkins Right, Lovell! We slept safe in our beds and were proud to be British.

Janet (*to Holly*) There's a lady comes already you know. And there's only so much spare cash.

Donna (*to Janet*) God, you're a misery-guts! (*to Holly*) She's been bringing the same old crap every month for hundreds of years. If you're selling the stuff that you've got on *your* face you're in business round here. (*She turns to Janet.*) And I know!

Emmett (*after a pause*) But the lady's not selling lipstick. (*Ominously, to Holly*) Are you?

Holly No.

Emmett (*proudly to all*) What did I tell you?

Silence in pub as Holly reads and sips her drink.

Dora (*shouting across to Holly*) Who *do* you work for, love?

Lovell (*to Tomkins*) She's guts has our Dora.

Tomkins (*to Lovell*) Can kill chickens, that woman, with her own bare hands.

Holly Me?

Dora Yes. I know who the others all work for. Them that's got jobs, that is.

Holly I'm in television, actually.

Dora Oooh! Fancy!

Janet Should have had your hair done, Dora!

Donna Television!

Lovell Never watch it.

Tomkins He does!

Stavely I do. All the time.

Emmett (*with authority*) Satellite? Cable?

Holly I work for an independent company. Fast Action Broadcasting Television. Ha ha. FAB TV!

Emmett FAB TV, eh? Oh yes.

Donna (*to Janet*) Interesting.

Janet (*to Donna*) Really interesting.

Holly The woman who runs the company, Kimberley Golden, she thinks the name's terribly funny.

Stavely Ha ha. Kimberley Golden. (*He laughs.*)

Emmett Cretin. FAB TV's what's meant to be funny.

Holly I mean, it's awful when someone says who do you work for and you have to say FAB TV!

Emmett Would we have seen you, you know –

Holly The programme I work on goes out terribly late.

Emmett I can stick with the boxing until it's time to get up.

Stavely But if you're already up –

Emmett Shut up, you.

Holly It's called *Teleport*. An in-depth look at hard news. Well, that's what it's supposed to be.

Dora And you, like – ? (*Dora mimes a bit of smiling and waving.*)

Emmett I bet she does it better than that. (*to Holly*) Do you? You know? (*assuming announcer's voice*) 'Good evening.'

Emmett laughs at himself and everyone laughs with him.

Holly Well, yes. I interview people who've been in the news.

Emmett (*with sudden ecstatic conviction*) I've seen you!

Stavely Yes! I think I've seen you 'n' all!

Lovell (*to all except Holly*) I recognized her minute she came in door.

Tomkins Liar.

Janet I wish I'd my camera.

Donna (*to Holly*) You've made our day!

Holly (*to all*) Good. Now, listen. I'm on expenses. Can I buy everybody a drink?

Donna and Janet Yes, please!

Lovell Women getting drinks in! World's gone all upside-down.

Dora (*to Lovell*) Nothing for you then, my dear?

Lovell I wasn't criticizing –

Everybody laughs.

Dora (*to Holly*) Before you spend all your company's money, love, tell us what brings you here to these parts.

Donna and Janet Yes!

Emmett Right!

Stavely Right! (*to Emmett*) Should have asked that before.

Lovell Have they heard about Dora's parkin in South?

Tomkins Heard about Lovell, oldest sex maniac in world, much more like!

General laughter.

Holly (*it costs her a lot to admit to professional failure*) I had – I had an appointment with Lord David Docherty. (*All laughter stops and pub goes silent at Docherty's name.*) But, but I couldn't find the entrance to his estate in that terrible fog out there. (*She tries to smile in the face of silent hostility.*) I'll tell you what I'm doing after I've eaten. Something happens to my blood sugar when I've been driving for hours. I'm feeling rather faint. (*unable to smile any more at their solemn faces, and speaking slowly*) That's why I asked for the crisps.

They look from one to the other as if deciding what they are going to do to Holly.
  Emmett, like a gang leader, clicks his fingers in the air to encourage the group to line up behind him. He sits astride a chair as if in the saddle. He pulls the chair closer to Holly.

Emmett (*to Holly*) You'll eat no beef, nor drink ale neither until you've heard a tale or two from us.

Holly stands and backs away.
Chairs are placed to mimic a group on horseback,
with Emmett as the leader.

Stavely (*sitting astride a chair*) Right!
Lovell (*sitting astride a chair*) True!
Tomkins (*sitting astride a chair*) Yes!
Donna (*sitting astride a chair*) You'll listen!
Janet (*sitting astride a chair*) Listen good!
Dora (*sitting astride a chair*) There are things that you
should hear, my dear.

Emmett, from the front of the pack, surveys the group.
He smiles, enjoying the fact that they suddenly look like
a posse of riders after a villain. He makes a clicking
sound with his tongue and lifts up and down in the
saddle. The others copy this. No one laughs.

Holly (*shaking her head*) Please stop. I don't like games.

Emmett holds up his hand to silence the group. They
obey.

Emmett This isn't a game. You've left the world of
television. You've got caught up in real life. (*He
dismounts and points to Lovell.*) Your story! You tell
her!

Lovell dismounts. As he speaks he slowly and sinisterly
encroaches on Holly.

Lovell Fifty years worked on estate. No pension. No
home. You should see where I live now. Damp place.
Gave me pneumonia. Killed my poor wife.
Emmett (*pointing to Tomkins*) And you!
Tomkins (*also dismounting and encroaching on Holly*)
You wouldn't notice. I'm blind in one eye. Happened
felling his trees. No compensation.

Movements of the speakers are sufficiently threatening

657

*for Holly to try and move out of their way. But they
follow her.*

Emmett (*pointing to Stavely*) Are you going to say nowt?
Stavely (*dismounting and slowly moving towards Holly*)
No! I'll talk 'n' all. There are things world should know
about bastard.
Donna (*Dismounting, unprompted, she moves towards
Holly.*) I couldn't say what he did to me. I've told no
one. There are things you can't tell.
Janet (*Dismounting, unprompted, she moves towards
Holly.*) I will tell you something. If there's a God, that
Docherty will get his comeuppance 'n' all.

Emmet suddenly jumps up on a table.

Emmett (*He throws his hand in air.*) Listen to me! Listen!
(*He points at Holly.*) I'll talk on your programme. I'll
tell you why my mum's in wheelchair! (*He jumps down,
pointing at Dora.*) And I bet you've got something to
say!

*All turn and look towards Dora, the only one still
seated.*
*Dora dismounts and slowly walks towards Holly.
Holly tries to escape but Dora catches her by her
shoulder.*

Dora I won't hurt you, love, I just want you to listen. (*She
lets go of Holly's shoulder.*) When you are talking about
Lord David Docherty you are naming landlord who
exploits every tenant. You are speaking of man with no
kindness in soul. But there's nowt we can do because he
owns half of England. (*Gesturing towards the group.*)
And more to the point, he owns all of us.
Lovell Well said!
Tomkins Bravely spoken!
All Off with his head!

Emmett (*miming the shotgun again and pointing it towards Holly*) Pow!

Holly screams.
She looks from one member of the threatening group to the other. They stare back at her silently.

Holly (*loudly, with terror*) Who *are* you?!

They answer quietly in turn.

Dora I'm Dora. Dora Biffin, love.
Lovell Lovell.
Tomkins Tomkins.
Stavely Stavely.
Donna Donna.
Janet Janet.
Emmett Emmett.

Holly is breathing heavily. She steps back from them, her breathing so heavy now she is almost hyperventilating.
Emmett speaks again with genuine concern:

What is it?
Holly I suddenly saw something terribly strange!
Emmett (*moving away from the group*) Tell *me* what you saw.
Holly (*to Emmett*) Well, when you all moved towards me – (*tearful*) I saw the past! It was so real! It was so real it turned into the present!
Emmett (*moving towards Holly*) And what were we doing in the past?
Holly You were – You were –
Emmett Yes?
Holly (*quietly*) You were Little John. Friar Tuck. Will Scarlet. Allen-a-dale. George-a-Green. And –
Emmett (*picking up Holly's quiet tone*) Robin Hood.

Everyone laughs at the idea, except Emmett. Holly collapses in tears. Emmett puts his arms around her.

You know there used to be a rumour that the grave of Robin Hood was on the Docherty estate. When we were kids we used to climb over the wall and look for signs on all those ancient oaks. So old those trees. They bear the scars of arrows –

Emmett and Holly regard each other in silence.

Holly (*in confidence to Emmett, but everyone is watching, listening*) I nearly died, you know. I can't do it. I can't bloody drive. I got stuck in the fast lane. I was indicating left. My exit was approaching. So I just sort of went for it. This huge supermarket on wheels nearly killed me –

Emmett (*to Holly*) You're safe now.

Holly breaks away from Emmett, suddenly aware she and Emmett have an audience.

Dora Take no notice of us, love. It's not you we don't like. It's that Lord David Docherty.

Holly I don't think I could face him tonight.

Dora We do rooms, you know.

Holly (*pulling herself together*) Do you?

Lovell (*leaving*) I'm off. (*to Tomkins*) Come on. Bring dominoes. Nowhere's safe any more. (*To Holly.*) I'd lay off gin, lass, if I were you.

Tomkins (*leaving*) Night all. (*to Holly*) Nice to make your acquaintance.

All Bye.

Janet (*leaving, to Holly*) Don't bother with Docherty, because you won't get in there. Not someone like you. Night, all.

Donna (*leaving, to Holly*) She means you'd have to be bloke and seven foot tall to cope with his guards at the door.

Emmett (*leaving, smiling at Holly*) Robin Hood, eh?
Holly (*smiling*) Good night.

Emmett goes up to Holly and, with an old-fashioned charm observed by all, extends his hand. Their eyes meet.

Emmett (*shaking her hand*) Good night.

They look at each other in silence.

Stavely (*to Emmett*) Got the van out there?
Emmett (*letting go of Holly's hand*) Don't fancy the forest in darkness?
Stavely (*leaving*) Shut up and give me a lift.
Dora (*to Emmett*) Give my love to your mother.
Emmett Sure thing.

Dora and Holly are now alone.

Dora Why don't you eat with me in the kitchen?
Holly (*cool now*) That would be lovely. We could have a nice talk. If I asked you some questions about Lord David Docherty, would you mind if I switched on my little recorder? I couldn't do justice to your lovely roast beef if I was busy making notes with a pen.
Dora I won't sully my kitchen with that villain's name. And if you've any sense you won't try and see him. He's not for you, a nervous little girl who can't handle motorway. (*laughing and picking up glasses*) Well, Maid Marian, if you cry like a baby when you meet Robin Hood, how can you cope with Sheriff of Nottingham?!
Holly (*with confident humour*) I'm a professional journalist. I'm invincible, Dora.
Dora Really? Come on. Help me get rid of pots. And enjoy your roast beef. Could be your last meal on earth if you won't listen to sense.

They leave.

SCENE THREE

Docherty estate. Day.

Estate guard, Crawshaw, enters. He is wearing a Securicor-style uniform and tall leather boots. He is obviously heavily armed and carries a police truncheon. He moves around with the authority of a Mafioso.

He goes to blackboard, takes duster from pocket, wipes board clean, then takes chalk and writes KEEP OUT, in letters big enough to fill board.

He bangs the odd table with his truncheon and hits the legs of chairs. He hits one leg, moves away suddenly, then returns and hits the leg even harder, as if surprising the chair. This makes him laugh.

With no respect for the furniture, he pushes a few pieces to the side.

In a space stage left he puts two tables together, making a desk. He places one chair behind the desk and one in front, creating Lord David Docherty's office. He bangs heavily on the desk top.

Crawshaw Yeh!

As Crawshaw continues to attack the furniture, Holly enters, carrying briefcase and mobile phone.

Holly (*cheerfully*) Excuse me –
Crawshaw (*pointing to blackboard with truncheon*) Can't you read?
Holly I had an appointment with Lord Docherty yesterday. I was delayed by fog. I spoke to his secretary. I understand he is at home today.
Crawshaw (*pointing at letters with truncheon but looking at Holly's legs*) I would have thought a lady with smart legs like yours could cope with words of one syllable.
Holly (*after a pause*) I think it says keep out.

Crawshaw Right! Well done! Now bugger off or I'll do something very nasty. You're trespassing. And that's against the law. (*He points the truncheon at Holly.*) Don't you think that you can get away with criminal behaviour just because you're wearing a tight skirt that shows your bum.

Holly (*after a pause*) I work for the Department of Transport.

Crawshaw I don't care who you work for!

Holly We are planning the construction of a new motorway. At this stage, of course, this is classified information.

Crawshaw Not another bloody motorway!

Holly If it goes ahead it would run right through your old medieval buildings, the Georgian mansion and the park. It would destroy all your agricultural areas. It would raze your forests to the ground. It would be the death of the Docherty estate.

Crawshaw walks away from Holly. He unclips a mobile phone at his waist and pulls up aerial.

Holly takes out computer notebook and punches in information. Crawshaw notices this and takes a few steps further away.

Crawshaw Sir. My apologies. Yes. I know you are shooting, but I have a woman here. (*He looks towards Holly and then walks a little further away.*) I know, sir. But I think you ought to see her. (*He looks towards Holly again and walks even further away.*) Classified information, sir. But if I may be a trifle impertinent, I'd keep your whisky decanter handy. (*Pause.*) I didn't mean that. With respect, it's you that shall be needing it, sir, not her.

Lord David Docherty enters and sits at desk. He has been shooting pheasants and still carries the gun; also several coils of thin rope. He puts stuff on desk. He stares into the middle distance, drumming fingers on the table.

    Crawshaw pushes down aerial and walks back to Holly. Holly puts her notebook away. Crawshaw waits for the notebook to be put back in the briefcase.

Holly Yes?

Crawshaw Come with me.

Crawshaw takes her across to Lord David Docherty's office. They stand for a moment outside.

Sir?

Docherty Come!

Crawshaw and Holly go into office.
    Docherty addresses Holly:

Sit down.

Holly sits. Crawshaw stands beside Docherty and observes Holly's every move with the assiduousness of a bodyguard.

Holly (*looking around*) Lord Docherty, your medieval tapestries are so beautifully preserved. And I have never seen them hung like that, from floor to ceiling. I feel I am in the company of knights in shining armour and damsels in distress! Look at him up on his horse! And her, with the bluebird in her hand! May I ask how long you've lived here?

Docherty We bought it on 18 December 1352. I still have the original conveyance. We got the whole place rather cheaply as it happened. We bought it from this character called Henry Dodd, who'd caught the plague. What's the saying, now? It is an ill wind that bloweth no man good? Truth is, the Dodd family were all layabouts, you know, even before the Black Death came their way.

Holly How wonderful. When you look at history it's not a book you see. You stare straight into the eyes of living men.

Crawshaw With respect, sir, this young lady is softening you up. I'd think you should get down to business.

Docherty I have noticed, Crawshaw, that you don't even wash your hands before you eat.

Crawshaw (*looking at his hands*) Don't get the meaning of that, sir.

Docherty In civilized behaviour there are procedures and courtesies. But you've got a point. (*to Holly*) Well?

Holly I wonder if I could ask you about the grave of Robin Hood?

Docherty No. Chitchat's over, I'm afraid. What brings you here? Be brief. As you can see, I should be shooting now.

Holly (*She stands and walks about the room with confidence.*) Your family is unique. It has kept company with kings. It has preserved the art and architecture of ancient England. You are a most articulate man with a valuable story to tell. In your domain, history lives and breathes and legends flower. I mean, have you ever stopped to wonder if Henry Dodd met Robin Hood?

Docherty stands and knocks over chair with barrel of gun. He then points shotgun at Holly.

Docherty I don't like women who assume the authority of men. It's a deceit that undermines the order of the world.

Crawshaw Right. She's dressed up like she's going shopping for new curtains but she's going to bulldoze Nottingham and raze the county to the ground.

Docherty This woman, Crawshaw, is a bloody journalist!

Crawshaw She works for the Department of Transport!

Docherty Who do you work for?

Holly (*to Docherty*) Fast Action Broadcasting Television.

Crawshaw You lied to me!

Holly (*to Crawshaw*) You should have asked to see my card.

Docherty (*to Crawshaw*) You did not even ask to see her card!

Crawshaw covers his face with his hands and rocks.

Holly (*to Crawshaw*) I'm sorry.

Crawshaw You're going to be much sorrier before this day is out!

Holly (*to Crawshaw*) I was so anxious to meet your employer. I'd heard so much about him.

Crawshaw Not enough, my girl. Or you wouldn't've wasted his time with all your little porky-pies.

Holly (*to Docherty*) Have you heard of *Teleport*? It's a serious programme that features interviews with prominent members of society.

Crawshaw (*to Docherty*) God! I can only apologize, sir. And let me say now, it's been a pleasure working for you.

Docherty I'm not going to sack you, Crawshaw. Just don't let it happen again.

Crawshaw That is very generous of you, sir! (*to Holly*) You! Come with me! I've plans for you. You won't trespass again. You won't have legs! And no more lying! I'm going to slit your tongue!

Docherty (*to Holly*) Don't let Crawshaw worry you. The man's a pussycat.

Crawshaw (*to Holly*) Come on!

Docherty No. She can stay. I didn't bag a single pheasant. So it's nice to see that fate has gone and trapped me something nice and tasty. As she's been caught I may as well enjoy her. You know me, Crawshaw, I never throw a catch back. It's bad luck.

Crawshaw (*leaving*) Nice one, gov'nor. Call me if you need me. (*to Holly*) I might be a pussycat, sweetheart, but my employer isn't.

Docherty One thing, Crawshaw. Make sure the lady's car is safely parked. You understand?

Crawshaw (*smiling*) I'll check it out, my lord.

Crawshaw marches smartly off and out of sight.
Docherty and Holly are now alone.

Holly (*taking out a notebook and placing it on the desk*) Well, Lord Docherty. *Have* you ever stopped to wonder if Henry Dodd met Robin Hood?

Docherty Oh no, my dear. You haven't bagged *your* pheasant. (*He gets up and walks around Holly.*)

Holly I can understand how you feel about journalists.

Docherty Can you?

Holly You think I might distort the truth. I wouldn't, but I could. However, if you spoke directly to the camera –

Docherty I've nothing to say.

Holly I've learned about Robin Hood from kids' books and silly films. But you've *seen* the evidence. The priory remains. The grave. The *facts* have been passed down to you.

Docherty The legend might be rich, my dear. But the true story's not worth telling.

Holly (*knowing this will provoke a response*) Robin Hood challenged the corruption of the state and the church. Although a nobleman himself, he defended the poor. He must have had tremendous integrity. Bravery too. What do you think?

Docherty (*angry*) Robin Hood, the erstwhile Earl of Huntingdon, was outlawed for his criminal behaviour. After years as a layabout and scrounger, the coward took refuge in a priory. He knew priories were run by women and so were really brothels. He got sick but the girls were without the skill or sense to cure the wretch. He died a dog's death and was buried on our ground. Nothing's in the grave. Foxes took his bones.

This is just the sort of soundbite that Holly is after. Very pleased with herself, she stands and moves quickly around the office, imagining the camera angles. She demonstrates this by holding up her hands to make an imaginary frame. She kneels down to view the low-angle shot of Docherty that would include his gun.

Holly (*standing*) Do you think that you could say that one more time?

Docherty I only say things once.

Holly I could get a crew up here this afternoon.

Docherty (*playfully holding gun to Holly's head*) Sit down, my darling.

Holly picks up her phone. Before she punches in the digits, Docherty grabs it from her. Holly gets up and goes towards the door. Docherty catches her by her wrist. He pushes the chair into the centre of the room and throws her back on to the seat.

Holly (*holding her wrist*) You hurt me!

Docherty You lied your way in here.

Holly I'm sorry. That was very wrong of me.

Docherty Your dishonesty continued. You said I was an articulate man with a valuable story to tell. That isn't what you think at all.

Holly I do! You speak exceptionally well, Lord Docherty. And what you have to say would interest lots of people!

Docherty Crawshaw said you're dressed up as if you're going shopping. Do you know what I think you look like? The prioress who used to take in vagabonds and strays. Her face would have been painted too. And she would have pulled up her skirt to attract the customers as well. Look at you! A slut.

After a silence, anger gives Holly the courage to stand. Docherty lets her move around.

Holly I've just realized something! Do you know why all the documentary evidence on Robin Hood has been destroyed?

Docherty He was just a petty criminal.

Holly He was a very dangerous man.

Docherty It would have been a waste of ink to write his name.

Holly He was the greatest revolutionary we've ever had in England.

Docherty How strange the Public Records Office has never even heard of him.

Holly Right! The ruling classes rubbed him out of history. They conveniently changed him from a hero to a joke. It really is the ultimate fudge, you know.

Docherty (*again holding gun to her head, no longer playful*) Sit down! (*after a pause*) Slut!

Holly (*standing and getting her things together*) I'm leaving now.

Docherty picks up the rope from the table and advances towards Holly. She runs away. He catches her. They struggle. Holly takes off a shoe and tries to hit him. He is obviously enjoying this. He releases her for a moment. Stealthily, she crawls towards the door. When she is almost there, Docherty pounces on her, pulling her back into the chair by her arm.

Docherty This is so much more fun than shooting pheasants. They are such lumpy birds, you know. Such easy targets.

Holly Do you want to read about yourself in all the daily papers? If you do something stupid to me all the world will know.

Docherty (*with slow pleasure*) Five hundred years after his death, still no one knows who murdered Robin Hood –

Holly fights as Docherty takes her hands and ties them behind the chair.

Holly I'm a journalist!
Docherty So who's going to care about a little bird like you?
Holly My best friends are in the media! (*She struggles manfully as Docherty ties her left leg to the chair.*)
Docherty I think of the local constabulary here as my blood brothers. Half the Cabinet were at my school. And I am a lord, you know. My colleagues are archbishops and royal dukes. My friends are earls, viscounts and barons.
Holly I don't know why you're doing this.

The struggle continues as Docherty ties Holly's right leg to the chair.

Docherty I've been asking myself why I've not done it *before*. I broke somebody's back once on the rack. Another time, when I was very bored, I pulled out fingernails. Tying a woman to a chair is almost a kindness by comparison, but it is very satisfying just the same. (*He stands back to relish the sight of the captive Holly.*)
Holly I don't believe you've any friends at all.

Docherty takes a large white handkerchief from his pocket.

Holly (*realizing that he is going to gag her and suddenly openly very frightened*) Please don't do that!
Docherty I think you've said enough.

Docherty gags her with handkerchief. Holly tries to make a noise but fails, then sits silently in terror. Docherty starts walking round her.

I shall keep you here. I shall watch you change from

confident slut to servile beggar. Your eyes will tell me of
the turmoil in your belly. You don't know what hunger
does, do you? It eats you alive. You feel its claws inside
you. Thirst is even worse. Your dry tongue swells and
chokes you. And I shall witness everything that happens,
right until your heart stops. You see, my dear, live
entertainment does beat television, every time. (*He
kneels on floor.*) Now I'm going to touch the sole of
your foot. Isn't it fascinating? This doesn't hurt at all
but already you are wishing you were dead.

*Docherty strokes the sole of her foot. Holly rocks from
side to side with horror as he tickles her.*
  Distant sound of three blasts on a horn.
  Docherty turns towards the sound.

Docherty Lovely! Someone has shot a stag. Shall I clothe
you in its bloody skin? That was once a popular prank
of your hero, Robin Hood. (*He stands.*) Look at you, a
doe if ever there was one! A dead woman in a deer skin!
Now, there's a thought –

Holly bows her head in horror.
  *Distant sound of heavy stakes pounding the ground
in a slow rhythm. The sound crescendos, from far away
to close. Docherty listens with pleasure.*

They are bringing the poor beast to me. Just as well that
you won't live to see it. I don't think that you've the
stomach to enjoy the spectacle of slaughter.

*Docherty unties Holly's legs and hands and pushes her on
to the floor. She stays there, on all fours, like an animal.*
  *Docherty gets his shotgun. He takes his time loading it,
smiling as he watches Holly's terror. He aims at Holly.
Crawling, she backs away. Docherty laughs. He prods her
so that she scuttles and scampers like a hunted animal. He
plays with her: a cat with a mouse.*

Simultaneously, outside on the estate, Emmett, Stavely, Lovell, Tomkins, Donna, Janet and Dora enter, all carrying pointed stakes and turning in a circle. They are banging the blunt ends upon the ground.

At their centre is Crawshaw, turning as if he is trapped at the hub of a wheel. *

Crawshaw screams.

In the office again, Docherty smiles on hearing the scream.

Docherty The shooting party's going well.

Outside, as Crawshaw screams, his assailants jump backwards and spear him at his waist with their stakes; the stakes now form the spokes of a giant wheel. The group move slowly around him in a circle, forcing Crawshaw to turn, like the hub of a wheel or the pole in a Maypole dance.

All (*chanting together as the wheel moves, their voices more animal than human*) Get him! Get him! Get him! Get him!

They turn about, moving backwards and forwards, like a powerful, slow-moving spinning-top. They chant until Crawshaw is dizzy and submits.

Crawshaw (*putting his hands in the air*) Stop!

The wheel stops moving. Slowly, the gang release Crawshaw from the stakes. They step backwards from him, still standing in a circle. Insecure and obviously terrified, Crawshaw backs out of the circle.

Crawshaw, fearful that the gang might still beat him to a pulp, walks slowly towards Docherty's office. With each slow step he takes, the gang beat their stakes on the ground.

* As 'the wheel' enters, Crawshaw is not immediately revealed as he is masked by his assailants and their weapons.

As Crawshaw reaches the office, the sticks go silent. He does not turn around. He stands outside the door.

In the office.

Docherty (*threateningly, to Holly*) My imagination is so wonderfully rich today!
Crawshaw (*outside office*) Sir!
Docherty Damn you, Crawshaw, go away!
Crawshaw (*outside office*) I have to speak!
Docherty Come!

As Crawshaw moves to enter the office, the gang bang their sticks several times on the ground, then march off slowly, banging sticks.
   Crawshaw enters.

Crawshaw I'm very sorry, sir.
Docherty I hope you have a damn good reason for this interruption.
Crawshaw (*breathless*) In all my years of working in security I've never seen anything quite like it. They've got these weapons, sir –
Docherty (*smiling*) Bren guns? AK-47s?
Crawshaw Stakes.
Docherty For God's sake, Crawshaw, they are the fencing contractors! I should have told you –
Crawshaw They aren't workmen. They've no respect at all.
Docherty Deal with them.
Crawshaw They want to speak to *you*.
Docherty How dare they ask to speak to me!
Crawshaw They've come with grievances.
Docherty Hoodlums, eh?
Crawshaw Shall I call the police, sir?
Docherty No! You have authority on my estate! Use it!
Crawshaw (*pleased*) I can shoot them?
Docherty Look, just tell them to piss off, OK?

Crawshaw They won't listen to reason.

Docherty Then set the dogs on them.

Crawshaw I did, sir. They, they have a way with dogs –

Docherty (*gun held to Holly*) You're fired, Crawshaw. No reference. I shall see you never work again.

Crawshaw (*bowing nervously*) But you've never turned your gun on me or lifted your hand in anger. I'll treasure that courtesy, sir. You are a true gentleman and no mistake.

Docherty (*pushing gun barrel to Holly's head*) I am an English lord, Crawshaw.

Distant sound of banging in solemn rhythm.
   Docherty listens, for the first time aware the noise means trouble.
   Banging stops.

Crawshaw (*pleased that Docherty has heard the noise*) And them out there are scum, sir! They have no breeding but they think they're safe in numbers. They spit in the face of authority and spray graffiti on the stable walls.

Docherty (*turning suddenly*) *Those* bastards!! You should have told me that before, Crawshaw! Those stables have survived from the Middle Ages, to be desecrated by aimless thugs today! I've been wanting to kill those vandals for some time! (*to Holly, as he throws her roughly back in the chair, lashes her ankles to the chair legs and ties her hands behind her back again*) This incident has made me very angry. You won't find me in such a playful mood when I return.

Docherty takes his shotgun and leaves with Crawshaw.

Outside, on the estate, Docherty keeps his gun at the ready. Crawshaw and Docherty proceed carefully.

Docherty I hope they haven't buggered off while you were stammering in the office!

Off stage, the sound of sticks banging in rhythm.

Crawshaw No! That's them, sir! Demanding your presence!

Banging stops.

Docherty (*stopping for a moment*) When I've shot the villains, call the police immediately, Crawshaw. Deal properly with the officers and you get your job back. Understand?

Crawshaw (*as they leave together*) A true gentleman you are, sir, and no mistake.

Crawshaw and Docherty leave hastily, stage left.
    Emmett runs on, stage right. He is now unarmed.

Emmett (*outside door*) You in there?

Horrified, Holly tries to move and speak.
    In spite of the silence, Emmett eventually opens the door into the office.

Thought you would be.

Emmett removes her gag first. Holly speaks as he releases the ropes.

Holly (*crying*) How did you know?

Emmett (*busy with ropes*) Stupid Crawshaw tried to move your Mercedes off the estate. I heard the alarm –

Holly (*crying*) Like three blasts on his horn –

Emmett (*working urgently with knots and looking anxiously towards door*) What? I went back to pub to get others. Fencing contractors said we could use posts. Good idea, eh?

Holly (*crying*) We wear different clothes and have cars and not horses but the same things happen over and over again! We don't move forward! We just stay trapped in history!

She stands. They stare at each other.

Emmett (*after a nervous glance towards door*) I found the place where Robin Hood's meant to be buried. The grave's been robbed and you can't read the stone. But –

Holly Yes?

Emmett I measured the distance from the priory remains to the tomb. It's an arrow's flight.

Holly
'But give me my bent bow in my hand,
And a broad arrow I'll let flee;
And where this arrow is taken up,
There shall my grave digged be.'

Emmett takes Holly's hands.

Emmett
'Let me have strength and breadth enough,
With a green sod under my head;
That they may say when I am dead
Here lies bold Robin Hood.'

They kiss.
Holly breaks away and looks around the room, at the tapestries.

Holly Look at those tapestries!

Emmett Docherty's a lunatic! He'll shoot us if he finds us.

She still doesn't move and continues to stare at the wall.

Holly Look at those knights in shining armour and damsels in distress. Can you hear them speaking?

Emmett (*looking towards door*) No! But I can hear someone coming! For heaven's sake –

Holly appears almost in a trance. With sudden inspiration Emmett addresses her:

Maid Marian!

Holly Yes!

Emmett Will you come with me to Sherwood?

676

Holly Yes!

Emmett takes her hand and pulls her quickly away.
They leave, running.
    Offstage, the sound of gunfire.
    Docherty enters, running, shotgun at the ready. He
stands in his empty office and kicks the chair over. He
then runs in the direction of Holly and Emmett's exit,
but stops very suddenly in his tracks. He takes careful
aim with his gun.

Docherty (*slowly, with venom*) Don't you take one further
step. And don't you touch that bloody phone! Don't
even bother to breathe. You've no more use for oxygen
because you're a corpse already. (*Docherty fires gun*
towards the offstage figure of Crawshaw.) Sorry to blow
out those pathetic brains of yours, Crawshaw, but
security's a high-risk business. I told you that the day I
took you on. (*Checking his gun, Docherty strides off.*)

SCENE FOUR

As Scene One.
    Amy, Laura and Hayley enter. Hayley goes to
blackboard, wipes it clean and chalks in blank squares to
be filled by details of the upcoming schedule. Amy and
Laura move away paraphernalia from previous scene, as
necessary. They put a few desks and chairs back in place.
    Chat starts as soon as girls enter.

Amy (*moving furniture*) Anyway, Killer Grannie got this
    great big advance from a publisher –
Laura (*moving furniture*) How big?
Amy Oh, a million or something.
Laura Pity she's too old to enjoy it.
Amy Wait till you see her at her party!

Laura Yes?

Amy She was on her yacht with this boy of sixteen!

Laura Steven get good stuff?

Amy He strapped a camera to the bonnet of her Lamborghini. He got the look in her eyes doing a ton!

Laura That's against the law.

Hayley (*turning from blackboard*) Did you hear about Holly's accident?

Laura Yes!

Amy After the shoot!

Hayley On her way back on the motorway!

Laura She always had a thing about cars, you know.

Hayley Right. Like a premonition –

Brandon enters wearing an I Love NY T-shirt and with baseball hat on back to front.

Brandon Hi, everybody!

Amy Well?

Laura How was it?

Hayley Come on!

Brandon (*after a pause during which he relishes his fame*) I just love that town! It's such a knock-out place! Second trip, of course. I know New York. And, more importantly, New York knows me now.

Amy Nice crew?

Brandon Milo Agostini. Punch that name in your notebooks. If you go to the Big Apple, use him. That cameraman is one bloody genius and knows everyone in town. He's a real news fiend. Knew about Holly's accident before it got on the Internet. What a guy!

Hayley (*who has gone for a notebook*) How do you spell Agostini?

Brandon Like it sounds.

Jodie and Shaun enter together and settle down at their desks.

Jodie (*on entering, to Hayley in a singsong I-know-it-all voice*) I've just been in the editing suite.

Hayley Are they still laughing?

Jodie 'Fraid so.

Hayley (*to all*) Mercy the Nursie?

Everyone Yes –

Hayley Her family? All estate agents! Her mother says stuff like 'The house Mercy was born in was walking distance from the station', then her dad butts in and says 'That killer grew up with a south-facing garden.'

Jodie Not right for *Teleport* but great for the Comedy Store.

Shaun You know who won't laugh?

Hayley I phoned Kimberley last night at home. She *did* laugh.

Shaun Always better to give her bad news after the Happy Hour.

Jodie Did you choose a *bad* moment?

Shaun Sure did. She'd just heard that we're right down to three million viewers.

Everyone reacts to this terrible news.

She said I must get the Cannibal if we're going to survive. She said I had to go back with a crew and an axe. She said just turn over and break down his door.

Brandon Throw a chop on his table! Say it's somebody's elbow!

Jodie It's OK for you. You've come back with a story. Brian's brains didn't work. The house where he cut off the heads is a garage now and no one remembers his name.

Laura (*after a pause*) Remember Martin the Mother? The man who gave birth? Well, he wasn't a man. Just a flat-chested girl called Veronica. She's married now! And living in Ealing!

Everyone sighs.

Amy Laura, how awful!

Neil enters and goes and sits at his desk.

Shaun (*to Neil*) I hope you've some good news for Kimberley. Most of us have just come back with shit.

Brandon Schwarz's Corpses could run for more than one show –

Amy So could the Killer Grannie! She's sweet!

Neil (*to Amy*) How many days' footage did Steven get?

Amy Listen! Every picture he took was a Rembrandt!

Neil Sorry, guys. I'm suicidal. The Rottweiler story was just a tabloid fudge. Sure, the nun's got a dog, but not the one in the photo. And the thought of Holly –

Kimberley enters with bundle of newspapers.

Kimberley (*on entering, to Brandon, giving him a quick kiss on he way to her desk*) They fitted perfectly, sweetheart. And I must say, you've got some good stuff.

Brandon I find I'm just that bit more alive when I'm on the other side of the pond.

Amy (*to Kimberley*) I should have something to show you this afternoon.

Neil Which is more than can be said for the rest of us.

Kimberley (*sitting on her desk and flicking through papers*) Don't worry, darlings. The figures actually went up last night.

Everyone reacts.

Neil What made them switch on?

Kimberley You kids do annoy me! Partying when you should be reading the papers! It was this. (*Kimberley holds up paper with trembling hand and reads to all:*) 'Physicists across the globe are studying this freak accident. The Mercedes hit the central reservation at such a speed that it achieved escape velocity and overcame the gravitational field. Observers saw it fly over the cathedral before landing safely on the empty tennis court. The driver –' (*showing them the paper*) Lovely picture of our Holly! – (*reading*) 'a journalist for *Teleport*, the cult news programme, said' – (*She puts the paper down, closes her eyes and hugs herself.*) Cult news programme! Cult! Oooh! What a lovely word!

Neil What did Holly say?

Kimberley (*not answering Neil*) Can you imagine how many viewers are going to watch Holly's piece on Robin Hood? (*She marches around with pleasure.*) It will be beamed by satellite across the world! It will be seen by *everyone*! It will be the show that saves us! (*changing to a more serious, voice-over style*) 'Tonight the cult news programme *Teleport* opens the grave of England's greatest hero. More than bones are found in the tomb. We reveal the answers to the questions that men have been asking for the last five hundred years. Was Robin Hood a real man with an agenda? Was he a bastard or a saint? Was he poisoned by a prostitute or silenced by a sheriff? In researching this story our reporter diced with death. Was she saved by a car that was top of the range or protected by an alien power?

Towards the end of Kimberley's speech, Holly enters. She is unnoticed as all eyes remain on Kimberley.

Holly Hi, everybody!

All Holly!

Neil Whatever happens to you, you just get more beautiful.

Amy You've lost weight, that's for sure.

Kimberley Come here and let me give you a big kiss.

Holly goes to Kimberley. Kimberley kisses her on both cheeks. Holly goes to her desk. All eyes are on her.

Neil (*pleased to see her safely back at her desk*) Holly.

Laura Did you think your number was up when you were flying through the sky?

Hayley You might need counselling, you know.

Kimberley All she needs is our lovely news.

Brandon The ratings, sweetheart!

Jodie Way up, Holly!

Brandon Thanks to you and your near-death experience!

Shaun We're a cult programme now!

Kimberley (*this is an offer of instant fame*) Would you like – the whole half-hour!

Brandon (*resentful*) You haven't seen the Schwarz assembly yet!

Amy (*pleading*) Killer Grannie has got guts as well!

Shaun (*to all*) Think of the viewers she'd pull in!

All agree with this sentiment.

Kimberley (*to Holly*) Go for it, darling! Use every bloody frame you've got. That bastard who owns half of Nottingham – set him up! Intercut the interview with shots of beggars starving on the streets.

Everyone, except Neil and Holly, think this is a good idea.

Brandon Nice one.

Kimberley For the priory sequence, shoot stuff in London too. Get wallpaper of prostitutes in miniskirts. In the commentary say, 'Did the Prioress who poisoned Robin Hood look anything like this?' (*She looks around to register the appreciation on the faces of her staff.*)

Shaun (*to Kimberley*) You're some kind of genius, girl.

Kimberley (*to Holly*) I can't wait to see your pictures of that neglected grave! How poignant. Have you thought of music?

Holly No.

Kimberley I have. Did you interview the locals? If they're very broad we can use subtitles (*laughing*) and the subtitles can say anything we like! (*A pause, during which she notices, for the first time, that Holly is rather silent. Suddenly confused as to why there are no rushes in the cutting room.*) Did you use a local crew?

Holly I didn't use a crew at all.

Kimberley I don't understand.

Holly I've come back without a story.

Shock horror from one and all to this. Except Neil, who begins to realize that Holly is a new person now.

Brandon (*to Hayley*) She *will* need counselling.

Holly It's only television.

Those who are standing collapse into chairs. All are stunned.

Neil (*knowing that something pretty horrible must have happened*) Lord David Docherty –

Kimberley walks up and down, very fast. Then stops.

Kimberley OK, so the bastard wouldn't let you shoot him. You still have a show, my dear. We get any old lords staggering into Parliament. We get the prostitutes and beggars, like I said. I mean, one ravaged grave is much like any other. Buy clips from Robin Hood movies and we're away!

Holly Kimberley, I'm leaving FAB TV.

Kimberley You've had a better offer!

Holly No.

Kimberley (*not believing her*) I can speak to the accountants!

Holly It's not the money.

Kimberley It's the Mercedes!

Holly I'm a terrible driver. The accident was all my fault.

Kimberley It's yours! Or would you prefer the sporty soft-top number?

Holly I'm never going to drive again.

All react to this catastrophic admission of defeat.

Hayley Counselling.

Kimberley Darling, I can hardly imagine the terror you must have felt when that car became a plane.

Holly Kimberley, how can you believe anything that's in the papers?

Kimberley You didn't fly?

Holly I went down the embankment and over a very low church wall.

All laugh.

Kimberley (*smiling with pleasure*) But no one knows that, do they!

Holly (*seriously*) I do.

Amy You *have* to drive again!

Holly I don't have to do anything that I don't want to.

Brandon I'd watch it, baby. In this business you're only as good as your last picture.

Kimberley Chauffeurs, Holly, are an arm and a bloody leg.

Holly There are far too many cars on planet earth. And from now on I plan to walk.

Kimberley Well, you won't get very far!

Holly stands. She takes her time before deciding to tell the truth.

Holly (*excited*) I've bought maps, Kimberley. Europe, Asia, Africa! I'm going to leave England with just a rucksack on my back! I'm going to be away for years!

All watch to see how Kimberley will cope with the loss of Holly. Kimberley is in despair, then suddenly inspired.

Kimberley Three reasons, Holly, that will make you change your mind. One. Some girl's already walked around the world. Two. They made a film of her. Three.

The book's already out. So give me one good reason
why you should turn your back on fame and go?

Holly (*after a pause*) *I've* never walked around the world
before.

*There is a silence, during which everyone takes this in.
Neil starts to clap. The others, except Kimberley, all join
in.*

Jodie I'd love to do that!

Brandon You've guts, baby!

Shaun You make it sound so easy.

Amy You'll get even thinner.

Laura Your hair will grow right down your back!

Hayley Your skin will turn a different colour!

Kimberley Your cat will die.

Holly My mother's going to take her. They'll be company
for each other.

Kimberley And what will happen to FAB TV?! To *Teleport*?
To all your lovely colleagues? What will become of me?

Brandon gives a little cough. Kimberley turns to him.

Brandon (*to Kimberley, in a hushed tone*) I've shot stuff
on Schwarz's Corpses that has never ever been
photographed before.

Amy Don't pull the plugs before you've seen my Killer
Grannie.

Shaun Now we're a cult programme, we could, you know,
invent the news.

Laura Right. There are stories out there just waiting to be
thought of!

Hayley I should go for it! Mercy the Nursie as a comedy
show! With music!

Jodie I could use the garage as the location for Brian's
Brains. Hire actors!

Kimberley (*after a pause*) I love it! We're going to break
the boundaries! Champagne?!

Everyone except Neil and Holly prepare to go.
Kimberley kisses Holly goodbye.

Bye-bye, darling. If I'm honest, you never seemed at home
in television. It's no business for a girl who just can't
drive.

All quickly hug Holly goodbye and leave.
  Neil and Holly are alone. They wait until there is
silence before they speak.

Neil (*quietly*) You're different.
Holly I know.
Neil (*quietly*) What happened to you?
Holly I found the estate. I met the owner. I was
kidnapped. Then I was rescued.
Neil Come on, Holly. You can talk to me.
Holly Some things that happen can't be told in words.
Neil Try.
Holly (*after a pause*) I've learned why no one knows who
murdered Robin Hood.
Neil You think he never existed?
Holly (*after a pause*) He never died, Neil. Robin Hood
lives. He's the spirit of truth. We try to kill it. But we
can't. The truth survives. And it's beautiful.
Neil (*putting his arms around her*) Dear Holly.
Holly That's why I want to walk right round the world
and look at everything. I want to stand in the sunlight
and wonder.
Neil I'll miss you.
Holly Will you stay here?
Neil (*sounding a bit defeated*) It's a living. I'll stick it out
until they publish my poems.
Holly They will!
Neil How can you be sure?
Holly Because your poems speak the truth! And that's
what everybody wants!

Neil My poems are mostly about love.

Holly (*preparing to go*) Exactly.

Neil Don't go! I want to know who kidnapped you! How you escaped! I want to hear about the accident!

Holly Have you time for a drink?

Neil Sure!

Holly (*holding out her hand to him*) You're not stuck at FAB TV! You'll hear three loud blasts on a bugle horn and fate will come to rescue you. No one's trapped, you know.

Neil (*taking her hand*) We'll drink a toast to Robin Hood, eh?

They leave together, hand in hand.

Holly Right! Robin Hood *and* his Merrie Men. Neil, I've got so much to tell you –

Why Sail on a Whaler When You Can Write Plays?

Jane Coles interviewed by Jim Mulligan

Everything in Jane Coles's childhood led her to become a
writer. It was the kind of lonely, introverted life that turns
a young person to writing and books. Her father, who was
a fan of Jack London, had the notion that the sooner a
would-be writer got out of education and into real life the
better. Consequently, by the time Jane was fifteen she had
completed a secretarial course and was working for the
Australian Broadcasting Commission, typing overtime
schedules and fetching and carrying – not exactly a life on
the San Francisco waterfront like Jack London at that age
or serving before the mast on a whaling boat, but it was
an independent life and there was always the writing.

> At twenty-one I returned to England and got a job with
> the BBC in the African Service, typing. This was in the
> 1960s. BBC2 had just begun and raw talent was being
> encouraged. I went to work for the Plays Department
> and then moved to the Music and Arts Department
> where I was able to progress from secretary to director.
> By 1985 the years of travelling, talking to strangers,
> hotel rooms and late nights didn't seem as thrilling as
> inventing my own reality – writing fiction is the best and
> biggest escape; it is lucid dreaming. So I resigned and I
> have earned my living as a writer since then.

Jane Coles started by writing radio plays. She has never
looked for recognition but a writer has to live and the
radio plays gave her the start she needed. In the past six
years there has been a flurry of activity with four plays
being produced in London theatres.

The Ultimate Fudge is a light play that deals with

serious issues. It is light in the sense that it tells a good story at a fast pace with characters that are clearly defined and nearly always amusing. It is serious in that it deals with such issues as inherited wealth and its abuse, tabloid journalism and popular television, the tyranny of the car, bullies and idiots of both sexes.

> I think *The Ultimate Fudge* is a very serious play. There are serious things in it like mass communication, truth, how much you have to compromise yourself in order to earn a living and, if you lose yourself by compromising, what happens to you. But that does not mean I am setting out to hit targets. I am reflecting the world in which these characters live. I don't see the play as drawing attention to them. One of the things I have become aware of as a writer is that the only people who will really understand what I am saying are those who already think a bit like me.

It is a paradox that a society which reveres Robin Hood is not prepared to reshape the structure that is based on inherited wealth and power. As an Australian Jane Coles is aware of this and takes on the paradox in her play.

> I find England very feudal and class ridden. I'm surprised at the power of the landed gentry and the respect of the ordinary person for them. Even the legend of Robin Hood is distorted and his bravery is accredited not to his wisdom and compassion but to his aristocratic blood, the last thing the legendary Robin Hood would have wanted. But as Holly says, 'They changed him from a hero to a joke, the ultimate fudge.' That's Holly talking. I don't think it is a fudge at all. It is the way our society deals with subversive heroes. Not that we have any, or at least, I can't think of any.

In the play, *Teleport* is a company that will stop at nothing to increase ratings. No lie or distortion is too extreme and the newsmakers are cynically aware of what they are doing. Jane Coles sees this attitude as a threat to our culture but one that can be resisted.

> If television is going to get worse, which sadly I think will happen, people may simply stop watching. They might go to the theatre or read. I don't think there is much that can be done about it but my belief is that television is not all that seductive in the end and there is probably a level of damage that can be done and then it stops.

At the end of the play Holly walks out of the job that is trapping her and takes off to walk round the world. It is an attractive proposition that people who are trapped can simply walk away but is it one that has any validity for ordinary people?

> I often wonder how much limitations are self-imposed. Of course you can't leave people who depend on you and you can't live without an income but, putting aside real poverty and severe illness, I don't think people are trapped. Most people live the kind of life they want to live and we probably have much more freedom than we think we have. The best thing is that we are here, wherever here is, because this is exactly the place that we want to be.

The positive thing in the play is that 'the truth survives'. But does it in reality? Does it even survive in the play?

> All it means in the play is that good triumphs over evil and I think it does. Not that I believe in good and evil and a war between the two. But I think human beings are capable of doing wonderful things – like loving each other – and in the end people prefer to do wonderful things rather than watch rubbish on television.

Although *The Ultimate Fudge* is written for young

people, the process of writing for this audience is not different from any other writing.

I don't think children are any different from adults. I think I am exactly the same person as an adult as I was when I was a child. I've written plays in which there have been parts for children and I've been amazed at the way children can grasp ideas of a complexity that many adults would give you a hard time about. What was difficult about this play was the opportunity I was given to write for a large cast. But once I'd come to terms with that and had created the characters I enjoyed it. Sometimes you get stuck in a world you don't like but I enjoyed the characters in this play.

Jane Coles's first play at the Bush Theatre, *Backstroke in a Crowded Pool*, won the Susan Smith Blackburn Prize, an international award for the best play written in English by a woman. She has directed documentary films for television and written extensively for both radio and the theatre.

Production Notes

STAGING AND SETTING

The Ultimate Fudge is a ripping yarn which requires bold
characterization and staging. It is set in the studio of FAB
TV, the Fox and Goose pub, and some exterior and
interior settings of the Docherty Estate near Sherwood.
These settings can be changed easily by the actors as part
of the action of the play. Much of the furniture and a
blackboard remain throughout and are multipurpose. The
play would work well within the conventions of a
proscenium stage. One approach would be to flatten out
the set two-dimensionally and to choose vivid colours and
bold lighting to give the piece a comic-strip quality.

CASTING

There are eighteen speaking parts, nine male and nine
female. Several of the reporters can be played by either
sex. The play is suitable for any cast with a feel for
comedy and a lot of energy.

QUESTIONS

1 What is the legend of Robin Hood?
2 Which of the legendary characters are most similar to
those in the pub?
3 What has Holly learned about herself by the end of the
play?
4 When are the serious moments in the play?

EXERCISES

1 Look at some of the many sitcoms that are set in TV studios, newsrooms and similar locations and discover how media people are portrayed and the comic timing needed when dealing with funny material.

2 Look at some of the early Robin Hood movies. Pay attention to the way the villain, the damsel in distress, the hero and his men are played.

3 In role as the wannabe researchers, create some of your own media stories that would please Kimberley Golden.

4 Experiment with ways of making Kimberley have even more high status. When she enters, have everyone lie on their stomachs, when she sits make everyone overattentive. Carry her everywhere so she has no need to walk or lift a finger. How might this exercise help you to find a way into playing the relationship between her and the other media obsessives?

5 In pairs, tell your partner a really funny story absolutely deadpan. Your partner is allowed to use any non-violent strategy to make you laugh or lose concentration.

6 Rehearse some of the scenes to a camcorder. Make sure the actors are very aware of where they are directing the action of the play. Experiment with other ways of giving the piece a more comic-strip quality?

7 Experiment with varying the speed of your performance. Discover what sections need to be played at a real pace and where you can afford to slow down.

8 Freeze a moment in the Fox and Goose pub. Have the characters gradually move into another tableau where they have obviously become Robin Hood and his associates. What physical changes are necessary to create the illusion that Holly sees something that disturbs her so much?

Suzy Graham-Adriani
February 1997